The timing of economic activities

T0340003

The timing of economic activities

Firms, households, and markets in time-specific analysis

GORDON C. WINSTON

Williams College
Williamstown, Massachusetts

CAMBRIDGE UNIVERSITY PRESS

Cambridge
London   New York   New Rochelle
Melbourne   Sydney

CAMBRIDGE UNIVERSITY PRESS
Cambridge, New York, Melbourne, Madrid, Cape Town, Singapore, São Paulo

Cambridge University Press
The Edinburgh Building, Cambridge CB2 8RU, UK

Published in the United States of America by Cambridge University Press, New York

www.cambridge.org
Information on this title: www.cambridge.org/9780521247207

First published 1982
This digitally printed version 2008

A catalogue record for this publication is available from the British Library

Library of Congress Cataloguing in Publication data
Winston, Gordon C.
The timing of economic activities.
Includes bibliographical references and
index.
1. Time and economic reactions. I. Title.
HB199.W54   330'.01   82–1328

ISBN 978-0-521-24720-7 hardback
ISBN 978-0-521-07092-8 paperback

to
MARY, VICTORIA, PARKER, and PAMELA

Contents

Preface   *page* xi

Part I. Economic events in time

1 Introduction   3
   1.1 *Time-specific analysis*   4
   1.2 *Time in economics: background*   7
   1.3 *The plan of the book*   10

2 Timing, information loss, and unit time in economic
   analysis   12
   2.1 *Time in economic analysis*   12
   2.2 *Time in economic behavior*   16
   2.3 *Unit time and loss of information*   17
   2.4 *The structure of time-specific analysis*   22
   2.5 *Economic rhythms: repetitive events in
        calendar unit time*   24
   2.6 *Music, electronics, and unit time: two illustrations*   27
   2.7 *Conclusions*   32

Part II. Time-specific analysis of production

3 Modeling the time-shape of processes, technology, and
   prices   37
   3.1 *The time context of time-specific models*   38
   3.2 *Production technology in specific time*   42
   3.3 *Characteristics of production flows*   47
   3.4 *Factor prices: duration-specific prices, time-specific
        prices, and time-invariant prices*   54
   3.5 *The time-shape of costs*   59
   3.6 *Summary*   65

4 Time-shaped costs: optimal scheduling of storable
   production   67
   4.1 *Timing and duration: the least-cost schedule of
        production in unit time*   68

4.2   *Least-cost speed of production in unit time: optimal
      factor flow rates*   76
4.3   *Least-cost timing of production in unit time*   82
4.4   *Summary and implications of the optimal schedule*   89
Appendix A: The formal model of time-specific
production   90

5 Time-shaped output: least-cost production of
   perishable peak-load products   100
   5.1   *The time-shape of output*   101
   5.2   *Least-cost tracking of time-shaped production*   102
   5.3   *Utilization tracking: adding and subtracting
         productive capacity*   105
   5.4   *Speed tracking: changing output speed with constant
         utilization*   109
   5.5   *Mixing utilization and speed tracking*   118
   5.6   *Time-shaped marginal costs*   119

Part III.   Applications of time-specific analysis

6 Shephard's dilemma: duality and the process of
   production   129
   6.1   *Mathematical duality theory and production in time*   129
   6.2   *Timing and duality*   131
   6.3   *Costs and free disposal*   135
   6.4   *The partitioned firm: the Purchasing Office and the
         Production Office*   136
   6.5   *Partly exogenous prices*   138
   6.6   *Conclusions*   139

7 Factor intensities, capacity, and the Leontief paradox   140
   7.1   *Optimal utilization and time-specific data*   140
   7.2   *The two meanings of factor proportions*   141
   7.3   *The Leontief paradox*   144
   7.4   *The idea of productive capacity and its utilization*   148
   7.5   *Conclusions*   154

Part IV.   Time-specific analysis of household activities

8 Modeling the time-shape of work and consumption:
   the optimal household schedule and the value of time   157
   8.1   *The model*   158
   8.2   *Time-shaped household production: the model structure* 159
   8.3   *Household labor as time*   162

8.4	*Time-shaped optimal behavior*	167
8.5	*The value of time in consumption and work*	171
8.6	*Work and consumption: timing and duration*	174
8.7	*Implications of the model*	180
8.8	*The Becker-Linder effect: the mix of activities*	183
8.9	*Summary and conclusions*	190

9 The anatomy of household activities: goal and process; work and home production; capital and self-control | 192

9.1	*Process utility and goal utility*	193
9.2	*Work: money income, job satisfaction, and goods*	197
9.3	*Home production or the market: an economics of do-it-yourself*	202
9.4	*Household capital and the economics of utilization*	206
9.5	*Rising incomes, household capital, and the logic of the Linder hypothesis*	212
9.6	*Adjustment costs, duration, and timing*	214
9.7	*Summary*	221

Part V. Time-specific markets

10 A theory of time-specific markets: generalized peak loads | 227

10.1	*A graphic representation of time-shaped markets*	227
10.2	*The time-specific market for labor services*	232
10.3	*The time-specific product market: peak-load pricing and "the capacity problem"*	239
10.4	*Producers' good market: toward a time-specific general equilibrium*	248

11 Welfare and distortions in time-specific exchange | 258

11.1	*Efficiency and welfare with time-specific pricing*	258
11.2	*Time-specific distortions and mismatch: the electric-power market*	268
11.3	*Time-specific distortions and mismatch: the labor market*	274
11.4	*Summary and conclusions*	283

Part VI. Postscript

12 Time-specific analysis of nonrhythmic events: relational exchange and the role of repetition | 287

12.1	*The illusion of constancy: nonrhythmic events within calendar unit time*	287

12.2 *An endogenous unit time: the case of*
       relational exchange   289
12.3 *Repetitiveness, neoclassical theory, and opportunism*   293
12.4 *Two notes on repetitiveness: reputations and liars as*
       free riders in time and space   295

Notes   298
References   327
Index   335

Preface

In 1965, Ragnar Frisch wrote that

in our enthusiasm for the powerful, modern means of calculation, we have run the risk of neglecting something essential which the good old "traditional" ways of reasoning brought home to us. These good old types of analyses we shall however never be able to dispense with. We will in the end always need to fall back on them.

One of the unexpected things I experienced in working through the analysis of this book was a growing appreciation for the way the best of the older economists – with their "good old traditional ways" of thinking – retained a wholeness in their representation of economic processes, even though it sometimes forced them to be vague, even sloppy, in the logic of their arguments. As one important instance (which is the subject of Chapter 6), economists' traditional representation of the production process – the one still embedded in undergraduate microeconomics texts – mixed stocks and flows, willy-nilly, leaving us with a description of "production technology" that had a lot in it that was economic and not purely technological. One objective in the application of mathematical duality theory to production was to clean all that up, to represent production technology in a pure form without any of that traditional contamination by economic influences.

Duality theory did that, but in the process it threw out the baby with the bathwater. The duality model of production purified its technological representation by leaving central parts of the production process entirely out of its analysis – parts, ironically, that are essential to the analysis of costs and technology to which modern duality theory is mainly addressed. Traditional analysis retained a fuller description of the production process at the cost of being imprecise; modern theory has achieved precision at the cost of seriously misrepresenting the process.

Relative to other social sciences, economics has done admirably in balancing these competing criteria. But needs for rigor and relevance change, and with them, analytical fashions. No "correct" balance – no steady-state equilibrium ratio of rigor to relevance – exists. Mainstream theory veers, instead, toward one extreme and then, compensating for its excesses, toward the other. Koopman's 1957 call to axiomatic arms was timely and has been immensely successful in encouraging careful economic reasoning. But in 25 years it has produced a sometimes excessive zeal for precision; by 1981, a healthy reaction had developed against that excess.

The shape of this new reaction is clear: Its unifying aspect is that it returns to people and processes, to observable human behavior and its consequences, to good old traditional types of analysis, with, however, a very modern respect for rigor. It reexamines the evidence on actual human motivation for its impact on the assumptions that underlie economic theory (Tversky and Kahneman, 1974; March, 1978); it borrows from psychology (Simon, 1959, 1978a, 1978b; Scitovsky, 1976; Leibenstein, 1976, 1979), from theories of organization (Williamson, 1971, 1975, 1979; Nelson and Winter, 1980; Barzel, 1980), from the law (Goldberg, 1980), from philosophy (Sen, 1964, 1975, 1977; Elster, 1977, 1979; McPherson, 1978, 1980, 1981), from ethics (Arrow, 1974, 1978; Reder, 1979; North, 1981), and from the philosophy of time (Shackle, 1958, 1972, 1973; Georgescu-Roegen, 1970, 1971, 1976). In all these borrowings, economic theory is moved toward closer contact with human complexity, sometimes even at the recognized price of less analytical precision.

This book is part of that reaction, but it also promises to reduce the price paid for increased relevance. It appears that to a remarkable extent (as reflected in the quotation from Marshall that begins Chapter 1) analytical imprecision about time and timing often has been the *source* of the dichotomy between descriptions of recognizable economic processes and logically tenable analyses. Choice often has been forced on us – choice between Good Old Theory and sometimes otherworldly abstractions – by failure to specify carefully the time dimensions of economic events and the analysis that deals with them. Time-specific analysis promises a significant reduction, over a wide range of theoretical issues, in the conflict between the good old objective of relevance in analysis and the modern objective of logical precision. There is something here – as with any technological change that shifts a production-possibilities curve outward – of being allowed to have one's cake and eat it too.

So this book is far more concrete in terms of the economic processes it describes than most studies in theory, and it is far more coherently theoretical than most studies of concrete economic processes. It presents a theory about actual production units, such as the International Paper Company mill in Ticonderoga, New York, and Tom McCoy's wheat farm in Wasco, Oregon, and the Stockholm bus system, and it presents a theory about actual households like mine and the reader's and that of the driver of a Stockholm bus. Yet the analysis is quite abstract, coherent, and even neoclassical; it aims at a high level of rigor, and it is related systematically to the mainstream literature on production, consumption, work, and markets.

The formal analysis is kept at a simple level – one that a well-trained undergraduate will not find impenetrable – for two good reasons. One, simply, is that the richer perspective provided by a time-specific analysis does not need an analytical setting more complicated than that of an undergraduate microeconomics course. It is more efficiently conveyed with as much simplicity as possible. Ideas, not apparatus, can then be central.

The second and more important reason for keeping things simple is that modern analytical sophistication and its sometimes abrupt discontinuity in imposing high abstraction and mathematical rigor can be a two-edged sword. GIGO – "garbage in, garbage out" – is the familiar warning to computer users who would hope to get powerful results from inappropriate analysis or from bad data by using sophisticated programming.

In economics, theory-GIGO is less celebrated and therefore probably more dangerous: Sophisticated and rigorous manipulation of fuzzy ideas about partially understood processes is hoped to be capable of yielding useful results – a view well served by high analytical altitudes and by a widespread impatience with methodological and conceptual niceties. But, obviously, implications derived from a highly complex, logically unassailable, rigorous analysis of inadequate and woolly concepts will be at best inadequate and woolly and at worst precisely and persuasively wrong. Because the objective in this study is to introduce a careful consideration of time and draw its implications, my aim has been to make only those minimal departures from textbook neoclassical analysis that are needed to make temporal dimensions clear.

The analysis is quite neoclassical. One rewarding discovery is how much richer an essentially orthodox neoclassical perspective on economic processes becomes when its time dimensions are laid out with unusual care. Seeing the neoclassical economic process "*in* time," in Hicks's phrase, gives that perspective an unexpected increase in analytical strength and concreteness. It simply becomes much easier to visualize it as a theory of real firms and real people.

But time-specific analysis also – and perhaps most usefully – defines limits of neoclassical analysis. It identifies a neglected aspect of economic events – whether they are repetitive or unique in time – that seems largely to determine the appropriateness of using neoclassical analysis in their modeling. It appears that repetitive events – repetitive decisions, transactions, and regular responses to rhythmic changes over the day or the week or the year – are the genuine stuff of neoclassical economics; unique, novel, one-shot events are not. Although this is a theme implied by Shackle, Simon, and Georgescu-Roegen, absent a time-specific representation of events, it has not been developed.

I hope this book will serve two purposes. It is intended to be a contribution to economics in the tradition of the Good Old Theory, carefully introducing aspects of economic reality that matter, both to people and to the logic of existing theory. If it is successful in that, its other contribution will be to help integrate the older and intuitively richer representations of that reality with newer and more rigorous representations.

I have been embarrassingly dependent on people and institutions in the writing of this book. Of Albert Hirschman, Mike McPherson, and Mary Lamb, I can say that without each of them – each in a different way – I would not have written it.

Albert Hirschman's tolerance (even enthusiasm) for offbeat ideas within essentially orthodox economics led him to invite me to be a member of the Institute for Advanced Study, Princeton, in 1978–9. That year allowed me to establish the direction and momentum of this study in a way that would have been impossible without that time and unlikely without the intellectually idyllic environment of the School of Social Sciences at the institute. Albert himself was largely responsible for that environment. But the results of his more direct and gently probing questions, his observations, and even his musings over lunch permeate the study, even if they are rarely acknowledged.

From adjoining offices at the institute – and at lunch and tea and running the towpath – Harvey Leibenstein, Dick Day, and Vic Goldberg spent hours discussing my ideas and theirs, leaving me with a pervasive debt to them that would be difficult to disentangle. Dick Day's Economic Modeling Consultants, under contract to the Electric Power Research Institute, supported the initial work on efficient time-shaped output of perishable products that became Chapter 5.

At Williams College, Mike McPherson barely escapes responsibility for joint authorship of much of this book. He acted as my sounding board, perceptive critic, and source of sustaining enthusiasm, encouraging me to think that these ideas might really be as exciting and novel and worthwhile as my paternal pride in them told me they were. He read repeated drafts and commented always with what can only be called wisdom. So he bears a heavy responsibility for the strengths, weaknesses, and existence of this book.

Tom McCoy does not escape responsibility for authorship. He was joint author and supplier of mathematical rigor to the 1974 *Review of Economic Studies* article that was the first careful statement of the continuous time-specific model. It is largely reproduced here as Appendix A to Chapter 4.

Virtually every step in the development of these ideas was tried out in the weekly Williams Economics Faculty Seminar, and hardly any member of the department escaped involvement; whole sections of the book owe their existence to things I learned from my colleagues in consequence. Mead Over frequently told me of ideas in the literature I had missed; Steve Lewis helped me focus the book; Rajhbendra Jha and Neil Grabois reassured me that my understanding of duality theory was essentially correct and my worries well-formed. The undergraduate seminar on The Economics of Time convinced me that these ideas are, indeed, accessible and even appealing to good college seniors. I have no doubt that a great liberal arts college with excellent students and demanding colleagues encourages a special sort of scholarship that is constrained by the compartmentalization of a great university. In this respect, Williams College seems to have not just a comparative advantage but an absolute advantage.

In Stockholm, the Institute for International Economic Studies generously supported my work, in 1979–80, on the analysis of the household. Assar Lindbeck, Ron Jones, Lars Svensson, Åke Blomqvist, and Hans Söderström read, commented on, and argued about the analysis, helping me to understand and sharpen the issues.

In my 10 years of fixation on these ideas, I have received help, encouragement, and insights at crucial moments from more people than I can mention, but among the most influential were Amartya Sen, Robin Marris, Mark Perlman, Julius Fraser, Mark Leiserson, Howard Kunreuther, Gene Winston, Nicholas Georgescu-Roegen, Rob Hollister, Romeo Bautista, and David Morawetz.

In addition to the institutes in Princeton and Stockholm, support was provided by the Warden and Fellows of Nuffield College and the Warden of Queen Elizabeth House, Oxford, by the Ford Foundation, through the Yale Pakistan Project and then directly by Grant

720-0234, by the World Bank's Capital Utilization Project, by the International Labour Office, and by the Edna McConnell Clark Foundation through the Williams College Center for Development Economics.

The manuscript was typed by Chris Naughton, Portia Edwards, and Mary Lamb, each of whom showed patience and a remarkable ability to penetrate my awful copy. Miriam Grabois corrected my persistent spelling errors, advised on musical scores, proofed endlessly retyped versions, and praised the occasional phrase. Andy Parnes, Bob Murphy, Pamela Winston, and Debbie Faunce served as highly capable research assistants, and Debbie read and commented on the entire manuscript in helpful detail.

Finally, Mary Lamb insisted that I had to overcome the constraint of my article-length mind and put these ideas together in book form, even though the consequent obsession with my clipboard altered her life. Without her support, I would not have done it; so the book is dedicated to her.

G.C.W.

PART I

Economic events in time

CHAPTER 1

Introduction

The element of Time . . . is the centre of the chief difficulty of almost every economic problem.

Alfred Marshall, 1890 (1961, p. vii)

Things happen – including economic events – at specific times. But modern economic analysis is constructed to reject a surprising amount of relevant information about that timing. This is as true for theoretical models as for empirical analyses, for models of firms and households as for descriptions of markets, for Austrian as for neoclassical analyses. In any day, an hour of work or the production of a ton of output is treated as analytically identical to any other hour of work or ton of output, whether it happens at midnight or 4:00 a.m. or in the middle of the afternoon. Although these marked differences in timing – time of day, in this case – matter very much to the worker who is working and to the firm that hires him, it is implicit in the standard methodology of economics that they do not matter to the economic processes with which our theories are concerned. Within the unit time of economic analysis, an hour of work is an hour of work, and production of a ton of output is a ton of output.

This lack of concern for when things happen within the unit time is not just a matter of analytical taste, but a far more fundamental matter of method or analytical technology. Information on the timing of events is lost in economic analysis not because it is selectively discarded after being judged irrelevant to the understanding of an economic issue; temporal information is lost automatically, filtered out by the way economics treats time. It would be reassuring if this were only a part of the process of abstraction inherent in any theory – that more information about timing would only reveal the "ceaseless oscillations" in economic variables that Hicks thought would be uninformative (Hicks, 1946, p. 122). Or it would be reassuring to believe that in those cases in which timing matters, astute

3

economic analysts usually will incorporate it. But neither, unfortunately, is the case.

A close consideration of the timing of economic activities shows that the structure of conventional analysis itself prevents information from getting past the barrier of the analytical time unit and that ad hoc adjustments of the theory in cases such as peak-load analysis, where timing matters centrally, have not been enough to prevent distortions of our understanding of familiar economic processes.

1.1   Time-specific analysis

This study introduces a time-specific analysis of economic processes. It presents a way of seeing and analyzing familiar processes – production, consumption, work, and exchange – with unfamiliar depth, detail, and insights. Time-specific models pay careful attention to time and the timing of economic events and develop the implications of that temporality. It is not always true that fresh insights into old theories and processes are introduced by time-specific analysis, but often it is. And then our orthodox atemporal habits of analysis can yield fundamentally misleading results based on a fundamentally misleading conception of an economic process.

It may seem strange to suggest that economic theorists have paid inadequate attention to time. Indeed, it would appear that there has been a persistent concern with time in economics. The list of those who have written explicitly on time in economic analysis includes Samuelson (1976), Hicks (1976), Frisch (1965), Arrow (1978), Georgescu-Roegen (1970, 1971), Hood (1948), and Rosenstein-Rodan (1934), not to mention those writing on subjects like information theory and expectations and disequilibrium analysis where time is always treated explicitly even if it is not the central subject. J. T. Fraser reported that there are 119 entries under "Time and Economic Reactions" in the 1966–80 *Social Science Index*.[1]

But the timing of economic events – like their distribution in social space – can be approached in either micro-detail or macro-inclusiveness, and the focus of economic theory has been almost exclusively on the latter. Economic processes are typically analyzed from one point in time to another over a series of time units. This *macro-time* or *extensive time* is familiarly represented by a simple time line (Figure 1.1) divided, explicitly or implicitly, into the time units needed to measure durations and flow rates. Then an economic process is ob-

Figure 1.1. Extensive or macro-time.

served and analyzed as it changes – or doesn't change, in static-equilibrium analysis – from one unit time to the next.

The subject of this study is complementary to this familiar temporal perspective, but different. Time-specific models analyze economic processes within the typical unit time – the day or week or year. They put events in *micro-time*, an *intensive* time. Time-specific models focus on the timing, duration, and sequence of economic events within the unit time, utilizing the information that is lost by the macro-time perspective of conventional theory. A simple diagram (Figure 1.2) shows the contrast in temporal scale and perspective between macro-timing in orthodox economic analysis (a) and the micro-timing of time-specific analysis (b). Conventional economic theory has guarded effectively against the temptation to see only immediate events to the neglect of foresight and the long view – temporal *myopia* – but it is seriously afflicted by a temporal *hyperopia*, the ability to see only distant events to the neglect of what is immediate. What time-specific analysis reveals are economic and technological characteristics of goods and services – prices and cost behavior and temporal mobility or immobility within the unit time – that affect factor productivity, optimal schedules of production and consumption, least-cost methods of producing time-shaped outputs, and efficient welfare-maximizing behavior in time-specific – including peak-load – markets.[2]

Time-specific models produce an analysis that is unique both in systematically incorporating the timing of events within the unit time and in providing a richer and more detailed representation of familiar economic processes. The first of these gives to the understanding of inherently time-dependent processes, such as the generation and sale of electric power or the demand for transportation services, a coherent analytical framework to replace the extensive adhocery of the past. But analysis of such processes, because they are so obviously dependent on timing – so evidently "time-shaped," in Frisch's phrase – often has already incorporated timing, one way or another. There is need for more coherence and refinement of that theory through time-specific representation before important issues can be understood, but less need for radical innovation.

So the more fundamental contribution of time-specific analysis lies

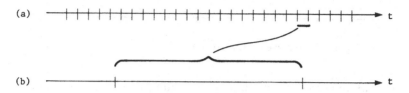

Figure 1.2. Temporal perspectives of macro-time (a) and time-specific analysis (b).

in its ability to provide an unusually rich and detailed anatomy of economic processes. It exposes unfamiliar characteristics of familiar economic variables that are hidden by the conventional time perspective. Two of the most important of such characteristics – two that figure prominently in the analysis that follows – will serve to illustrate and introduce the time-specific anatomy of process. They are the nature of capital and labor inputs to production and the perishability of outputs within unit time.

Capital services and labor services enter neoclassical production functions as parallel arguments. Yet some time ago Jorgenson and Griliches (1967) argued that capital services are derived from stocks that are owned by the firm, so that the capital-utilization decision is internal to the firm. Labor services are bought as such by the firm. The two factors therefore have essentially different characteristics with essentially different economic implications: For an idealized competitive firm the price of its capital services is determined in part internally – by the duration of production within the unit time – whereas the price of labor services is determined exogenously by the labor (service) market. Add to that the fact, identified by Eels (1956) and Marris (1964), that the exogenous market price for labor services is time-specific – different at different times of the day (and week and year) – and the economics of the production process is revealed in a quite unconventional perspective: The price of one input in the two-factor production analysis is seen to be sensitive to the *duration of production,* whereas the price of the other is sensitive to the *timing of production,* both within the day or usual unit time. This, it will be shown, both complicates production theory and makes sense of much that escapes conventional analysis.

The other characteristic of goods and services that a time-specific analysis shows to have unexpected analytical importance is a product's perishability or storability – its "temporal mobility" – over the day or week or year. A bicycle made at 2:00 a.m. can be kept at negligible storage costs until it is sold the next afternoon, but a kilowatt of electric power made at 2:00 a.m. will perish immediately, absent an elaborate and expensive storage system. So the least-cost production of storable bicycles is essentially different in its timing and technology – again within the unit time – from the least-cost production of perishable electric power. The first will be determined by the time pattern of costs, the second by the time pattern of demand. This has a number of implications, among them that the applicabilities of marginal-cost pricing rules in the two processes are less similar than has been assumed: The absence of a careful time-specific conception of production and exchange explains why the Holy Grail of a nice, clean application of marginal-cost pricing principles to electric power generation, for instance, has proved to be so persistently elusive. Chapters 5 and 10 address these issues.

For those steeped in the neoclassical tradition, the only thing inherently unusual about time-specific analysis per se is its representation of time and timing, and even that is, at one level, only a matter of a greater generality of the familiar analysis. Whenever temporal details are not important in a time-specific neoclassical model – when nothing of relevance to the economic process is identified by time-specific modeling – the analysis collapses back into a strictly orthodox and quite simple sort of neoclassical representation.

1.2   Time in economics: background

Aside from the efforts of Hicks (1946, 1976, 1979), Shackle (1958), and Hood (1948) to focus economists' attention on time, the main lines of economic theory that influenced the development of time-specific analysis – and the clearest anticipation of the importance of what I have called "micro-timing" in economic processes – were those of Frisch and Georgescu-Roegen. In his *Theory of Production*, Frisch devoted a chapter to "time-shaped" production – the felicitous phrase I will borrow frequently in what follows – although finally he despaired of its careful development as requiring too much analytical complexity. Georgescu, from the timing-conscious tradition of agricultural economics, meticulously described production as a process in time. His representation of production in *The Entropy Law and the Economic Process* is deeply embedded in the time-specific models of this study. Indeed, had Georgescu considered prices and economic incentives with the same care he used in describing production technology in time, he would certainly have discovered much of what is presented here.

Combining Georgescu's description of technology with Robin Marris's attention to time-specific labor costs and adding the cost implications of Jorgenson and Griliches's attention to the source of capital services yielded the time-specific analysis of this study. The first full-blown time-specific model described the optimal utilization and idleness of production. In a discrete-time form, it modeled optimal shift-working (Winston, 1970);[3] in a more general continuous-time form, it was the optimal-utilization model (Winston and McCoy, 1974) that is central to this analysis. Hutt (1939), J. M. Clark (1923), Eels (1956), and Marris (1964) anticipated this concern with the utilization and idleness of productive resources, but they did so without benefit of a careful time-specific representation of production.

Becker's incorporation of production theory into the analysis of household time allocation (1965) was essential to the creation of time-specific analysis of work and consumption behavior. The time-specific household model of Chapter 8, however, departs significantly from Becker's model in making time the context within which household activities take place – as it is the context within which firms' production activities take place – instead of being the mysteriously reified Thing that gets used up in time-allocation models. Although a time-specific model replicates the main results of Becker's analysis, it also defines the "value of time" and gives a clearer understanding of the household's optimizing process. It identifies different utility, input, and activity characteristics that generalize the household model: Linder's harried leisure class (1970) can escape its torments, Scitovsky's self-discipline (1975) is seen explicitly as part of the household's activity-timing decision, and Gronau's analysis (1977) of household do-it-yourself decisions can be integrated.

Time-shaped "peak-load" markets – in which time-specific demand meets time-specific output – have been studied since Houthakker (1951), largely in the context of the electric power industry and largely addressing questions of optimal generating capacity, temporal cost patterns, and efficient pricing. A general theory of time-shaped markets is derived from time-specific analysis of exchange. It incorporates that large peak-load literature but also and more generally the analysis of markets for labor services, for transportation, for the exchange of any perishable good with either a time-shaped supply or demand.

The curious role of repetitive – rhythmic – economic events within the unit time was anticipated by J. M. Clark in *The Economics of Overhead Costs* (1923). But it is rather remarkable that since then the primary analytical attention that has been paid to rhythmic variables has been intended mainly to remove their temporal information. "Seasonal-adjustment" techniques transform actual time-specific information into its unit-time equivalents; September's actual auto sales, when seasonally adjusted, will describe yearly auto sales, but not September's.

Finally, the Austrian tradition has a sufficient proprietary claim on the subject of "time in economics" that I should be explicit about how the very neoclassical time-specific models of this study relate to Austrian concerns and treatment of time. A key aspect of Austrian capital theory is its appreciation – from Böhm-Bawerk to Mises to Shackle and Lachmann – of the inherent delay in payoff to durable capital – the period of production – that necessitates waiting for output with resources tied up for some period of time. Investment is therefore a precommitment of resources, and the corollary of any precommitment is that it is made under uncertainty. The Austrian tradition emphasizes this, rejecting analyses of investment under certainty in order to stress that the inherent technological delays in payoffs to durable capital push its analysis into an inherently unknowable future: The use of capital requires waiting and also not really knowing.

But a tendency to slip from this emphasis on uncertainty to a denial of any regularities in the future has come to characterize the rhetoric of much neo-Austrian writing on time – not only can the future not be known with certainty, but nothing in the future can even be usefully guessed at. This ultimate temporal nihilism appears, for instance, in some of the writings of Shackle (1973) and Lachmann (1976).

The premise of this study is that among actual economic events there is a continuum from repetitive to unique events – from those that take place day after day or year after year with a fixed rhythmic periodicity to, at the other end of the continuum, those utterly unique events that happen only once in a lifetime for a person or family or society. Most events and certainly most economic events lie somewhere in between. But the pure extremes define the appropriateness of the pure models economists use: Austrian analysis is appropriate to unique nonrepetitive events with their inevitable uncertainties and the dark importance of future ignorance; time-specific neoclassical analysis is appropriate to repetitive, rhythmic events with their high degree of predictability and even equilibria and perfect knowledge. These are two ends of a continuum, the same continuum. So long as actual economic events are found all along that continuum, neither the Austrian's unique unknowability nor the neoclassicist's predictable certainty can be The Correct analytical model. Each is correct for quite different economic events and processes; neither is entirely appropriate for most events and processes; the two approaches are complementary; they talk about different things. It will be argued later that this temporal aspect of repetitiveness and predictability goes far to determine the relevance of neoclassical models for economic events in the world.

1.3   The plan of the book

The organization of this book is straightforward. In the next chapter, the role of time in economic analysis and behavior is examined, and the analytical unit time is seen to be an abstracting device that discards temporal information. Time-specific analysis – as the method of retaining and analyzing that information – is described briefly in that chapter.

Part II develops time-specific analysis with care in the context of production, showing the central characteristics of goods and services that are hidden by the time frame of orthodox analysis and are revealed clearly in a time-specific model (Chapter 3). That analytical structure is then used to examine the time-shape of efficient production of storable output (Chapter 4) and perishable output (Chapter 5). The central issues of Chapters 3 and 4 are introduced with an accessible informality that relies mostly on familiar-looking average cost curves; the core of that analysis is presented with more rigor in the Appendix to Chapter 4.

Part III uses this time-specific production analysis first to examine the logic of modern duality modeling when production is explicitly seen to be a process in time (Chapter 6) and then (Chapter 7) to look at the empirical problems caused by ambiguities in the familiar idea of "factor proportions" in international trade and in measures of "productive capacity" and "capacity utilization."

Part IV deals with consumption and work activities. The household model of Chapter 8 is a model of time-specific activity choice with the appealingly intuitive feature that the household will optimally choose, at each moment, to do that activity in which time has the greatest value. The same choice rule applies all of the time, differentiating among consumption activities and between work and consumption – so the only distinction among household activities that need be imposed from outside is that work does and consumption does not earn a money wage. In Chapter 9, the time-specific model is used to analyze household utility, distinguishing between "process utility" and "goal utility" – the pleasures of doing and having done – to examine the effects on household behavior of job satisfaction, of changing opportunities to purchase or make commodities at home, of the characteristics of goods that determine the time-shapes of their costs. The household production model examines, in the household, the implications of those differences in the characteristics of capital, labor, and goods inputs that first appear in the time-specific production analysis of Chapter 3.

Part V analyzes time-specific exchange. The optimal household activity schedules that emerge from Part IV generate time-shaped demands for consumption goods and a time-shaped supply of labor services. The firm's optimal production schedule that emerges from Part II describes a time-shaped demand for labor services and a time-shaped supply of output. Households and firms must trade perishable goods and services at specific times. But their optimal schedules do not match. So the analysis of time-shaped markets examines ways to reconcile these time-specific differences, alternatives that include peak-load pricing and time-specific quantity rationing. Representation of the process of exchange in explicit temporal detail makes it possible to see the unique problems of time-shaped markets and why that temporal characteristic is quite fundamental to their economic analysis. The electric power and labor markets serve as primary examples in the discussions of Chapters 10 and 11, and the efficiencies, distortions, and welfare implications of alternative time-specific allocation devices are illustrated nicely in these two markets; the general analysis, of course, is relevant to any market with a time-shaped supply or demand.

Finally, Part VI is a postscript, added to suggest the kinds of economic issues to which the time-specific perspective can be applied when it is not restricted – as it is throughout the main part of this book – to the analysis of regular, repetitive, rhythmic events. The two related themes of that chapter are a time-specific analysis of "relational exchange" and the role of repetitiveness, per se, both in disciplining market transactions and in justifying neoclassical analysis. The first is a time-shaped view of ordinary market transactions that reveals, especially for unique transactions, a set of incentives that modify orthodox exchange theory. The second examines the parallels between repetitive transactions in time and competitive transactions in market space, suggesting that it is only the analysis of repetitive transactions to which neoclassical analysis is entirely appropriate.

CHAPTER 2

Timing, information loss, and unit time in economic analysis

The central theme of this study is that important aspects of economic processes often are obscured in modern economic analysis by its too-casual treatment of time and the timing of economic events. Although it is widespread, the assumption that such things are always quite obvious appears not to be justified. So it is important that this study begin with an uncharacteristically careful and explicit discussion of the role of time in conventional analysis – why it creates problems and how the treatment of time in the time-specific models developed here deals with those problems. That is the business of this chapter.

The first two sections describe the three different roles that time plays both in modern economic analysis and in economic behavior. The next section introduces a central aspect of the study: the powerful but unacknowledged role played by the choice of an analytical "unit time" in determining what information enters the analysis of an economic process. The fourth section introduces time-specific modeling of economic process to retain and utilize the temporal information lost in conventional analysis; it produces formal theories of time-shaped production, consumption, work, and exchange, and it provides the criteria by which a given unit time can be judged appropriate to a particular analysis. The next section restricts the set of questions to which time-specific models will be applied in this study; until the postscript at the end of the book, I will consider only the analysis of regular, repetitive, rhythmic events in calendar time units. Finally, in the last section of the chapter, two brief illustrations of the analytical effects of the choice of unit time are taken from areas usefully foreign to economic analysis: the production of music and of electronic calculations.

2.1   Time in economic analysis

Unsettling questions about the fundamental nature of time have disturbed physicists and philosophers since Einstein's special theory

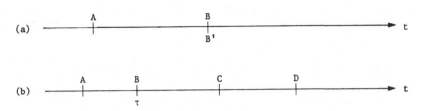

Figure 2.1. Temporal order, perspective, and measure.

of relativity, but the economist's uses of time are very little concerned with those metaphysics.[1] A simple conception of time per se – a human and social conception – is adequate in describing economic behavior and our analysis of it. Time in economics is a simple unidirectional linear flow, exogenous to the economic actors – even a Newtonian absolute time serves us nicely, as if a cosmic clock ticked away somewhere.[2]

Three characteristics of time are essential to economic analysis: (a) that time orders events sequentially as before, after, and simultaneous; (b) that because of time's irreversibility, people individually and collectively perceive events as being in the past, present, and future; (c) that measures of time employ the usual metric of the real numbers. The first two of these characterize order; the last establishes a measure.[3] These characteristics can be represented graphically on time lines (Figure 2.1). In Figure 2.1(a), events A and B – which could be production (A) of a product and its consumption (B) – are simply ordered as "A is before B" ("B is after A") and "B is simultaneous with B'." With a person on the time line – an economic actor – whose temporal perspective, Now, is represented by the moving point τ in Figure 2.1(b), past, present, and future are defined: From the perspective of τ, "A is a past event," "C and D are in the future," and "B is happening now." A measure and the real-number metric, finally, underlie any statement such as "At $t = \tau$, D is twice as far in the future as C," or, with a different measure, "In the long run, we are all dead."

Economic analysis utilizes these characteristics of time in three distinct ways:

Analytical time

Analytical time describes the temporal framework of any economic analysis, theoretical or empirical. Its components are (a) the *unit time*

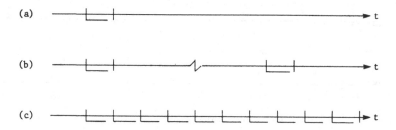

Figure 2.2. Analytical time: statics, comparative statics, and dynamics.

in which economic events are to be measured and (b) the *time range* or *horizon* that describes the number of such units time the analytical structure is to encompass. Either or both may be explicitly or only implicitly specified. Flow variables like output or saving are measured as accumulated flows – rates – per unit time, like a day; stock variables like wealth or inventories are measured at some specified moment of the unit time, like the beginning or end of the day or high noon. The temporal range of the analysis may be a single unit time (static analysis), two or more discrete units time (comparative statics), or a series, finite or infinite, of units time (dynamics). Event order – including the order of units time – is retained as before/after.

Analytical time, then, describes the way time is divided up and over what duration those divisions are of analytical interest to the economic problem. Static analysis is represented graphically by a single unit time as in Figure 2.2(a); comparative statics is represented by two separated units time as in Figure 2.2(b), with indefinite separation for pure comparative statics; dynamics is represented by a range divided into a series of units of time as in Figure 2.2(c). The measure of analytical time may be exogenous to the process being analyzed, using clock or calendar time, like days or years or instants, or it may be endogenous, using an economically functional measure of time such as the familiar long run and short run (Hood, 1948). With regard to the analytical time dimensions of an economic analysis, the economist stands aloof, specifying the temporal dimensions needed to reveal those economic relationships he seeks to understand: He ranges freely, as Omniscient Analyst, back and forth over the time line.[4]

Perspective time

Perspective time puts an economic actor into time and describes his behavior as it is influenced by his temporal position; perspective time introduces the Now, τ, that is the basis of the second kind of temporal ordering, the ordering of events into past, present, and future. This is the use of time Hicks (1976) aptly described as "economics *in* time" – in contrast to an "economics *of* time" – in which the temporal perspective of the economic actor is, itself, of central importance to his behavior. This time dimension is, of course, involved in much of recent economic theory, in the analysis of information and uncertainty, hence of expectations, of learning in adaptive systems, and of some but not all discussions of time preferences and the relationships between present and future. Attention to perspective time has led Shackle (1958) to the nihilistic position that economic analysis is essentially impossible because the future is of necessity unknown; it led Strotz (1955), Pollak (1968), and McPherson (1978), among others, to consider the conflicts generated when things do not look the same at the time of planning an optimal course of action as they do in the actual living of it because judgments change with temporal perspective; it led to a different and more realistic picture of "relational-exchange" markets when market transactions were seen in perspective time, because changing τ changes the incentives and opportunities of the traders (Williamson, 1979; Goldberg, 1980; Kornai, 1971). And so on. Perspective time is represented graphically simply by the way events look when viewed from τ and by the movement of τ toward and then past events A and B and C on a time line like that of Figure 2.1(b). The analytical observer can still move freely over the time line, but the subject of analysis cannot.

Commodity time

Commodity time describes a quite different use of time in economics in which time is treated as A Thing like a case of beer or a ton of steel – "reified" in the philosopher's usually derisive phrase. As a valuable and scarce commodity,[5] time is seen to be allocated among competing uses on the same principles of economic rationality that are applied to any other scarce thing of value. Economic theories of "time allocation" were first embedded in analyses of labor-supply behavior intended to understand the division of time between work and leisure (Robbins, 1930; Dalton, 1932; Winston, 1963). Since Becker's important article (1965), they have included, too, the time component of nonlabor activities – originally a "time price" of consumption. Time-allocation theory has employed insights from consumer-demand analysis to say things of considerable usefulness about the way people spend their scarce time and the way they change their time allocation when conditions change: Linder's study of the harried leisure class (1970) focused on long-term changes in the way time is spent as it becomes increasingly scarce relative to goods, and Becker and his students have generalized the analysis of how time is spent into an analysis of human behavior (Becker, 1976; Michael and Becker, 1973). These are issues to be considered in Part IV.[6]

2.2   Time in economic behavior

It is useful to emphasize that these are not simply analytical constructs that classify the uses of time in economic analysis. The fact that these same three dimensions of temporality are clear to the economic actors we study is important – that they (we) are simultaneously aware of these rather different aspects of people's temporal existence and that that awareness is often central to understanding their economic behavior.

So people know that they exist in "analytical time," that different units time and time horizons are appropriate to different decisions: The year as unit time and a decade as the range may be appropriate to a family's planning of its house-painting expenditures, whereas an hour as the unit time and four days as the range are appropriate to planning the family's menus. For the same household, the Now is seen to be very different from any other moment, and the distinction of perspective time between past and future is fundamental to rational behavior, as is the fact that there are some things, contra Shackle, that remain the same between past and future (Arrow and Kurz, 1970; Hicks, 1976).[7] Finally, the family's behavior is affected by an awareness that "time is of the essence"; so its not-too-careless allocation among alternative activities is a matter of considerable importance to rational behavior.

Because the economic actors whose behavior economic theory hopes to understand are simultaneously aware of these different aspects of time, it is important that economic analysis recognize and incorporate that awareness. When we envision the people we analyze as being guided by only one aspect of time alone, the result often is an analysis that is at once plausible and misleading: Although it describes an aspect of time that is influential, it ignores other temporal influences on behavior.

It has often been argued, for instance (Böhm-Bawerk, 1891; Jevons, 1888; Maital and Maital, 1978), that the discounting of future events – time preference – is irrational because it is logically indefensible to assert that an event at time t is in any essential way different from the same event at some other time $t + m$ – apart from the negligible chance that one will die in the interim. That argument, however, rests on an exclusive if implicit preoccupation with analytical time. From its Olympian perspective, time preferences are indeed irrational, because any one point on the analytical time line is no different from any other. But that argument is false in terms of perspective time, in which the moment Now is distinct from all other moments and the future is quite different from the past. This is the thrust of much of Shackle's argument (1958); see, too, Lachmann (1976) and Mises (1947). For "economics *in* time," time preferences are entirely reasonable, and indeed it is their absence that would appear difficult to explain. Or, as another and different illustration, the total neglect until recently of the time costs of transactions made a number of quite rational activities – like paying a higher price rather than search further for a bargain – look foolish because the analysis ignored commodity time as a scarce and valuable input to transactions. In general, the uses of time in economic analysis appear to be the same as the influences of time on economic behavior.

2.3   Unit time and loss of information

The unit time has a surprisingly fundamental significance for economic analysis; the selection of a specific unit time reveals or obscures a great deal about economic reality and relationships. That fact appears not to be at all obvious. The choice of a day or a year or a week or an instant as the elementary analytical time unit seems to be innocent enough – a fairly trivial matter of convention, convenience, or availability of data. Yet the unit time acts as an analytical filter that determines what temporal information the analysis includes and what it leaves out. This is so because all temporal information about events within units time is lost; only changes between units time are revealed.

The unit time is the period over which economic flows are measured; it denominates, as noted earlier, the "rate of flow per unit time." But familiar though it is, such a rate of flow is itself an abstraction that reduces an ordered series of events to a single number. Sometimes the temporal information that is thereby lost is not important to understanding an economic process. Sometimes it is.

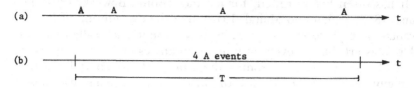

Figure 2.3. The information loss in unit time.

Economic events occur, of course, in time, in ordered sequences, separated by various durations. Leaving aside the specific nature of events for now – so all similar events can be represented by anonymous A's – and dealing only in analytical time so that there is no problem of an economic actor's perspective, such an ordered set of economic events is shown in Figure 2.3(a). There is a good deal of information in that representation of events. In the time horizon encompassed by Figure 2.3, four A events happened, one after the other. They are differentiated both by the order in which they occurred and by the durations of the periods between them: The second event came quite soon after the first (one unit of time), whereas the third came only much later (five time units), and the fourth followed long after the third (also by five time units).

The time line of Figure 2.3(b), coincidental with that of Figure 2.3(a), introduces a conventional analytical unit time of duration T. The unit time T is of such duration and timing that it encompasses all the events A. The A events are then represented as a rate of flow per unit time T, with the inevitable result that all information about the sequence (order) and timing (measure) of the A events is lost. All that remains of the original temporal information about those events can be put in the statement "In the period T, four similar events, A, happened." Nothing else is left. All temporal individuation of those events is lost: There is no differentiation, for instance, between the first and second of the ordered events, should differentiation or sequence be of analytical value; it is impossible to say when any event happened or what the differences were in the timing of the events within T, should that be of analytical value. All temporal information about A events is compressed into the single number 4, a simple count over duration T that abstracts both from order and from measure.

The parallel with a statistical mean is obvious. A "rate of flow per unit time, T," is like an average over a population; it summarizes events occurring over the period T; $N\overline{x} = \sum_{i=1}^{N} x_i$ is a summary of the characteristic x_i occurring in the population of size N. Temporal information about individual events is lost in the flow-rate statistic, with only the fact of their occurrence within T being retained; information about variations in characteristic among individuals is lost in the population mean. In both, the use of finer subdivisions – of the population N or of the elementary time unit T – will increasingly reveal the underlying facts about individual characteristics or the timing of individual events. The extreme of information retention is a full individual enumeration of characteristics in population N or a full time-specific enumeration of when events occur within unit time T, a fully time-shaped description of events.

The elementary time unit of any analysis establishes its level of temporal abstraction: Anything less than full time-specific enumeration of events loses information. The point is not, of course, that information loss is necessarily undesirable, because abstraction is the essence of theory. It is, rather, that

Influential choices about the degree of analytical abstraction – what temporal detail to leave out of an analysis and what to include – are typically made unwittingly, because the unit time is only casually specified when it is made explicit at all. What should be a conscious decision about the level of analytical abstraction appropriate to a given economic problem is too often a matter of unexamined convention.

There is considerable potential for mischief in this practice, as it is an aim of this study to show.[8]

As the unit time is made shorter, more temporal information about economic variables and economic processes is revealed. At one extreme, finely delineated time units generate an undigestible mass of temporal information about economic events – a collection of trees that might make up a forest if only one could see it. This is the "ceaseless oscillation" of economic variables that Hicks (1946), in one of the rare analytical considerations of the length of unit time, saw as the irrelevant noise resulting from use of a too-small unit time. But the more subtle and more serious problem exists at the other extreme. A too-long unit time obliterates the temporality of events and makes it impossible to see change, causality, or sequence, no matter how central they may be to the process being studied. Everything appears to happen all at once or constantly, and although exogenous common sense can be imposed to sort out the timing – "everyone knows" that daily food consumption is not spread evenly over the 24 hours – that timing cannot be considered analytically, so its implications cannot be developed. The convention of using calendar periods as the unit time does not avoid but instead exacerbates these problems.

Figure 2.4 shows one hypothetical economic variable over time – a series of events A, again – and the effect of choosing analytical units time of different lengths to describe it. The actual sequence and timing are shown on time line (a) in time-specific detail. Time lines

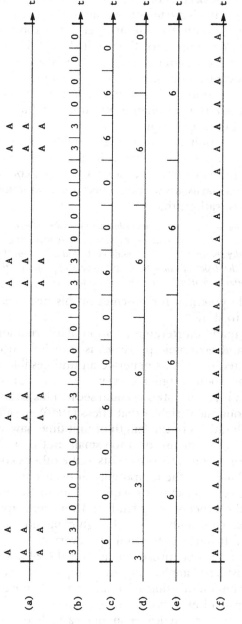

Figure 2.4. A single-event sequence (a) represented in different units time (b)–(e).

20

(b) through (e) show the very different representations that the same events in (a) get under different choices of analytical units time. Each of the very different patterns of flow rates pictured might imply a quite different set of economic relationships, of course, yet their variety is only an analytical fiction, due to differences in the unit time used to describe the actual sequence (a). Changing the unit time changes the representation of an underlying reality: In general, the larger is the unit time, the more temporal detail is lost and the more "constant" any events will seem to be.

And the information lost by a larger unit time is truly lost. As an alternative to (a), a different sequence of A events is shown on time line (f); here the A events occur continuously. But sequence (f), despite its quite fundamental difference from sequence (a), would appear to be identical to (a) when represented in the large unit time of (e) – both would be seen as constant flows at a rate of "six A's per unit time" despite their underlying dissimilarities. In the other direction, it is impossible to tell with the analytical unit time of (e) whether the underlying process is the very discontinuous one of (a) or the wholly constant one of (f).

In production, for one relevant example, it is impossible to know whether a statement like "twenty-four tons of output per day" describes output produced at a constant rate of 1 ton per hour over the whole day or output at a rate of 3 tons per hour on a single eight-hour shift or output at a rate of 24 tons, all in one hour. Yet these very different time-shapes of production carry very different implications for costs, capital stocks, capacity, capital productivity, labor use, and factor intensities – economic variables that often are of considerable analytical importance.[9]

In econometrics there is a closely related issue. Geweke's recent work (1978) on temporal aggregation, following Theil (1954), has been concerned with the information loss when econometric estimation is based on data in which large time units are used to measure flow rates. The information loss leads to "contamination" of parameter estimates, in Geweke's terminology, and it proves to be greater the more oscillation there is within the time unit of the data. Whatever the degree of contamination of estimates, contamination is a decreasing function of the fineness of temporal detail in the series, the size of the unit time.

Despite its considerable similarity, this econometric question is different in a fundamental sense from the issue of this study. The econometric analysis concerns the accuracy with which a hypothesized, hence already recognized, economic relationship is estimated empirically. The vector of independent variables is not at issue; only the accuracy of estimation of their coefficients is at issue. This study, in contrast, deals with the recognition and specification of economic variables in the first place when they are hidden by aggregation in an inappropriate unit time; the analytical unit time will determine which variable will show up in the theory that in turn specifies the independent variables to be tested econometrically. So time-specific modeling seeks to avoid an initial "conceptual contamination" that can obscure underlying economic relationships: It deals with a seemingly more basic problem than the econometric contamination that interferes with estimation of already hypothesized relationships.

2.4   The structure of time-specific analysis

I have said that time-specific models retain and analyze the temporal information about events within unit time that is lost in conventional analysis. They bring that information into formal models and determine, thereby, whether or not the timing and sequence of events within the orthodox unit time have significance for the economic problems being examined. This is not simply a matter of using finer and finer time units to reveal more and more temporal detail – Hicks's "ceaseless oscillations," again. Instead, time-specific analysis is distinguished structurally by simultaneously retaining both the orthodox unit time, like a day or year – a "calendar unit time," always denoted by T in what follows – and a much smaller unit time into which that calendar unit is divided, like an instant or minute within a day or a day within a year – an "elementary unit time," denoted by t in what follows. In time-specific analysis, then, every orthodox unit time T is broken down into its elementary units time t, so that every process is seen both conventionally and in its detailed time-shape within that orthodox unit time. Put the other way around, the economic process is described in elementary time units t and then is always explicitly described over the whole of the orthodox calendar unit time T. It is the simultaneous use of these two nested analytical units time that reveals what is happening within the temporal boundaries of the conventional calendar unit time of conventional analysis.

Hood's analysis of time in economics (1948) drew the important distinction between an exogenous time measure and an endogenous time measure, between an external and essentially geophysical numeraire, like a calendar or clock unit, and a functional time unit defined by the economic process itself, like "the long run." In time-specific analysis, the elementary unit time t is always an endogenous functional time unit – whatever name it is given – because it is the largest unit time that can be used and still fully reveal the economic relationships under study. So *the appropriate elementary time unit will vary from one problem to the next because different degrees of temporal detail are functionally relevant to different analytical issues.* If the appropriate elementary time unit is the calendar unit time T, then a time-specific model is identical to that of ordinary analysis.

The time unit T usually will be the exogenous geophysical *calendar* unit time of conventional analysis – it always will be in the models of this study. But it need not be. As illustrated in the postscript (Chapter 12), T can also be endogenous, as it is in the analysis of the relational exchange contract or of Kornai's goods transactions, where it is the duration of a period that encompasses all transactions events.

The familiar question "How long is the long run?" asks about the relationship between an economically functional time unit and exogenous geophysical time units. It can be paraphrased generally: "How many exogenous calendar time units are there in that given endogenous functional time unit?" A similar question, but in the opposite analytical direction, is important in time-specific analysis: *How finely must the calendar unit time be divided to fully reveal the relationships of a given economic process?* In any time-specific model, the elementary time unit must be chosen to be sufficiently small that no information of analytical importance is lost. The principle is easy, but its application requires some trial and error. In terms used in the first section of this chapter, the familiar calendar time unit T is the analytical range of time-specific analysis; its analytical unit time is a functional subdivision t. "Instant" and "moment" are usefully imprecise phrases to describe that small but functionally varying unit time.

All economic events are identifiable in time-specific analysis, with explicit clock times and flow rates per elementary unit time – typically instantaneous rates. From these, the timing, duration, and sequence of events can be derived. The familiar "rate of flow of output per day, Q" of conventional analysis, for instance, appears in a time-specific representation as the accumulated daily flow Q, explicitly decomposed into its instantaneous rate of flow, $q(t)$, at each instant t ($t_0 \leq t \leq t_T$) over the day T ($= t_T - t_0$). If Q is produced during only a part of the day, T_p ($= t_p - t_0$), then the process is idle the rest of the day. As noted in the last chapter and as developed in the next, time-specific analysis reveals that the cost behaviors of inputs to production are different in fundamental ways – that the price of capital services is sensitive to the duration of their use in T, whereas the price of labor services is sensitive to the timing of their use in T. So what appears in conventional analysis as simply Q appears in time-specific analysis as

$$Q = \int_{t_0}^{t_p} q(t)\, dt,$$

and the capital service price is dependent on duration $T_p = t_p - t_0$, whereas the labor service price depended on specific time t.

The defining characteristics of a time-specific analysis are these:

1. Two analytical time units are used simultaneously, the familiar calendar unit time T, of conventional analysis, and a smaller elementary unit time t, into which T is exhaustively divided.

2. The elementary unit time t is always a functional endogenous interval determined by the particular economic process under study, the largest time unit that can be used to decompose T and still reveal all the relevant economic relationships: At one extreme, $t = T$. The conventional unit time T can be either a geophysical unit such as the day or year or an endogenous unit such as the short run.

3. Analytical attention is focused within the ordinary unit time T; time-specific analysis looks internally at the timing of events within T, rather than externally over a series of time units T as does conventional analysis.

4. Events that appear as simple accumulated "rate of flow X per unit time T" in conventional analysis are decomposed into instantaneous rates of flow $x(t)$ at each moment t over T to retain and reveal information about their timing, sequence, and duration: Where $X = x(t)T$, t and T are the nested elementary and calendar time units, respectively.

It is important to stress that within this unconventional temporal context, time-specific models in this study are wholly and neoclassically orthodox.[10] Their function is solely to allow careful examination of economic processes within the unit time T. If, in a particular case, nothing of analytical interest is revealed by time-specific analysis, $t = T$, and the model's structure is such that it reverts to an entirely familiar and orthodox neoclassical form. So the only thing that necessarily distinguishes time-specific modeling is the foregoing list of characteristics that allow its unusual retention of the temporal information about events within the unit time that conventional analysis loses.

2.5   Economic rhythms: repetitive events in calendar unit time

In the body of this study, time-specific analysis will be used to model an important but quite restricted set of economic events. It will concentrate on the implications of regular, repetitive, wholly predicted changes in economic variables and environment within geophysical calendar units time, changes that depend on night and day, winter and summer, that occur with rhythmic regularity and in the same way within each of a series of conventional units time. These variations will always be hidden in the temporal abstraction of that orthodox unit time: The regular rise and fall of the hourly wage rate from night to day will appear as *the* unchanging wage rate for each 24-hour day, and the regular weekly change in demand for electric power or transportation services will be lost in a single number of kilowatt-hours or person-miles per week.

Concentration initially on these regular, rhythmic variations of economic events within calendar units time is recommended simply because this seems the most modest and most effective way to introduce a new sort of analytical perspective. But a more basic justification for this limited focus is that rhythmic variables are of considerable and often unrecognized importance to economic behavior and processes. For instance, it was impossible to understand investment behavior in underdeveloped countries – with its concomitant political and international ramifications – without understanding the determinants of multiple-shift-working, because the prevalence of shift-working (the utilization and idleness of the capital stock) determined capacity, capital productivity, and its contribution to economic growth (Winston, 1968). But because shift-working is a time-specific activity within the day, the established production theory of 1968 was totally silent on its determinants.[11] The night–day wage and productivity differentials that are its main determinants were simply ignored.

An interesting attribute of these repetitive, rhythmic events is that they induce behavior that justifies to a remarkable degree the usually unjustifiable assumptions of textbook neoclassical economics: the assumptions that information is perfect, that economic actors adjust fully to an optimal pattern of behavior, that preferences are stable, that relative prices change less rapidly than people can adapt to them, etc. These ordinarily sticky assertions about human behavior become markedly less objectionable when they describe economic behavior with respect to regular, repetitive events that occur at predictable times and with predictable magnitudes: Learning, search, and adjustment are inherent in the highly repetitive nature of the choices being made. Simply through repetition, people making such decisions will improve their knowledge. In every one of many unit times T, they face the same events at the same time t with the same constraints and the same objective functions. In that wholly repetitive context, even the dullest economic actor will likely come to know what to expect. Indeed, it appears that repetitive events may be the only economic events to which neoclassical analysis really applies (this is pursued further in Chapter 12).

So one can support, as I would, the relevance of an unreconstructed and quite simplistic neoclassical choice theory for analysis of these repetitive rhythmic decisions, but at the same time, and with no inconsistency, hold that a highly bounded rationality and limited cognitive capacities must underlie nonrepetitive choices (March, 1978; Simon, 1978a). For the class of events that is the subject of the rhythmic analysis of this book, therefore, the rationality of firms and households appears to be defensibly unbounded.

Equilibrium, in this context of repetitive choice, is very much a Hahn full-information equilibrium in which economic actors can be seen fully to have adjusted to their (rhythmic) environment so that no additional knowledge or new discovery about that environment will modify their behavior (Hahn, 1973). Of course, in this context, that equilibrium behavior is itself time-specific and rhythmic rather than time-invariant: Although it is stable from one calendar unit time to the next and would appear to be constant in the usual representation, it is nonconstant, in fact, within any unit time. To Hahn's description would be added "full information with respect to time." It is interesting, too, that if one accepts Samuelson's schema (1947, Chapter XI), a time-specific analysis of repetitive events is neither "statical" nor "dynamical," but something in between (I've flirted with "rhythmical").

The fact that perfect knowledge about rhythmic events can reasonably be assumed simplifies the time dimensions of this analysis. In the first part of this chapter, I was at pains to distinguish between *analytical time*, in which events are represented as they are viewed by an omniscient analyst standing above the action of the time line, and *perspective time*, in which the unfolding events are seen from the temporal perspective of the decision maker moving through time. But now, with the assumption of perfect knowledge justified by the repetitive nature of the decisions modeled, this distinction is virtually eliminated. Until we turn to the different and nonrhythmic time-specific events considered in the postscript (Chapter 12), therefore, perspective time will be put aside, and only analytical time will be employed.

Finally, in dealing only with rhythmic and repetitive events, we clearly rule out uncertainty and with it any consideration of its effects (excepting only the occasional lapse in a footnote); the models of this study incorporate a purely deterministic analysis.

2.6   Music, electronics, and unit time: two illustrations

It is useful to end this introduction of timing and unit-time-as-an-abstracting-device with two illustrations, one brief and one very brief. Each can be seen as describing a production process, although both are drawn from outside of economics. One is Bach's Suite for Solo Cello as it would appear if it were to be represented in the same way that production processes are represented in economic analysis. The other is the internal functioning of the small hand-held electronic calculator, which becomes comprehensible only with a proper choice of the elementary unit time. Modern music and electronics, it is not irrelevant to note, employ time in highly sophisticated and self-conscious ways that are reflected, if only dimly, in stereophonic broadcasting, digital sound recording, and computer design and in the operas of Phillip Glass or the music of John Cage and Terry Riley.

Bach's Suite No. 1 for Solo Cello

It is not necessary to belabor the point that comes through clearly, I think, in a comparison of Figures 2.5 and 2.6, where the score of the prelude and first minuet from Bach's Suite No. 1 for Solo Cello is first reproduced in full as two and a half pages of musical notation (Figure 2.5) and then is represented as simple rates of flow per unit time (Figure 2.6), where the unit time is here defined as $T = 280$ beats (an endogenous interval). When all information about the sequence, timing, and duration within that unit time T is suppressed, so is all the essential information about the musical process. Whereas simple common sense might assure that such extensive damage is rarely done to the description of economic processes by temporal abstraction, it is clear that the scope for misrepresentation and the potential for misunderstanding of underlying processes are very great. The score itself in Figure 2.5 is a time-specific representation, revealing the anatomy of the musical process.

The electronic calculator[12]

The second and richer illustration describes the problem of trying to understand, de novo, how the hand-held electronic calculator works. A striking paradox would be encountered at the outset of any investigation: It doesn't have enough parts – enough capital equipment – to do all the things that in fact it does. The calculator reads informa-

Prelude

Figure 2.5. Bach's Suite No. 1 for Solo Violoncello. (From Eisenberg's Bach: Six Suites for Solo Violoncello, copyright 1975 by Paganiniana Publications Inc. Reprinted by permission of the publisher).

tion from keystrokes, performs a set of mathematical operations, and displays the results of those operations by using light-emitting diodes (LED) to form numerals. But there are only four electrical terminals available to transmit information from the 20 input keys to the processing unit of the machine, and there are only eight terminals available to light up any or all of the 72 diodes needed to show nine-place numbers in the lighted display.[13] In both cases it simply cannot be done – it is impossible for so few terminals to differentiate among that many inputs or outputs.

NOTE	RATE PER UNIT TIME
G´	0.02500
F#´	0.00625
F´	0.00089
E´	0.00268
E$^{b´}$	0.00179
D´	0.02589
C#´	0.00714
Middle C	0.06161
B	0.08571
A#	0.00268
A	0.13929
G#	0.00625
G	0.09196
F#	0.09464
F	0.01250
E	0.07321
E^b	0.00714
D	0.11607
C#	0.01071
C	0.02500
b	0.03214
a#	0.00000
a	0.02321
g#	0.00000
g	0.05446
f#	0.00357
f	0.00000
e	0.00982
d#	0.00000
d	0.01161
c#	0.00179
c	0.00446

Figure 2.6. Bach's Suite No. 1 for Solo Violoncello.

In contrast to an economic process, in the understanding of an electronic process we can get help from its designers. From them we learn that the secret to the workings of the calculator lies in the fact that its limited physical capital is used *seriatim* to control the input and display, one piece at a time. Only a small part of the display or keystroke capital is in use at any one moment. Two components of the calculator make this *seriatim* job assignment possible: (a) a storage register that holds numbers in inventory until they can be processed

or displayed and (b) a clock signal that switches the same eight circuits of the display function (on which we will further concentrate)
from illuminating one digit to illuminating the next. Over a whole
cycle of such switches, all nine display digits are lighted up *seriatim;*
at no moment is more than one digit lighted. Each displayed number, then, has its moment in the cycle when it is turned on; all are
lighted, one after the other, so that each position in the display –
each digit – gets its information in its turn and appropriately turns
on some or all of its diodes using the eight circuits. Eight circuits are
enough to light up one numeral, but not more than one. At any
moment, only one is needed.

So the calculator operates rhythmically. The "main clock signal"
lets it use the same capital stock (the processor and eight terminals)
to do a number of different tasks (light up some or all of the 72
different diodes) by specialization of functions within time. Simultaneously inconsistent activities (lighting more than eight diodes with
eight terminals) are accommodated one after the other.[14] The main
clock signal that controls job assignments among circuits generates a
natural frequency from an electronic oscillator circuit – a geophysical
rhythm. It is like the day–night rhythm relevant to economic processes, only too fast, of course, for human perception; it operates at
250 kilohertz, each rhythm lasting 1/250,000th of a second.

It is the brevity of these periods that makes calculator technology
so useful in illustrating the analytical role of unit time. Each digit of
the display is lighted for only 132 microseconds – 33 cycles of the
main clock – before the system is reassigned to display the next digit.
With six clock cycles of idleness between each separate digit display,
the whole scanning cycle that covers all nine digits takes 429 clock
cycles.[15] Even though each digit on the calculator display is actually
lighted only 8% of the time, human perception sees a constant,
nonflickering numeral in the display; we sense that all digits are
lighted simultaneously and constantly, but in fact that is not true.
The parallel with our economic perception of constancy over the
reality of daily change is too tempting not to point out. So is the fact
that major technical advances in electronics – which is certainly the
Schumpeterian leading sector of the last half century – have rested
on the same sort of explicit attention to time as that of time-specific
economic analysis.[16]

Armed with a description of how the calculator *does* work, now
consider the effect that different choices of an analytical unit time
would have on our ability to comprehend the working of that calculator if, as with a social process, we could not get any insights or

hints from its designer. How might we model the calculator as a production process if we were not already warned of its temporal subtleties?

Within any selected analytical unit time t, all events would, of course, be accumulated and would appear as a single number; no information on order or sequence of activities would be retained. So any effort to analyze the calculator's operation using a unit time longer than $t = 1.7$ milliseconds – the duration of the 429 vibrations of the oscillator – would leave the analyst boggled about its operation. Paradoxes would abound; eight circuits would magically differentiate among and turn on and off 72 circuits in defiance of the rules of electricity. Of course, an analysis based on a unit time somewhat shorter than 429 clock cycles would begin to unravel the mystery, and progressively shorter units time would progressively reveal the underlying fact that the capital stock of the calculator's processing unit and terminals is utilized more intensively by sequencing activities than we would expect on the assumption of the single-purpose tasks typical of specialized capital. Ultimately, as t was made smaller and smaller, we would discover that display capital is idle 92% of the time, despite its apparent constancy of use.

Timing and sequence are crucial to understanding the way the calculator works, but these are the temporal characteristics of events that are always suppressed within any unit time.

The elementary unit time appropriate to fully comprehending the calculator's operation is the basic one-frequency rhythm of the oscillation of its main clock – the unit time of $t = 1/250,000$th of a second.[17] Whereas any longer unit time would obscure important production relationships, any shorter unit time (like that appropriate to a computer, with its higher-frequency clock) would risk confusing the analysis by revealing the "ceaseless oscillations" that would provide too much detail and not help in understanding the calculator's operation.[18]

2.7   Conclusions

Starting in the next chapter, a series of explicitly time-specific models of familiar economic processes is developed: a time-specific production theory in Part II, a time-specific theory of household behavior – of work and consumption – in Part IV, and a time-specific theory of markets for factors and for production in Part V. All of these models are of the sort described in this chapter, in which the economic process is described simultaneously in two nested units time to reveal the timing of activities within the orthodox unit time. All are highly conventional in their neoclassical assumptions in order to focus clearly on their unique treatment of time. The temporal abstraction and information loss of ordinary analysis are avoided – the elementary unit time is selected with explicit attention to what information it suppresses – and the often misleading results of that conventional abstraction are revealed. So production – to which we turn in the next chapter – is analyzed as a time-shaped process in which the familiar cost-minimizing firm will, if it can, minimize costs with respect to the timing of its production within the unit time, as well as the more familiar variables. When work and consumption are recognized as time-shaped, the household's behavior can be seen to be importantly conditioned by its highly time-specific environment.

The order of the development of time-specific theory – from production theory to the household and then to markets – is useful despite the fact that a powerful underlying source of variation in economic behavior within calendar units time – the main source of daily economic rhythms – is certainly the households' responses to their time-specific geophysical and social environment. It is important, though, that the time-specific production theory be laid out clearly at the outset, both because it establishes essential characteristics of inputs and products that remain central in all the time-specific modeling and because the "new" household production analysis – in a time-specific version – is used subsequently to describe time-shaped consumption and work behavior.

PART II

Time-specific analysis of production

Modeling the time-shape of processes, technology, and prices

If we were to formulate an entirely general theory of production, all inputs would have to be regarded as more or less continuous time functions, and the product quantity . . . would likewise have to be considered as [a] more or less continuous time function . . . This would involve a study of how a change in the shape of one or several of the factor time curves would influence the shape of the production time curve.

Ragnar Frisch (1965)

The same perspective on economic processes and the same analytical elements are used to develop a time-specific analysis of production, of household work and consumption behavior, and finally of markets. That perspective is set out in this chapter. It is used in Chapters 4 and 5 to describe the time-specific production theory, in Chapter 8 to develop the time-specific theory of the household, and in Chapter 10 as the basis of the time-specific theory of markets. Rather than start with totally disembodied abstractions, however, the common structure and perspective of time-specific analysis are developed here, embedded in the theory of production. Firms are represented while producing goods or services under technological and economic constraints; this is the process at the core of the time-specific production model.

The first section of this chapter makes explicit the time dimensions of the analysis. The next establishes the instantaneous production function as the way of representing technology, so that production is described as a purely technological process at a moment of time, then integrated over the unit time, making explicit the relationships among stocks and flow rates and their timing, durations, time profiles, and accumulated flows. The third section links the strictly technological stuff of the second section and the price behavior of the fourth, identifying those crucial technological and economic characteristics that differentiate among inputs and outputs in time. The fourth section develops the implications for input prices of those factor characteristics – perishability, market institutions, and ownership – hence their effects on the behavior of costs. In the last section, the time-shapes of cost flows over the unit time are derived from production processes that combine inputs with different characteristics; this last section prepares the way for discussion of optimal production scheduling in Chapter 4 and the discussion of cost-minimization in Chapter 5.

3.1   The time context of time-specific models

The purpose of time-specific analysis is to expose what happens within the familiar unit time so that the implications of those events and their timing can be examined. To do so, it uses, simultaneously, two analytical time units, the calendar unit time T of orthodox analysis, like a day or week or year, and its subdivisions into elementary time units t, like an hour or a moment. Representing economic process in this time frame decomposes each of the familiar summary variables, like output per day, Q, into its instantaneous rate of flow $q(t)$ at each moment t over the day T. If the instantaneous flow rate is either ON at a constant rate $q(t)$ or OFF at rate zero, then the accumulated daily output flow, Q, is simply the product $q(t)T_p$ of production within the day T.

Figure 3.1 shows the same output per day, Q, as it could be generated by four quite different time-shapes of production: (a) a constant output flow rate over the whole day, T; (b) a higher constant rate, but for only one shift out of a possible three, so that $T_p/T = \frac{1}{3}$; (c) a constantly changing rate, but over the entire day, T; and (d) the whole of Q concentrated into two glorious if brief hours of production, T_p. In each, $T = t_T - t_0$. Although these relationships are described for flow rates and duration of output per day, they apply with equal force to yearly man-hours of labor service flow or weekly machine-hours of capital services or any other ordinary economic flow variable. Because all four of the output profiles pictured in Figure 3.1 describe the same accumulated daily output, Q, the areas under the curves are the same, and they would not be distinguished in ordinary analysis. Yet each of these time-shapes of production carries very different implications for the flows and timing of inputs into the production process – they imply different capital productivities, labor-force behavior, and costs, even though by the end of the day each has produced the same accumulated amount of output.

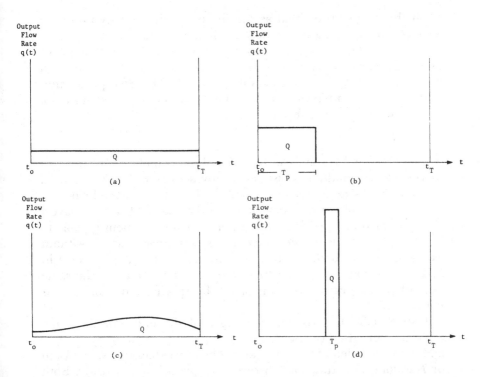

Figure 3.1. Alternative time-shapes of a given daily output Q.

So in time-specific analysis, those familiar accumulated quantities, "flow per unit time, T," are represented as the explicit result of explicit rates of flow per the explicit elementary time units (ETU), t, that compose the unit time T. Those instantaneous flow rates can change from one moment to the next and can be positive or zero. The unit time T is exhaustively divided into its constituent ETUs t, so that any economic process that is traditionally reported in summary form for unit time T gets spread out, in a time-specific model, to reveal the explicit temporal detail or time-shape of that process.

The ETUs t of this analysis – the instants in the production model – have the two analytical functions described in the last chapter: (a) The duration of the ETU is the elementary endogenous measure of the analysis, and (b) each ETU carries an implicit label, specifying its timing within the unit time, its clock or calendar time. In a daily production analysis ($T = 24$ hours), t_i might be 4:17:31

when the second is defined as the "instant" t_i in a yearly unit time ($T = 365$ days), t_i might be a day like January 14th.

There are two aspects of this specification of ETUs that prove useful. First, within the unit time T, any two specified ETUs define a duration, the length of an interval on the time line. So if production starts at time t_0 within the day T and continues until t_p, the duration of production is the difference

$$T_p = t_p - t_0.$$

(In general – and certainly at first – I will not complicate the analysis by considering multiple episodes of any activity within T.) Second, it is not always necessary to be explicit about the specified clock or calendar time, but only to bear in mind that any ETU t_i does have a clock or calendar specificity. So although it is convenient initially to let t_0 be that moment when production starts every day T without worrying about whether it is 5:45 a.m. or 8:00 p.m., whatever it is, t_0 is understood to be some specific time of day, and it is the same time of day every day. (Later, t_0 will be specified in a daily T as midnight.)

Time-specific analysis lets the length of the unit time T be any arbitrary period – a calendar day or week or year, most typically – and it lets the elementary time units t be any exhaustive subdivision of T so long as it functions to reveal the process under study. Both of these choices have important effects in any particular application of the theory.

The time-specific models of this study concentrate on the behavior of economic events within a typical unit time T; so they describe, over a whole sequence of units T, repetitive, rhythmic changes of price, environment, costs, etc. The value of any variable is fully specified within any unit time by a value of the ETU – things are assumed always exactly the same every day at 12:15 p.m. (with t a minute and T a day). So the selection of a particular calendar unit time T – say a day instead of a week – will determine the nature of the rhythmic phenomena in any analysis – light, dark, and pronounced diurnal biological and social rhythms will affect economic behavior with $T = 24$ hours; snow, hydroelectric potential, farm-price rhythms, and school schedules will affect economic behavior within $T =$ the year. For many economic questions, the relevant rhythmic events will be obvious, and the appropriate analytical period T will be that of a single calendar unit time; for other questions, the rhythmic events may be subtle and may reflect a time-shape defined over more than one calendar time unit – consideration of shift-working, electric-power demand, or travel timing suggests that complex time-shapes are most common.

Selection of an elementary time unit, t, even in time-specific analysis, determines the level of temporal abstraction as described in the last chapter. It is still true that events even within t are aggregated; so all information about their timing within that ETU is lost. A time-specific analysis, therefore, must still self-consciously select as the ETU a unit of time sufficiently small that, for the analytical purposes at hand, nothing of economic interest changes within it. There remains the same potential for unwitting abstraction as in orthodox analysis.[1] So the explicit assumption in analyzing production is that all prices, input flow rates, and technological input and output relationships remain entirely unchanged within the "instant."[2] (Lest this seem a trivial point, note in Chapter 6 Shephard's serious problems with it in applying mathematical duality theory to production.)

The notation used throughout this study is designed to reflect the time-specific dimensions of the analysis; so it is well to make its conventions clear.

> *Elementary time units,* ETUs, are denoted by lower-case t, whether an instant or a day is the ETU. They are subscripted by specific clock or calendar or functional labels, i, j, p, where it matters.
>
> *Calendar units time* – the units time of orthodox analysis – are always T.
>
> *Durations* of periods within the calendar unit time are capital T's. T is the duration of the calendar unit time; any specific functional duration within T, like that of production, T_p, is subscripted (and must lie between zero and T).
>
> *Rates of flow of economic variables* per ETU – of output, factor inputs, costs, utilities, goods used in household production, etc. – are indicated by lower-case letters. If they change over the unit period T, they are made explicit functions of time in ETU, t. So $q(t)$ and $l(t)$ are the rates of flow of output and labor services, respectively, at time t. Without an argument, a flow variable is constant; so k will describe a time-invariant rate of capital service flow.
>
> *The prices of those flows* are indicated, too, by lower-case letters, with $p(t)$ indicating, further, that the price is time-specific, varying within T; $\bar{p}$ indicates a price that remains time-invariant over T.
>
> *Accumulated flows* over specified periods – the whole unit period T if not otherwise specified – are denoted by capital letters: K is accumulated machine-hours of capital service flow, and L is accumulated man-hours per T.

Stocks – of capital or workers – are denoted by barred capital letters; so $\bar{K}$ is the capital stock and $\bar{L}$ the size of the labor crew.

The prices of stocks, like the purchase price of a unit of capital stock, are barred capitals, $\bar{P}$, subscripted for identification; so $\bar{P}_m$ is the purchase price of a machine.

Notation, added as needed, will fall within this general convention.

3.2   Production technology in specific time

The production process is defined by instantaneous flow rates and their time profile over the unit time T; so the basic element of time-specific production analysis is the instantaneous production function

$$q(t) = f(x_1(t), x_2(t)), \quad \partial f/\partial x_1, \partial f/\partial x_2 \geq 0,$$
$$\partial^2 f/\partial x_1^2, \partial^2 f/\partial x_2^2 < 0,$$
$$f(0, x_2(t)) = f(x_1(t), 0) = 0. \tag{3.1}$$

This is a purely technological relationship, uninfluenced by economic choices, by the specific conditions of particular firms or adjustment periods like the short run or long run. It conforms to Shephard's conception of the production function as describing the entire, unconstrained set of purely technical relationships between inputs and outputs that has been the standard of modern production theory (Shephard, 1970, Chapter 1).

The production function (3.1) is unchanged over T. All variables are instantaneous rates of flow at the specific time t, and output and input flows are assumed to be homogeneous.[3] The production function is linear homogeneous and has the usual well-behaved properties with respect to factor and output flow rates. It is represented graphically by an ordinary-looking isoquant map in $x_1(t), x_2(t)$ space like that of Figure 3.2; only the explicit use of instantaneous and time-specified rates of flow is different from the familiar representation. And because the established tradition of two-factor models serves our initial purposes well, until it is modified at a later point in this chapter, $x_1(t)$ is seen as the rate of flow of capital services, $k(t)$, and $x_2(t)$ as the rate of flow of labor services, $l(t)$.

But because these are truly instantaneous flow rates, they seem more familiar than they are. $l(t)$ is the rate of flow of labor services at t. Assuming (as I will until Chapter 11) constant levels of effort per worker, both among workers and for a given worker over time, $l(t)$ is the same thing as the crew size, $\bar{L}(t)$. Crew size is defined as the number of workers working in that production process at time t.

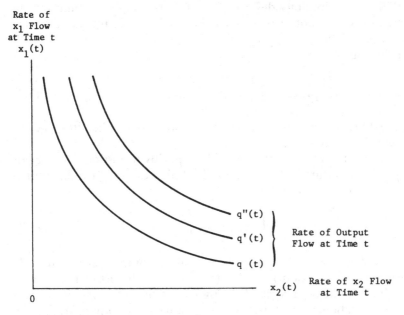

Figure 3.2. Instantaneous isoquant map.

The crew, $\bar{L}(t)$, therefore does not include all the employees ($\bar{E}$) who work for the firm but may be absent at that moment, t, from the job – because they are on a later shift or on vacation or for whatever reason – but only those at work at t, producing output. $k(t)$ is the capital service flow rate at t. It is equal to the size of the capital stock in operation at t, because, again, I will simplify by assuming that all of the capital stock owned or rented by a firm is at work during periods of operation.[4] Finally, the rate of flow of output, $q(t)$, at time t is the "speed" of production.

So a strictly interpreted instantaneous production function (3.1) says that the rate of output flow at t depends on the rate of flow of capital and labor services to the production process then, that, *ceteris paribus*, increasing either capital or labor service flow rate – the amount of equipment each crew member works with or the number of crew members tending a given set of machines – will speed up production, but the increase in speed obtained with increased input flow rates diminishes. There are assumed to be no lags in response to flow-rate changes. Equation (3.1) allows for the possibility of fixed flow coefficients – that "a machine must be operated by a crew of fixed size," in Solow's phrase (1962) – but certainly not their necessity.

With the technology described by (3.1) relating input and output flows at each instant over the unit time T, it is a simple matter to get onto the familiar ground of an accumulated output per unit time T, like "output per day,"

$$Q = \int_{t_0}^{t_T} q(t) \, dt = \int_{t_0}^{t_T} f(k(t), l(t)) \, dt, \qquad (3.2)$$

where t_T is the moment at which T ends.[5] Q is "the time rate of output flow" when the unit time is T.

Because it is important to be able explicitly to distinguish periods of production during T from periods of idleness, (3.2) can be written in more useful temporal detail as

$$Q = \int_{t_0}^{t_p} q(t) \, dt + \int_{t_p}^{t_T} q(t) \, dt = \int_{t_0}^{t_p} q(t) \, dt, \qquad (3.3)$$

because there is a positive rate of flow of output, $q(t) > 0$, only during the production period $T_p (= t_p - t_0)$. This sort of production schedule would be described by Figure 3.1(b) or 3.1(d), with different specifications of $t_p < t_T$: an 8-hour shift, a 12-hour shift, or, if T were a week, a five-day week of 24-hour operation. With $t_p = t_T$, the plant operates all the unit time – Figure 3.1(a) or 3.1(c). It is necessary only that the period T_p describe uninterrupted operation, so that $q(t) > 0$ in $t_p - t_0$ and that the duration of that period be clear and explicit.[6] So all of the variety of Figure 3.1, and more, lies beneath the familiar "output, Q, per unit time." The "utilization of the production process" – or, equivalently, "capital utilization" – is defined as T_p/T.[7]

Input flows are accumulated over the unit time in the same straightforward way as output flows. So the accumulated flows of capital services per unit time and of labor services per unit time are

$$K = \int_{t_0}^{t_T} k(t) \, dt = \int_{t_0}^{t_p} k(t) \, dt \quad \text{and} \quad L = \int_{t_0}^{t_T} l(t) \, dt = \int_{t_0}^{t_p} l(t) \, dt,$$

respectively. When input flow rates are constant during production,

$$K = k(t)T_p \quad \text{and} \quad L = l(t)T_p.$$

Then the production function can be written in accumulated-flow form,

$$Q = T_p f(k(t), l(t)) = f(K, L), \qquad (3.4)$$

by virtue of the homogeneity of (3.1).

But it is clear that the accumulated-flow production function (3.4) is not a generally valid description of production; in general, it is not permissible to show daily accumulated output as a unique and strictly technical function of daily accumulated input flows. Adding up flow rates over T to get (3.4) is an acceptable and familiar matter of accounting or summarizing. But breaking down (3.4) into implicit flow rates – though also familiar – requires that the timing of each flow must be known somehow so that $k(t)$ and $l(t)$, hence $q(t)$, can be known at each moment over T. There is no information in the accumulated input flows K and L to tell when these flows take place; yet that timing is crucial to their contributions to daily output. If a tractor and driver are both in the field for 10 hours in a given day but they are not the same 10 hours, little plowing will get done. Or, more familiarly, if a plant is run for two shifts with a crew of eight men on each shift or alternatively with a crew of one man on the first shift and fifteen on the second shift, the resulting outputs will be quite different, given our usual assumption of diminishing returns.

This is the first concrete illustration of the way the information loss inherent in selection of an elementary analytical unit time affects economic understanding. To use the familiar flow production function (3.4), where T is the elementary unit time (because it is the only unit time), it is necessary to assume implicitly that the time profiles of $k(t)$ and $l(t)$, hence $q(t)$, are strictly independent of all economic influences, including their own time-specific and duration-specific price behavior (described in Section 3.4), and that is inconsistent with our more basic assumption of cost-minimization or profit-maximization motivations. If the time-shape of these flows is not wholly independent of all costs and prices, the accumulated flow production function (3.4) cannot satisfy the requirement that the production function be purely technological in nature, because its technical relationships are contaminated by economic choices on timing. That Shephard himself used equation (3.4) is central to the criticism of duality theory in Chapter 6.

Figure 3.3 shows the three dimensions in which the two-factor production process has now been described. The instantaneous isoquants of Figure 3.2 are extended into a time dimension, t. Only one, for an arbitrary output rate $q_\alpha(t)$, is shown. The accumulated input flows K and L, used during operation for T_p of the period T, appear as areas on the $k(t),t$ and $l(t),t$ planes. The accumulated output over a period of operation is a path in the isoquant space. Any point like ω on an isoquant surface defines an instantaneous rate of

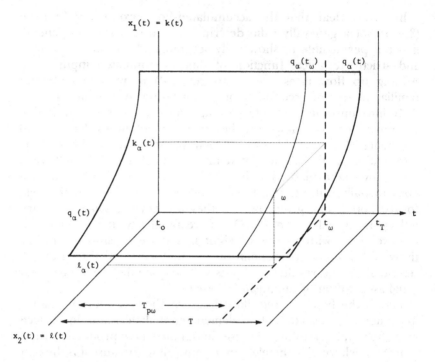

Figure 3.3. An isoquant surface: the time-shape of production within unit time.

output flow $q_\alpha(t_\omega)$ at a moment t_ω and its minimal supporting factor service flow rates $k_\alpha(t_\omega)$ and $l_\alpha(t_\omega)$. If production starts at t_0 and continues without interruption until t_ω, $T_{p\omega} = t_\omega - t_0$. So ω also defines the duration of production over the day, $T_{p\omega}$, and the utilization rate $T_{p\omega}/T$. If there were a constant rate of production at $q_\alpha(t)$ over all of $T_{p\omega}$, the accumulated output per unit time T would be $Q = T_{p\omega}q_\alpha(t)$, and daily factor service use would be K_α and L_α, the areas of the rectangles enclosed by dotted lines on the $k(t),t$ and $l(t),t$ planes. Varying rates of output and factor use over $T_{p\omega}$ would describe non-rectangular output rates off of the $q_\alpha(t)$ isoquant surface. The additive separability of the instantaneous production function (3.1) in time is responsible for the isoquant surfaces being simple extensions of the instantaneous isoquants in the t dimension. So the production process defined by (3.1) goes on without inherent change; given the technical flow relationships, the rate of output at t is determined solely by the rates of flow of inputs at t.[8]

3.3   Characteristics of production flows

A main source of the economic insights of time-specific analysis is its
ability to identify temporal characteristics of inputs and outputs – of
the flows into and out of the production process – that get lost in the
unit time of orthodox analysis. It was noted in Chapter 1 that in its
fruitful attention to distinguishing characteristics of inputs, time-
specific analysis is doing much the same thing as recent pure trade
theory; both draw the significant implications of a more careful attention to neglected aspects of inputs and outputs. In trade theory,
those characteristics are defined by spatial mobility or immobility; in
time-specific analysis, they are defined by temporal mobility or immobility. In both, the mobility affects an input's price characteristics.

Flows to and from the production process have four closely related characteristics that are central to their economic behavior in
time: (a) the nature of the flow (whether in the form of services or
goods); (b) the source of service flows (whether from the same unit
of stock over T or from different units); (c) the ownership and
markets in input stocks and flows (what is owned by the producer,
what is owned by others, and what it is that is traded in input markets); (d) the perishability of accumulated flows over the unit time T
(whether or not inputs and outputs can be cheaply stored over T).
Together, these characteristics determine importantly different
time-specific price characteristics and cost behavior of the inputs to
and outputs from production over T. The costs of inputs with different characteristics behave differently, and systematically so, within
the calendar unit time, and the rational economic actor will adjust to
these time-specific facts just as he adjusts to other technical and
economic aspects of his environment in familiar microeconomic theory. Time-specific output flow characteristics add further constraints
to the decisions of rational actors.

The nature of flows

Production flows are divided into (a) service flows, including capital
and labor services and inputs like electric power, and (b) goods
flows, including nuts and bolts and cloth and sugar. When capital
and labor services are used in the instantaneous production function
(3.1), both of the explicit input arguments are service flows, and the
output can be either a service flow or a goods flow. Differently
specified, $x_1(t)$ or $x_2(t)$ could describe the rate of flow of either services or goods.

Sources of flows: stocks, flow rates, and accumulated flows per unit time

Georgescu's meticulous description of the production process in time made the distinction between service flows and goods flows on the basis of their sources in "funds" and "stocks," respectively.[9] While retaining the spirit of that analysis, it is not necessary to worry about the distinction between drawing down goods inventories (his "stocks") and the utilization in production of the services of capital equipment of a labor crew (his "fund"): Their relevant differences are reflected in time-specific analysis in their price behavior. What is important here is to spell out the various relationships, for the different service inputs to production, between stocks, flow rates at time t, and accumulated flows over T. There are marked and significant differences in these relationships between capital and labor as the two primary service flows relevant to production. These differences stem from the fact that capital services are derived from insensate capital stocks, whereas labor services are derived from often too-human labor stocks. Because these complementary factor services must – explicitly in time-specific modeling – meet simultaneously in producing output, such differences have a very fundamental and time-specific effect on the production process. This central fact needs to be spelled out.

For both capital and labor, the rate of service flow from a unit of stock during production – of capital stock, $\bar{K}$, or the labor crew, $\bar{L}(t)$ – is assumed always the same both over period T and between homogeneous units of those stocks. So, whereas the measured "rate of flow of capital services" will be the same whenever a given stock of capital is used in production, the productivity of that capital service flow will vary in the familiar, elementary textbook sort of way, as more or less labor services are combined with it. This is explicit in equation (3.1), and it conforms to ordinary usage, but it is now in a pure flow-rate context. The same is true for labor services. "Work effort" from all crew members is constant and identical (that assumption will be dropped in a later chapter). Finally, it was assumed earlier, and still is, that during production there are no idle machines or crew members; this is a reasonable concomitant of the assumption of homogeneity.

Together, these give a very simple relationship between factor stocks and factor flow rates:

$$k(t) = \bar{K}; \quad l(t) = \bar{L}(t) > 0 \quad \text{for} \quad t_0 \geqslant t \geqslant t_p, \tag{3.5}$$

and

$$k(t), \, l(t), \, \bar{L}(t) = 0 \quad \text{for} \quad t_p > t \geq t_T.$$

During production at time t, a unit of capital stock $\bar{K}^{10}$ yields a unit of capital service flow, $k(t)$, and a member of the labor crew, $\bar{L}(t)$, yields a unit of labor service flow, $l(t)$. When the production process is idle, both capital and labor service flows are zero, and so is the size of the work crew – so even temporary stockpiling of labor is ruled out for simplicity. Both the capital stock and the rate of flow of its capital services are constant over T_p because of its durability over T; both crew size, $\bar{L}(t)$, and the rate of flow of labor services can vary.

Then, K, the accumulated flow of capital services over T, is related to the size of the capital stock, $\bar{K}$, by

$$K = T_p k(t) = T_p \bar{K}, \tag{3.6}$$

where $k(t)$ is rate and T_p is duration of flow in T. It is clear that the accumulated flow of capital services K per unit time can be varied *ex ante* by varying either the size of the capital stock $\bar{K}$ or, alternatively, the rate of its utilization, T_p.[11] Put the other way around, the same accumulated capital service flow per unit time can be got from an infinite set of pairs, (K, T_p); even though $T_p \leq T$, $\bar{K}$ and T_p can be varied widely while maintaining the same daily flow of capital services.

With the explicit capital-utilization relationship (3.6), the capital *stock* can be used in an accumulated-flow production function (3.4) as

$$Q = f(T_p \bar{K}, L), \tag{3.7}$$

which is very close to the familiar production function that casually mixes stocks and accumulated flows,

$$Q = G(\bar{K}, L). \tag{3.8}$$

Both (3.7) and (3.8), of course, violate the requirement that production functions be purely technological relationships by including economic influences. Equation (3.7) makes an implicit assumption about the time-shape of the input flows over T_p; equation (3.8) makes implicit assumptions about that and, in addition, about the duration of production, T_p. Because the optimal duration emerges in the next chapter as the result of a least-cost schedule for producing Q over T, the technological relationships in (3.8) are even a bit more contaminated with economic responses than those in (3.7). (As an unsatisfactory escape, one might assert that capital stocks somehow produce output regardless of their periods of use–a very Austrian view in which the world of production is a great big wine barrel.)

For the labor input, the labor crew, $\bar{L}(t)$, is the group of workers providing labor services to production at time t. The relationship among alternative measures of labor input – stocks, flow rates, accumulated flows – is complicated by the fact of the *seriatim* and partial participation of individual workers (employees) in the production process. The total accumulated flow of labor services, L, used in production in period T is simply related to crew size and flow rate by

$$L = \int_{t_0}^{t_p} \bar{L}(t) \, dt = \int_{t_0}^{t_p} l(t) \, dt. \tag{3.9}$$

Of course, crew size is not often a central concern about labor. Interest usually centers on employment, and that is clearly a different thing. Individuals replace each other, *seriatim*, in their membership on a labor crew of unchanged size, when the duration of production, T_p, is sufficiently long. That, of course, is shift-working. So the number of crew slots, $\bar{L}(t)$, is not the same thing as the number of individual employees, $\bar{E}$, who may fill those slots at different times over T. For the labor input, therefore, it is necessary to distinguish among the following: (a) crew size, $\bar{L}(t) = l(t)$, which describes the number of workers providing labor services to the production process at any moment t during T, hence the rate of labor service flow; (b) employment, $\bar{E}$, which describes the whole set of individuals who provide labor services at one time or another during T; (c) the familiar accumulated man-hours of labor services, L, which measure the total of accumulated labor service flow used in production at any time during T.

Although employment, $\bar{E}$, must always be at least as large as crew size, $\bar{L}(t)$, and the rate of flow of labor services, $l(t)$, is identical with crew size, the accumulated flow of labor services, L, has no simple relationship to employment, crew size, or rate of labor services in production. Employees, $\bar{E}$, can follow each other in their participation in the labor crew, $\bar{L}(t)$, so even if crew size is constant during operation, employment depends on much else besides:

$$\bar{E} = T_p \bar{L}/T_w = L/T_w, \tag{3.10}$$

over T, where T_w is the average duration of work per worker – the work day, when T is a day. With a crew $(\bar{L})$ of 100 on two-shift operation $(T_p = 16$ hours) and an eight-hour workday $(T_w = 8)$, 1,600 daily man-hours of labor services (L) are provided by 200 employees

($\bar{E}$). On a single shift, a crew of 200 would produce that same accumulated flow. But if T is a year, instead, and L is measured in man-years (T_w') of accumulated labor service flows, seasonal concentration of production implies

$$\bar{E} = T_w'L/T_p = \bar{L}.$$

With a crew ($\bar{L}$) of 100 workers working for only 1,000 hours in the year ($T_p = 1,000$), only 50 man-years ($100 \times {}^{1000}/_{2000}$) are provided by the 100 employees. This has been a considerable source of mischief in empirical studies of factor use – a problem to which we return in Chapter 7.

For now, it is necessary only to stress that capital and labor service inputs have quite different relationships to their stock sources and accumulated flows, the insensate one being operable with little regard for preferences or fatigue,[12] the human one having both preferences and physiological limitations that often require *seriatim* participation in the production process. And both are embedded in rhythms that often impose seasonality of utilization.

Perishability or storability of flows over unit time

A central characteristic that distinguishes among the flows in production is their storability over the calendar time unit T, whether accumulated flows like Q or K actually can accumulate (or deplete) or whether "accumulated flow" simply describes an accounting convention, summarizing what has happened during T. For instance, does the flow of output, $q(t)$, that (3.3) accumulates to Q over T actually exist at the end of that period, at t_T? Or is Q simply the record of a set of ephemeral events – the $q(t)$ – that happened between t_0 and t_T? For $q(t)$ of bicycles, Q exists at t_T; for $q(t)$ of electric power, Q does not exist. If flows actually do accumulate (or deplete), they will be called storable flows; if they do not accumulate, they will be called perishable flows.

This is an oversimplification, but a useful one; what is involved often is not an inherently binary characteristic of input or output flows but rather the result of a decision based on the costs of storage over the unit period, T. Electric energy, for instance, can be stored over the day or the week and often is, but only at a cost so high that it is optimal for producers and users typically to treat electric power as if it were a strictly perishable output or input. So assumptions about storage costs will be implicit in the classification of commodities as perishable or storable, and a change in, for instance, storage technology can alter that classification. This becomes relevant in the discussion of Chapters 10 and 11, but initially all goods and services will be either storable at no cost or perishable.

Storable flows are, within unit time T, "temporally footloose"; perishable flows are time-specific. So this characteristic of flows determines the necessity for simultaneity in the timing within T of the separate economic activities of production, sale, purchase, and use. A unit of perishable input must be produced and used at the same moment within T; a unit of perishable output must be produced at that moment during T that it is used: No matter how acute the shortage of local transportation during the morning rush hour, it will not be alleviated by driving more buses through empty streets at 2:00 a.m. Perishable products must be produced and consumed coincidentally; storable products can be made when they are cheapest and used when they are most valuable. Storability removes the need for simultaneity in production and use, breaking the temporal link between them. Schedules of production, marketing, and use of perishable flows must be coordinated; schedules of production, marketing, and use of storable flows can be temporally independent. This is the basis for the quite fundamental distinction in time-specific production theory between the production of storable commodities made with perishable inputs (Chapter 4) and the production of perishable commodities made with storable inputs (Chapter 5).

Factor ownership and markets

The final characteristic of inputs to production that time-specific analysis shows to play a central economic role is that identified by Jorgenson and Griliches – that in a capitalist nonslave economy, ownership institutions are typically such that capital stocks are owned by firms, whereas labor stocks are owned outside the firm.

If capital services were bought and sold by distinct economic units in the same way as labour services, there would be no conceptual or empirical difference . . . The measurement of capital services is less straightforward than the measurement of labor services because the consumer of a capital service is usually also the supplier of the service; the whole transaction is recorded only in the internal accounts of individual economic units [Jorgenson and Griliches, 1967, p. 254].

This difference has profound and only partially appreciated influence on the economics of the production process. Although both capital and labor stocks contribute their service flows to the production process in (3.1), they differ significantly in the structures of their markets, hence the behaviors of their prices and costs within the unit time T.

Capital *stocks* are bought and sold. Labor *service flows* are bought and sold. For both factors, owners make decisions on the utilization of their stocks – the amount of factor service flow per unit time, T, to contribute to production. In the case of capital, that utilization decision is internal to the producing firm – it is the optimal-utilization decision, the optimal time period, T_p, to utilize the capital stock in production. In the case of labor, that utilization decision is internal to the household – it is the worker's familiar decision on the optimal time period, T_w, to work, his work–leisure choice. The factor market in productive capital is a market in capital *stocks;* the factor market in productive labor is a market in labor *service flows.*

It might appear that this distinction is eroded by the existence of rental markets for capital, but that is not necessarily the case. Rental markets force the distinction to a deeper level, however, than simply that of ownership. Most generally, the relevant distinction between factor-markets institutions rests on *who pays for periods of idleness of stocks of productive resources during the unit time T.* Ownership of capital stocks requires the payment of a fixed amount per unit time T (ignoring use-depreciation). The firm (or household) pays whether or not the capital is utilized, whether it is yielding a flow of services or is idle; the firm pays for the idleness of its capital. In contrast, the firm buys labor service flows as such, paying only for what it uses; the worker pays for his own idleness. This has long been seen as the central fact in analyses of the optimal work–leisure decision.

So capital rental is analytically the same as capital ownership *if* the firm's rental pays for its right to use the capital stock for the unit time, T, and not just for that part of T in which it is actually utilized, T_p. This, of course, is the practice in most productive capital rental markets. So "ownership" and "rental" are not as relevant to the economics of production as are "payment for unit period, T" and "payment for use, T_p."

In the production analysis that follows, therefore, salaried workers, slaves, and capital equipment owned or rented over T all have the same essential cost characteristic of being paid for per unit time T regardless of the amount of their productive use, T_p. In contrast, hired labor services, computer time, and electric power have the same essential cost characteristic of being paid for only in the amount used in production. Although it appears superficially that all that is involved is the familiar difference between "fixed costs" and "variable costs," it will become clear that those ideas convey only a small and often misleading part of what is economically relevant about the different input ownership and market characteristics.[13]

3.4   Factor prices: duration-specific prices, time-specific prices, and time-invariant prices

We can now describe the prices of the arguments of the instantaneous production function (3.1) and how they behave over unit time. Their specification is neither trivial nor obvious, despite the general conviction to the contrary, because the prices of capital service flows, labor service flows, and goods flows behave quite differently. These are the economic consequences of the different flow characteristics that time-specific analysis identifies.

The conventional treatment of the price of labor service flows is appropriate to time-specific analysis of production because market transactions take place typically in labor services, per se, so that we deal naturally with a wage rate that is the price of a unit of labor service flow – a man-hour.

But because market transactions in capital inputs typically take place in capital stocks, the decision on how much factor service flow that stock will yield per unit time T is hidden in the bowels of the firm.[14] As noted earlier, Jorgenson and Griliches first described the effect that this institutional characteristic of inputs has had in obscuring the analysis of capital service flows in production, specifically the variable utilization of capital stocks that is central to time-specific production analysis. But its fuller implications were not developed. Especially powerful are those deriving from the fact that these ownership institutions and the internal nature of the utilization decision have obscured the nature of the capital service prices to which producers respond. We deal quite unnaturally with the unit price of capital service flows as a simple price per machine-hour, a measure wholly analogous to the wage rate as the unit price of the labor service flow. Yet that is the price of the capital argument of a flow production function.

Duration-specific prices: the prices of capital

The price of capital services is typically not well specified. When they incorporated plant and equipment price, interest rate, depreciation, and taxes in a single "price of capital," Jorgenson and Griliches (1967) and Williamson (1971) significantly clarified that important part of production theory. Unfortunately, they chose to call that integrated capital price "the price of capital services," implying that it described the price of a capital service flow, the argument of a flow production function (3.1). Instead, what they had specified was the price of owning a unit of capital stock for a period of unit time T, the price of having access to its services. Because capital utilization, T_p/T, is implicitly assumed to be a constant in orthodox production analysis, the inconsistency of this specification is not obvious: With an unchanged utilization rate, T_p/T, the price of a machine hour, p_k, is simply a scalar of the cost of owning the capital stock for period T. But when production is recognized as a process in time where the duration of production, T_p, is explicitly variable – indeed, is subject to optimization – the error is seen to be less than innocent. Its ramifications are wide.

It is useful, therefore, to be explicit about the existence of three quite different "prices of capital" in time-specific production:

(a) The purchase price of a unit ("machine") of capital stock, $\bar{P}_m$, is the market price of "a machine," determined by the supply of and demand for machines. $\bar{P}_m\bar{K}$ is the purchase price of a (homogeneous) capital stock of size $\bar{K}$.

(b) The price of owning a unit of capital stock for a period of unit time, T, $\bar{P}_m(r_T + \delta_T)$. Then $\bar{P}_m(r_T + \delta_T)\bar{K}$ is the cost of owning a capital stock of size $\bar{K}$ for a period of duration T. It reflects the opportunity cost, r_T, of tying up resources and the loss in value due to depreciation, δ_T, for that period, T (r_T and δ_T are measured appropriately, always, to T, taxes being ignored). If δ_T represents depreciation due only to obsolescence and deterioration, then $\bar{P}_m(r_T + \delta_T)$, the "owner cost of capital," is wholly independent of the amount of capital service the stock provides to production during T. $\bar{P}_m(r_T + \delta_T)$, as used earlier, is the familiar "rental rate of capital" that would emerge in a competitive rental market. Denote the unit owner cost or rental rate of capital for the period T as

$$P_k = \bar{P}_m(r_T + \delta_T). \tag{3.11}$$

(c) The price of the capital service flows used in production, P_k/T_p, is a price of capital services entirely analogous to the wage rate, and therefore the price appropriate to $k(t)$ in the pure flow production function (3.1). The firm owns (or rents) the capital stock $\bar{K}$ at a cost of $\bar{P}_m(r_T + \delta_T)\bar{K}$ over T, whether it is used ($T_p > 0$) or not ($T_p = 0$), so P_k/T_p reflects the fact that the price of the capital services used in production is inversely dependent on the rate of utilization of the capital stock. For simplicity, assume that δ_T is unaffected by use

(which is not crucial to the analysis).[15] Then the price of a unit of capital service flow to production is

$$p_k(T_p) = \frac{P_k}{T_p} = \frac{\bar{P}_m(r_T + \delta_T)}{T_p} . \tag{3.12}$$

This capital service price is unconventional enough and its behavior is important enough to all that follows in time-specific analysis that I will risk belaboring the issue. Consider two identical machines with the same sales price, $\bar{P}_m$, bought at the same time, with r_T and δ_T identical for both. So both have the same yearly owner cost or rental rate. But machine No. 1 is operated one hour every year, whereas machine No. 2 is operated flat out, 8,760 hours every year. So machine No. 1 provides one machine-hour of capital service flow per year. Machine No. 2 provides 8,760 times as much. Clearly, the prices per machine-hour of their services – the price of the argument of a flow production function (3.1) – must be different by the nontrivial factor of 8,760. This difference is reflected in $p_k(T_p)$, but not in the traditional "rental rate," P_k.

This important relationship between capital service price and utilization rests, of course, on the fact that the cost of capital rolls on over T, no matter how much it is used; whether owned or rented, capital is paid for per unit time T. And capital is always durable over T. The same relationship would hold for labor under slavery, where the stock of labor would be owned by the firm. Then the distinction between crew size and employment would vanish, because at all times the labor stock is being paid for by the producer. The cost of owning a slave (the stock) would then depend on his supply price, costs of maintenance, depreciation (appreciation), and the rate of interest per unit time T. The price per man-hour of labor services – the effective wage rate, ignoring fatigue – would vary inversely with the man-hours of labor service flow the slave provided per unit time T; his wage rate, like the price of capital service flow, would be a decreasing function of his utilization – the duration of his average workday, T_w. In the other direction, capital and labor would also be treated symmetrically if capital were rented only for the time it was in use – if capital service flows, per se, were always bought and sold, as in the market for computer services.[16]

So the price of the capital service flows that are an input to the production process – the price of $k(t)$ of (3.1) – is duration-specific. It is expressed, therefore, as an explicit function of the duration of utilization of the capital stock, $p_k(T_p)$.

Time-specific prices: the price of labor service flows[17]

The price of the labor service argument of the production function (3.1) has different characteristics. A wage rate like an ordinary hourly wage is conceptually appropriate as the price of the labor service flow, $l(t)$ in (3.1): Labor markets ordinarily buy and sell labor services, per se.

The distinctive aspect of the wage rate is its time specificity, that it changes regularly by time of day (or week or possibly year), t. Most people have strong opinions about when they prefer to schedule their work and consumption activities within the unit time; to be induced to schedule work regularly at night or on weekends or holidays, most of us have to be paid a premium wage over that for "normal" timing of work. The underlying reasons for this are subjected to close examination in time-specific analysis of the household in Part IV; here, work timing preferences and the time-specific wage rates they induce are taken simply as data to the firm – as a major rhythmic aspect of the firm's economic environment.

Although specific time patterns of wage rates will be considered in the next chapter and in the later discussion of time-specific markets, for now it is important only that the wage rate, $w(t)$, be made an explicit function of time t within the unit time T. This describes a wage rate that is predictably different at different times of day (or the week or year) – a regular night-shift wage premium or a higher wage rate for work on Sunday or Christmas. It is a wage for a given amount of work, but one that is sensitive to and is defined by when the person works.[18]

Time-invariant prices: the prices of goods inputs

When goods flows enter as inputs into the instantaneous production function (3.1), they add a third type of price behavior over T to time-specific analysis. Goods prices often are time-invariant, changing neither by time of day (or year) nor by duration of their use. The price of a good will be time-invariant over T either if the good is subject to no rhythmic influences in its supply or demand over T – an unlikely prospect, according to Chapter 10 – or if the good is cheaply storable and hence temporally footloose in T – a quite likely prospect, especially when T represents a short calendar period like a day.

Goods prices can be time-specific, and they will be if the goods flow is subject to sufficiently strong rhythmic influences in its own supply or demand over T (sufficient to justify time-specific metering

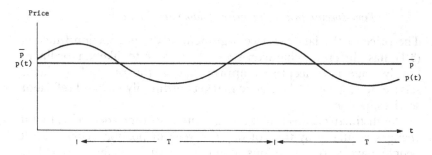

Figure 3.4. A rhythmic price in orthodox, $\bar{p}$, and time-specific, $p(t)$, representations.

costs) and if storage costs over T are significant. A time-specific purchase price alone is not enough to establish a time-specific price of the flow that enters the production function (3.1) at time t: If a good can be stored at no cost over T, it can be made available to production at any time at a time-invariant price – it is the temporally footloose input in what follows. The longer the unit time T, the longer the period of storage required and the more prevalent will be time-specific prices for goods flows. The price of cane to a Louisiana sugar mill is highly time-specific over the year but not over the day; the price of clothing to a household is time-specific over seasonal "sales" but not over a week.

Because a time-specific price is a rhythmic price when viewed over a sequence of time units T, rising and falling in a regular, repetitive, and wholly predictable pattern with no trends and no uncertainty, in conventional analysis this regularity has justified using an average price over T, a "constant" price that does not change from one T to the next. In Figure 3.4, the rhythmic pattern of a time-specific price profile within T is shown, along with the time-invariant representation it gets in orthodox analysis as a constant price, $\bar{p}$. This conventional use of "constant" has recommended use here of the more awkward but explicit phrase "time-invariant" to describe a price that is truly unchanged over all t.

Prices of the arguments of an instantaneous production function: summary

Three very different patterns of price behavior in time, therefore, characterize the goods and services in the production process as it operates over the unit time. Some prices are time-invariant, the same at all moments during T; some prices are time-specific, varying rhythmically and predictably according to the specific time of day or time of year; some prices are duration-specific, varying systematically with the utilization of factor stocks. These price behaviors and the interaction among them are the essential links between the strictly technological aspect of production of (3.1) and the costs of production essential to the economics of time-specific analysis that describes firms (and households) adjusting to this time-specific price environment. The remainder of this study is, in its essentials, an examination of the implications of these fundamental differences in price behavior within the unit time, differences that are neglected because of the temporal abstraction of orthodox economic analysis. This time- and duration-specific price behavior is the basic economic component of the answer to the question implicit since Chapter 1: What of economic interest happens within the unit time of orthodox analysis? The answer: Prices change systematically because of both timing and duration, and people adapt to those changes.

3.5   The time-shape of costs

Because key factors of production have time-specific and duration-specific prices over the unit time T, production costs vary over T, with time-shapes that depend on the characteristics of these factor inputs. In general, the instantaneous rate of flow of costs at t is simply

$$c(t) = p_1(t)x_1(t) + p_2(t)x_2(t) \tag{3.13}$$

in production with two factors. The cost of production of conventional interest – that which is to be minimized by a cost-minimizing firm – is the accumulated cost flow per unit time T, which is

$$C = \int_{t_0}^{t_T} c(t) \, dt = \int_{t_0}^{t_p} c(t) \, dt. \tag{3.14}$$

It is the relationship between this familiar summary cost measure, C, and its time distribution over T – the time-shape of the $c(t)$ – that can now be examined. In this concluding section of this chapter, that relationship is seen as it describes a time-specific cost profile, per se; in Chapter 4 it is a determinant of the optimal utilization and idleness of production, and in Chapter 5 it is a determinant of optimal tracking and technology in producing a time-shaped output.

An important aspect of the temporal distribution of costs over unit time is reflected in the second identity in (3.14). It implies that costs are incurred only during production, from t_0 to t_p, that the rate of flow of costs, $c(t)$, is zero when the production process is idle, from t_p to t_T. This is assured by the fact in (3.5) that factor input flows are nonzero only during production.[19] So, again, costs per unit time T are determined by their rate of flow, $c(t)$, and their duration, T_p. This is explicit when the instantaneous time rate of cost flow, $c(t)$, is constant over the period of production, so that (3.14) becomes simply

$$C = c(t)T_p. \tag{3.15}$$

Given the three different sorts of input price behaviors, there are six permutations possible in a two-factor production analysis. It is useful to consider four of them: (a) that both input prices are time-invariant; (b) that one input has a time-specific price; (c) that one input has a duration-specific price; (d) that one input has a time-specific price and one a duration-specific price. These would describe production using, respectively, (a) only storable inputs, (b) a storable input combined only with labor services, (c) capital services and storable input, and (d) capital and labor services. The other two possibilities pair two duration-specific inputs (two capital service flows) or two time-specific inputs (labor and electricity), price behaviors that may well be of interest in particular cases, but seem not to be in general.

Time-invariant input prices

In this case, $p_1 = \bar{p}_1$ and $p_2 = \bar{p}_2$ are both time-invariant; so $c(t)$ in (3.13) is a simple linear function of $x_1(t)$ and $x_2(t)$, both at time t and over T. Any $c(t)$ will generate a familiar isocost curve in instantaneous factor flow space, given input prices at t; $c(t_0)$ is the isocost curve on the $x_1(t_0),x_2(t_0)$ plane at t_0 in Figure 3.5. With all prices time-invariant, that instantaneous isocost curve will, with $c(t)$ constant, trace out over T an isocost surface like that of Figure 3.5. The cost surface drawn is only one of the infinite number, with given prices, that would correspond to different values of $c(t)$. But all of them have the same time-shape over T because that time-shape is determined by $\bar{p}_1$ and $\bar{p}_2$. Note that the cost surface describes costs, C, per unit time, T; so the surface of Figure 3.5 describes production costs per T only when production is continuous throughout all of T. The smaller surface truncated at t_p shows the more typical case where production is scheduled for only a part, T_p, of the unit time. With the same

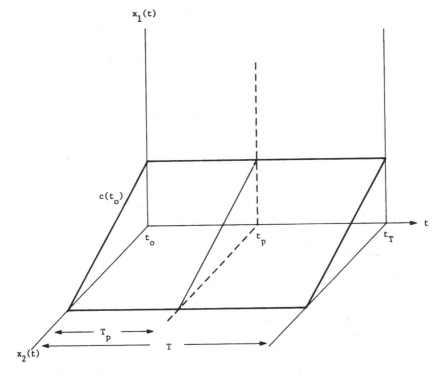

Figure 3.5. An isocost surface for time-invariant input prices $\bar{p}_1$, $\bar{p}_2$.

instantaneous rate of cost flow $c(t)$, cost per unit time, C, depends on factor prices and utilization, together.

Time-specific and time-invariant input prices

Replace one of the inputs in (3.13) so that $x_2(t)$ has a time-specific price, $p_2(t)$ – rising monotonically from t_0 to t_T as shown in Figure 3.6 – but leave $\bar{p}_1$ as time-invariant. That time specificity of $p_2(t)$ means (a) that the isocost surface for a constant $c(t)$ shows changing relative input prices over T – as a function of t – and (b) that the given rate of cost flow, $c(t)$, buys smaller and smaller input flow rates between t_0 and t_T. This possibility is more useful to orderly exposition than to actual analysis of production because, it may be apparent, cost-minimizing production would all have to be concentrated at t_0.

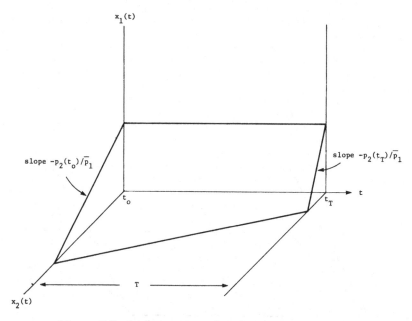

Figure 3.6. An isoquant surface for time-specific, $p_2(t)$, and time-invariant, $\bar{p}_1$, input prices.

Duration-specific and time-invariant input prices

In this case, let $p_1 = p_k(T_p)$ be the price of the capital service flow ($x_1(t) = k(t)$) that therefore depends inversely on the duration of production T_p per unit time; $p_2 = \bar{p}_2$ is now assumed time-invariant. Then a key aspect of production costs in unit time is immediately evident in Figure 3.7. The cost flow $c(t)$ at any time t depends on what will happen both before and after t, because one of the input prices in $c(t)$ is sensitive to the total duration of production T_p, to when it starts and when it stops. If the process starts at t_0 and ends at t_a in Figure 3.7, then the duration of production will be T_{pa}, the price of capital services will be $p_k(T_{pa})$, and the given cost flow rate $c(t)$ will buy a flow $k_a(t)$ of capital services.

Note that if production stops at t_a, the price of capital services is established thereby for all of the period of operation, T_{pa}, up to t_a; so $c(t)$ buys $k_a(t)$ of capital services at any time from t_0 to t_a, and the lowest plane in Figure 3.7, reflecting the highest capital service price, is relevant for the whole of that production period T_{pa}. The repetitive nature of the process, of course, assures perfect knowl-

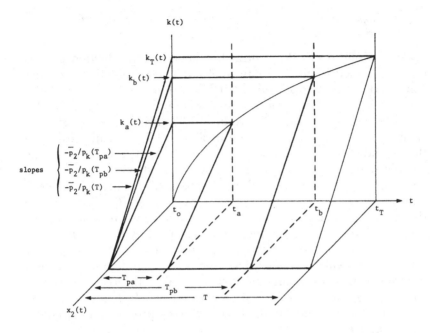

Figure 3.7. Isocost surfaces for duration-specific, $p_k(T_p)$, and time-invariant, $\bar{p}_2$, input prices.

edge before t_a of the price $p_k(T_{pa})$, but that, strictly speaking, is a matter of response to these cost shapes and not their shapes per se – a matter for the next chapter.

If production is extended to t_b for a duration of T_{pb}, then the price of capital service flow falls to $p_k(T_{pb})$; again, because that price is applicable to all capital service flows from t_0 to t_b, $c(t)$ buys a capital service flow rate during that period of $k_b(t)$. Its flow rate is higher than for duration T_{pa} because capital service prices are lower. Finally, if the capital stock is utilized over the whole of the unit time period T, the relevant isocost surface is the top one in the figure that reflects the lowest possible capital service price; $c(t)$ buys $k_T(t)$ of capital services at the low price, $p_k(T)$.

Clearly, $c(t)$ buys more capital services and no less of the other input with the highest utilization of production. When the other input has a time-invariant price, maximum utilization will always be optimal, because only maximum utilization will minimize production costs. But the analysis is very different when the other input has a time-specific price.

Capital and labor: duration-specific and time-specific input prices

Figure 3.8 illustrates the central fact about the production process that is revealed by time-specific analysis. There, capital services are combined with an input flow that has a time-specific price; this is two-factor production, where labor's wage rate, $w(t)$, is time-specific. Then, extended duration of production, T_p, brings the reduction in capital service price just pictured in Figure 3.7, reducing costs. But the extended duration of production also brings the increasing time-specific wage rates pictured in Figure 3.6, and they increase costs. The capital service price is duration-specific, and the wage rate is time-specific; so any given duration of production, T_p, will determine the capital service price for all production between t_0 and t_p, but wage rates during that period are determined by the specific time, $t_0 \leq t \leq t_p$. The isocost surface for production all of the time, duration $T_p = T$, will be that of Figure 3.6; having minimized capital service prices by operating all of the period T, the rising wage rate from t_0 to t_T still twists the resulting cost surface. In Figure 3.8, three such surfaces are shown for three different production durations, T_{pa}, T_{pb}, and T.

Again, anticipating the next chapter, it is clear that maximum utilization will no longer necessarily be optimal. Operating all the time, $T_p = T$, capital service prices are minimized, as before, but labor service prices are at their highest. With increasing utilization, the isocost surface in Figure 3.8 has twisted, pulling in toward the origin in the labor service dimension at the same time that it shifted out from the origin in the capital service dimension. How these two movements will shape the isocost surface and then interact with any given technology – described by an isoquant surface like that of Figure 3.3 – determines the optimal schedule of production, to which we turn next.

Whatever the limitations of three-dimensional graphs, Figure 3.8 makes it difficult to maintain the convention that nothing of economic significance happens within the unit time; it suggests why the relationship between production and costs is a simple matter of a simple price vector only under very restrictive circumstances and with a very limited range of factor input characteristics. The effect of extending utilization, per se, on time-marginal relative input prices is shown in Figure 3.9, where the changes in instantaneous isocosts with increasing utilization are made explicit in the "isocost" lines along that twisting surface.

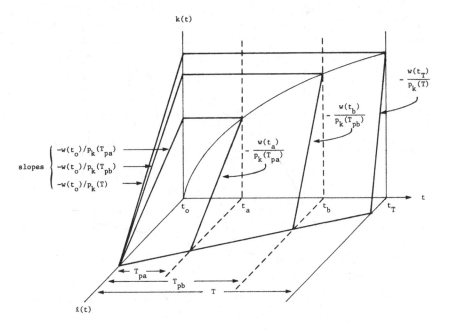

Figure 3.8. Isocost surfaces for capital and labor service inputs.

3.6   Summary

These are the basic materials of time-specific analysis: giving simultaneous attention to familiar accumulated flows per unit time and to the way those flows accumulate, moment by moment, within that unit time; basing the description of purely technical production relationships on truly instantaneous production functions, with no unintended incorporation of economic decisions; examining the arguments to that purely technological production function to reveal the characteristics of factors of production that determine their price behaviors over the unit time; identifying the three markedly different input price patterns over the unit time, because some prices are time-specific, some are duration-specific, and some are time-invariant; deriving the implications of these price patterns for the time-shape of production costs within unit time.

Much has been implied about the optimal response – especially in this last section – of the firm living in this time-specific cost environment. Superimposing Figures 3.3 and, say, 3.8, with their time-shaped production and cost functions, would suggest a great deal

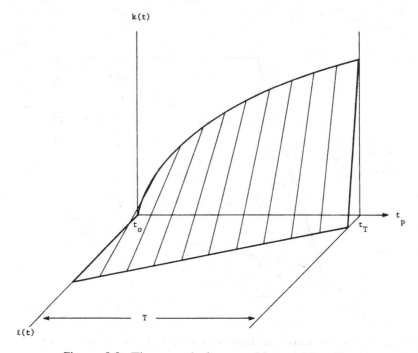

Figure 3.9. Time-marginal costs with variable utilization: capital and labor inputs.

more. In the next two chapters, that optimal, cost-minimizing response will be embodied in optimal production. In Chapter 4, the firm uses time-specific labor services and duration-specific capital services to produce a storable output flow; so cost-minimizing production of any Q per unit time must include optimal production scheduling decisions. In Chapter 5, the firm produces a perishable output flow that has a time-specific demand (like electric power), using duration-specific capital services and a time-invariant input flow (like fuel); least-cost production then centers on the optimal tracking and truncating of the time-specific demand profile.

CHAPTER 4

Time-shaped costs: optimal scheduling of storable production

A firm making a product that is storable over the unit time can schedule production within that unit time so as to minimize costs. In this chapter we will examine that optimal, least-cost schedule for producing a storable output. In the next chapter we will look at the more constrained technological and scheduling choices faced by the producer of a perishable product whose production schedule must adjust simultaneously to the time-shapes of both costs and the demand for its output.

The least-cost production of any given output Q per unit time T involves choices of optimal factor input flow rates, $k^*(t)$ and $l^*(t)$ – thus the speed of production, $q^*(t)$, at each moment t – and the optimal length of the production period, T_p^*, within the unit time T. These are the time-specific intensity and duration of production. All of this takes place in an exogenous time frame that shares clocks and calendars with the world outside the firm. So the optimal scheduling of a given output involves when the production process is operated, t_0 to t_p, for how long, T_p, per unit time, and at what rate, $q(t)$, at each moment of the unit time.

Because it describes so familiar an economic process from so unfamiliar an analytical perspective, this chapter requires special pains in its exposition. The discussion proceeds in three steps in order to separate analysis of the optimal duration of production – the decision on utilization and idleness – from that of the optimal intensity of production, and only when each has been described separately are they joined in a full representation of time-shaped production. This makes it possible to use much of the logic and intuition of familiar unit cost geometry to deal first with optimal utilization, then with optimal intensity, and then – in the three dimensions that are implicit in any time-shaped process – with these aspects of unit cost together.

So Section 4.1 describes the firm's decision on the optimal duration of production within the unit time with intensity fixed; Section 4.2 defines the optimal intensity of production at each moment within the unit time with utilization fixed; Section 4.3 combines optimal utilization and speed to define the optimal, least-cost schedule within T for producing the given output Q per T. Appendix A provides a suitably rigorous restatement of the basic analysis of the chapter.

4.1   Timing and duration: the least-cost schedule of production in unit time

Because this section concentrates on the optimal duration of production, T_p^*, within the unit time T, the intensity of production, $q(t)$, during T is assumed to be fixed by a strict Leontief relationship: Any time the production process is operated, it operates at the same speed with the same factor flow intensities. This allows a nice simple use of familiar-looking, but time-specific, average-cost curves to illustrate the economics of optimal utilization. With speed fixed over any period of operation, output per unit time T is simply a scalar of the duration of production; so they can both be represented on the same axis. This section starts with the structure of efficient production, then describes the limiting case where optimal duration is not an issue – the case where the temporal detail of time-specific analysis adds nothing to the usual orthodox model of production. This artificial situation demonstrates the strange conditions that have to prevail to make time-specific analysis irrelevant. The following part, then, introduces the more reasonable circumstances in which it is optimal to produce less than all the time – where days and nights and seasons exist and firms respond to their time-specific price rhythms by optimally leaving the production processes idle some of the time.

Technology, prices, and costs

The production of a flow of output, $q(t)$, at time t using capital services, k, and a variable input flow, $x_2(t)$ (initially unspecified) that has a unit price p_2 is described by an instantaneous production function like that of (3.1). The $q(t)$ of this chapter can be stored costlessly over the unit time T; so the production schedule for Q per T can attend only to cost minimization. Because the instantaneous production function is restricted, in this initial section, to strictly fixed flow coefficients, (3.1) can be written as

$$q(t) = \min\ [a_k k, a_2 x_2(t)]; \tag{4.1}$$

scale economies are assumed absent.[1] The capital service flow rate is shown as time-invariant, because all of the homogeneous capital stock owned (or rented) by the firm is in use at any moment of operation, and the size of the capital stock is fixed over the unit time by the T-durability of capital. Making (4.1) an instantaneous Leontief production function in this section eliminates from the producer's optimization problem the choice of factor use and speed of output. And without scale economies, the size of the output per unit time – the size of Q – is irrelevant: Whatever timing and duration are optimal for production of one level of output per unit time are optimal for any other.

The total cost flow rate from operating the production process in (4.1) at t is simply

$$c(t,T_p) = p_k(T_p)k + p_2x_2(t), \qquad (4.2)$$

where $p_k(T_p) = P_k/T_p$, with P_k fixed and exogenous to the firm. The unit cost flow rate at t is generally

$$ac(q,T_p,t) = p_k(T_p)[k/q(t)] + p_2x_2(t)/q(t)$$
$$= c_k(q,T_p) + c_2(q,t), \qquad (4.3)$$

where the last two terms are unit capital service costs and unit costs of the x_2 input flow, respectively.

Now consider any given instantaneous rate of output flow, $q(t)$. Let production start at time t_0 and continue, uninterrupted, at the same rate of flow into the unit time T until it stops at time $t_p \leq t_T$. Because it is assumed that the given output rate is time-invariant over T_p, denote it q. The longer q lasts – the greater T_p, the duration of production within T – the more output is produced. The level of output per unit time T, of course, is simply $Q = qT_p$; so with q fixed, accumulated output per unit time T changes proportionately, and only, with duration of production per T. This fact conveniently allows duration of production, T_p, to be represented on the Q axis of an ordinary average-cost curve ("ordinary," given the explicit conditions under which it is here defined): So long as q cannot change over T, Q defines T_p, and the cost-minimizing output per T, Q^*, defines the cost-minimizing duration of production T_p^*. And optimal utilization, T_p^*/T. Only two slight modifications to an elementary textbook unit cost graph are needed: (a) "Costs" are explicitly a unit cost flow rate per ETU, equation (4.3); (b) the horizontal quantity axis, $Q = qT_p$, has a maximum value at qT because, given q fixed, Q varies only with T_p, and no more than qT of output can possibly be produced in T.

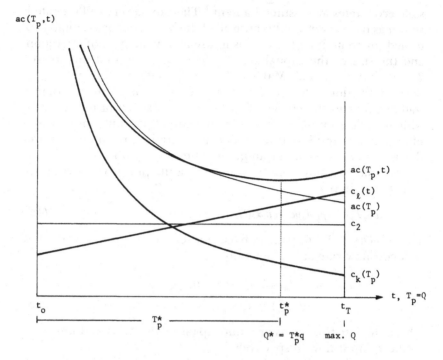

Figure 4.1. Duration of production and unit costs.

Now turn to efficiency. Efficient production of the given rate of flow of output, $q(t)$, requires a given capital service flow, k – which in turn defines a given-size capital stock, $\bar{K}$ – and a given flow of $x_2(t)$, all fixed by the Leontief production function (4.1). Because the flow rate of x_2 also is time-invariant during production, denote it x_2.

The unit costs of capital services are

$$c_k(T_p) = (P_k/T_p)(k/q) = p_k(T_p)k/q, \qquad (4.4)$$

and unit variable costs are

$$c_2(t) = p_2 x_2/q. \qquad (4.5)$$

These costs are drawn in Figure 4.1. Unit capital service costs, $c_k(T_p)$, fall with increasing output per unit time, despite the fixed capital/output flow ratio. The increased duration of production, T_p, reduces the price of the capital service flow, $p_k(T_p)$, hence the costs of a constant rate of flow of capital services, k – mimicking one of the familiar behaviors of a "fixed cost." Unit variable costs, $c_2(t)$, are less straightforward.

The case of constant production, $T_p^* = T$

One possible behavior of unit variable costs – based on one possible set of variable input characteristics – is reflected in the light lines of Figure 4.1. It is the simplest case – and the one case where no insights are derived from time-specific analysis – because the variable input is such that its price is time-invariant, $\bar{p}_2$. Then the unit cost of x_2, $c_2 = \bar{p}_2 x_2/q$, is constant over both time and duration. The total unit cost flow (4.3), the vertical sum of unit capital and unit variable costs, falls from $Q = 0$ to max $Q = qT$, the output level when the process is operated all the time, T.

The optimal schedule implied by the light cost curves of Figure 4.1 is obvious: With the price of the variable input, $\bar{p}_2$, time-invariant, it will always be optimal to produce any given daily output level Q at maximum utilization. The optimal duration of production is $T_p^* = T$; so optimal utilization is $T_p^*/T = 1$. Extending the duration of production, increasing T_p, has lowered capital service costs throughout the unit time interval without affecting the costs of the variable input flow, x_2, and cost minimization clearly requires maximum exploitation of that unit capital cost reduction. This is the same result we noted for this same combination of factor characteristics in Chapter 3, with reference to Figure 3.7. Combining an input like capital services that has a duration-specific price with an input that has a time-invariant price will always lead to maximum utilization as the least-cost schedule of operation. This is the case implicit in all orthodox analysis; it is justified if, but only if, price changes within unit time are absent (and not simply deemed "uninformative").

So when capital services are combined with temporally footloose inputs whose prices do not vary over unit time in the production of a storable output, the optimal schedule of production is always and unambiguously to operate at a constant rate for the entire unit time. The optimal output profile is that of Figure 3.1(a) of the last chapter – a straight line over t_0 to t_T. Note that this conclusion would apply to the usual two-factor production analysis with use of capital and labor services in production only if the wage rate were time-invariant over the unit time. And because the arguments in a two-factor production function are surrogates for many similar inputs, the maximum optimal-utilization rule applies only when all noncapital inputs have time-invariant prices – when production uses no labor, no sugar cane, seasonal weather, or other input with rhythmic prices.

The case of cost-minimizing idleness, $T_p^* < T$

Consider the less artificial and more useful case where the variable input x_2 is explicitly identified as a labor service flow $l(t)$, so that its price is the time-specific wage rate, $w(t)$. Everything else remains the same. Now something can be said about the timing of production in relation to exogenous clock or calendar time, because the moment of the lowest wage rate during T is specifically time t_0, and that – along with all of the time-shape of wages, $w(t)$ – is exogenous to the firm. If the wage rate increases from t_0 onward to t_T, efficient production must be scheduled to start, always, at t_0.[2] So identifying t_0 as the moment of the lowest exogenous wage rate also identifies it as the moment when endogenous least-cost production begins: It can never be optimal for the firm to produce a unit of storable output at a high-cost moment instead of at a low-cost moment. The unit cost function for capital, $c_k(T_p)$, is unchanged, of course, by this different identification of the variable input, but the unit variable cost function (4.5) becomes

$$c_l(t) = w(t)l/q, \quad \partial c(t)/\partial t, \ \partial w/\partial t > 0 \quad \text{for} \quad t_0 < t \leq t_T. \quad (4.6)$$

Were substitution possible, relative factor flow rates, k/l, would vary over T in response both to the falling price of capital services and to the rising price of labor service. But substitution is not possible so long as (4.1) is a Leontief production function; so both k and l are time-invariant and appropriate to the given and time-invariant rate of output flow q.

Starting at t_0, then, as production is extended further into the unit time, it will still bring falling unit capital costs as before, but because of the time-specific wage rate, it will now also bring rising labor costs. The longer the duration of production, T_p, the lower the price of capital services, $p_k(T_p)$, but the longer the duration of production, the higher the wage rate, $w(t)$, and so the higher the labor costs $w(t)l(t)$. Total unit costs for the given rate of output flow, q, then become

$$ac(T_p,t) = c_k(T_p) + c_l(t).$$

The heavy lines of Figure 4.1 show those unit costs when capital and labor services are combined. Unit capital costs are unchanged as $c_k(T_p)$. But now, instead of a time-invariant unit variable cost curve, c_2, the unit labor cost curve, $c_l(t)$, is shown to rise throughout T, from t_0 to t_T, because the only way T_p can be increased is to operate in higher-wage periods. Total unit costs, $ac(T_p,t)$, may thereby be increased, so that least costs are no longer got by operating all of the unit time but, instead, by running the production process only T_p^* out of T — producing from time t_0 to t_p^* and then shutting down from t_p^* to t_T within unit time T. It is optimal to leave the production process idle for $T - T_p^*$ of each unit time; to operate more would save on capital costs but it would incur more than offsetting increases in labor costs because it would necessitate operating during the high-priced period, t_p^* to t_T. That, in a nutshell, is why it is often optimal for a firm to schedule production of a storable output so as to leave the capital stock idle a good part of the time – the extremely important insight that came from the original Marris study of capital utilization.

It might be emphasized that the analysis to this point has adhered strictly to the admonition not to constrain a technological description of the production process by considerations of particular firms or locations or endowments or time periods. The average-cost curves of Figure 4.1 (and those that follow) show neither short-run nor long-run costs, in the usual dichotomy; they are *unit time average costs*, equally relevant to both the short run and the long run. The reason, discussed in Chapter 3, is that within any unit time T, whether it occurs in the short run or in the long run, any capital stocks will be durable, and hence fixed, enduring for the full duration of the unit time; "long run" and "short run" serve only to describe the variability – or lack of it – of the level at which those fixed capital stocks are fixed over T.

Determinants of the optimal duration of production

Figure 4.1 nicely suggests the economic and technological characteristics of production that determine optimal utilization and idleness – optimal duration, T_p^* – of the process over unit time T. They are, simply, the characteristics that determine the shape and position of the unit cost curve, the same characteristics that emerge from the more rigorous model in Appendix A.

The optimal schedule of operation and idleness in the production of a commodity that is storable over unit time T is determined by the following:

(a) The amplitude of wage rate (time-specific price) variations. Because a rhythmic, time-specific price is a necessary condition for less-than-maximum utilization to be optimal, the magnitude of that time-specific price change over T – the amplitude of a time-specific price over a series of units time, denoted as β in Appendix A – will quite reasonably affect optimal utilization. The greater the amplitude, the greater the relative cost penalty for producing during high-cost peri-

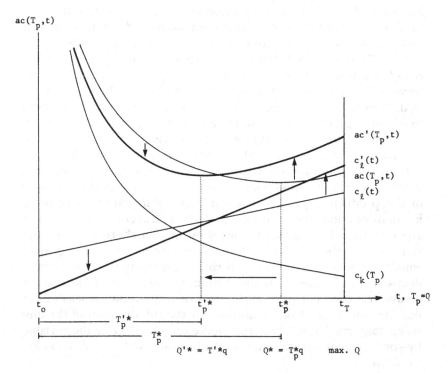

Figure 4.2. Duration of production and unit costs: increased time-specific price rhythm.

ods and the more they are to be avoided. Figure 4.2 illustrates the effect of an increase in amplitude of a time-specific wage rate. With a greater amplitude, unit labor costs rise more sharply with T_p and Q; so $c_l(t)$ becomes steeper, rolling average total costs $ac(T_p,t)$ to the left, thereby reducing the optimal duration of production T_p^* that describes lowest unit costs. Both "before" and "after" in Figure 4.2, the average wage rate over T is the same, and so are p_k, k^*, and l^*. So the first relationship between price parameters and the optimal production schedule is this:

The greater the amplitude of the time-specific price, the lower the optimal duration of production.

   (b) *The relative importance of capital (duration-specific) and labor (time-specific) costs.* Figure 4.3 shows that a rise in capital costs and a decline in labor costs increase the optimal duration of production. Sensibly, the more important are capital costs, the more important it

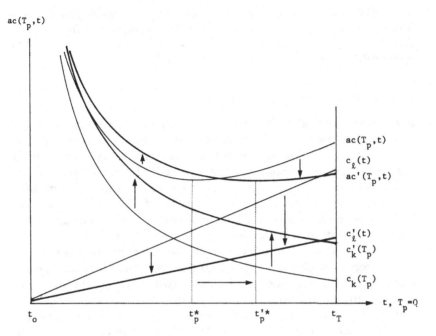

Figure 4.3. Duration of production and unit costs: increasing the importance of capital.

becomes to economize on them through higher utilization. Put the other way, the less important are the time-specific input costs, the less incentive there is to leave capital stocks idle in order to avoid periods of high time-specific prices – even a very large time-specific wage increase will not make much difference in unit costs if labor is an insignificant part of production costs.

But this relationship rests in turn on more fundamental economic and technical parameters of production. The relative costs of duration-specific and time-specific inputs depend on two things:

(a) *Relative factor prices, P_k/W*, where W is an accumulated wage over T_p and P_k is the owner cost or rental rate of a unit of capital stock per unit time T. Relative factor prices influence optimal utilization even in the Leontief case, influencing the relative importance of duration- and time-specific costs. These are the economic parameters that influence relative costs.

(b) *Factor intensities* of the production process, k/l, will, *ceteris paribus*, determine the relative importance of duration- and time-specific costs. These are the technological parameters that influence relative costs.

So the more important are capital (duration-specific) costs – either because capital is expensive or because a lot of it is used in the production process – relative to the costs of the time-specific input, the greater will be the optimal duration of production, T_p^*, in producing any given level of output per unit time T.

Summary: the optimal duration of production

It becomes optimal to leave a production process idle part of the time, despite the waste of capital that this entails, because periods of high prices of time-specific inputs can thereby be avoided. This is the essence of the economics of an optimal schedule of production within unit time T when the output is storable. Costs change with both time and duration of production over T. Because the product can be stored cheaply over T, the least-cost production of any given quantity of output requires least-cost scheduling. Least-cost production must start at the moment of lowest time-specific costs, t_0. As production is extended further into the unit time, duration-specific input costs fall, but time-specific input costs rise. The optimal moment to stop production, t_p^*, is when these two are equal on the time and duration margins;[3] then the increment in capital cost saving is exactly offset by the increment in labor cost increase. The resulting optimal duration of production, T_p^*, determines (a) optimal utilization as T_p^*/T and idleness as its complement $(T - T_p^*)/T$ and (b) the optimal timing, as the moments – in a time frame exogenous to the firm and production process – to stop production, t_p^*, because the starting time, $t_0 = t_p^* - T_p^*$, is exogenous to the firm.

4.2   Least-cost speed of production in unit time: optimal factor flow rates

This second section concentrates on the optimal intensity of production; so the duration of production per unit time, T_p, is assumed fixed. All variations in costs of producing Q considered in this section, then, are got – because duration, T_p, and hence utilization, is fixed – by variations in the speed of output, $q(t)$. The Leontief form of the production function (4.1) obviously is inappropriate to this discussion of the choice of least-cost technology and rate of output because it does not allow any choice of technique with its fixed factor flow proportions at each instant over T both in the short run (*ex post*) and in the long run (*ex ante*).[4]

Fortunately, and in contrast to the optimal-utilization decision, the criterion for choice of factor proportions is, at base, the familiar one from standard analysis, complicated only by the greater detail in which the production process is revealed in a time-specific perspective. That detail shows some ambiguities underlying the orthodox description of production, and it requires that some additional restrictions on optimization be made or dismissed explicitly. But, in general, factor flow proportions are optimal at time t when their relative marginal (flow) products equal their relative prices,[5]

$$w(t)/p_k(T_p) = [\partial f/\partial l(t)]/[\partial f/\partial k(t)]. \tag{4.7}$$

But the temporal details of the production process that inhibit a simple, straightforward adherence to (4.7) at each instant during unit time T are important:

1. The capital stock is always durable over T; hence the maximum capital service flow rate, k^*, will be the same at every time t over any unit time T, whether in the long run (*ex ante*) or in the short-run (*ex post*). (This is true, too, for other capitallike inputs like services of salaried employees that also have duration-specific prices.)

2. Relative input prices at t in (4.7) combine duration-specific and time-specific prices; so they depend both on what time it is, t, and on the duration of production within T, T_p.

3. The ability technologically to substitute inputs in adhering to (4.7) – described by the instantaneous elasticity of factor service flow substitution, σ – depends on the time period allowed for adjustment in the familiar way: The *ex ante* (long-run) elasticity of substitution is different from and often greater than the *ex post* (short-run) elasticity. But a third elasticity is relevant in time-specific analysis, defined by the unit time. It is an "*ex die*" elasticity of substitution that describes the technological factor flow substitution possibilities within the unit time T. These elasticities of factor flow substitution will be denoted σ_a, σ_p, and σ_T, respectively.[6]

The first temporal characteristic, durability of the capital stock over any T, implies that, within any unit time, any adjustment of factor proportions can only take the form of changing the labor input flow with a fixed rate of flow of capital services: Changing the size of the crew, $\bar{L}(t)$, at t to change the rate of labor service flow, $l(t)$, is the only way to change factor flow proportions, $k/l(t)$. What is more, over T, changing $l(t)$ is the only way to vary the rate of output, $q(t)$. Of course in the usual way, the level at which k is fixed over T can be changed in the long run but not in the short run, but whatever its level it is fixed within any T.

The second temporal characteristic, mixing duration- and time-specific prices in (4.7), implies the need for much more specificity and consistency about the time dimensions in which optimization takes place and a corresponding care about the meaning of such comfortable and apparently innocent phrases as "the marginal product of capital." It will be shown later in the chapter that there are, in fact, three quite different "marginal product of capitals," and although each adheres to a variant of the familiar rule of (4.7), the marginal product and its appropriate price ratio are different in each case. Such dissection of the production process reveals sources of ambiguity and potential confusion, especially in analyses like that of peak-load pricing, where the time dimension is important.

The last time-specific modification – the introduction of a third time frame over which substitution possibilities must be defined – is of immediate relevance to optimal factor use and the optimal timing of production. It suggests not only that *ex ante, ex post,* and *ex die* elasticities can differ or can be the same – they were all equal to zero under the Leontief production function (4.1) – but also that all of them, in different ways, affect the ability of the firm optimally to adjust factor proportions. The elasticity of substitution affects the optimal timing of production (a) through *ex ante* and *ex post* elasticities as they define the ability to respond in k/l and T_p to changing relative factor prices or price amplitude and (b) through the *ex die* elasticity of substitution as it defines the ability to adjust k/l to track factor price changes, moment by moment, within time unit T. The first of these relationships will be emphasized formally and the second only informally, because it is both more obvious in its effects on optimal scheduling and more intractable in formal modeling with the tools used here. So, explicitly, we will consider σ_a and σ_p to have the same (denoted simply σ), and typically nonzero, value in what follows, but $\sigma_T = 0$. This means that factor proportions can be changed from one day to the next, if T is a day, in response to a change in factor prices or amplitude of the wage rate, but throughout any single day's operation, factor flow proportions must remain unchanged.

Now, with those temporal characteristics spelled out, the instantaneous production function at t can be expressed in a general form like that used in the last chapter.

$$q(t) = f(k,l(t)); \quad \partial f/\partial k, \ \partial f/\partial l(t) \geqslant 0, \quad \partial^2 f/\partial l(t)^2 < 0, \qquad (4.8)$$

with $\sigma_a = \sigma_p \geqslant 0$ and $\sigma_T = 0$. Because the rate of capital service flow, k, is fixed during T, different rates of output flow at t, $q(t)$, are got by varying the labor service flow rate: More labor increases the speed of production; less slows it down. The output rate can be varied from

$q(t) = 0$ to $q(t) = \max q(t)$ by applying more labor $l(t) = \bar{L}(t)$. The speed at which the marginal product of the labor service flow rate becomes zero – max $q(t)$ – is the most that can be got from that given k of capital. The greater the elasticity of substitution, σ, the wider the range from 0 to max $q(t)$ over which labor's marginal product is positive.

Since the duration of production is specified at some given value T_p, then with given capital services k at any time t, the cost of producing the output flow rate $q(t)$ is

$$c(q,t) = \dot{p}_k(T_p)k + w(t)l(t),$$

and average costs depend on the rate of output, q, and time, t,

$$ac(q,t) = \dot{p}_k k/q(t) + w(t)l(t)/q(t)$$
$$= c_k(q) + c_1(q,t).$$

The cost of the given capital service flow is unaffected by the rate of output; a faster output rate simply spreads the fixed rate of capital service flow costs over a higher rate of output flow in a most familiar fashion. So unit capital costs, $c_k(q)$, are a negative function of output. The cost of labor rises with output rate. At time t, the wage rate, $w(t)$, is unaffected by the output rate, but given diminishing returns, the rate of flow of labor services must rise faster than the output rate; so unit labor costs, $c_l(q,t)$, increase with increasing output rates.

The optimal rate of output at t, $q^*(t)$, is shown in Figure 4.4 as the least-cost output rate at t, given the production function, the fixed rate of capital service flow, k, and the specified duration of production, T_p. This $q^*(t)$ is the rate of output at t at which the negative marginal unit capital cost and positive marginal unit labor cost are equal; it is the rate of output generated by k^* of capital services combined, implicitly, with the optimal rates of factor service flows, $k^*/l^*(t)$.

Figure 4.4 describes the unit costs of the rate of output flow $q(t)$ at a moment t. It becomes a description of the unit costs of the accumulated flow of output Q per unit time T simply by multiplying the $q(t)$ units on the horizontal axis by the scalar, T_p, the given duration of production. Because $\sigma_T = 0$, factor proportions and, given k, factor flow rates and hence $q(t)$ must be the same over all of the production period in any unit time T. Given T_p and an accumulated wage payment per crew member over T_p,

$$W(T_p) = \int_{t_0}^{t_p} w(t)\, dt, \qquad (4.9)$$

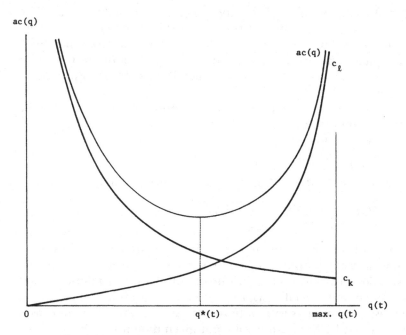

Figure 4.4. Speed of production and unit costs.

the least-cost output per unit time T is $Q^* = q^*(t)T_p$. It uses a constant k^* and $l^*(t)$ of factor services from (4.7) for P_k and $W(T_p)$.

Just as in the earlier discussion of optimal duration, the unit time/ unit cost representation leads quite naturally to seeing the determinants of the shapes and positions of the unit cost curves as the determinants of the optimal intensity of production and factor flow rates – whatever shifts or alters the shape of unit capital or labor costs will shift the unit cost curve, changing the optimal speed of production and, implicitly, the optimal factor flow rate proportions.

The unit capital cost curve is a familiar rectangular hyperbola in cost and rate of output space at t, because the owner cost of capital, P_k, is exogenous to the firm, and both duration of production, T_p, and flow of capital services at t are given over all $q(t)$. But the position of that rectangular hyperbola, and hence the influence of capital costs on the unit cost curve, $ac(q)$, is affected by those exogenous and given values. So, *ceteris paribus*, the higher the owner cost of capital, P_k, the higher will be the optimal rate of output, $q^*(t)$, and the lower will be the optimal factor flow rate proportions, $k^*/l^*(t)$ at t. Increased duration of production, T_p, will have the opposite effect, lowering unit capital service costs at t, hence lowering optimal intensity of output, $q^*(t)$, and raising the optimal capital service intensity, $k^*/l^*(t)$. So optimal factor use and speed at time t depend on when, after t, the process will be shut down. Both owner cost and duration of production cause shifts in unit capital costs; both alter the relative importance of capital and labor cost flows, and hence the relative importance of the diminishing productivity of the labor service flow. The shape of the unit capital cost, it should be noted, would be distorted from a rectangular hyperbola – lifted in the $q(t)$ dimension – if we were to acknowledge the engineering evidence (Eary and Johnson, 1962) that depreciation often is a positive function of the speed of output, $q(t)$, even though it appears impervious to differences in the duration of output.[7]

The unit labor cost curve rises from zero at $q(t) = 0$ – because we assume $f(0,l(t)) = f(k(t),0) = 0$ – to infinity at $\partial q(t)/\partial l(t) = 0$, which defines the maximum rate of output flow, given the fixed capital service flow at t. How fast unit labor costs rise depends on the instantaneous elasticity of substitution, *ex post*, σ_p: The higher its value, the more gently will unit labor costs increase at higher output rates, and the greater will be the optimal rate of output, $q^*(t)$. Given an elasticity of substitution and the fixed capital flow at t, the relationship between labor service flow rate $l(t)$ and output flow rate $q(t)$ is determined. Then the position of the unit labor cost curve at t depends only on the wage rate function and time t. A higher general level of wages will reduce $q^*(t)$ at any t. And with the time-specific wage rate increasing throughout T, the unit labor cost curve at t will shift upward as t increases from t_0 to t_T, reducing, therefore, the optimal rate of output flow, $q^*(t)$, and bringing higher optimal capital intensity, $k^*/l^*(t)$. So "later" moments in T carry higher unit labor costs and hence lower optimal output rates, $q^*(t)$, but under the assumption that $\sigma_T = 0$, the firm is unable to accommodate them.

Finally, the response to an average wage $W(T_p)$. There is a question of appropriateness of variables in the specification of optimal factor flows in (4.7). At time t, flow rates will optimally be adjusted to (4.7), as set out there. If they can be. But the degree to which they can be is determined by the instantaneous elasticity of substitution. So (4.7) describes the ultimately efficient factor flow rates at t that may or may not be achievable by the firm: When all instantaneous elasticities of substitution were assumed to be zero in Section 4.1, equation (4.7) was irrelevant, because no adjustment of factor flow rate proportions was possible, and variations in factor flow prices could only affect costs. With all three elasticities of substitution greater than zero, at the other extreme, optimal factor flow rates must be adjusted to factor prices at each instant over T to satisfy equation (4.7).

But this section and Appendix A describe an intermediate situation in which adjustment is possible from one unit time T to the next, but not from one moment t to the next within any unit time. So the optimality condition of (4.7) is modified so that the prices and factor flows are appropriate both to the possibilities for adjustment and to each other. The fact that $\sigma_T = 0$ implies an optimal factor mix condition much like (4.7), but based on the owner cost of capital, P_k, and the average or accumulated wage payment per crew member over the period of operation, W, because the best the firm can do, under $\sigma_T = 0$, is to adjust the constant rates of factor flow over all of any T_p to some average of factor prices over that whole period. Given the exogenous P_k, $p_k(T_p)$, of course, is defined by T_p. But $w(t)$ keeps changing over t_0 to t_p; so what is relevant with $\sigma_T = 0$ is equation (4.9), the wage payment per crew member per T.

4.3   Least-cost timing of production in unit time

The duration of production, of course, is not given; it, too, is a variable in the optimization. So for each possible duration of production $0 < T_p \leqslant T$, there is an equivalent to Figure 4.4. And for each possible rate of output $0 < q(t) \leqslant \max q(t)$, there is an equivalent to Figure 4.1 describing the least-cost duration of production with a given output rate, and hence a least-cost output per unit time. The dimension of production described by Figure 4.4 uses changes in factor proportions to alter the speed of output during production; the dimension of production described by Figure 4.1 uses changes in the duration of production to alter the total output flow per unit time. The first, certainly, is familiar from production theory; the second, certainly, is familiar from observation of actual utilization practices. They generate very similar-appearing but fundamentally different cost behaviors. Together, they determine the least-cost arrangement of production within the unit time; both factor proportions and the timing of production within the unit time have to be adjusted to achieve least-cost output.

The determinants of the simultaneously optimal timing and duration of production, T_p^*, and the optimal factor flows, $k^*(t)$ and $l^*(t)$, implicit in $q^*(t)$ are reflected in the unit cost surface of Figure 4.7. Underlying any unit cost surface, of course, are implicit unit labor cost and unit capital cost surfaces. These have been made explicit in Figures 4.5 and 4.6, respectively. It is useful to consider them briefly first.

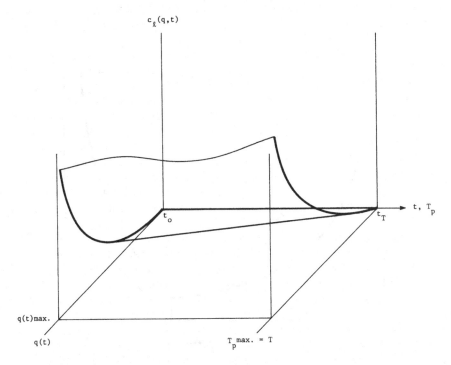

Figure 4.5. Unit labor costs: duration and speed of production.

Unit labor costs behave as described earlier: They increase with both increasing duration and increasing speed of production, as in Figure 4.5. Because production always starts at t_0, the moment of lowest time-specific wage rate within the unit time, continued operation necessitates higher wage rates; so for any rate of output, unit labor costs rise with the duration of production. For a given duration of production, in the other direction, unit labor costs rise with an increasing rate of output as a result of the diminishing marginal product of labor services combined with a fixed capital service flow. So, on both counts – in both dimensions – the unit labor cost surface rises as it moves away from the origin. It can rise at a constant rate in the T_p direction, but it will rise at an increasing rate in the $q(t)$ direction, where the rate of increase will depend on the elasticity of substitution.

Unit capital costs behave even more simply, as indicated in Figure 4.6. Because capital costs are always fixed per unit time at $P_k\overline{K}^*$, regardless of duration or rate of output, unit capital costs fall in both

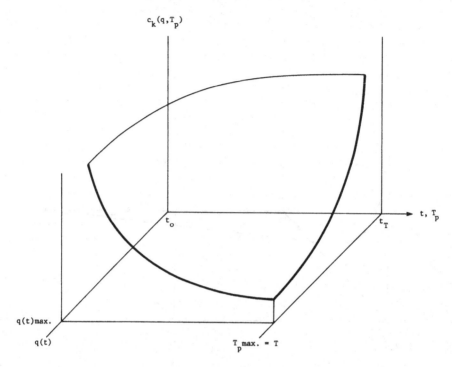

Figure 4.6. Unit capital costs: duration and speed of production.

directions in Figure 4.6; they fall with T_p because increasing the duration of output at a constant speed spreads those fixed capital costs over more production; they fall with $q(t)$ because increasing the speed of output at any moment spreads those fixed capital costs over more production. So the unit capital cost surface falls with movement away from either axis; hence its truncated bowl shape in Figure 4.6.

Added vertically, these two cost components yield the unit cost surface of Figure 4.7. It incorporates the two adjustments to production described by Figures 4.1 and 4.4: Along the T_p axis, a perpendicular plane – a slice – will hold the duration of production per unit time constant and generate a set of unit cost curves like those of Figure 4.4; along the $q(t)$ axis, a perpendicular plane will hold the speed of output constant and generate unit cost curves like those of Figure 4.1. Letting both duration and factor proportions vary lets the firm move to the least-cost combination of timing and intensity of production, T_p^* and $q^*(t)$ implying $k^*/l^*(t)$. With the assumed ab-

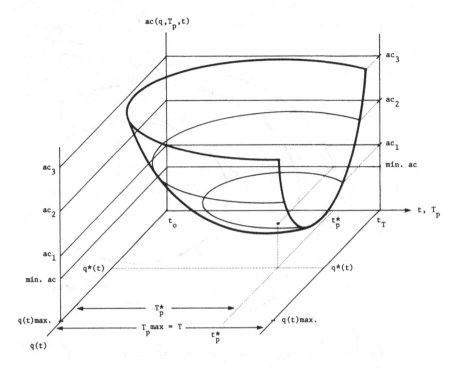

Figure 4.7. Unit total costs: duration and speed of production.

sence of scale economies, proportional adjustment of k and l would adjust $q(t)$ proportionately to produce any output, Q, per unit time over an unchanged T_p with the price and production parameters underlying Figure 4.7. So the same optimal duration of production T_p^* and the same optimal factor proportions $k^*/l^*(t)$ are appropriate to any output per unit time Q, given the parameters implicit in Figure 4.6.

The minimum point of the unit cost surface, $ac(q, T_p, t)$, in Figure 4.7 defines the optimal duration and intensity of production within T. The shape of the unit cost surface is determined by the economic and technological parameters of the process that affect unit capital and labor costs described earlier:

1. An increased wage amplitude β, over T, will lift the unit labor cost surface along $T_p = T$, lifting the unit cost surface and moving the minimum cost point toward the origin; so T_p^* and $q^*(t)$ will fall.

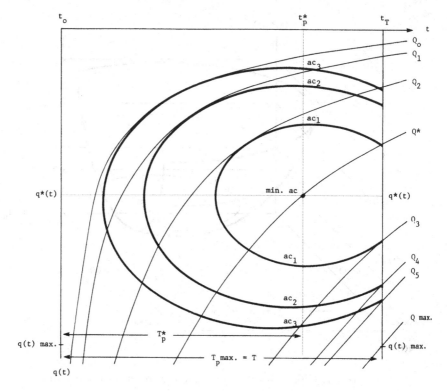

Figure 4.8. Unit cost contours: duration and speed of production.

2. An increase in the relative price of capital, P_k/W (or, *ceteris paribus,* an increase in the capital intensity of production) will lift the unit capital cost surface throughout, tilting the unit cost surface away from the origin; so T_p^* and $q^*(t)$ will rise, and $k^*/l^*(t)$ will fall.

3. An increase in the elasticity of substitution, σ (with σ_T still zero), will lower the unit labor cost surface in the $q(t)$ direction, tilting $ac(q,T_p,t)$ away from the origin and increasing T_p^* and $q^*(t)$, but without reducing $k^*/l^*(t)$ – because a higher σ allows a higher $q(t)$ to be got with any given $k^*/l^*(t)$.

It may be useful – as a graphic alternative to Figure 4.7 – to let the unit cost surface, $ac(q,T_p,t)$, be reflected simply as a set of constant unit cost contours on the duration-intensity plane, $T_p,q(t)$. For Figure 4.7, they would appear as in Figure 4.8, with the point $T_p^*,q^*(t)$ as the least-cost schedule of production and the encircling contours de-

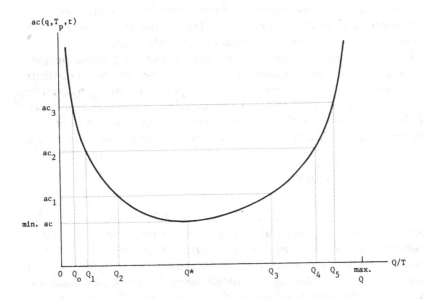

Figure 4.9. Unit costs of output Q per unit time T.

scribing increasing unit costs. Then, because accumulated output per unit time is $Q = T_p q(t)$, for any constant $q(t)$ over T_p, each rectangular hyperbola, $Q_1, Q_2, \ldots$ reflects a given level of output per unit time – the familiar datum of orthodox analysis. Movement away from the origin in Figure 4.8, as in a familiar isoquant diagram, reflects a higher level of accumulated output per unit time. These are not, of course, isoquants in any but the most literal sense – because T_p and $q(t)$ are not factor inputs – but alternative ways to produce and schedule a given daily output within the unit time. The strange shape of the appropriate unit cost contours emphasizes that. So although a wide range of output levels per unit time can be produced with the time-specific price and technology constraints that underlie Figures 4.7 and 4.8, only Q^* represents a least-cost level of output per unit time in the face of those constraints, and to achieve least cost, Q^* must be made at $q^*(t)$ for T_p^* of the unit time.[8]

It is clear now how much is implicit in an orthodox average cost curve of the sort that is a staple in an undergraduate economics course. A line in Figure 4.8 connecting tangencies would show the adjustments of duration and intensity of production within the unit time needed to produce the "outputs per unit time" of the orthodox average cost curve (Figure 4.9) without violating its explicit assumption that each point on an average cost curve is a least-cost point for that level of output per unit time. This is the set of adjustments masked by the unit time convention of orthodox analysis.

Finally, consider briefly the possibility of changing factor proportions within unit time dismissed until now. Then the *ex die* elasticity of substitution σ_T is not zero, and output per unit time, Q, will not be the simple product of duration and speed of output, because speed is changing over T_p with changing factor proportions in response to changing factor flow prices (4.7). So least-cost output per unit time is

$$Q^* = \int_{t_0}^{t_p^*} q^*(t)\, dt.$$

And, importantly, it is possible to satisfy (4.7) throughout T. This flexibility will, of course, always allow lower-cost production – least costs will be less – because the firm can at least partially accommodate the rising time-specific wage rate over T_p by shifting out of labor use while exploiting the duration-specific price of capital services by continuing production. So production will start at t_0 with the greatest labor intensity and, given the fixed capital service flow, the greatest rate of output. As production continues and the wage rate rises, the labor service flow – the crew size $\bar{L}(t)$ – will be cut back to maintain equation (4.7).[9]

If the opportunity for substitution is sufficient, it will be possible always to offset a higher time-specific wage rate by reductions in labor service flow, preventing the rise in unit costs. Because capital service price $p_k(T_p)$ is unaffected by adjustments in the labor input, it continues to fall with increasing T_p, and given enough elasticity of substitution, it will always be optimal to operate all of the unit time T. Production and employment, to be sure, will be concentrated – as higher $q^*(t)$ and $l^*(t)$ – in the low-wage periods, "early" in the unit time, but utilization per se and the use of capital services will be spread over the whole of the unit time. This, of course, is what happens when multiple-shift plants are run with a large crew in the day and a smaller crew throughout the night, with its premium time-specific wage rates. Intermediate values of the *ex die* elasticity of substitution will yield intermediate cases – some adjustment of factor proportions over T with some concentration of production in lower-wage periods but not enough ability to substitute capital always to justify operating the entire unit time T. Again, this is illustrated by two-shift operation, with a reduced crew on the second shift but shut down on the third.

4.4 Summary and implications of the optimal schedule

The efficient production of any given quantity per unit time of a storable product requires a least-cost schedule within that unit time. That, in turn, requires selecting optimal values for duration of production, T_p^*, factor input flow rates, $k^*/l^*(t)$, and consequent intensity of production, $q^*(t)$, at each moment t during the unit time. The optimal duration of production, T_p^*, often will see the production process left idle some of the unit time; the optimal utilization of that process will be $T_p^*/T \leq 1$. With this simple wage function, the timing of the firm's production is tied to exogenous clock and calendar time by the requirement of efficient production that it start at t_0, the moment of lowest exogenous time-specific input price. The optimal factor use, $k^*/l^*(t)$, and its timing determine the optimal intensity or speed of production, $q^*(t)$, given technical parameters, at each moment of the unit time, and that, in turn, specifies the optimal timing of the variable input flows $l^*(t)$ over the unit time. The economic and technical parameters that determine optimal utilization, factor proportions, and intensity of production are the severity of the time-specific input price changes within unit time – the amplitude of such price rhythms – relative factor prices, the factor intensity of the production process, and the instantaneous elasticities of substitution.

The discussion of optimal scheduling in this chapter, including the graphs and Appendix A, deals with continuous variables; so the duration of production and the flows of factor inputs – both their rates and flows over time – are all considered to be incrementally adjustable. This is consistent with use of the instant as the elementary time unit. But a major source of time specificity in production actually takes the form of discrete shifts of operation – usually of 8 or 10 hours – that divide the day up into very nonincremental time units. Time-specific analysis is relevant to the discrete case, too. Indeed, the earliest explicit specification of an optimal time-specific model of production took the form of an optimal shift-working model that used discrete shifts as the elementary time unit within the day as unit time (Winston, 1970). That discrete time model spurred other developments and extensions of that optimal shift-work analysis, especially by Baily (1974), Goppers (1972), and Betancourt and Clague (1975, 1981), who extended it to include economies of scale, applied it to the incentive environment of worker-controlled firms, and subjected it to careful international comparative analysis. So it will frequently be useful in what follows to use discrete shift-working decisions as illustrations of time-specific decisions, and the later discussion of time-specific markets will consider the underlying motivations for that discreteness. The continuous model remains the most general case.

This chapter has described the optimal schedule of production when the firm has complete discretion over when to produce within unit time and can adjust that schedule to minimize costs. That discretion depends crucially on the nature of the output – that it is storable at no cost over the unit time – so that the timing of production is entirely divorced from the timing of its sale and use. We turn in the next chapter to the much more constrained choices faced by the producer of a perishable product whose optimal schedule of production within the unit time is heavily conditioned by the schedule of demand for its product within the unit time.

Appendix A: The formal model of time-specific production

The model described here is a slightly edited version of one developed with Thomas McCoy and published in the *Review of Economic Studies* (Winston and McCoy, 1974). The notation has been changed from the original to conform to that of the last two chapters, except that the instantaneous production function denoted $f(\cdot)$ here is in ratio form, in contrast to the production functions of Chapters 2 and 3; so $q(t)/l(t) = f(k/l)$ here, and $f(k(t),l(t))$ from equation (3.1) or (4.1) is here denoted $F(k(t),l(t))$. This should not prove confusing.

The firm produces a product that is storable over unit time using one input with a time-specific price – labor services, $l(t)$ – and another with a duration-specific price – capital services, $k(t)$. The firm is a price taker in input and product markets; so the time shape of the wage rate and its level are both determined exogenously, as is the owner cost of the capital stock; the capital service price, of course, is an endogenous function of the production schedule. The cost-minimizing schedule of production of any given Q_0 of output per unit time is defined by the optimal duration of production, T_p^*, and factor service flow rates, $k^*(t)$ and $l^*(t)$. In the fully repetitive environment described by the time-specific model with its regular rhythmic changes within unit time, the firm's optimal schedule is a rhythmic equilibrium – one that changes constantly, adapting to the time-specific environment, but changing in exactly the same way in each unit time T. The *ex ante* perspective of the model makes it descriptive of the firm's investment decision if desired.

In the first section the model is formulated. In the second section the effects of factor prices on optimal duration of production are shown to depend on the elasticity of substitution. In the third section the implications of the model for capital productivity and employment are presented.

The model

Consider a firm with a pure flow instantaneous production function,

$$q(t) = F(k(t),l(t)),$$

where $q(t)$ is the rate of flow of output, $k(t)$ is the rate of capital service flow, and $l(t)$ is the rate of labor service flow, all at time t. $F(\cdot)$ is linear and homogeneous; so we can write

$$F(k(t),l(t)) = l(t)f(y(t)), \qquad (A.1)$$

where $y(t) = k(t)/l(t)$, $f(y(t)) \equiv F(y(t),1)$, and $f(\cdot)$ has the usual properties, $f' > 0$ and $f'' > 0$.[1]

The amount of output produced per unit time T is

$$Q = \int_{t_0}^{t_p} q(t)\ dt = \int_{t_0}^{t_p} l(t)f(y(t))\ dt. \qquad (A.2)$$

Production starts at time t_0 and continues without interruption until it stops at time $t_p = t_0 + T_p$. T_p is the duration of production in unit time T, and if $T = 1$, T_p is also the rate of utilization, the proportion of the time the process is operated: $0 \leqslant T_p \leqslant 1$.

The ratio of capital and labor service flow rates, $y(t)$, is assumed to be variable from one unit time to the next, to the extent described by the elasticity of substitution. Within any period of operation, T_p, however, $y(t)$ is assumed to be constant;[2] so the *ex post* instantaneous elasticity of substitution $\sigma_p > 0$, and the *ex die* instantaneous elasticity of substitution $\sigma_T = 0$; *ex ante* and *ex post* elasticities are assumed equal.

So $l(t)$, $k(t)$, and $y(t)$ are constants to be determined, and equation (A.2) can be rewritten as

$$Q = T_p lf(y). \qquad (A.3)$$

The capital service flow, k, is derived by the firm from a stock, $\overline{K}$, that is purchased (or rented) as such and is retained by the firm throughout the whole of T, whether yielding capital services (in operation) or not (idle), and the capital service flow is assumed homogeneous. The rate of flow of capital services, k, equals the number of homogeneous machines, $\overline{K}$, during operation and zero during idleness; thus,

$$k(t) = \overline{K} \quad \text{when} \quad t_0 \le t \le t_p$$
$$= 0 \quad \text{when} \quad t_p < t. \tag{A.4}$$

The cost of owning (renting) a unit of capital stock per unit time T (exogenously determined) is P_k.[3] The labor service flow, l, is purchased by the firm as a flow of services (man-hours) *per se*. The firm pays for labor services only during the period of operation, and the instantaneous wage rate, $w(t)$, that must be paid to each (homogeneous) worker at time t varies rhythmically over T with exogenous time-shape. Assume that within each day $w(t)$ is positive and is a continuous function of t. Also assume that within each day $w(t)$ reaches a minimum at time t_m and a maximum at time t_x; so

$$w'(t) \le 0 \quad \text{for} \quad t_x \le t \le t_m$$
$$w'(t) \ge 0 \quad \text{for} \quad t_m < t < t_x.$$

Hence the wage declines monotonically to time t_m and rises monotonically throughout the rest of T. The firm will pick its period of operation within T so as to minimize labor cost. Let $W(T_p)$ be the total daily wage payment per worker when the period of utilization is T_p. Then

$$W(T_p) = \min_{t_\phi} \int_{t_\phi}^{t_\phi + T_p} w(t) \, dt,$$

where t_ϕ is the time of day when use of the capital stock (production) starts. To be optimal, the starting time t_ϕ^* must satisfy the first-order condition

$$w(t_\phi^* + T_p) = w(t_\phi^*). \tag{A.5}$$

Now,

$$W'(T_p) = w(t_\phi^* + T_p)\frac{d(t_\phi^* + T_p)}{dT_p} - w(t_\phi^*)\frac{dt_\phi^*}{dT_p}$$
$$= w(t_\phi^*) > 0,$$

and

$$W''(T_p) = \frac{w'(t_\phi^*)w'(t_\phi^* + T_p)}{w'(t_\phi^*) - w'(t_\phi^* + T_p)} \geq 0,$$

because $w'(t_\phi^*) \leq 0$ and $w'(t_\phi^* + T_p) \geq 0$.

Without loss of generality we can write the wage payment per crew member per unit time in the form

$$W(T_p) = w_0 T_p + w_0 \beta B(T_p), \qquad (A.6)$$

where w_0, β, $B'(T_p) > 0$ and $B''(T_p) \geq 0$; w_0 can be interpreted as the *level* of the wage rate, and $\beta B(T_p)$ is a determinant of its *amplitude* over unit time T.

The firm's cost of producing Q per T is

$$C = lW(T_p) + P_k \bar{K}.$$

Substituting in (A.4),

$$C = l\psi(y, T_p), \qquad (A.7)$$

where

$$\psi(y, T_p) = W(T_p) + P_k y \qquad (A.8)$$

is the cost (both wage and capital) of using a crew member over the period of production, T_p. We will assume that the output per unit time is given at Q_0, so that from (A.3),

$$l = l(y, T_p) = Q_0 / T_p f(y). \qquad (A.9)$$

Then the firm's optimal schedule embedded in its investment decision[4] involves picking the capital-labor ratio, y, and level of utilization, T_p – the period of operation – to minimize

$$C = C(y, T_p) = l(y, T_p)\psi(y, T_p). \qquad (A.10)$$

Factor prices, wage rhythms, and elasticities of substitution

This section will show how the optimal level of utilization *changes* in response to changes in relative factor prices, p_k / w_0, and changes in the amplitude of the wage rate rhythm, β.

Changes in relative factor prices and wage rhythm amplitude. Let T_p^* and y^* be the values of T_p and y that minimize (A.10), and assume that $T_p^* < 1$.[5] Let σ be the instantaneous flow elasticity of substitution, *ex ante* and *ex post;* but still, $\sigma_T = 0$. In general, the elasticity of substitution is defined as

$$\sigma = -\frac{f'(f - yf')}{yff''}.$$ (A.11)

Then we can prove the following two theorems:

    Theorem 1: If T_p^* and y^* are values of T_p and y that minimize (A.10), and if $T_p^* < 1$,

$$\frac{dT_p^*}{d(P_k/w_0)} = A(1 - \sigma),$$

where $A > 0$.

    Proof: Because T_p^* and y^* minimize (A.10) at an internal point ($T_p^* < 1$), the following first-[6] and second-order conditions hold:

$$C_y = l(y^*, T_p^*)w_0\left\{\frac{P_k}{w_0} - \frac{T_p^* + \beta B(T_p^*) + (P_k/w_0)y^*}{f/f'}\right\} = 0,$$ (A.12)

$$C_T = l(y^*, T_p^*)w_0\left\{\beta B'(T_p^*) - \frac{\beta B(T_p^*) + (P_k/w_0)y^*}{T_p^*}\right\},$$ (A.13)

and

$$C_{yy} = -l(y^*, T_p^*)\psi(y^*, T_p^*)(f''/f) > 0,$$ (A.14)

$$C_{TT} = l(y^*, T_p^*)W''(T_p^*) > 0,$$ (A.15)

$$D = C_{yy}C_{TT} - C_{yT}C_{Ty}$$
$$= (-l\psi f''/f)(lW''(T_p^*)) - (lW'(T_p^*)f''/f)(lP_k/T_p^*) > 0.$$ (A.16)

Totally differentiating (A.12) and (A.13) with respect to relative factor prices, P_k/w_0, we get

$$\begin{bmatrix} C_{yy} & C_{yT} \\ C_{Ty} & C_{TT} \end{bmatrix} \begin{bmatrix} \dfrac{dy^*}{d(P_k/w_0)} \\ \dfrac{dT_p^*}{d(P_k/w_0)} \end{bmatrix} = -lw_0 \begin{bmatrix} 1 - y^*(f'/f) \\ -y^*/T_p^* \end{bmatrix}.$$ (A.17)

Solving (A.16) for $dT_p^*/d(P_k/w_0)$,

$$\frac{dT_p^*}{d(P_k/w_0)} = \frac{lw_0}{D}[(lP_k/T_p^*)(1 - y^*(f'/f)) + (l\psi f''/f)(y^*/T_p^*)].$$

From (A.12),

$$lP_k = l\psi f'/f; \tag{A.18}$$

hence

$$\frac{dT_p^*}{d(P_k/w_0)} = -(l^2\psi w_0 y^* f''/DT_p^* f)(1 + f'/y^* f'' - (f')^2/ff'').$$

Using the definition of the elasticity of substitution, (A.11),

$$\frac{dT_p^*}{d(P_k/w_0)} = A(1 - \sigma),$$

where $A = -(l^2\psi w_0 y^* f''/DT_p^* f) > 0$.

Theorem 2: If T_p^* and y^* are values of T_p and y that minimize (A.10), and if $T_p^* < 1$, then

$$dT_p^*/d\beta < 0,$$

if $\sigma \leq 1$.

Proof: Following the procedure in the previous proof and totally differentiating (A.12) and (A.13) with respect to β, we get

$$\begin{bmatrix} C_{yy} C_{yT} \\ \\ C_{Ty} C_{TT} \end{bmatrix} \begin{bmatrix} \dfrac{dy^*}{d\beta} \\ \\ \dfrac{dT_p^*}{d\beta} \end{bmatrix} = -lw_0 \begin{bmatrix} -Bf'/f \\ \\ B' - B/T_p^* \end{bmatrix}. \tag{A.19}$$

Solving (A.19) for $dT_p^*/d\beta$,

$$dT_p^*/d\beta = -lw_0/D[-(lP_k/T_p^*)(Bf'/f) - (l\psi f''/f)(B' - B/T_p^*)]. \tag{A.20}$$

From (A.12),

$$lB = l/\beta[P_k/w_0(f/f' - y^*) - T_p^*], \tag{A.21}$$

and from (A.13),

$$l(B/T_p^* - B') = -l\frac{(P_k/w_0)y^*}{\beta T_p^*}. \tag{A.22}$$

Substituting (A.18), (A.21), and (A.22) into (A.20),

$$\frac{dT_p^*}{d\beta} = \frac{l^2 \psi P_k f'' y^*}{DT_p^* f\beta}(1 - \sigma) - \frac{l^2 \psi w_0}{D\beta}(f'f)^2.$$

So, if $\sigma \leq 1$, $dT_p^*/d\beta < 0$.

Effect of the instantaneous elasticity of substitution on the optimal schedule.
The effects of both relative factor prices and amplitude of the wage
rate on optimal utilization – the duration of production – depend on
whether the *ex ante* (and *ex post*, with $\sigma_T = 0$ still) elasticity of factor
service substitution is greater or less than 1. The economics of this
are easy to visualize.

If the elasticity is less than 1, an increase in the relative price of
capital, P_k/w_0, will reduce the importance in costs of the time-specifically priced input and therefore reduce the justification for leaving
the capital stock idle. A smaller amplitude, β, of the cost rhythm
reduces the relative importance of rhythmic costs and hence increases optimal utilization. The less important is the cost rhythm, the
less reason there is to shut down production in order to avoid high-
cost operating periods.

If the elasticity is greater than 1, an increase in the relative price
of capital will *reduce* optimal utilization, because substitution out of
capital services is so great that it lowers capital's share, and it pays to
economize on labor (as the now-larger share of costs) even though it
means using the capital stock less of the time. Again, most generally,
for instantaneous elasticities greater than 1, an increase in the price
of capital increases the relative importance (cost share) of the rhythmic factor and therefore increases the incentive to leave the capital
stock idle: The more important is the cost rhythm, the more reason
there is to shut down production to avoid high-cost operating periods. When $\sigma > 1$, the response of utilization to increased amplitude
β is indeterminate, because the sharper amplitude of the factor *price*
rhythm can, in this elasticity range, be offset in part by substitution
out of the rhythmically varying factor.

If the elasticity equals 1, relative factor prices do not affect the
optimal utilization of capital. A higher (lower) relative capital price
leaves the relative importance (cost shares) of capital and the rhythmic input unchanged; therefore, relative factor prices do not alter
the incentive to use the capital stock or to leave it idle.[7]

This is of considerable interest and quite likely explains why the formal analysis of optimal utilization has proved so elusive – even if framed correctly in all other respects, the crucial influence of relative factor prices on capital utilization evaporates in an analysis based on a Cobb-Douglas production function.

Capital productivity and employment

The optimal schedule of production describes the cost-minimizing relationship between a capital *stock* and its daily capital service *flow*. The fact that this relationship is a *variable* influenced by factor prices is important; *ex ante*, under the influence of varying factor prices, a given capital stock (investment) will yield varying amounts of daily capital service flow, it will employ varying amounts of labor, and it will produce varying amounts of daily output.

Optimal productivity of investment. The optimal productivity of a capital stock (investment) changes with varying relative factor prices and amplitude of the wage rhythm, even in the extreme case when $\sigma = 0$, that is, when the (instantaneous) capital-labor ratio is fixed *ex ante*. In this case, (A.13) and (A.15) hold with y^* set at some given value, y_0. Now, totally differentiating (A.13) with respect to P_k/w_0 and β yields

$$\frac{dT_p^*}{d(P_k/w_0)} = \frac{w_0 y_0}{T_p^* W''} > 0, \quad \frac{dT_p^*}{d\beta} = -\frac{P_k y_0}{\beta T_p^* W''} < 0. \tag{A.23}$$

With $\sigma = 0$,

$$k/l = y_0. \tag{A.24}$$

Substituting (A.4) into (A.24) and the result into (A.9) yields

$$Q_0/\overline{K} = T_p^* f(y_0)/y_0. \tag{A.25}$$

An increase (decrease) in the relative price of capital will increase (decrease) the optimal productivity of the capital stock,[8]

$$\frac{d(Q_0/\overline{K})}{d(P_k/w_0)} = \frac{f(y_0)}{y_0} \frac{dT_p^*}{d(P_k/w_0)} > 0,$$

even though we have assumed $\sigma = 0$. The "capital output ratio" defined on a capital *stock* clearly will fall with an increase in the relative price of capital, even though a machine technically must be operated by a crew of fixed size.

The optimal productivity of the capital stock falls, too, with increasing amplitude of the wage rate, because, differentiating (A.25) with respect to β,

$$\frac{d(Q_0/\overline{K})}{d\beta} = \frac{f(y_0)}{y_0} \frac{dT_p^*}{d\beta} < 0. \tag{A.26}$$

Employment creation of investment. The amount of employment generated by a unit of capital *stock* (investment) will clearly vary in response to changes in utilization. The instantaneous rate of flow of labor service, $l(t)$, describes l men at work providing labor services at time t. Each day, a labor service flow rate of l yields $T_p l$ man-hours of labor per day when T_p is expressed in hours, assuming that l remains constant over the period of operation. The total number $\overline{E}$ of individual people *employed* per day is then

$$\overline{E} = lT_p/T_w,$$

where T_w is the average number of hours worked per person. Then, given y_0 fixed,

$$y_0 = \frac{k}{l} = \frac{\overline{K}}{l} = \frac{\overline{K}}{\overline{E}(T_w/T_p)}.$$

Employment per unit of capital *stock* is

$$\overline{E}/\overline{K} = T_p/T_w y_0,$$

so that

$$\frac{d(\overline{E}/\overline{K})}{d(P_k/w_0)} = \frac{1}{T_w y_0} \frac{dT_p^*}{d(P_k/w_0)} > 0$$

and

$$\frac{d(\overline{E}/\overline{K})}{d\beta} = \frac{1}{T_w y_0} \frac{dT_p^*}{d\beta} < 0.$$

So the capital-labor ratio, too, is always sensitive to factor prices, even when each unit of capital stock must be operated by a crew of fixed size.

Finally, it is useful to note that this model is formally similar to vintage capital models; the primary difference is in their time frame. In the vintage model, plants representing different ages of capital and technologies experience a secular decline in the relative price of capital. The oldest plants (the smallest y_0) become unprofitable and are shut down. At any time, a plant is either operated (T_p^* = 1) or idle (T_p^* = 0); hence Solow's statement (1962) that "less-than-capacity-utilization is uninteresting" (p. 208). In the optimal-utilization model, a plant (or set of plants) will experience a decline in the relative price of capital within each T. To continue operation beyond time t_p^* would be unprofitable; so the plant is shut down. The lower is y_0, *ceteris paribus*, the earlier in the "day" will production be stopped. In the vintage model, capital retired from production stays idle unless the relative factor price movement is reversed; in the time-specific model, the relative factor price movement is reversed every "day," T; so a plant retired from production one evening is brought out of retirement the next morning. In both models, utilization (hence the average age of the capital stock in a vintage model) is not sensitive to relative factor prices when a Cobb-Douglas production function is used.

CHAPTER 5

Time-shaped output: least-cost production of perishable peak-load products

The firm that produces a nonstorable output can rarely schedule its production within the unit time so as to minimize costs. It would like to, given its least-cost objectives, but its production timing decisions are constrained by when the product can be sold. Nonstorable output can be made only when it will be used; its perishability requires that production and use be simultaneous. In this chapter, the time-specific model is used to examine least-cost production within the unit time for a firm that uses capital services and a flow of storable variable input to produce a flow of nonstorable output with a fixed time-shape over the unit time. Electric-power generation is the archetypical example – and the one that has been the subject of the largest analytical literature as "the peak-load problem" – but the analysis is applicable to a wide range of products from restaurant and transportation services to irrigation water. It is quite general.

It is important to be clear about what is being changed in this chapter and what is not. Capital services and the capital stocks that provide them are still central to the production process, and, of course, capital stocks are always durable over the unit time T. The production process is still described by a two-factor instantaneous pure flow production function like that introduced in (3.1). But the noncapital input in this chapter will be the flow of a temporally footloose variable input like fuel or materials that can be used in production at any time during the unit time T at the same time-invariant price. On the input side, that is the only change – that footloose "fuel" is the variable input instead of time-specific labor. On the output side, the only change is product perishability that requires that it be produced at the same instant that it is used by the firm's customers. This simultaneity introduces a new constraint on the firm in the form of a time-shaped output – an exogenously given production schedule. So this chapter examines the firm's cost-minimizing choices within that time-specific output constraint. The firm of Chapter 4 could vary both its schedule and its technology of production to minimize costs; this one, because its production schedule is given, can adjust only its technology – how to produce that time-shaped output – to minimize costs.

The analysis of this chapter takes the time-shape of output as entirely exogenous to the firm: The firm is required to adhere to a given time-shape of demand without the chance to modify it even through time-differentiated pricing. In Chapter 10, where the analysis of time-specific markets leads to peak-load pricing, we will consider the broader questions of the firm's optimal output and capacity decisions when it has some discretion over the time-shape of its output under a given time-shaped demand. In this initial discussion, output and demand time-shapes then are the same, exogenous and given, and the firm minimizes the cost of production.

5.1 The time-shape of output

The time-shape of output is fully specified – as in an output time-profile like that of Figure 5.1 – by the rate of flow of output, $q(t)$, at each moment t during the unit time T. Special significance attaches to the minimum "base-load" rate of flow, $q_b(t)$, and to the maximum "peak-load" rate, $q_p(t)$. Of course, the accumulated output flow, Q, per unit time T is the area under the output time-profile. Because of its frequent appearance in the electric-power literature, this output curve will also be referred to as a "load curve." Furthermore, to avoid a needless sense of abstraction, Figure 5.1 has been given a stylized shape of a stylized daily load curve for electric power. Although the relationship between this time-shape of output and the time-shape of the demand is the subject of extensive discussion in Chapters 10 and 11, for now the time-profile of output is taken as given; so the question of this chapter is how the firm optimally alters the rate of its output flow to track that given time-shape over the unit time.

It is useful to recall one conclusion of Chapter 3: that any cost-minimizing firm using capital services along with a time-invariant-priced input like fuel to produce a given accumulated output flow, Q, over the unit time will – if it has the option – always schedule its

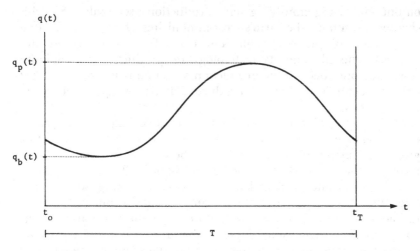

Figure 5.1. Time-shaped output: the load curve.

production at an even, time-invariant rate, q, over the whole unit time T. That production schedule will achieve maximum economies in the capital service price with no diseconomies in the cost of the other, temporally footloose input. So the factor characteristics assumed in this chapter, considered alone, will lead to a least-cost production schedule involving both full utilization, $T_p^* = T$, and a constant output rate, $q^* = q$ – a schedule that yields a nice straight-line time-shape of output like Figure 3.1(a). Of course, the fact that its output is time-shaped constrains the firm of this chapter from deciding on its own output schedule. Yet that constant-rate full-utilization schedule still represents the target toward which it will want to adjust its schedule, to the extent it can. It is useful to keep those cost-minimizing incentives in mind – their direction and source – even though we deal here with a firm that cannot do anything about them.

5.2   Least-cost tracking of time-shaped production

The firm has to track the changing output rates of the time-profile of output over T. It can do this either by altering the number of units of productive capacity in operation, $\overline{K}_i$, or by changing the speed, $q(t)$, with which a given capital stock is operated. Or both. These alternatives, however, involve quite different technological and cost adjustments, with quite different implications for familiar questions. The first way of conforming output to the load curve we will call "utilization tracking." In its simplest form, utilization tracking involves a divisible capital stock from which all variations in output flow rate, $q(t)$, can be got simply by adding and subtracting the output, $q_i(t)$, of different productive units. The second way of matching output to load curve we will call "speed tracking." In its simplest form, speed tracking involves a single piece of capital stock that is run all the time, $T_p = T$, so that all variations in the rate of output flow, $q(t)$, are got simply by changing the speed at which it is operated. This is done, of course, by changing the rate of flow of the variable input, $v(t)$.

Each of these methods of changing the output flow rate to track the time-shaped production over the unit time T involves costs – different costs. They are the subject of analysis in this section.

With one modification and one slight shift in interpretation, the average-cost surface of Figure 4.7 indicates the nature of these alternative tracking methods and their costs. The minor modification is reflected in Figure 5.2, where the unit cost surface is shown, as it was in Figure 4.7, to depend on the duration of production, T_p, and on the rate of flow of output, $q(t)$. But because the variable input of this chapter has a time-invariant price, the average-cost surface of Figure 5.2 slopes down, always, in the T_p direction: A maximum duration, $T_p^* = T$, is always optimal, because increased utilization always reduces the capital service price, but without, in this case, an offsetting cost penalty from rising variable costs. In the $q(t)$ dimension, of course, the average-cost surface is still forced up (to infinity at max $q(t)$) by diminishing returns to $v(t)$ reflected in $c_v(q)$. Unit capital and unit variable cost surfaces are shown in Figure 5.2. So with these inputs, the optimal speed and duration of output are $q^*(t)$, where the factor flow-rates $k/v(t)$, are proportional to relative factor prices, $p_k(T)/\bar{p}_v$, and duration is at its maximum, $T_p^* = T$; $p_k(T)$, of course, is the lowest possible capital service price, and $\bar{p}_v$ is the time-invariant price of the variable input. So $q^*(t)$ satisfies (4.7), given the nature of the inputs.

It is immediately apparent from Figure 5.2 that the firm may be able to follow the time-profile of output over T simply by altering $q(t)$, changing the rate of flow of the variable input $v(t)$ used with the flow of capital services k (from a capital stock that must be constant over T). That is speed tracking of the load curve, changing the rate of output with a production process that is always utilized. It is clear,

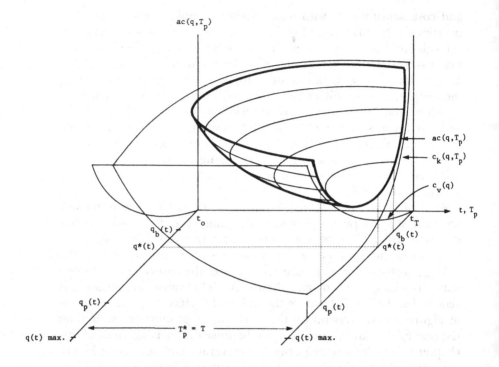

Figure 5.2. Unit total cost: footloose variable input.

too, from Figure 5.2 that when $q(t)$ is varied above and below $q^*(t)$ during T in order to track the time-shape of output, unit costs are higher than the minimum costs of the optimal rate of output, $q^*(t)$; how much higher depends on the flexibility of the technology reflected in the *ex die* elasticity of substitution discussed in the last chapter.

The alternative way to track the time-shape of output over T is also pictured in Figure 5.2 if it is seen as the unit cost surface associated with *one* of those many pieces of capacity, $\overline{K}_i$, that together produce any given output rate, $q(t)$, at time t. Each of those (small) units of capital stock can be seen as a separate plant, each with a unit cost surface like that of Figure 5.2. Then any given total rate of output at t, $q(t)$, is the sum of the contributions of all of those "plants" in operation at t, and changes in $q(t)$ are accomplished by starting up or shutting down some of those plants. That is utilization tracking of the load curve over T. When Figure 5.2 describes unit costs for the ith plant, its optimal rate of output, $q_i^*(t)$, is added to or subtracted from the output rate $q(t)$ at any time t.[1] But because it is then operated only part of the time, the resulting reduction in its utilization inevitably raises the price of its capital services as $p_{ki}(T_{pi}) > p_{ki}(T)$ always for $T_{pi} < T$. So, again, to track the time-shape of output over T, unit costs are higher than the minimum costs of an optimal output rate, $q_i^*(t)$; how much they rise depends on the factor prices and factor proportions of the ith technology.

Now we can turn to a closer examination of these two alternatives.

5.3 Utilization tracking: adding and subtracting productive capacity

Consider the firm's capital, $\overline{K}$, to be highly divisible; so

$$\overline{K} = \sum_{i=1}^{p} \overline{K}_i, \tag{5.1}$$

each unit of which can be operated separately. Each is the capital stock of a separate plant within the firm whose output time-shape is to be tracked. The full analysis of Chapters 3 and 4 applies to that ith plant individually; it will produce a rate of flow of output, $\dot{q}_i(t)$, using capital services and variable input flows at rates k_i and $v_i(t)$, constrained by an instantaneous pure flow production function $f_i(\cdot)$ like (3.1). The variable input price, $\overline{p}_v$, is time-invariant, whereas the capital service price depends on the duration of production by that ith plant, T_{pi}. Because $\overline{K}_i$ is always durable over T, the rate of capital services flow its $k_i = \overline{K}_i$ during production and $k_i = 0$ when the ith plant is idle.

At any moment, t, the firm's total rate of output flow, $q(t)$, will simply be the sum of rates of output flow from each of the plants that is in operation – "on stream" – at t. Except at the peak output rate $q_p(t)$, some plants will be in operation and some will not.[2] Assume that when any plant is operated under this scheme, it runs constantly at its optimal speed, $\dot{q}_i^*(t)$; when it is not run at that speed, it is shut down. There is nothing in between. Then all tracking of $q(t)$ over T is utilization tracking: All variations in the rate of total output flow over T are achieved by changes in the number of plants on stream that contribute to production of $q(t)$ at that moment. Any particular rate of total output flow, $q_m(t)$, at t is achieved by using m

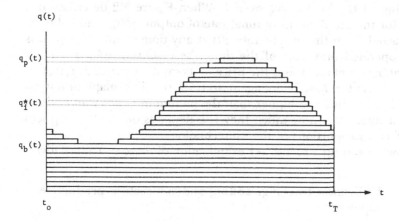

Figure 5.3. Stratification of a load curve into separate "plants."

plants with units of capital $\overline{K}_i$, $i = 1,...,m$, each producing at its optimal rate of output $\dot{q}_i^*(t)$; so

$$q_m(t) = \sum_{i=1}^{m} \dot{q}_i^*(t) = \sum_{i=1}^{m} f_i(k_i, v_i^*(t)). \qquad (5.2)$$

All deviations from $q_m(t)$ in output flow rate over T are obtained simply by starting up $(m + j)$ or shutting down $(m - h)$ plants. Clearly, the divisibility of capital must be fine enough – under pure utilization tracking – that the $\dot{q}_i^*(t)$ yield "acceptably" fine adjustments in $q(t)$ with which to track its time-shape.

Graphically, the area under the output load curve of Figure 5.1 can be stratified with the ith stratum representing the ith plant's contribution, $\dot{q}_i^*(t)$, to the total output flow at t, $q(t)$. For reasons that will soon become apparent, a given plant, its capital stock, and its output, $\dot{q}_i^*(t)$, will be associated with a specific stratum in the time-output space. The (crudely) stratified version of the time-shaped output of Figure 5.1 is shown in Figure 5.3. At any moment during T when its output stratum, $\dot{q}_i^*(t)$, lies below the load curve, the ith plant will be operating, contributing to the total flow rate; when the load curve drops below its output stratum, the ith plant will be shut down.

The total output flow rate never falls below the base rate, $q_b(t)$, nor does it rise above the peak rate, $q_p(t)$.[3] So capital used to produce output strata below the base-load rate will be utilized all the time $(T_{pi} = T$ for $q_i \leq q_b)$, and plants used to meet above-base output

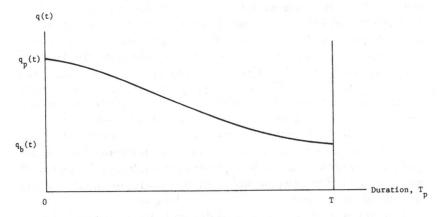

Figure 5.4. Load duration curve.

rates – those between $q_b(t)$ and $q_p(t)$ – will be utilized only part of the time ($T_{pi} < T$). The utilization rate associated with the marginal stratum $\dot{q}_i(t)$ will decline with increasing rates of total output flow – T_{pi} falls as $q_i(t)$ increases from $q_b(t)$ to $q_p(t)$. This is explicit when strata durations are mapped into the "load duration curve" of Figure 5.4, a curve widely used to represent the duration of production in electric-power generation.

It is important that the reasons why these stratum-specific utilization rates are less than 1 ($T_{pi} < T$) are quite different from the reasons for less-than-unitary utilization rates in the firms of Chapter 4. For those firms that used labor to produce a storable output, often it was optimal to operate with idle periods during T; $T_p^* < T$ minimized production costs in a world of time-specific labor costs. But for the firms of this chapter that use fuel to produce a perishable output there are no time-specific input costs, and it is optimal for any plant to operate all the time – $T_{pi}^* = T$ always minimizes costs. But a time-shape constraint on the output of a perishable product means that a plant supplying above-base output cannot operate all the time because its perishable output cannot be sold at every moment of the unit time T, $\dot{q}_i^*(t)$ can be sold only during those periods when the output rate is $q_m(t)$, where $m \geq i$. So the duration of production from the ith plant is constrained by the time-shape of output and is less than its cost-minimizing duration $T_{pi} \leq T_{pi}^* = T$. The load duration curve states, quite uncompromisingly, that given the specified time-shape of output, an output rate sufficient to utilize the output of the ith stratum will be sustained for only $T_{pi} < T$, even though optimal $T^*_{pi} = T$. For each plant stratum, its production duration is imposed by the time-shaped output profile.

Because each stratum of output rate is subject to the rules of Chapters 3 and 4, it is clear why the capital service price, $p_{ki}(T_{pi})$, plays a central role in time-specific modeling of production in the tracking of variable output loads. *The price of capital services used in the different output strata systematically rises as their rates of utilization fall.*[4] Plants used to produce the base-load rate of output carry a lower price of capital services than identical plants used to generate the above-base output rates, simply because above-base plants are used less of the time, and $p_{ki}(T_{pi}) > p_{ki}(T)$. The price of capital services, therefore, increases with the rate of output beyond the level of the base load: In electric-power production, a generator that provides an hour of base-load capital services at a given cost per kilowatt will provide an hour per day of peak-load capital service only at a cost 24 times as great.[5]

In predictable response to these systematic differences in stratum-specific input prices, firms will try to use stratum-specific technologies. If firms have a choice among technologies, *ex ante*, they can use different factor proportions to produce the different output strata, with each technology appropriate to the stratum's relative factor prices. So between output rate strata, not only different pieces of capital but also different technologies will be found in an optimal use of utilization tracking. This is the reason it was useful to associate a stratum with a capital stock and its output—because each stratum may be technologically distinct.

Because the plants used to produce during higher total output rates will be utilized less of the unit time and their capital service prices will therefore be higher, they will use less capital-intensive— more fuel-intensive—technologies. Base-load plants have the lowest capital service price, $p_{ki}(T)$, but (in our simple model) the same fuel price, $\bar{p}_v$; so on grounds of relative factor prices, base-load plants will be the most capital-intensive. In electric-power production, these are nuclear and large thermal plants. The plants that operate only at peak loads have very high capital service prices because of their low utilization. Because they, too, pay the same fuel prices, they will be the most fuel-intensive—the least capital-intensive. "Peaking capacity" in electric-power generation involves technologies like gas-fired turbines.

The greater is the range of technological choice available to the firm—the greater is the *ex ante* instantaneous elasticity of substitution – the greater will be the differences in the technologies used simultaneously by the cost-minimizing firm in tracking the time-shape of output, and the less costly will be the constraint imposed by any given time-shape of output over the unit time. The relevant elasticity of substitution for using different technologies in tracking a fully predictable, rhythmic time-shape of output is the *ex ante* instantaneous elasticity, because it describes possibilities for factor substitution embodied in different plants. But a high *ex ante* elasticity will assure use of a wide array of technologies only if those processes are sufficiently divisible to track the load curve with acceptable precision; for this reason alone, we would expect pure utilization tracking in fact to be rare. *Ex post* and *ex die* elasticities are not relevant to pure utilization tracking; even if both are zero, mixed-technology production will still be optimal, with utilization tracking of the load curve.

The costs of tracking any given time-shape of output will be lower the greater is the *ex ante* choice of technologies to differentiate among output strata. Using different factor proportions allows the firm to reduce the impact of rising capital service prices with falling strata duration. The greater that ability, the less the cost penalty inherent in idle capital. In peaking strata, where capital is idle much of the time, not much capital is used; in base strata, where it is fully and optimally utilized, capital is used heavily. In terms of Figure 5.2, again with nonzero *ex ante* elasticity, unit cost surfaces will be different for different strata technologies – unit costs will fall steeply to T_p = T for a base-load technology; for a peaking technology, unit costs will be higher at T but will rise much less sharply over lower durations and so will be lower than the base technology's unit costs at some $T_{pi} < T$. The next sections look more closely at average and marginal costs in producing time-shaped output. First it is necessary to describe the alternative to utilization tracking.

5.4 Speed tracking: changing output speed with constant utilization

Variations in the rate of output that follow the time-shape of output over the unit time can be got from a given plant by changes solely in the speed of its operation.[6] This section describes a pure speed tracking model. With a given capital stock $\overline{K}$ utilized all the time to yield a constant rate of capital service flow k, changes in variable inputs flows $v(t)$ induce changes in output flow rates $q(t)$, and these may be varied enough to track the load curve. This very neoclassical[7] speed tracking is – as noted before – described as movements of output rate along the plane $T_p = T$ of Figure 5.2, where utilization is constant and at a maximum over the unit time T, and the rate of output flow varies around an optimal level $q^*(t)$.

Speed tracking seems to conjure up a much more familiar, even textbook-level, neoclassical analysis of production, in contrast to utilization tracking. But, in fact, it does not, and that appearance of familiarity may obscure much that is to be revealed about time-shaped output and technology. The basic complication of the time-shaped production of perishable products remains: Although accumulated output is identical from one unit time to the next, it is time-shaped within the unit time. Our well-schooled intuition about production simply is not embedded in those circumstances.

Because plant utilization is constant at its maximum with speed tracking, unit production costs for any output rate are simply the sum of unit capital costs, $p_k(T)k/q(t)$, and unit variable costs, $\bar{p}_v v(t)/q(t)$. The rates of output, $q(t)$, and variable input flows, $v(t)$, are variable: Unit costs $ac(q,t)$ generate a very ordinary-looking two-dimensional average-cost curve like the heavy $ac(q,t,k)$ of Figure 5.5. But much is not ordinary about Figure 5.5. What is represented in the $T_p = T$ plane of Figure 5.2 that is isolated in Figure 5.5 is, of course, the *instantaneous rate of flow* of output and costs with the given capital stock operated all the time. The requirement that the firm track a time-shaped output pattern over T means that it must change rates of output $q(t)$ on an exogenously set schedule throughout the unit time. So least-cost production involves a least-cost time-shape of output, not a least-cost rate or level of output.

The unique least-cost rate of flow of output with a capital stock of given size is, of course, the familiar $q^*(t)$ in Figure 5.2 – the lowest point on a U-shaped average-cost curve. But in the unfamiliar world of time-shaped output, the plant will have to vary output rates during T to produce rates of output as high as the peak rate $q_p(t)$ and as low as the base rate $q_b(t)$ described by the load curve. Those departures from the plant's optimal speed encounter increased unit costs in both directions: Below $q^*(t)$, reduced unit variable costs are more than offset by increased unit capital costs; above $q^*(t)$, diminishing marginal product of the variable input $v(t)$ with the given capital service flow rate k offsets the declining unit capital costs. And at max $q(t)$, of course, variable costs and hence unit costs become infinite. So changing output rates during T to track the time-shape of output increases costs.

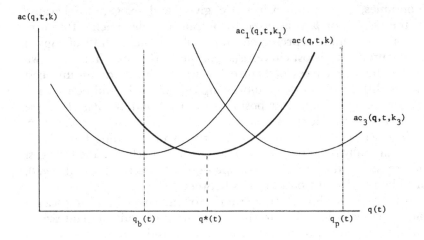

Figure 5.5. Speed and unit costs with varying plant scale.

The time-shape of production over T can usefully be described by duration-weighted rates of output flow. The issue of this section, then, is how to track all of that given time-shaped output over T at least cost, changing only the rate of output flow from a capital stock that is durable and hence must remain constant over T. The key questions are (a) how to minimize the costs of producing a time-shaped output of given shape and (b) what parameters determine the level of the resulting minimized cost. The first of these is a decision variable to the firm; it involves picking the optimal plant scale. The second involves the exogenous parameters: technology, factor prices, and the time-shape of the output.

Least-cost plant size to track a given time-shaped output with given technology and factor prices

Whatever the scale of the capital stock, $\overline{K}$, it must be the same over the whole of the unit time, but that scale, despite its fixity throughout T, can be freely adjusted *ex ante* to minimize the costs of producing any given time-shape of output. The optimal scale, $\overline{K}^*$, is the firm's basic optimizing choice in speed tracking the load curve.

Assume initially that there is only a single technology defined by an instantaneous production function with the usual properties, including *ex post* and *ex die* factor flow substitution. There are no scale economies, and factor prices are given and exogenous, because neither $p_k(T)$ nor $\bar{p}_v$ is affected by output or scale. Then differences in scale are simply represented graphically as lateral shifts of a given short-run average-cost curve, $ac(q,t,k)$, with different k. This is shown in the three ac curves of Figure 5.5, where the short-run unit cost curves differ only in their underlying capital stocks and hence capital service flow rates and positions vis-à-vis output rates. In these conveniently simple terms, the selection of an optimal scale, $\bar{K}^* = k^*$, with which to track a given load curve involves sliding the $ac(q,t,k)$ curve laterally by adjustments of $k = \bar{K}$ until it achieves the least cost of producing the given time-shaped output described by $q_p(t)$, $q_b(t)$, and the duration of output rates between.

It is useful to describe the criteria for the cost-minimizing scale a bit less casually and then to show the choice of optimal plant size in an instantaneous isoquant map like that introduced in Chapter 3 in order to reveal the other dimensions of optimal speed tracking. To simplify, a discretely time-shaped output can be represented fully as a set of n different output flow rates, $q_j(t)$, $j = 1,...,n$, each of which lasts for T_{pj} of the unit time T; so $T = \Sigma_{j=1}^n T_{pj}$. Then the cost flow rate associated with the production of any jth rate of output, $q_j(t)$, is

$$c_j(t) = p_k(T)k + \bar{p}_v v_j(t). \tag{5.3}$$

Because k is the same over T, any output rate $q_j(t)$ on the load curve will be got by using a larger or smaller variable input flow rate, $v_j(t)$. The particular value of $v_j(t)$ needed to produce $q_j(t)$ depends on technology and the size of that unchanged rate of capital service flow; the larger the capital service flow rate, k, the smaller the variable input flow rate, $v_j(t)$, needed to produce any given $q_j(t)$, because *ex die* substitution is assumed. So, for a given production function,

$$v_j(t) = v_j(k,t). \tag{5.4}$$

Then the accumulated cost of producing all of the given time-shaped output over T is simply

$$C = \sum_{j=1}^n T_{pj} c_j(t)$$

$$= \sum_{j=1}^n T_{pj}[p_k(T)k + \bar{p}_v v_j(k,t)]$$

$$= P_k k + \bar{p}_v \sum_{j=1}^n T_{pj} v_j(k,t). \tag{5.5}$$

This is what is to be minimized. It is minimized when scale is adjusted so that

$$\partial C/\partial k = P_k + \overline{p}_v \sum_{j=1}^{n} T_{pj}(\partial v_j(t)/\partial k) = 0, \tag{5.6}$$

which implies the following first-order condition for optimal scale:

$$\frac{P_k}{\overline{p}_v} = -\sum_{j=1}^{n} T_{pj}(\partial v_j(t)/\partial k) = \sum_{j=1}^{n} T_{pj}[(\partial f/\partial k)/(\partial f/\partial v_j(t))]. \tag{5.7}$$

The slope of the jth instantaneous isoquant is $-1/(\partial v_j(t)/\partial k)$; so it equals the relative marginal products of the variable input and capital service flows – their marginal rate of substitution. The second-order conditions are assured by the convexity of the isoquants.

Expression (5.7) defines the conditions of the least-cost production of any given (discretely) time-shaped output over T when the scale of the plant is adjusted *ex ante* to minimize the costs of producing those output rates and durations that track the given load curve. The condition is, simply, that the duration-weighted sum of relative marginal products of variable input and capital service flow rates be set equal to their (exogenous) relative prices.

When the load tracking problem is trivialized to its familiar form by assuming a "load curve" with a single rate of output that is maintained over all of T – the horizontal load curve of Figure 3.1(a), again – then $n = 1$, $T_p = T$, and (5.7) reduces to the condition for cost minimization from elementary textbooks,

$$p_k(t)/\overline{p}_v = (\partial f/\partial k)/(\partial f/\partial v);$$

in average-cost diagrammatics, it is the simple matter of adjusting the position of a U-shaped average-cost curve so that its minimum point coincides with the single given rate of output as the heavy cost curve, $ac(q,t,k)$, does with $q^*(t)$ in Figure 5.5.

The instantaneous isoquant map of Figure 5.6 shows the dimensions of the optimal speed tracking choice more completely. Capital service and variable input flow rates are on the axes, and the isoquants describe output flow rates; some substitution is possible. The number and range of isoquants that are relevant are determined by the load curve; in the trivial case of a flat load curve, again, only a single isoquant matters, and cost minimization determines k^* (and $v^*(t)$) by tangency with that isoquant. More generally, the range of output rates incorporated in the load curve explicitly bounds the set of relevant isoquants by base and peak rates, $q_b(t)$ and $q_p(t)$, as in

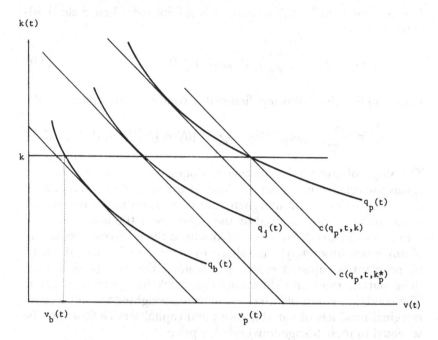

Figure 5.6. Optimal scale in speed tracking time-shaped output.

Figure 5.6. Their duration-weights, of course, are not explicit in the figure.[8] The relative prices of input flows are described by the slopes of the isocost curves, and the rate of cost flow, $c_j(t)$, is described by their positions. Finally, the need to use the same plant to track the whole of the variation in output flow rates from $q_b(t)$ to $q_p(t)$ over T requires that the capital service flow rate, k, be the same over all output rates and that their variations from $q_b(t)$ to $q_p(t)$ be got by changing variable input flow rates from $v_b(t)$ to $v_p(t)$ as indicated.

The cost-minimization process of the earlier paragraphs, of course, was intended to solve for the optimal size of the capital stock and hence the rate of flow of capital services, k^*, that would produce at least cost the full range of (weighted) output rates given by the load curve. A number of aspects of that choice are apparent in Figure 5.6. The fact that the capital stock is durable over T prevents the firm from operating at least cost for most output rates. In fact, as drawn, the capital stock that yields k of capital service flows will achieve least cost for none of the three rates of output posited for that load curve. Furthermore, it is clear that the optimal scale implied by the duration-weighted sum of marginal rates of substitution is not the same, generally, as the scale optimal to produce the duration-weighted average level of output. So it is not generally useful to collapse the time-shape of output into a single weighted-average output rate. And because of the fixity of the capital service flow rate, the variable input flows change more in tracking the load curve than they would have to if capital services were also variable – that would maintain optimal factor flow proportions.

The intersection of any fixed capital service flow rate, k, with the jth isoquant specifies the relevant marginal rate of substitution for that rate of output and scale, and the horizontal distance at k between that isoquant and its tangent isocost curve measures the cost penalty of producing $q_j(t)$ with k instead of using the scale optimal for that output level; (5.7) can be interpreted as adjusting k to minimize the duration-weighted sum of these cost penalty distances over all the isoquants relevant to the load curve. The cost penalty is the distance between $c(q_p,t,k_p^*)$ and $c(q_p,t,k)$.

Figure 5.6 also reflects the exogenous determinants of the level of costs with an optimal speed tracking choice of k^* that we will now consider briefly.

Parameters of optimal speed tracking

Although the choice of the optimal scale may be the only variable the firm can control, the total cost of tracking the load curve will be influenced by (a) production technology, (b) factor prices, and (c) the shape of the load curve. Each of these is relevant to speed tracking.

Technology. The degree of *ex die* factor substitutability – "flexibility" – determines the costs of tracking any given load curve with given factor prices. Costs are higher the less is the ability to substitute factor flows; so if there are two technologies with the same minimum costs of $q^*(t)$, the one with the greater flexibility will always dominate the one with the lesser in tracking any nontrivial load curve. That, of course, suggests the relevance to time-shaped production of Stigler's classic argument (1939) that with two technologies with different minimum average costs – like ac_1 and ac_2 of Figure 5.7 – the one with higher minimum costs but greater flexibility will, for some load curves, dominate the one with lower minimum unit costs but more expensive output variations.[9] A load curve of $\frac{1}{2}Tq_b(t)$, $\frac{1}{2}Tq_p(t)$ would, in terms of Figure 5.7, be made more cheaply by the flexible technology, ac_1, even though $ac_1(q^*(t)) > ac_2(q^*(t))$.

In instantaneous isoquant terms, inflexibility appears as reduced

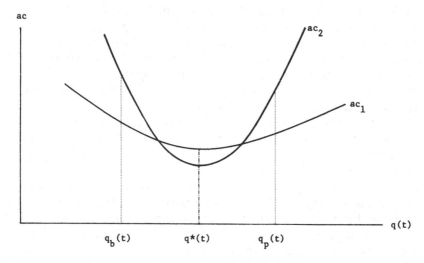

Figure 5.7. Speed tracking with flexible or low-cost plant.

factor substitutability and a consequent increase in the curvature of the isoquants, and hence, for any given k and $p_k/\bar{p}_v$, a greater accumulated cost penalty of the variations in output rates called for by a given load curve.

Factor prices. A change in factor prices will affect optimal speed tracking in entirely predictable ways that are reflected in any one of the representations used – average cost or isoquant diagrams or conditions (5.7). An uncompensated rise in input price will increase costs of tracking any given load curve; a change in relative prices will alter optimal scale, reducing (increasing) it with a higher (lower) relative price of capital services.[10]

Time-shape of output. The load curve determines the range of output rates that must be produced and the weights attached to them in (5.7); so a change in the shape of the load curve will alter both costs and the optimal capital scale with which to track output over T. Increasing the range of output rates – the amplitude of the output rhythm – will increase costs; increasing the duration-weights of output rates near the boundaries of the range will increase costs. These, of course, are simply the obverse of the fact first pointed out in Chapter 3 that, absent time-specific input prices, costs are always minimized when the time-shape of output is flat over T. A biased shift in weighting, *ceteris paribus*, clearly will alter the optimal scale.

Although the time-shape of output over T is exogenous to the firm in this chapter, efforts to modify that shape are central to the discussion of peak-load pricing and load management in Chapters 10 and 11; so it is useful to have noted, now, the role that time-shape plays in influencing both optimal scale and average costs.

A simple Cobb-Douglas example

The things that affect speed tracking of a time-shaped output are illustrated nicely by the simple example summarized in Table 5.1. The first five columns of the table describe different load curves, and the rows describe different plant scales. Cell entries are the average cost of tracking the specified load curve over T with the specified amount of capital using the same Cobb-Douglas production function, $q_j(t) = k^{1/3} v_j^{2/3}$. Factor prices are the same, $P_k = 1 = \bar{p}_v$, for the first five columns; in the sixth, the price of capital is doubled to reevaluate the cost of an earlier load curve. Each of the first five columns describes a different load curve; each is defined by three rates of output, q_j, and their associated durations, T_{pj}, as shown at the head of the column. The first three load curves differ only in rates of output; the next two repeat the rate pattern from column (1), but with different durations; the last column reports the costs of producing the load curve of column (1) with a higher price of capital, $P_k = 2$. For each load curve and factor price variant in a column, unit production costs are reported for capital stock of size $\underline{K} = 1$ through $\bar{K} = 5$.

The table illustrates the main dimensions of speed tracking. Reading down any column, it is clear that the cost of tracking any time-shaped output falls at first with increasing scale and then rises; plant size can be too large or too small for efficient production of a given load curve. The flat load curve of column (3) yields the same pattern of falling and rising cost, but, again, its costs are lower than those of any other time-shaped output. In a comparison of columns (1), (2), and (3), it is clear that even though both duration and total output per unit time are the same, the amplitude of output rate variations can change the level of minimum unit costs attainable. Columns (1), (4), and (5) differ only in the durations of their three similar output rates, but that changes both the level of minimum unit cost and their optimal scale. Finally, column (6) repeats the load curve of column (1) but produces it with capital that is twice as expensive, with the predictable result that a smaller optimal scale only partially reduces the impact of higher capital costs.

Table 5.1. *Speed tracking time-shaped outputs: average costs*

	Time-shape of output					
	(1)	(2)	(3)	(4)	(5)[c]	(6)[d]
	2,4,6[a]	½,½,11	4,4,4	2,4,6	2,4,6	2,4,6
$\bar{K}$	8,8,8[b]	8,8,8	8,8,8	2,2,20	20,2,2	8,8,8
1	2.38	3.35	2.25	2.57	2.10	2.63
2	2.00	2.69	1.91	2.05	2.00	2.50
3	1.98	2.54	1.90	1.93	2.18	2.73
4	2.06	2.55	2.00	1.92	2.45	3.06
5	2.20	2.64	2.14	1.98	2.75	3.45

[a]Output rates, q_1, q_2, q_3; $q_j = k_h^{1/3} v_j^{2/3}$; $j = 1,2,3$; $h = 1,2,3,4,5$.
[b]Durations, T_{p1}, T_{p2}, T_{p3}.
[c]$P_k = 1 = \bar{p}_v$ for columns (1) to (5).
[d]$P_k = 2, \bar{p}_v = 1$ for column (6).

5.5   Mixing utilization and speed tracking

It would be rare for a cost-minimizing producer of a perishable output with a time-shaped demand to follow my expositional convenience, relying solely on either utilization or speed tracking. Typically, the least-cost tracking of any given time-shaped output will use both methods: To track an increasing output rate, the firm will first increase the rate of output from a given plant over some range beyond its least-cost output rate and then bring an additional unit of capacity into production while cutting the original plant back so that both produce at less than their least-cost rates of output. If there is scope for *ex ante* factor substitution, the second plant may bring with it a technology and a cost structure quite different from those of the first. Further increases in output rate will be got by speed tracking as both plants increase output (probably at different rates). When their two output rates have been increased to some levels, a third unit of plant will be brought on stream, at a less-than-optimal rate, while the first two are cut back. And so on. The tracking of decreasing output rates will be symmetric.

So the tracking of a time-shaped output will involve both the mix of tracking methods – varying utilization rates of different units of capacity and varying the rate of output of each – and the mix of technologies among the plants. A careful analysis of the conditions for optimal switching between speed tracking and utilization tracking with changing output rates is well beyond the aims of this chapter, but its main dimensions seem clear.[11] Relative *ex ante* and *ex die* elasticities of substitution are central. The *ex ante* elasticity is relevant to the costs of utilization tracking; the *ex die* elasticity is relevant to the costs of speed tracking. So very different characteristics of a production technology are involved in the two alternatives. It seems unlikely that their relative balance would be the same over the whole of a load curve: Two different *ex ante* technologies that fit nicely into utilization tracking may have very different *ex die* substitution characteristics – flexibility – and hence quite different abilities to speed track output at low cost. Scale gaps – lumpiness – between *ex ante* technologies may be different over different portions of the load curve.

In general, the balance between utilization tracking and speed tracking will be tipped toward the former for any load curve, or part of a load curve, where the technology is quite divisible with high *ex ante* elasticity of substitution and a low *ex die* elasticity; under these circumstances, low-cost tracking is got by additions and subtractions of fine gradations of differentiated technologies, adapted to their different factor prices, and each carries high cost penalties for deviations from its optimal rate of output.

Each tracking method implies specific limitations. Utilization tracking will be inadequate if minimum plant scale generates gaps – discrete jumps – in output rate that are unacceptable in the load tracking. Only speed tracking can fill in such gaps. On the other hand, with speed tracking, all output rate variation is to be got from a single plant, but the range of output rates required by the load curve may exceed the output rates achievable at noninfinite cost with a particular technology. Only utilization tracking with multiple units of small plants would fill in those extremes. So mixed tracking might be imposed by a technology, even in the absence of assiduous cost minimization.

5.6 Time-shaped marginal costs

Special significance attaches to the marginal cost of producing a time-shaped output. It has been a persistent concern and an elusive objective of the literature on peak-load pricing to apply the welfare criteria of orthodox analysis to the pricing of perishable and time-shaped products, and that requires adapting the idea of marginal costs to the complexities of a time-shaped production process. That objective has had greater urgency for the fact that important time-shaped perishable products like transportation services and electric power often are made by regulated firms; so public agencies have had responsibility for pricing decisions. The adaptation of the marginal-cost concept to time-shaped output has so far been only partly successful, and the theory of efficient production of time-shaped output developed in this chapter appears useful both in showing why and in achieving some greater measure of success.

"Marginal cost" ordinarily means the minimum cost of producing an increment to output, $dQ = q(t)$ within T. In the production of a storable commodity, the scheduling of that increment is assumed to yield the least cost of producing $q(t)$ within the unit time T. It is a function of quantity, Q. In the production of a product with a time-shaped output, the least cost of such a temporally footloose output increment – although it can be readily identified – is rarely of interest. Instead, we usually care about the marginal cost of producing an increment to output at a specific moment during T – at a specific place on the load curve – because production, supply, demand, and use are all time-specific. So the marginal cost is a function of timing, $t,$ and quantity, $q(t),$ and there will be an infinite number of such marginal costs, differentiated by the specific timing of the output increment, $dQ = q(t)$. Finally, our analysis of methods of tracking time-shaped output shows that the cost of producing a specified increment to output at a specified moment on the load curve can depend on the shape of the entire load curve; so the load curve must be fully specified, too.

The time-shaped marginal cost of a perishable product, then, should be defined as the increment to cost, C, per unit time, T, consequent on producing an increment, q(t), to output Q per unit time at a specific moment on a specific time-shaped load curve.

The marginal cost of a time-shaped output is conditioned by the rate and timing of that increment of output and by the whole time-shape of output over T. Long- and short-run time-shaped marginal costs can be separated on the usual basis of the variability of the capital stock. We will concentrate on the long run as appropriate to the questions raised by the peak-load literature.

The components of time-shaped marginal costs: Who pays the capacity costs?

The last two sections of this chapter have shown that the technological characteristics of production described by elasticities of factor flow substitution *ex ante, ex post,* and *ex die* play a central role in determining the optimal method of tracking a time-shaped output. The method of tracking a time-shaped output largely determines the components of long-run marginal costs. So therein lies the answer to the persistent question of which customers of a time-shaped product should pay the capital costs. If the technology allows factor service substitution *ex ante*, but none either *ex post* or *ex die*, the time-shape of output has to be tracked by utilization tracking; if the technology allows substitution *ex die*, but not *ex ante*, the time-shaped output has to be tracked by speed tracking. And in the real world, it has just been argued, both methods will typically be found. But consider the long-run time-shaped marginal costs for each of these in turn.

Rigid technologies ex post: *utilization tracking.* If *ex ante*, *ex post*, and *ex die* substitutions are all impossible, the load curve's time-shape must be produced by utilization tracking. All marginal capital costs will then fall on the peak-load users. In this familiar scenario, the peak output rate alone determines the size of the capital stock – "capacity" – via the fixed coefficient production function assumed, $\dot{q}(t) = \min[ak,bv(t)]$; so $q_p(t)$ implies a unique $k_p(t)$ and hence $\bar{K}_p$. Long-run marginal costs of the peak output rate, therefore, include both capital and variable cost components. Off-peak rates of output costlessly use the extant capital stock left over from producing $q_p(t)$, because capital is durable over T. So off-peak marginal costs include only variable costs. Those variable costs, furthermore, will be the same for all output rates, absent substitution possibilities all around. So a rigid technology yields two long-run time-shaped marginal costs: a marginal cost of the peak-load output rate that includes capital and variable costs and a marginal cost of all off-peak output rates that includes only the (constant) variable input costs. Such crisp conclusions, unfortunately, rest entirely on the rigidity of the technology assumed.

If there is scope for *ex ante* substitution, utilization tracking is still the only option, but different strata of output will be made with different technologies. Long-run time-shaped marginal costs are altered considerably even though *ex post* and *ex die* elasticities of substitution are still assumed to be zero. Any increment to the peak output bears capital costs, but that cost is lowered, *ceteris paribus*, by substituting the variable input, $v(t)$, for expensive, little-utilized capital. More important, off-peak increments also incur capital costs. Finally, variable costs will differ by output rate.

The cost of producing any time-specific increment to the rate of output will now depend on the whole time-shape of output, because that will determine production costs through technological differentiation among strata, owing, in turn, to their different utilization rates, capital prices, and optimal strata technologies. So although only the *ex ante* elasticity of substitution is nonzero, a time-specified increment to output will carry variable costs that depend on the rest of the load curve shape, because that increment in output increases the duration of production for an off-peak stratum: In altering the stratum utilization rate, the output increment will reduce capital service prices for that stratum, increasing the optimal capital use. So as long as all substitution possibilities are continuous, *ex ante*, the output increment $\dot{q}_i(t)$ will therefore increase the optimal amount of capital used to produce that stratum of output; even if only *ex ante* elasticity of substitution is positive, there is a capital cost component to off-peak long-run marginal costs. Note that the adjustment in variable costs consequent on adapting a more capital-intensive technology (as increment $\dot{q}_i(t)$ reduces i-stratum capital costs) might well be negative.

Substitution ex post: *speed tracking*. Now let *ex ante* substitution be zero but *ex die* (and *ex post*) substitution be positive. Then the only option is to track the time-shape of output by speed tracking. Marginal costs are, again, the conditional costs of producing increment $q_i(t)$, given the entire time-shape of producing Q. Long-run marginal costs clearly include capital costs as well as variable costs, and this is true for all levels of output. This is exactly the issue addressed by equation (5.7): the optimal capital stock for a given time-shape of output. With speed tracking and an optimal capital stock, the peak output rate, $q_p(t)$, has no special significance; its role in determining the optimal capital stock, and hence marginal capital costs, is – like that of all other output rates on the load curve – limited to its weighted contribution to the cost of the whole curve. Because the peak rate, $q_p(t)$, is always far less than max $q(t)$ when there is *ex die* substitution, it is like all the other output rates. Any $q_i(t)$, the time-specified increment to output, will alter the optimal capital stock by changing the weights attached to the output rates of the load curve. The long-run marginal capital cost of $q_i(t)$ can be positive, zero, or negative, depending on where the increment $q_i(t)$ falls relative to the rest of the time-shaped output. Variable costs, of course, are relevant to the long-run marginal cost of all $q_i(t)$, but they are the marginal variable costs associated not only with that isolated increment to output but also with the whole of the change in variable costs incurred in producing optimally the entire altered load curve.

Substitution all around. Finally, the nasty implication of all this derives from the fact that even this set of increasingly complicated conclusions about what to include in long-run time-shaped marginal costs rests on the artificial separation of tracking methods got by specifying that only one sort of elasticity can be positive at a time. We have seen that the typical least-cost tracking of a time-shaped output will merge both methods of tracking.[12] That means, simply, that, *in general, even identifying the components of the long-run marginal cost of time-shaped output is an empirical issue that varies case by case.*

The problem with "the bridge problem" and the public goods analogy

The earliest successes in understanding the costs of time-shaped production borrowed effectively from the logic of public goods in the form of The Bridge Problem. It was argued – and is now the standard stuff of textbooks – that all capital costs should be assigned to the users of peak output rates, and off-peak users should pay, on social-welfare/marginal-cost criteria, only the variable costs. This has had a sufficiently strong influence on the analysis of peak-load costs to warrant a closer examination in light of our fuller understanding of time-shaped production.

The bridge problem analogy argues simply that once it has been built, a bridge will serve less-than-peak rates of output with the same durable-over-T capital stock used for peak output rates. Because the size of the needed capital stock (bridge) is determined solely by the peak output rate, all capital costs fall on the peak-rate users, and only variable costs fall on the off-peak customers: Off-peak capital services from the bridge are free as public goods; their use is nonrivalrous. This is, of course, the same conclusion just reached for the case of no substitution, but it appears that the bridge problem analogy, although successful for rigid technologies, may have hampered seriously the extension of understanding of time-shaped marginal costs: The bridge is an entirely apt illustration, and the *ex die* time perspective it embodies is quite appealing, but only in the strictly limited case of utilization tracking with no input substitution. The other situations can also be nicely illustrated by bridges, but only with considerable reconstruction and further specification of their operation to convey the dimensions of less simplistic production processes.

The bridge of the preceding paragraph, with its rigid technology, had, perhaps, a number of traffic lanes, but all of them, because *ex ante* substitution was zero, were the same, and each lane (stratum, if you will) carried the same maximum traffic flow rate, $q_i(t)$. So the total width of the bridge, $\bar{K}$ – the number of lanes or strata – was determined by the peak output flow the bridge was to produce.

Once there is *ex ante* technological substitution, a different bridge is needed – it must embody different technologies in the different lanes that handle different levels of output flow. The left-hand lane, perhaps, is well and solidly built, with good paving and ample space for the ordinary nonprofessional driver to negotiate the bridge crossing safely under his own power. So that lane (stratum) uses a great deal of bridge capital and economizes on variable inputs. Because it is the base-load stratum, used all the time, the capital service price of that lane is low, making that capital-intensive technology optimal. But the next lane, designed for use less of the time, may be narrower and unpaved, using an open steel grating that will unnerve the average driver. So that lane of traffic uses hired skilled drivers to take the cars across the bridge. These paid drivers are able to achieve a high rate of traffic flow with the same safety as in the base-load lane, but at a considerable saving in capital costs in the bridge (lane) construction. And, of course, because that lane is needed only during rush hours, these drivers do not have to be paid except when the lane is in use.[13]

Now, in this form, the bridge illustration describes utilization tracking with *ex ante* factor substitution, but it is quite a different bridge. The pure public goods aspect of nonrivalrous consumption no longer is so relevant. To be sure, the services of the peak-load lane – the narrow, unpaved one – are a free good off peak, but it is not true that all off-peak output rates can be increased without capital cost. To increase the base rate of traffic flow might require another wide, paved lane as the least-cost way of increasing that off-peak output, and that could clearly incur capital costs. Variable costs – the drivers' wage bill – might be either reduced or increased by an increment to off-peak output, whereas capital costs might be positive.

A final reconstruction of the bridge describes speed tracking of the load curve over T. With zero *ex ante* substitution, all lanes must be of the same design, but because of positive *ex post* and *ex die* substitution, $\sigma_p, \sigma_t > 0$, output variations are got by hiring more or fewer drivers. With low traffic volume, amateurs can get their own cars across the bridge safely (zero variable cost), perhaps requiring lots of room (capital) in which to maneuver. As the volume of traffic increases, larger numbers of paid drivers are employed, because they are able to drive more closely and carefully, increasing the flow rate of cars over the given bridge. Of course, the bridge will not be designed to have its engineering capacity, max $q(t)$, coincide with the peak output flow, $q_p(t)$, because that would mean that the marginal product of the hired drivers had been driven to zero. So at the peak rates of output the bridge can still handle more traffic at higher (short-run) marginal cost. The optimal width of the bridge – the optimal-size capital stock with the single technology – will depend very much on the time-pattern of traffic flows. An increment to output can increase the optimal width of the bridge (if it comes at peak periods) or decrease it (if the increment comes at the base period). It is quite clear that, *ex die,* the bridge exists and that its services are "free" in the familiar sense that *ex post* marginal costs do not include capital costs. But it is also quite clear that long-run marginal costs must include a capital cost component for all increments to time-shaped output; that capital component may turn out to be negative or zero, but whether or not it does will depend on the existing time-shape of output, and not in any predictable way.

This cavalier reengineering of The Bridge has served to make it fit the relevant complexity of the time-shaped production problem instead of fitting the public goods problem. It is clear, I think, that the bridge and public goods logic is applicable only to a world of totally fixed coefficients and therefore that the bridge analogy probably has not helped the efforts to extend the analysis of the costs of time-shaped production beyond that rigidly restricted world – the grip of the bridge analogy on the imagination and analytical structure of the problem appears to have been strong.

PART III

Applications of time-specific analysis

Shephard's dilemma: duality and the process of production

This chapter and the next illustrate the way the time-specific production models just developed impinge on issues in the center of mainstream economics. Three specific issues are considered. This chapter looks carefully at the process of production implied by the use of mathematical duality theory to represent the behavior of firms. The next chapter shows that the familiar one-dimensional, timeless representation of economic variables – like output and capital and employment – inherent in orthodox theory leads to frequent ambiguities in the meanings of those variables that in turn result in errors, biases, and noise in their measurement. The time-specific perspective is used in Chapter 7 to identify the sources of ambiguity in the concepts and measurement of "factor proportions" and "productive capacity."

6.1   Mathematical duality theory and production in time

Chapter 3, through its attention to the timing of factor use within the orthodox unit time, showed that inputs to production differ essentially in their technological and economic characteristics. Those differences make the use of mathematical duality theory generally inappropriate to production analysis.[1] The representations of technology and input prices, and hence costs, that underlie and justify duality theory are either internally inconsistent or else applicable only to a firm that is, in very central ways, unlike any we know. In commenting on the economics of the duality model, I will rely largely on Shephard's work (1970) as a pioneering contribution and the one that often goes furthest in explicit detail.[2] It is useful, briefly, to review that contribution and the relevant aspects of production introduced in Chapters 3 and 4.

In Shephard's production function, "both the input and output variables [are] defined as time rates ... per some unit time interval" (Shephard, 1970, p. 5). Using flows to describe technology achieves the laudable aim set out in the opening sentence of his Chapter 1: It makes the production function "a mathematical statement relating quantitatively the purely technological relationships between the output of a process and the inputs of the factors of production" (Shephard, 1970, p. 3).

But, of course, the inputs to that pure flow production function differ in essential characteristics: A capital service flow argument is derived from durable capital stocks owned or rented by the firm, whereas in any nonslave society a labor service flow argument is purchased by the firm as a labor service flow per se. In its primary factor markets, then, the firm buys capital stocks and labor service flows; it purchases the source of the argument of its production function in one case and the argument itself in the other. This is the insight of Jorgenson and Griliches (1967). From this fundamental technical-institutional difference between capital services and labor services comes an equally fundamental difference in their price behaviors in production.

As developed with care in Chapter 3, at any given unit rental rate, P_k, per unit time T for a durable capital stock, the firm will pay the price $p_k = P_k/T_p$ for a unit of the capital service flow that is the argument of its production function. T_p is the duration of production per unit time T, like a day or year; so T_p/T is the rate of capital utilization. The price of capital services, $p_k(P_k,T_p)$, falls with increasing utilization: The price of capital services is duration-specific, dependent on the duration of production, T_p, within the unit time T.

Labor service flows, in contrast, are traded in service flow markets; so the price, $w(t)$, the firm pays for its labor input is appropriate to that argument of its pure flow production function. But the price of labor services depends, *inter alia*, on when, t, during the unit time T the labor service is used: A wage rate that appears to be wholly "stationary" from one day to the next will mask the time-specific variation in the price of labor services to which any cost-minimizing firm must respond in its production schedule and utilization decision. The price of the labor service argument of a pure flow production function is thus time-specific, dependent on the timing of production within the unit time T.

Finally, any temporally footloose input, like a flow of cheaply storable materials (flour or steel or paint or tires), enters the pure flow production function with a time-invariant price, dependent on neither timing nor duration of production within the unit time.

6.2   Timing and duality

Shephard made the unit time neither an infinitesimal nor an elementary time unit for the analysis of production; he introduced technologies that could be operated for only a part of the unit time:

> Property P.8 is valid for time divisibly-operated technologies. For example, in [input vector] $\mathbf{x} \ \varepsilon \ L(u)$, $\mathbf{y} \ \varepsilon \ L(u)$ and $\theta \ \varepsilon \ [0,1]$, the input vector $[(1 - \theta)\mathbf{x} + \theta\mathbf{y}]$ may be interpreted as an operation of the technology a fraction $(1 - \theta)$ of some unit time interval with the input vector $\mathbf{x}$ and a fraction θ with $\mathbf{y}$, assuring at least the output rate u [Shephard, 1970, p. 15].

So those "time rates" of input and output flows are more specifically accumulated flows over the unit time T, not instantaneous rates of flow at time t. An accumulated flow production function is appropriate to the duality model's representation of production because it is time-divisible, whereas an instantaneous production function is not.[3]

Finally, the "time divisibility" of technology is not differentiated in Shephard's representation from the physical divisibility of the factor flows themselves; only accumulated quanta matter:

> If $\mathbf{x}$, $\mathbf{y}$ . . . are two input vectors, the input vector $[(1 - \theta)\mathbf{x} + \theta\mathbf{y}]$, where $\theta \ \varepsilon$ [0,1], may be interpreted *either* as a single input vector $\mathbf{z}$ *or* that the input vector $\mathbf{x}$ is used a fraction $(1 - \theta)$ of the time interval and the input $\mathbf{y}$ is used the remaining fraction θ [emphasis added].

He then continued with the important assertion that the cost implications of these two alternatives are equally undifferentiated:

> In either case, the cost per unit time of the input $[(1 - \theta)\mathbf{x} + \theta\mathbf{y}]$ is calculated by the inner product $\mathbf{p} \cdot [(1 - \theta)\mathbf{x} + \theta\mathbf{y}]$. As a combined input, the interpretation of this cost is straightforward. The capital service components imply [that] certain amounts of those services are inputed per unit time, and the corresponding components of the price vector $\mathbf{p}$ denote the costs per unit of those services calculated by whatever practices may be used for amortization of investments involved. If the input $[(1 - \theta)\mathbf{x} + \theta\mathbf{y}]$ is regarded as time fractional applications of two distinct input vectors, the costing of the capital service components of each input vector is time prorated [Shephard, 1970, p. 79].

This, of course, underlines the second deficiency of the production duality analysis, the failure to recognize that input flows to production differ in essential respects in their technological and ownership characteristics and that those differences are an integral part of the production process that must be captured either in its technological representation or in the representation of its prices and costs. These characteristics are central to any analysis of the relationship between technology and costs in production.

To see how this indifference to factor characteristics undermines the duality model, consider in time-specific detail Shephard's assertion that there is no meaningful difference between *seriatim* changes in factor inputs during the unit time and the simultaneous blending of two different input vectors, each at reduced rates, continuously over the unit time. Decomposing the accumulated flows of duality theory into explicit instantaneous flow rates and duration within unit time T reveals what lies beneath this assertion.

Process X uses input vector $\mathbf{x}$ – now precisely specified as a vector of instantaneous flow rates of factor inputs – to produce an output at instantaneous rate q_x. $Tq_x = Q_u$ is then Shephard's "time rate" of output per unit time T when using process X. Alternatively, process Y can be used with its instantaneous input vector $\mathbf{y}$, producing output at the instantaneous rate q_y. Define $\mathbf{x}$ and $\mathbf{y}$ so that $q_y = q_x$; then $Q_u = Tq_y = Tq_x$. Absent scale economies, $(1 - \theta)\mathbf{x}$ produces output at rate $(1 - \theta)q_x$, and $\theta\mathbf{y}$ produces at rate θq_y; so if both processes are used simultaneously over unit time T, $[T(1 - \theta)\mathbf{x} + T\theta\mathbf{y}] = T[(1 - \theta)\mathbf{x} + \theta\mathbf{y}]$ will yield an accumulated flow of output over T of $T(1 - \theta)q_x + T\theta q_y = Q_u$. Alternatively, if X produces output at rate q_x for $(1 - \theta)T$ of the unit time, the input flow $(1 - \theta)T\mathbf{x}$ will produce $(1 - \theta)Tq_x = (1 - \theta)Q_u$ of output, and, similarly, $\theta T\mathbf{y}$ will produce θTq_y over the interval θ of T. So again, $[(1 - \theta)T\mathbf{x} + \theta T\mathbf{y}] = T[(1 - \theta)\mathbf{x} + \theta\mathbf{y}]$ will yield $(1 - \theta)Tq_x = \theta Tq_y = Q_u$ of output per unit time T. Superficially, the asserted equivalence seems clear.

But now say that vector $\mathbf{x}$ includes as one input element the rate of capital service flow k_x from a machine $\overline{K}_x$. Vector $\mathbf{y}$ does not. Further, assume that $\overline{K}_x$ is entirely divisible in size, yielding proportional service flow rates, so that the stock $\overline{K}_x$ yields a rate of capital service flow k_x, and a stock $(1 - \theta)\overline{K}_x$ yields a rate of capital service flow $(1 - \theta)k_x$.

Now the equivalence between using process X for the period $(1 - \theta)T$ and Y for θT and running both simultaneously over θT at reduced rates $(1 - \theta)\mathbf{x}$ and $\theta\mathbf{y}$ breaks down. Although in terms of service flows, per se, there is still no distinction between these alternative ways to produce Q_u, that is not all there is to production. Service flows come from somewhere. In this case, some of the service flows of vector $\mathbf{x}$ come from the capital stock $\overline{K}_x$; so the size of the requisite capital stock needed by the firm is very different under the two alternative ways to produce Q_u. With *seriatim* production using $\mathbf{x}$ for $(1 - \theta)T$ of the time, and then $\mathbf{y}$ for θT, the full $\overline{K}_x$ must be in place during both periods, $(1 - \theta)T$ and θT, even though it is utilized only during $(1 - \theta)T$. $\bar{K}_x$ is idle during θT. But with simultaneous production using both $\mathbf{x}$ and $\mathbf{y}$ over T, only $(1 - \theta)\bar{K}_x$ of capital stock is needed, and it is utilized throughout T. So very different factor stock levels are required to support these two alternatives that the duality model takes to be identical. And *capital costs are determined by capital stocks, not by accumulated capital service flows.*

Carelessness about production as a process in time would be innocent in duality theory were it not for the differences in technology and ownership, and hence price behavior, of the inputs that are the elements of the vectors $\mathbf{x}$ and $\mathbf{y}$. If all input flows in $\mathbf{x}$ and $\mathbf{y}$ were simple, temporally footloose goods flows with time-invariant prices, there would be no problem – spigots would be turned on and off at $(1 - \theta)T$ or let run throughout T at rates $(1 - \theta)\mathbf{x}$ and $\theta\mathbf{y}$ with identical results in both technology and costs. Inconsistencies enter when some inputs, like capital services, have duration-specific prices and some, like labor services, have time-specific prices.

One can argue that these are aspects not of the production process per se but of ownership institutions, to which a strictly technological description of production should be indifferent, that these are just the sorts of contamination of technology with institutional characteristics that Shephard sought so carefully to purge from the production function. But valid though that is, it does not go very far, because (a) there is a clearly technological aspect to the differences in input characteristics – a technological basis for separating capital services derived from capital stocks on the one hand from labor services or goods flows derived from inventory depletion – that must surely be accommodated somehow as an aspect of "production technology," and (b) even when "technology" is defined carefully to exclude those technological characteristics of input flows – as it is in both time-specific and duality models – those same characteristics must reappear as soon as the prices of input flows are examined. Differences in input characteristics are centrally relevant to the relationship between production technology and costs, however that centrality is represented. So, either way, timing and factor characteristics remain sticking points for duality theory.

Which gets to the issue of input prices, the prices of the elements of the input vectors. As developed, duality theory assumes, with very little explicit justification, both that all input prices are exogenous – unaffected by the firm's decisions – and that all input prices are denominated per unit flow of the inputs in a vector like $\mathbf{x}$. These are, of course, perfectly ordinary assumptions about the input prices paid by a competitive price-taking firm. But in ordinary usage, these assumptions are not combined with Shephard's meticulous representation of the production technology in terms of flows only; ordinarily, the technology described in a production function is highly "contaminated" with economic influences, because stocks and flows are mixed among the inputs. But those arguments are often appropriate to the exogeneity of the input prices – labor services appear along with capital stocks, because the cost of labor services is exogenous to the firm, and the cost of owning capital stocks is exogenous to the firm.

If the production technology is specified only in flows, input prices cannot be exogenous; if input prices are exogenous, the production technology cannot be specified only in flows. When both of these are maintained simultaneously, the analysis is applicable only to processes that use neither labor nor capital inputs.

Unit input prices are exogenous to the competitive, price-taking firm only for the limited subset of inputs of goods or service flows with time-invariant prices. Unit prices are not exogenous to the firm for either capital or labor service inputs: Because the price of capital service flow is $p_k(P_k, T_p)$ and that of the labor service flow is $w(t)$, both depend on the least-cost production schedule – on the timing and duration of production. The prices that are exogenous to the price-taking firm are $P_k = p_k T_p$ and the schedule of the $w(t)$ over T. *The input prices that are exogenous to price-taking firms are specific to different aspects of time, to timing t and duration, T_p.[4] There is therefore no temporal specification of the production function – neither in instantaneous, t, flow rates nor in accumulated flows over T_p in the unit time T – that will simultaneously make both capital and labor service prices exogenous to the firm. Duration-specific input prices and time-specific input prices together make endogeneity of input prices to the production process unavoidable.* Such are the characteristics of inputs and their markets.

The time dimension of duality analysis is no more nor less naive than that of much economic theory, but temporal inconsistencies stand here in sharper contrast to the elegance and rigor of the mathematics, and they carry a significantly higher cost. Indeed, it appears that a good measure of the imprecision of the "good old traditional types" of production analysis that Frisch praised and that Shephard sought to correct reflected an intuitive recognition of the realities of the production process in time and the consequent differences in characteristics of its inputs. That intuitively guided sloth, difficult to justify in isolation, partly compensated for an incomplete specification of production as a process operating in time. Shephard purged the theory of its intuitive carelessness, but without augmenting our understanding of the underlying process – a clear illustration in methodology of the pitfalls of the second best.

6.3   Costs and free disposal

The "property of disposability" in duality theory – Shephard's property 2 and later the "property of free disposal" – may reflect an uneasy awareness of this inconsistency. It makes two sorts of assertions: (a) that any excess flows of inputs will not get in the way of production, "unutilized capacity of a physical item is merely excess input flow of the related capital service which does not hinder output" (Shephard, 1970, p. 5), and (b) that any excess flows can be disposed of at no cost – there is no rubbish-removal charge. These are not unreasonable propositions – apart from environmentalists' concerns – but they are irrelevant to the problem of technology and costs that we have identified. Because that problem stems from the essentially different characteristics of inputs, the irrelevance of free disposal is certainly implicit in Shephard's indifferent choice of goods inputs or capital services to illustrate the free disposal property:

P.2 implies disposability of inputs. For example, if chemical fertilizer is used as an input with land to produce a crop and excessive amounts of fertilizer have been provided, one merely disposes of the surplus . . . Excess capacity of machinery and equipment imply merely that the services of such capital are foregone [Shephard, 1970, p. 14].

The source of persistent difficulty, of course, is that the technological implications of the free disposal proposition are unexceptionable in a pure flow representation of production technology – excess input flows can be ignored – but the price-cost implications are not. Although free disposal may assure that the firm does not have to pay a trucker to cart off any unutilized inputs, they are not costless to the firm; someone has to pay for those inputs if they have a nonzero price, despite zero disposal costs. For goods inputs with a positive price, like chemical fertilizer, of course, efficiency nicely rules out such excess flows. For free inputs like sunlight and warmth, the nonhindrance aspect of the free disposal property makes their excess flows a matter of no moment.

But for capital whose price is exogenous to the firm over the unit time, excess flows are expensive – there is an opportunity cost to "excess capacity" that is not eliminated by productive efficiency (indeed, Chapter 4 has shown that "excess" capital capacity often is assured by productive efficiency). This must be reflected either in the duration-specific price of capital service flow, as it is in $p_k(P_k,T_p)$ of the time-specific model,[5] or in the incorporation of the capital stock itself in the production function – with all the attendant contamination – as it often is in orthodox, nonduality production theory. The opportunity cost of idle capital cannot simply be wished away with the exogenous capital service price assumption of duality theory, because to do so leaves the very large question raised earlier: Who pays for the idle resources? Who pays for the excess flows of capital services that can be costlessly got rid of and that do not hinder output but that cost the firm, nonetheless? In duality theory, the firm does not pay. So who does?

6.4   The partitioned firm: the Purchasing Office and the Production Office

The production processes to which duality theory applies are a very small subset of those of traditional concern in production theory; indeed, there is no assurance that that set is not empty, because it excludes all production processes that use owned or rented capital or hired labor inputs, leaving only those that rely solely on inputs with exogenous and time-invariant prices.

Duality theory has evolved as if firms could be partitioned into two parts, one part – a Production Office – that buys input flows from another part – the Purchasing Office – at constant unit prices regardless of its production decisions. Then all decisions made in the Production Office will be well and truly modeled by duality theory. Technology is well specified by the production function as a purely technological process defined on pure flows. Prices are exogenous to the Production Office at constant unit values. The cost function is demonstrably the dual of the production function.

But that other part of the firm still remains – or what we traditionally considered a part of the firm in production theory. The Purchasing Office, unnoticed, silently absorbs all the costs and inefficiencies inherent in inducing the Production Office to think that all input prices are time- and duration-invariant when they are not. The Purchasing Office – of this perfectly competitive, price-taking firm – pays for its capital purchases a rental rate or owner cost per unit time that is exogenous and given, but it turns around and resells the services of that capital stock to the Production Office at a constant price, no matter how much or how little of the time the Production Office chooses to use it, 1 hour per year or 8,760 hours. And the Purchasing Office buys labor services at the exogenous but time-specific wage rates it must pay, then turns around and delivers them to the Production Office at the same price, regardless of timing, t.

On the basis of sterilized and distorted price information, the Production Office makes its decisions with inescapable inefficiency – all production decisions are made by actors denied information about the costs of the inputs used in production. In its antiseptic environment, the Production Office is aptly modeled by the duality model, but the firm as a whole produces with steadfast ignorance of the economic characteristics of its inputs and its actual costs. Indeed, of all the aspects of the production process one might model with this sort of partitioning of the functions of the firm, the efficient relationship between technology and costs would seem to be among the least appropriate.

What duality does with very great rigor is to establish the relationships between production and these pseudocosts, leaving the unseen Purchasing Office to subsidize the resulting inefficiency.[6]

This functional perspective on the production process is useful. It suggests that good old traditional production theory from Smith through Marshall to Frisch has tried to grapple with a set of questions about the efficient operation of firms that combine purchased inputs with their own resources to produce output of various types. The good old orthodox production theory that has evolved has been imprecise in dimensions that are sometimes quite important to understanding the production process – the thrust of time-specific analysis is that a too-casual consideration of timing of the production process has obscured much that is important.

But the modification of production theory to utilize the mathematical theory of duality has produced a more fundamental change in the theory than is generally recognized. Behind its formidable mathematical apparatus and emphasis on rigorous axiomatic derivations of all mathematical results, it has sharply limited the scope of production theory, lopping off those inconvenient parts of the production process, like the relationship between stocks and flows, that make the mathematics intractable. The result is an elegant theory of virtually nonexistent production processes in which central functions of the traditional firm are simply assumed to be taken care of outside the firm somehow.

Time-specific modeling has taken a quite different route. It has retained the compass of the orthodox theory of production and tried, like duality theory, to inject more care and specificity in the technological description of production. But it has been able to give

careful attention, too, to the other technical and ownership characteristics of both inputs and outputs of production, developing the
implications of the important differences among input flows from
capital stocks, those from labor, and those from materials inputs
and, for output, drawing the implications of the markedly different
storage characteristics that determine production costs within the
unit time.

6.5   Partly exogenous prices

In part, it appears that the time-shape of production, and hence
differing economic characteristics of inputs, can be incorporated
into the structure of duality logic to include these neglected aspects.
Whether or not that part is enough is not clear.

In describing the input price vector, Shephard wrote:

In effect, it is assumed that the prices p_i ($i = 1, 2,\ldots,n$) do not depend upon
the amounts x_i ($i = 1,2,\ldots,n$) of the inputs of the factors of production. But
this is apparently not a serious loss of generality for the economic theory of
production, because, if the price of a factor varies stepwise with the amount
demanded, each quantity range may be considered qualitatively as a different factor of production with inputs of multiples of this level treated as
replications of use. The most economic of these so considered qualitatively
different levels will be chosen for any output rate sought. The dependence
of price of a factor upon the amount used has primary significance for the
analysis of the total economy. We do not consider stocks explicitly [Shep-
hard, 1970, p. 80].

Although Shephard saw this proliferation of inputs on the basis of
different (stepwise) prices as the result solely of quantity variations –
either volume discounts on input purchases or rising supply prices –
the possibility of specifying separate inputs on the basis of different
prices meets, within the duality logic, the strictly logical objections to
the model in this chapter. It would be messy but might be permissible to define different inputs on the basis of both when and how
much of the time – timing and duration – a given input is used per
unit time T. For a time-specific input like labor, one input would be
defined as "an hour of labor services from 9:00 a.m. to 10:00 a.m."
with its corresponding and exogenous price and another input as
"an hour of labor services between 9:00 and 10:00 p.m.," again with
corresponding time-specific price: Labor service prices and their
time shapes are clearly exogenous, like Shephard's pattern of volume discounts. But there still remains the endogeneity of the capital
service price. It is the price of "one hour of services from machine $\bar{K}_x$

if it is used T_p hours out of the 24, T," $p_k = P_k/T_p$. Endogeneity appears unavoidable so long as the utilization rate, T_p/T, that determines p_k depends on the firm's cost-minimizing response to that exogenous, time-specific wage schedule. For a discrete time schedule of wage rates, a discrete set of relative input price pairs – labor and capital service price – can be enumerated, but the capital service price remains endogenous, nonetheless.

Even if the logical problem were ignored, the increase in dimensionality required by those time-specific relative prices would clearly be extreme, the more so because T must be allowed to represent a day or week or year and time-specific input price schedules other than that of labor must certainly be allowed for. So, on grounds of dimensionality alone, the rigorous link between analytical structure and existing empirical data – sometimes invoked in praise of duality models[7] – is broken by the absence of time-specific production data.[8]

6.6   Conclusions

It is clear, I think, that a careful specification, like Shephard's, of technology in terms of pure flows – so that none of the functions of the Purchasing Office are left mixed in with those of the Production Office – makes it more important that time-specific considerations of stocks and flows and their economic relationships be incorporated in the analysis. Conventional, preduality production theory is less wrong in the scope of its representation of the production process than is its modern replacement; duality theory has narrowed the compass of what is included in "production technology" but has found no place for what was thereby left out. As a result, the duality representation of production appears to be widely misapplied. It has been purged of so much of what is involved in the process of economically efficient production as to be inapplicable to most of production.

CHAPTER 7

Factor intensities, capacity, and the Leontief paradox

Any attempt to embody in the time-specific analysis of production actual numbers for actual economic magnitudes immediately confronts the paucity of time-specific data noted at the end of the last chapter. That absence of data is explained, of course, by the absence hitherto of a time-specific economic analysis that could show why anyone would want to collect temporally more detailed information on economic processes: the empirical chicken and the theoretical egg. So in this chapter, the significance of two main revelations of time-specific analysis is developed where numbers do exist so that their implications can be given some welcome concreteness. These are the issues of factor intensities and productive capacity.[1]

7.1 Optimal utilization and time-specific data

The one aspect of time-specific modeling that has thus far generated enough concern to justify collection of data on the timing of production is the utilization and idleness of production and hence of productive capital stocks (given the inherent T-durability of those stocks). The optimal-utilization model of Chapter 4 – the optimal shift-working model in discrete form – is the time-specific model that succeeded in attracting attention because it showed that any firm operating in an environment of time-specific and rhythmic costs (i.e., any firm) might *optimally* leave its capital stock idle much of the time. How much of the time that capital is optimally idle will depend on time-specific economic and technical parameters facing the firm.

So a time-specific model showed that the firm would alter its optimal utilization, and hence the productivity of its capital stocks and its employment, in ways not previously identified. And among the parameters of that decision were economic variables that are routinely affected by the policies of governments and international agencies, especially in the context of economic development. The particular worrisome prospect identified by this analysis was that the low capital prices that were intended to increase investment might well have the unintended effect of reducing the utilization of capital and

140

hence its productivity and output growth and employment. Utilization effects tend to offset, maybe more than offset, the intended
investment effects of low capital prices.[2] It is understandable, then,
that the World Bank sponsored the first large empirical study of
capital utilization and generated the first general production data
explicitly tailored to a time-specific description of production.

The optimal-utilization model – describing the responses of firms'
production schedules to those economic variables identified by time-
specific analysis – has been nicely supported by empirical studies,
starting with Mary Ann Baily's early work (1974) on Kenyan manufacturing, the World Bank's preliminary analysis of its data (Hughes
et al., 1976), and my small and less formal study of Nigerian manufacturing done for the ILO in 1976 (Winston, 1978). The most complete and most careful test of the optimal-utilization analysis so far –
Betancourt and Clague's recent study (1981) using UNIDO data –
also gives the model reassuringly strong empirical support.

This chapter exploits data that were generated by those studies.
As described in Chapter 4, one of the key technical parameters
whose influence on optimal utilization the time-specific analysis hypothesized is the instantaneous factor intensity of production,
$k/l(t)$ – the "degree of mechanization," or a "capital/crew-size ratio"
in the vocabulary of Chapter 3. The data from utilization studies,
then, let us examine some of the problems inherent in the usual but
ambiguous concept of "factor intensities" and in addition say something about the seriousness of those ambiguities. Those are the questions of this chapter.

We will first review why the simple, widely used, and appealing
idea of "factor proportions" is not so simple and appealing in its
actual measurement and use. In the next section we show how that
ambiguity has affected important issues of empirical and theoretical
understanding, how, particularly, the famed Leontief paradox that
has preoccupied trade theorists for more than 25 years may be explained solely by the questionable way sectoral factor proportions
are measured. Finally, in the last part of this chapter, we use different data to examine the concept of a firm's productive capacity and
the implications of that idea for its measurement.

7.2   The two meanings of factor proportions

The source of ambiguity in the concept and measurement of factor
proportions is that identified in Chapter 3: Although a unit of insensate capital stock can typically be worked all of the unit time T, a

worker cannot.[3] A worker's duration of work activity per period T is limited – the result of this optimal "work–leisure choice" (about which more in Part IV) – so to operate production longer within the unit time than one worker will work requires shift-working, the *seriatim* replacement of one individual worker by another. To keep one crew member working on one machine, so that $k = l(t) = \bar{L}(t) = k/l(t) = 1$, for $T = 24$ hours, requires three employees, $\bar{E} = 3$, *seriatim* if each works an 8-hour day. Continuous operation over a week, so that $T = 168$ hours, would require four workers, each putting in a 40-hour work week. It clearly matters very much (by about 400%) whether "factor intensity" measures the amount of capital each worker is equipped with when working – capital per crew member, $k/l(t)$ – or whether it measures capital per employee, $k/\bar{E}$. In this illustration, $k/l(t) = 1.0$, whereas $k/\bar{E} = 0.25$. The traditional (but by no means consistent) practice of calling the second of these the industry's "factor intensity" clearly and seriously misrepresents that aspect of the industry's technology $k/l(t)$.[4]

The ratio of the value of an industry's capital stock to the number of its employees is an inappropriate measure of the industry's production technology, understating the capital/labor ratio if there is multiple-shift-working. The measure confuses the sharing of capital sequentially between shifts with simultaneous sharing between the members of a larger crew. The degree of error in this conventional measure depends on the number of shifts worked.

Human capital is liable to the same mismeasurement as labor. Because a worker's human capital is "embedded in his own person," his human capital is involved in production only while he is; he takes it home at the end of his shift, leaving the physical capital for use by workers on any subsequent shift.

With seasonal variations in production and crew size, traditional measures of factor intensities that rely on man-years of labor will understate the labor input, because each man-year describes more than one man working with the capital stock over less than one year; were a $10,000 farm machine to be operated by one man for one month each year, the measured ratio of capital to labor would not be $10,000, but $120,000.

The empirical significance of these mismeasurements hinges on the extent of variation in shift and seasonal production patterns between products and, if the mismeasurement is to be relevant to international trade, between countries.

The two sets of available data indicate that variations in the timing of production and hence factor inputs are sufficient to cause serious mismeasurement of technical factor intensities both among products and between countries: the World Bank study of capital utilization in 73 industries in four countries (Hughes et al., 1976) and the much smaller study (Winston, 1977b) of 44 manufacturing firms in Nigeria that recorded data on crew size and utilization as well as on capital stock and employment.

The World Bank data show that capital-utilization rates vary both among the 73 sectors of the study and within each sector among its four countries (Hughes et al., 1976, Table 2). For those who accept capital utilization as an aspect of production that may vary between products but is expected, on technical grounds, to be quite stable for a given product, it will be surprising that the amounts of variation in these two dimensions appear to be about the same. The coefficients of variation between sectors within each country ranged from 0.28 (Colombia) to 0.38 (Malaysia), with an average intersectoral variation of 0.32 for the four countries. The coefficients of variation among countries within each sector ranged from 0.05 (oils and fats) to 0.88 (electrical apparatus), with an average intercountry variation of 0.33 for the 73 sectors. Thus, intercountry differences in utilization rates within a sector are as pronounced as are the more familiar differences among sectors within a country. These differences in levels of capital utilization among products and countries have a considerable effect on measured factor intensities. If all these utilization variations were attributable to differences in shift patterns, the degree of understatement of capital intensity implicit in the conventional measure would range, across individual sectors, from zero to 67%. The average understatement is 50%, and 67% is the maximum possible under the procedures used.

The Nigerian survey included questions on maximum crew size and utilization as well as value of capital and total production employment, so that the true technological factor intensities could be compared directly to those generated by traditional measures. In these firms, each crew member actually had, on the average, almost twice as much capital to work with as would have been shown by the traditional ratio of capital per employee. Put the other way around, as we did earlier with the World Bank data, the true capital intensity was understated by 45% on the average by the traditional measure, a figure intriguingly close to that implicit in the larger World Bank sample. The range of understatement for individual firms was from zero to 74%. For the 32 firms operating multiple shifts, the technological capital/labor ratio was understated by 53% by the traditional measure.

7.3   The Leontief paradox

Although a firm's or sector's factor proportions are widely accepted as one of its basic technological characteristics – in regional economics, economic development, income distribution, and growth – that characteristic has surely played its most central role in the theory of international trade. So this section reexamines the Leontief paradox in light of carefully specified sectoral factor intensities and in light of the predictable interaction of utilization and sectoral characteristics. The potential range of error introduced by using the wrong measure of factor proportions is infinite; its actual range is large, and its distribution among industries appears to be biased in such a way as to have created the illusion of paradoxical patterns of trade. It seems that had factor proportions been measured as a technological characteristic of production in the first place, there might never have been a paradox.

Leontief's finding that U.S. imports were more capital-intensive than its exports (Leontief, 1954) was based on a study that classified traded products according to the factor intensities of their manufacture using ratios of capital stock per man-year. Other studies of factor intensities in trade have used capital-stock/employment ratios. For instance, Baldwin (1971) used the first, Hufbauer (1970) the second.[5] With a standard number of hours per man-year, these two traditional measures come to the same thing. Such factor intensities are seen to describe the relative amounts of capital stock and labor required for the manufacture of a unit of product or, equivalently, the amount of capital stock with which a typical worker is equipped in making the product. But they do not. What is more, the utilization variations that introduce these differences are systematically related to industry characteristics that are themselves relevant to trade patterns.

Recall from Chapter 4 that the optimal level of utilization is related (a) positively to the ratio of factor shares, $P_k k / W l$ (if capital is cheap or small, it can be left idle at lower cost than if it is dear or extensive) and (b) negatively to the amplitude of the rhythmic price movement, β. A larger night wage premium (in a two-factor model) does more to discourage nighttime operation than does a smaller one.[6]

Thus factor prices and factor intensities together – the stuff of the theory of comparative advantage – systematically affect capital utilization. By this route, errors in the measurement of capital intensity may explain "paradoxical" trade patterns. The connection is simple.

A capital-rich country that follows Heckscher-Ohlin logic and concentrates its exports in products made with high capital intensity (k/l) and its imports in products made with low capital intensity will tend to utilize the capital in its export industries more of the time than the capital in its import competing industries. Higher utilization brings greater understatement of factor intensities. So, in traditional measures, relatively capital-intensive exports may not be seen to be relatively capital-intensive, whereas relatively labor-intensive imports are, by virtue of the lower utilization of the cooperating capital, revealed for what they are. If each worker used $120,000 in capital to make an export product on three-shift operation and an import competing product was made by workers each using $50,000 in capital on one-shift operation, a Leontief paradox would appear; the ratio of import to export capital intensities would be measured as 1.25 rather than 0.42. So an actual Heckscher-Ohlin trade pattern can be obscured by traditional measures of factor intensities, which may show, instead, the paradox of a country exporting those products that use less of its relatively abundant factor and importing those that use more.

As for the seasonal distribution of production, an optimal-utilization model can, of course, explain it as the result of rhythmic variations in input prices, but the inputs whose prices vary rhythmically over the year are warmth and rain and wind instead of the labor and capital that fit the basic theory of comparative advantage. This may be of small concern, however, because two useful facts remain: (a) that the agriculture and fisheries sector loomed very large in the data that generated the original Leontief paradox and (b) that the seasonally uneven production typical of that sector causes the traditional measures to overstate its capital intensity. Baldwin (1971) and Hufbauer (1970), and Leontief (1966) before them, separated out the agricultural sector for special consideration as a producer of "natural" products, but without recognizing that it is the time-shape of production and its effect on the measurement of factor porportions that distinguish the products of this sector.

Agriculture and fisheries accounted for roughly 20% of the capital in exports and 40% in imports in Leontief's original study. Although these include both direct and indirect capital, a crude adjustment can treat them as if they were direct inputs only. If the typical operation in U.S. agriculture and fisheries were staffed at full strength for three months of the year and not all the other nine months (an oversimplification, but the magnitudes probably are not terribly wrong), then the measured factor intensities in this sector would have to be reduced by three-quarters, and Leontief's paradox would all but disappear for U.S. data on this account alone. Capital/labor ratios in his data would become $11,510 for aggregate imports and $11,300 for aggregate exports, giving a ratio of import to export factor intensities of approximately 1.0, as against Leontief's 1.3 ratio that supported the initial paradox.

For the United States, only highly aggregated figures – and only those for shift-working – are available to test the hypothesis developed so far by reestimating the Leontief results on their home ground. But the shift-work data can be used to estimate "corrected" factor inputs, which can then be used to reestimate the relationship between commodity trade and factor inputs to see what difference such a crude timing correction makes.

To do this, I have reestimated a recent analysis of trade patterns and the Leontief paradox by Branson and Monoyios (1977).[7] A main objective of that study was to see if physical capital and human capital behaved similarly and hence could be aggregated. They concluded that when human capital is treated separately, physical capital behaves paradoxically, the amount used falling significantly as the net exports of a sector rise. Their analysis relied on linear regressions of factor inputs on net exports. Their results (with t values) are given in Table 7.1 in roman type. Equations (7.4) and (7.5) in the table are scaled by value of shipments.

In its extreme form, the hypothesis of this discussion would require that once labor and human capital input measures have been corrected for differences in shift patterns and seasonal timing among commodities, the data on factor intensities should reveal a pure Heckscher-Ohlin pattern of trade – that (under the usual assumption that the United States has relatively more human and physical capital and less labor) its net exports should be significantly negatively correlated with raw labor and positively correlated with both physical and human capital. Compared with the Branson-Monoyios results, then, regressions on timing-corrected data should have the same signs on labor and human capital inputs, but a positive sign on physical capital. More modestly, however, the hypothesis would suggest that use of timing-corrected labor and human capital data would generally move the regression coefficients in the "right" (Heckscher-Ohlin) direction. Compared with Branson-Monoyios's results, these corrected data should increase the already negative coefficient on labor and the positive coefficient on human capital, while moving the coefficient on physical capital toward the positive range.

Table 7.1. *Relationships between net exports (NX) and factor inputs with traditional and timing-corrected (italicized) measures*[a]

Regression equation number	Dependent variable	K[b]	H	L	S	S^{-t}	C	R^2
7.1	NX(1963)	−0.05	0.04	−0.67	–	–	18.54	0.45
		(2.18)	(6.87)	(3.99)				
7.1(c)	*NX(1963)*	*−0.03*	*0.06*	*−0.88*	–	–	*15.61*	*0.45*
		(1.64)	*(6.94)*	*(4.41)*				
7.2	NX(1967)	−0.04	0.04	−0.69	–	–	19.05	0.34
		(2.33)	(6.02)	(3.21)				
7.2(c)	*NX(1967)*	*−0.01*	*0.04*	*−0.79*	–	–	*−2.93*	*0.25*
		(0.40)	*(4.77)*	*(2.99)*				
7.3	NX(1963)	−0.07	0.04	−0.79	0.02	–	19.68	0.48
		(2.98)	(6.57)	(4.58)	(2.28)			
7.3(c)	*NX(1963)*	*−0.05*	*0.05*	*−1.10*	*0.03*	–	*17.55*	*0.48*
		(2.46)	*(6.60)*	*(5.12)*	*(2.41)*			
7.4	NX(1963)	−0.08	0.04	−0.90	–	−53.48	2.81	0.22
		(2.27)	(3.63)	(2.63)		(3.0)		
7.4(c)	*NX(1963)*	*−0.07*	*0.06*	*−1.37*	–	*−70.25*	*4.21*	*0.27*
		(2.58)	*(3.86)*	*(2.88)*		*(3.95)*		
7.5	NX(1967)	−0.04	0.04	−1.06	–	−84.38	2.78	0.32
		(2.01)	(3.94)	(2.80)		(3.80)		
7.5(c)	*NX(1967)*	*−0.02*	*0.04*	*−1.25*	–	*−85.06*	*3.24*	*0.31*
		(1.46)	*(3.03)*	*(2.32)*		*(4.09)*		

[a]From Winston (1979c).
[b]K, physical capital; H, human capital; L, labor; S, shipments; C, constant term.

The italicized entries in Table 7.1 report the same regressions run with the corrected labor and human capital measures. They show the hypothesized pattern clearly and rather consistently, although the sizes of the changes in coefficients and significance are not very great. Nonetheless, for the five comparisons, use of corrected input data moved the regression coefficient for physical capital toward the positive range in every case and reduced its negative significance in four of five comparisons; corrected data either increased the coefficient of human capital or left it unchanged, while increasing its positive significance in three of five equations; finally, corrected inputs increased the negative value of the raw labor coefficient, while increasing its significance in three of five equations. Comparative R^2 values are a mixed bag: Two values are increased by the corrected data, two are decreased, and one is left unchanged. It is important to keep in mind that the paradoxical results of Branson and Monoyios are those involving the physical capital coefficient for which both regression coefficient and significance are moved most consistently in the right direction by even this crude and incomplete timing correction.

Reestimation of the relationships between factor intensities and commodity trade patterns using timing-corrected data does not produce a statistical tour de force in support of the hypothesis that mismeasurement has created a Leontief paradox where none in fact exists. The results, however, are certainly consistent with that possibility, and until better data on the timing of factor use have been collected, not much more than that can be expected.

7.4   The idea of productive capacity and its utilization

A similar sort of ambiguity afflicts the important concepts of "productive capacity" and, when capacity is contrasted with actual output, "capacity utilization." Conveying the sense of exasperation often associated with that idea, Alan Greenspan, chairman of President Ford's Council of Economic Advisors, said, "In principle, 'capacity' has meaning. . .," but implicitly, only in principle. Productive capacity is an essentially macroeconomic concept that lacks a clear microeconomic rationale or foundation. The analysis of Chapters 3 and 4 provides that foundation. As in the case of factor intensities, a time-specific analysis of capacity decomposes an aspect of the production process – in this case output, Q, per unit time, T – into its underlying intensity and duration dimensions to identify the sources of ambiguity. In the case of capacity, an added dimension is that of costs.

Macroeconomic capacity

In macroeconomics, "capacity has meaning" in a number of areas of analysis:

Some idea of capacity and its utilization is central in investment demand analysis; the accelerator is damped by excess capacity, because, in its presence, increases in product demand do not induce further demand for investment goods.

Some idea of a capacity ceiling to real output is embodied in analyses of the real causes of price inflation.

Capacity helps explain variations in trade flows, because excess capacity acts as an inducement to increase exports.

Changes in factor productivity over the business cycle that result in changes in income shares are intimately related to changes in utilization of capacity.

Underlying these applications is a generally accepted idea of aggregate productive capacity that would go something like this:

Capacity is the maximum sustainable level of output (per year) that can be got when an economy's available resources are fully and efficiently employed, given tastes and technology.

Microeconomic capacity

Although there is little difficulty with this idea of capacity on a macro level, it creates problems at a micro level, because it has in it two aspects that conflict within an individual firm. First, it says that capacity is a maximum output. This implies a technical definition of capacity for the firm, an engineering capacity. But at the same time, it says that capacity is a most efficient level of output, and that, for the individual firm, suggests an economic capacity, which is quite a different thing. In economic capacity, costs become important. J. M. Cassels, Lawrence Klein, George Perry, and others have therefore suggested that the firm's capacity should be defined as the output that achieves lowest average costs. Frank de Leeuw defined the firm's capacity with respect to its marginal costs and their relation to average costs. Both of these concepts imply that the firm's level of economic capacity is significantly below what technically it could produce as an engineering maximum. Thus, one major source of contradiction has been that the macroeconomic concept of capacity rests on both maximum and efficient output, but these goals are in conflict at the level of the firm. And firms provide the data for the macroeconomic measure.

The nature of that conflict is clear from Chapters 3 and 4. Central is the fact that any accumulated output, Q, per unit time T can always be expressed in time-specific analysis as the product of the intensity (speed) of production, $q(t)$, and its duration, T_p, within the unit time T: $Q = q(t)T_p$ when $q(t)$ is constant, or Q is the integral of $q(t)$ over T_p when it is not. So there are two dimensions into which any "output per unit time" can always be decomposed: speed of production and its duration. Each implies a different adjustment mechanism for Q.

But the time-specified description of production showed, too, that changes on either of these dimensions of Q bring changes in unit costs. This was pictured graphically in the bowl-shaped unit cost surface of Figure 4.7. An increase in $q(t)$, *ceteris paribus* (given capital stock and production function), reduces unit capital costs, whereas it increases unit variable costs because of the diminishing marginal product of the variable input flow. Any optimal rate of output flow, $q^*(t)$, will balance these against input prices to minimize unit costs. The extreme value – max $q(t)$ – is that speed of output flow at the outer limit of the given technology and plant, the speed at which the marginal product of the variable input flow has been driven to zero so that unit costs have been driven to infinity.

In the other dimension, an increase in the duration of production, T_p, *ceteris paribus*, again reduces unit capital costs, but it increases unit costs of any input with a time-specific price like labor. The optimal duration of production, T_p^*, will balance these costs to minimize unit costs, often leaving production idle some of the time ($T - T_p^* > 0$) in order to avoid periods of high time-specific input prices. At the extreme value in this dimension, max $T_p = T$, and the production process is operated all the time with higher unit costs if $T_p^* < T$.

So continuous, full-time operation (T_p = max $T_p = T$) in the one dimension and top speed ($q(t)$ = max $q(t)$) in the other set the boundaries that limit feasible output per unit time T. Maximum output per unit time – max Q = max $q(t)T$ – is got by a process operated at top speed, all the time, and that requires the use of all variable inputs until their marginal products are zero. Maximum output per unit time T is always at the southeast corner of the feasible space in Figure 4.7, where unit costs are infinite. Unit costs typically reach an interior minimum in both dimensions at $q^*(t),T_p^*$ – reflected in the bowl-shaped unit cost surface. So the two quite different ideas of "capacity" output are nicely pictured in Figure 4.7: max Q = max $q(t)T$ is engineering capacity, whereas $Q^* = q^*(t)T_p^*$ is cost-minimizing economic capacity.[8]

Compounding the frustration of having two conflicting measures of capacity is a sense frequently encountered in the literature that productive capacity should be a straightforward technical matter, like the capacity of a bucket, not something we have to haggle over with economic subtleties. A five-gallon bucket has a capacity of five gallons, and a 100-ton/day plant should, by the same persuasive reasoning, have a capacity of 100 tons per day. That should be the end of that. It follows that capacity output should be determined solely by the capital stock – by the bucket – both for the firm and for the economy as a whole. But this leads to two further questions relevant to capacity measures. First, what about other resources? In the macroeconomic concept of capacity, the concern is certainly with the availability and use of all of the economy's resources, not with capital alone. Second, how can it be that society's capital is idle much of the time if capital stocks define output capacity?

An integrated concept of capacity

Macroeconomic capacity (a) is a general-equilibrium concept, and (b) in that general equilibrium, as time-specific analysis makes clear, resource allocation is efficient only if plants' capital stocks are idle much of the time. The first of these assertions is familiar; it has been said frequently by Lawrence Klein, among others. The second, of course, follows directly from the analysis of optimal utilization. The firms in a society where, at the minimum, people have work-timing preferences – where they care about when they work – will efficiently adjust to factor prices not only by allocation among factors and among products and firms but also by time-specific allocation throughout T, and that will typically mean idle capital.

When the economy as a whole is operating at its macroeconomic capacity level of output, the individual firms that make up that economy are operating at an economic capacity level of output, therefore with a good deal of idle capital. Idle plants and maximum aggregate output coincide, because it is efficient for firms not to use their capital all the time. The efficient economy, in turn, will have adjusted its resource allocation to reflect that fact, and maximum aggregate output will not require (indeed, would be inconsistent with) maximum output from each individual firm.[9] A potential fallacy of composition is involved because in an aggregate general equilibrium at full capacity, any one firm, alone, typically can increase its output beyond its economic capacity – even to its engineering capacity – but all firms considered together cannot, simply because in the aggregate there are not enough available resources. Resources will have been allocated efficiently so that firms are operating at their economic capacities, with – because they are operating efficiently – a good deal of idle capital. The sum of firms' feasible maximum outputs is greater (by far) than the feasible maximum output of the sum of firms because of the interdependence inherent in allocating limited aggregate resources.

The significance of a time-specific model of capacity

There are a number of useful implications of an integrated time-specific conception of productive capacity in which macroeconomic behavior and microeconomic behavior are consistent and derive from the same incentives working on the same sorts of people. Most important, profit-maximizing firms behave with respect to their capacity exactly the way we expect an economy to behave with respect to its aggregate capacity:

A firm will operate at a level of output above capacity if it is paid a high enough price for its product to cover the increased marginal costs. So operation at outputs in excess of capacity levels is, indeed, to be expected under some conditions, but it is, indeed, also inflationary.

Sustained operation in excess of capacity will induce the firm to expand its capital stock by investment in order to reduce utilization back to its least-cost level.[10]

Whether one firm alone or many firms together operate above their capacity levels is important, because that will determine how steeply their marginal costs will rise after economic capacity levels are reached.

Exports are encouraged by excess economic capacity as firms seek to expand output.

Cyclical labor (and capital) productivity changes will result if firms are reluctant to adjust their labor input as output varies around economic capacity levels (Oi, 1962).

In all these respects, firms' microeconomic behavior parallels what we have come to expect for the economy as a whole.

Second, this analysis emphasizes that capacity should be defined, at both micro and macro levels, with respect to all resources, not with respect simply to capital stock. This supports the warnings (by Perry, Klein, and others) that overestimation of capacities will result when individual sectors are considered in isolation from the rest of the economy.

Third, this analysis shows that the empirical capacity-utilization measures typically generated in the United States simply measure different things. The McGraw-Hill capacity-utilization series is widely believed to measure firms' current operations relative to their most economical, least-cost levels of output; in our terms, McGraw-Hill is an estimate of firms' economic capacity utilization. The Wharton utilization series, in contrast, takes as capacity observed past peak output (at the two-digit level, then aggregated) and expresses current output as a percentage of that; in our terms, Wharton capacity is based on firm's marginal costs.

Wharton and McGraw-Hill measures, therefore, will frequently differ, both in magnitude and direction, depending on the data served up by recent history.[11] The McGraw-Hill estimates of economic capacity are believed to be influenced by animal spirits – by optimism or pessimism based on current output. They measure, in principle, something quite solidly defined at the level of the firm. The Wharton series, in contrast, reports on movements of output up and down firms' marginal cost curves relative to movements of peaks up and down firms' marginal cost curves, while the shape of those curves is itself being affected by the proportion of the economy that is trying to move in the same direction at the same time. Even with constant capacity, different patterns of fluctuation in output will generate quite different Wharton utilization rates. So it seems inevitable that the vagaries of history will have generated disparities between these two indices in both trend and level, disparities that only an integrated model might hope to sort out.

Fourth, in this analysis, there are seen to be three kinds of social excess capacity, two of which are familiar and one that is not. The most familiar is the excess capacity that occurs when firms do not produce up to their targets of economic capacity output, a problem that results from Keynesian deficient demand (typical in advanced countries) or from deficient supplies of inputs (typical in less developed countries) – both, of course, at prevailing prices. A different, but still familiar, sort of excess capacity appears when firms face scale economies with limited product markets and therefore operate a "too-large" plant at less than its economic capacity because that minimizes cost – in textbook graphics, they operate at a Viner tangency of falling long- and short-run average costs. The third and unfamiliar kind of social excess capacity appears when firms set their economic capacity targets too low in light of society's real scarcities; they may report "full utilization of capacity," but what the firms see as "full" is not full enough, because they base their private calculations of economic capacity on input prices that do not reflect real scarcities – the integrated capacity analysis shows that artificially cheap capital, for an important instance, will induce firms to set full-capacity targets lower than they should.

The Nigerian survey generated data on this. Although Nigeria, as an oil-rich underdeveloped country, was typical of neither developed nor underdeveloped countries, the sample showed firms operating with 7% to 12% excess capacity when their own economic capacity at market prices was used as the denominator, but with 16% to 21% excess capacity when the denominator was an economic capacity based on socially appropriate shadow prices (Winston, in Phan-Thuy et al., 1981, Table V.1, p. 136). In a more typical less developed country – one with more distortions in factor prices and more quantity intervention in markets like Pakistan – these gaps would certainly have been larger. Finally, in the Nigerian data, as in other data (Betancourt and Clague, 1981), it is clear that most idleness of capital stocks is intentional – firms' optimal utilization under market prices leaves the average firm's capital idle 53% of the time (Winston, 1977b, Table IV.1, p. 112).

The final implication to be drawn from the time-specific analysis of capacity is that if they hope to get more reliable estimates, designers of survey-based measures of capacity and excess capacity such as McGraw-Hill's will have to give their respondents in the firms more guidance about the conditions they are supposed to assume in making their estimates of capacity output. Now they are expected to use a "common-sense" concept of capacity. But common sense does not specify the period of adjustment nor factor prices nor hours of work nor product mix nor overtime nor conditions of demand nor its time-shape. Yet these, and more, inescapably condition any estimates of economic capacity output from even the most knowledgeable respondent.

7.5   Conclusions

What the applications of this chapter have in common is that they show how the time-specific description of production, by adding an important dimension to the representation of the production process, identifies ambiguities in what seem to be unambiguous concepts until they develop puzzling uncertainties in their measurement. When ordinary yearly output, Q, is seen through time-specific modeling to be $Q = q(t)T_p$, the product of intensity and duration of production, it is apparent that a lot of differences in production behavior – with very different implications for important economic variables like factor proportions and employment and capital productivity and unit costs and capacity – are typically obscured by the simple, one-dimensional measure Q. It is in this sense that time-specific analysis describes an "anatomy" of familiar economic variables and processes.

These applications, of course, barely scratch the surface of the pragmatic insights of time-specific analysis. More will be discussed in Part IV concerning analysis of the household, and Part V will discuss time-specific markets.

PART IV

Time-specific analysis of household activities

Modeling the time-shape of work and consumption: the optimal household schedule and the value of time

In the next two chapters, the time-specific apparatus of Chapters 3–5 is applied to the analysis of household behavior, to household decisions about work and consumption activities. Again, the explicit analytical recognition that these familiar economic processes take place "*in* time" adds surprising dimensions to their understanding.

The household makes its economic decisions while embedded in an environment of nights and days and weekends and weekdays and winters and summers that crucially condition those decisions. Indeed, rhythmic and largely geophysical changes in the household's economic environment – that affect household activities both directly and indirectly through their effects on other households, and hence society – are the sole driving force for the rhythmic behavior in the simple time-specific models of firms and markets of this study. In Chapters 4 and 5, household work- and consumption-timing preferences determined firms' optimal production schedules or their least-cost technologies and tracking methods; in Chapters 10 and 11, households' timing preferences will be shown to interact with firms' optimal schedules in time-specific markets. All this happens – in the present simplified models – solely because households recognize their highly time-shaped environment and they respond to it.

This chapter describes the time-specific household model that sees work and consumption activities as processes in time. An explicit temporal context makes it possible both to say something about why activities are done when they are done during a calendar unit time, T, and to describe a meaningful "value of time." This was the simplest model I could devise that adequately showed the detail and role of timing in optimal household behavior; it will bear considerable future expansion. In this chapter, the model itself is described, and its implications for the orthodox time-allocation questions are examined. In the next chapter, the model is elaborated and extended (at a less formal level), and its richer implications for the timing of work and consumption activities are developed.

Although it started as a straightforward merger of time-specific production analysis and the "time-allocation" and household production models descendent from Becker (1965), Linder (1970), and Lancaster (1966), this model has become far more differentiated from that tradition than I anticipated. As I tried carefully to analyze the process of household choice in time that must underlie those atemporal models, it became increasingly evident that existing time-allocation models cast the description of that process in ways that importantly restrict its analysis. This has been a recurrent theme – though often more in spirit than in specific detail, and not always with especially productive remedies – of the critical literature on the Becker models (Pollak and Wachter, 1975). Put in an explicitly time-specific setting, it becomes clear that the main problems of these now-traditional models lie in their representation of time and "time" allocation. So this chapter describes the process and timing of household work and consumption choices and at the same time establishes its time dimensions in a new and considerably less mysterious way. When time is "de-reified," household-production analysis becomes a good deal more ordinary and useful.

8.1   The model

Like the time-specific models of cost-minimizing firms, this one analyzes not only how much time and goods households allocate to various consumption and work activities but also when. It adds temporal detail – an optimal household activity schedule – to the usual analysis of allocation of resources and time over the day or year.

The now-familiar elements of time-specific analysis appear again: Optimal economic processes are examined at each moment over a typical, repetitive calendar period, T, like a day or year, and are explicitly related to the accumulated daily (yearly) flows they generate; instantaneous flow rates and their daily (yearly) accumulations are nested; flow rates are identified by when they occur within the day or year, T; so events are explicitly embedded in an exogenous time context common to all economic actors and sectors. Standard "time-allocation" analysis, of course, deals only with accumulated totals – of time, goods, commodities – in the calendar unit time. Those summary statistics are often useful but sometimes insufficient for answering questions of considerable importance.

The only truly unique postulate of this model is that households operate in a rhythmically changing geophysical, social, and economic environment that systematically affects economic magnitudes. In Part II, that environment acted on firms either through time-specific changes in perishable input prices, $p(t)$, or through time-specific changes in the demand for perishable output, $q(t)$: All environmental rhythms appeared as price or quantity rhythms. Here we have tracked the source of those rhythms to the household – the household as supplier of perishable labor services and the household as demander of perishable output. The genesis of those rhythms, in turn, is the rhythmic environment in which the household functions.

The environment is assumed to change constantly throughout the unit time, T, but always in the same way within one T and the next; day by day, year by year, the environmental patterns repeat themselves. These environmental rhythms are exogenous to the household. Other things surely influence optimal activity scheduling, but we will continue to focus on the effects of those aspects of the economic environment that are stable from one "day" to the next, but non-constant within each – repetitive, rhythmic, fully predictable events. The household is assumed to be fully aware of these environmental changes and their economic significance and to have fully adjusted to them in a Hahn full-information equilibrium.

Other than the rhythmic environment and time-specific representation of the economic process that links instantaneous and calendar periods – and some significant changes from traditional vocabulary – the model is essentially quite orthodox: Neoclassical, utility-maximizing households adapt to an exogenous economic and technical environment under perfect information.

8.2   Time-shaped household production: the model structure

The model uses a household production framework.[1] Households do not consume goods and services, deriving utility from them directly. Instead, the act of consumption is separated into two tiers: On one tier, the household acts as pure producer, combining purchased goods with its own labor to produce a "commodity," in Becker's term, under the technological constraint of a household production function; on the other tier, the household acts as pure consumer, using that home-produced commodity to derive utility. In the time-specific model, these two activities are explicitly simultaneous. This artificial separation of consumption into two separate activities usefully (a) makes explicit and derives implications from the fact that consumption requires both purchased goods and household inputs and (b) reduces as much as possible the amorphous black box of "preferences," allowing for consideration of technical efficiency and the environment of consumption.

Although it is not always made explicit, another tier – an "input tier" – precedes the two tiers described. In the input tier, the household adjusts its resource endowments through trade. It has fixed initial daily endowments of labor services and money income that can then be adjusted in composition by trading labor for income in the external labor market at an exogenously given wage rate. This composite commodity is the household's ultimate resource constraint; it can be expressed in terms of money or labor.

So in the input tier, the household adjusts the composition of its initial resource endowment bundle to get the optimal mix of labor and purchased goods and services to be used in the second tier for household production of the commodities that, in the third tier, yield household utility.[2] There are considerable advantages to this roundabout description of consumption and work.

Production in a time-specific environment

A one-person household has a set of pure flow instantaneous production functions

$$z_i(t) = f_i(x_i(t), l_i)E_i(t) = f_i(x_i(t), l_i; t), \quad i = 1, \ldots, m, \qquad (8.1)$$

each of which describes the technology of producing a commodity, i – of doing consumption activity i – at a rate or intensity $z_i(t)$ using a flow of purchased goods and services at rate $x_i(t)$ and labor services at rate l_i; $x_i(t)$ is the vector of inputs specific to activity i. The production function is assumed to have diminishing marginal product with respect to all input flows.

$E(t)$ is a vector describing the production environment that affects the efficiency of household activity production – $E(t)$ describes light, dark, open schools, availability of friends, bus schedules, etc. $E_i(t)$ is the subset of $E(t)$ that affects the efficiency of consumption activity i. It does not matter whether the influence of the time-specific environment is explicit and multiplicative, as in the middle term of (8.1), or implicit, as on the right-hand side.[3] The household production environment, $E(t)$ (or $f_i(\cdot; t)$), is in constant rhythmic flux over the day, altering the relative efficiency of production of the m activities the household can do. This wholly repetitive environmental change is the main driving force in the model.

Goods inputs to activity i are assumed to be available at a time-invariant unit price, $\bar{p}_i$; they are always temporally footloose.[4] The household's labor service input flow costs w per unit, where w is the wage rate; its temporal character will be specified later. Finally, the rate of flow of labor services to production at any moment for a one-person household is 1; so $l_i = 1$ for all i, and the instantaneous production functions can be written simply as

$$z_i(t) = z_i(x_i(t);t), \quad i = 1, \ldots, m,$$
$$z' = \partial z_i(t)/\partial x_i(t) > 0,$$
$$z'' = \partial^2 z_i(t)/\partial x_i(t)^2 < 0,$$
$$\partial z_i(t)/\partial t = dE_i(t)/dt \gtreqless 0. \qquad (8.2)$$

Time-shaped utility

An instantaneous utility function assigns to each activity at any moment t a rate of flow of satisfaction that depends only on the activity, i, and its intensity, $z_i(t)$:

$$u(t) = u_i(z_i(t)), \quad i = 1, \ldots, m,$$
$$u' = \partial u_i(t)/\partial z_i(t) > 0, \qquad (8.3)$$
$$u'' = \partial^2 u_i(t)/\partial z_i(t)^2 < 0.$$

By assumption, the marginal utility of the intensity of consumption is always positive – more intensity is better – but diminishing. The instantaneous utility function itself is assumed not to change over the day, T.[5] Utility is time-additive and -separable, so that the accumulated flow of utility from any activity over any period depends on how intensely and how long it is done:

$$U_i = \int_{t_{i-1}}^{t_i} u_i(z_i(t)) \, dt, \qquad (8.4)$$

where the limits to integration are the times at which the household starts, t_{i-1}, and stops, t_i, doing i.

It is assumed that the household can do only one thing at a time. This can always be justified by appropriately defining activities. Then the accumulated utility per unit time T – the stuff of any standard time-allocation model, usually expressed as a daily utility flow – is

$$U = \int_{t_0}^{t_1} u_1(z_1(t)) \, dt + \int_{t_1}^{t_2} u_2(z_2(t)) \, dt + \ldots + \int_{t_{h-1}}^{t_h} u_h(z_h(t)) \, dt. \qquad (8.5)$$

Now t_0 is the time at the beginning of the uninterrupted consumption period – the period of household production – and t_h is the time at the end; $h \leqslant m$ consumption activities have been done during the day in (8.5). It is initially implicit – as usual, if not entirely defensibly – that utility is derived only from consumption activities.

It should be emphasized that the sequence of the activities that fill in the spaces in (8.5) is not imposed exogenously but emerges from the process of optimal activity choice through the day. This will be clear as the analysis develops, but at this stage, without resorting to cumbersome notation it might appear that identified activities, $i = 1, \ldots, m$ from (8.1) to (8.4), must be assigned to specific places in the sequence. That is not the case.

8.3   Household labor as time

Although each household activity in this model is identified with a specific starting time and stopping time, standard time-allocation analysis deals only with the duration of activities, $T_i = t_i - t_{i-1}$. When temporal detail is thereby suppressed by reducing timing and sequence to durations, total daily consumption or household production time is

$$T_h = \sum_{i=1}^{h} T_i, \tag{8.6}$$

and what is left of the day, T, is then work time, T_w, giving

$$T = T_h + T_w \tag{8.7}$$

as the familiar household "time constraint," expressed in durations. In standard time-allocation analysis, all commodities, inputs, production, and utility functions are defined over the duration of activities; so "commodities," "goods inputs," "time inputs," etc., are, respectively,

$$Z_i = \int_{t_{i-1}}^{t_i} z_i(t) \, dt; \quad X_i = \int_{t_{i-1}}^{t_i} x_i(t) \, dt; \quad L_i = \int_{t_{i-1}}^{t_i} 1 \, dt = T_i.$$

If rates of flow are constant, of course, $Z_i = z_i T_i$, $X_i = x_i T_i$, and $L_i = T_i$.

Time as a thing versus time as a context

It is useful, before going further, to clarify an aspect of the Becker tradition of household time-allocation analysis that has created some confusion: It is the way time is incorporated in that analysis, both as part of the household's initial endowment and as an input to its production processes and its consumption. The most striking aspects of Becker's treatment of time are two:

(a) Analytically, time has been treated very differently in household production models and in analyses of traditional production by a firm. In household production, time has been fully "reified," treated as a "thing." It is an input that is used up in the production process, like a worker's effort or 100 pounds of sheet steel. Time is an explicit argument of the household production function. Contrast this to production theory, in which time is always the context within which the production process takes place; it is not some sort of concrete if mysterious input to production. This sharp break with tradition by household time-allocation analysis is unacknowledged; instead, Becker implied a close similarity of household production analysis and the standard production theory of the firm (Becker, 1965; Michael and Becker, 1973).

(b) But odd though this representation of time may be, the Becker analysis has proved extremely powerful. From that, it would appear that it must be doing something right.

The explanation for this paradox is implicit in the last mathematical expression of the preceding section, where, for a one-person household, the accumulated daily flow of labor services in household production of a consumption activity is, simply, the duration of that production: $L_i = T_i$. More generally, for a household with l members (on the same activity schedule), the total amount of labor services used in producing activity i is

$$L_i = lT_i = \int_{t_{i-1}}^{t_i} l\, dt.$$

In the Becker representation, time and accumulated labor service flows are the same thing by a scalar.

The important implication of this fact is that Becker's time-allocation model does not allocate time. It allocates, less metaphysically, the household's labor supply. This is a fixed daily quantum of household labor services per unit time, T, measured, as usual, in man-hours; it can be used in household production or sold on a labor market in exchange for command over goods and services. Labor services are, like any constant flow (of irrigation water or electric power or television programming), measurable in time units, but that does not make them into time. The depth of potential confusion was suggested by Pollak and Wachter's statement (1975, p. 276) that in the Becker model, "technically, the household time devoted to an activity is both an input and an output."

Yet – and this is the second aspect of the Becker tradition – even with the wrong name attached to the main variable, Becker's analysis has proved exceptionally powerful because the insights it provides into households' optimal allocation of limited labor supplies have opened a number of new areas to fruitful economic analysis. The fact that labor services are called "time" has done little to reduce the value of that analysis in examining household behavior – so long as no other aspect of time in household behavior can be confused with it.[6]

At its base, the key difficulty with all this is that in the Becker analysis, not only is labor seen as time, but time can be seen *only* as labor. Yet "time spent in consumption activities" must both measure labor service allocation and describe the context in which household work, production, and consumption take place. That is why the misspecification is not entirely innocent: The Becker model seems to be analyzing time in household behavior, when instead it is analyzing labor in household behavior – because it is measurable in time units. This is what confronted Pollak and Wachter when they tried to identify "the value of time," per se, in Becker's model. A time-specific model – where time is once again part of the analytical context – can describe "the value of time." A Becker model – where time is reified – cannot.

It is clear, then, why the reified time of those traditional time-allocation models fits so well and fruitfully into the established analytical techniques as an argument in a two-factor production function: "time" behaves as if it were a familiar factor input, like labor services, because it is. It is clear, too, that time, in fact, is the context within which all this household work-production-consumption process takes place – just as in the familiar theory of the production process in firms – and not a "thing" with mysterious properties that give it a unique role in production analysis of the household but not in production analysis of the firm.

Marketed labor: endowments, trade, and constraints

The household has a daily resource endowment of L man-hours of labor services and Y_p dollars of unearned income. The labor supply of a one-person household is fixed at $L = T$ per unit time T;[7] unearned income, Y_p, can be positive (property income) or negative (taxation). Income is used to buy goods inputs for household production of consumption activities. Labor services are either used directly in household production or sold on the labor market to earn additional income with which to buy goods and services for household production. The optimal allocation of the fixed labor supply between household and market production is, of course, the familiar work–leisure choice expressed in slightly different form.

The existence of a market in endowments – the labor market – with exogenously determined trading possibilities,

$$Y_w = \bar{w}L_w,$$

allows the household to transform the composition of its initial endowment (L,Y_p) into (L_h,Y), where

$$L = L_w + L_h$$

is equivalent to (8.7), the time constraint, and income from earnings and endowment, together, is

$$Y = Y_p + Y_w.$$

The wage rate, w, is assumed for now to be time-invariant.

In the goods market, money income is further transformed by exchange for purchased inputs to household production at given prices, $\bar{p}_i$. The availability of goods inputs to production is, of course, constrained by money income,

$$Y = \sum_{i=1}^{h} \bar{p}_i X_i = \sum_{i=1}^{h} \int_{t_{i-1}}^{t_i} \bar{p}_i x_i(t) \, dt. \tag{8.8}$$

Because market prices $\bar{w}$ and the $\bar{p}_i$ are all exogenous to the household, this entire tier of endowment/labor market/goods-market can be reduced to a single aggregated resource constraint to household production (hence utility). When valued in money income, it is Becker's "full income constraint,"

$$S = \bar{w}L + Y_p = \sum_{i=1}^{h} (\bar{p}_i X_i + \bar{w}T_i)$$

$$= \sum_{i=1}^{h} \int_{t_{i-1}}^{t_i} (\bar{p}_i x_i + \bar{w}) \, dt. \tag{8.9}$$

When valued in labor services, in the tradition of Lionel Robbins (1930), it is a "full-effort constraint,"

$$R = L + Y_p/\bar{w} = \sum_{i=1}^{h} ((\bar{p}_i/\bar{w})X_i + L_i)$$

$$= \sum_{i=1}^{h} \int_{t_{i-1}}^{t_i} ((\bar{p}_i/\bar{w})x_i + 1) \, dt, \tag{8.10}$$

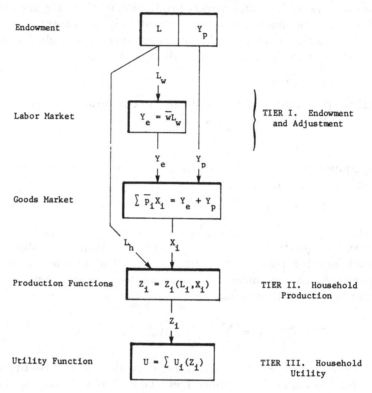

Figure 8.1. Structure of household production models (in accumulated flows).

with $Y_p/\bar{w}$ and the $\bar{p}_i/\bar{w}$ as the "effort prices" of income and goods, respectively. Convention recommends use of the full-income version, even though it is important that the choice between the two forms of endowment for the numeraire is arbitrary.

So two markets with exogenous prices intervene between the household's resource endowment and the inputs to its production tier, allowing optimal adjustment of the composition of its initial endowment in light of production and utility functions and the environment. The flow diagram of Figure 8.1 makes this explicit.

Reduction of all this to a single constraint, as in Becker models, stresses the market equivalence of labor and goods inputs to household production, but it obscures very important differences between them – differences that are obscured, too, in the atemporal models of orthodox analysis. Their critical role is revealed in a time-specific model; these endowment characteristics are, indeed, reminiscent of those identified for production inputs in Chapter 3.

Money income and the purchased goods it buys are generally temporally footloose. Goods purchase and use can be can be shifted about over the day to maximize household satisfaction; a penny saved at 10:00 in the morning can be available to spend at 10:00 at night. In terms of Part II, money and goods are essentially storable over T. But household labor services are time-specific – they cannot be moved about over the unit time T. The hour of labor services available from 10:00 to 11:00 in the morning is wholly time-specific; it cannot be made available between 3:00 and 4:00 in the afternoon. Labor services are perishable. Their supply and use must be simultaneous.

The constant rate of flow of labor services over T and their perishability, together, are responsible for an odd but important change of perspective; these characteristics make labor the fixed (flow) factor input in household production to which variable goods flow rates adjust. In its rhythmic environment, the time specificity of labor inputs and the time flexibility of goods inputs importantly influence the process of optimal behavior for the household. In light of the fixed and time-invariant flow of labor services, the changing production environment over T calls for an optimal temporal allocation of goods as part of the process – constrained by production and utility functions – from which an optimal household activity schedule emerges.

8.4   Time-shaped optimal behavior

Rather than continue with discussion of the large number, h, of household activities, we will switch to two consumption activities, 1 and 2, and work activity; three activities are more easily visualized and no less general. Then accumulated household utility,

$$U = \int_{t_0}^{t_1} u_1(z_1(x_1(t);t)) \, dt + \int_{t_1}^{t_h} u_2(z_2(x_2(t);t)) \, dt, \qquad (8.11)$$

is to be maximized subject to a resource constraint,

$$\int_{t_0}^{t_1} \bar{p}_1 x_1(t) \, dt + \int_{t_1}^{t_h} \bar{p}_2 x_2(t) \, dt = \int_{t_h}^{t_T} \bar{w} \, dt + Y_p, \qquad (8.12)$$

where it is implicit that

$$L = L_h + L_w = T_1 + T_2 + T_w = (t_1 - t_0) + (t_h - t_1) + (t_T - t_h). \quad (8.13)$$

The solution will yield optimal values x_1^*, x_2^*, t_1^*, and t_h^* and a Lagrange multiplier, λ. From these, we can derive the following: accumulated goods consumption over T, X_1^*, X_2^*; the allocation of time and labor among consumption and work activities, T_1^*, T_2^*, T_w^* (i.e., L_1^*, L_2^*, L_w^*); the "quantities of commodities," Z_1^*, Z_2^*, produced and consumed by the household; the satisfactions they yield, U_1 and U_2, all per unit time T. This information is the standard stuff of standard time-allocation analysis. In addition, from the time-specific model we can see the optimal activity sequence and timing, showing in temporal order what specific time each activity is started, t_0^*, t_1^*, and t_h^* ($= t_2^*$), and stopped, t_1^*, t_2^* ($= t_h^*$), and t_T and its optimal intensity at each moment, z_1^* and z_2^*. This is the household's optimal activity schedule.

The first-order conditions for optimal activity choice have useful economic interpretation. With respect to goods allocation,

$$u_1'z_1'(x_1^*(t)) - \overline{p}_1\lambda = 0 \quad \text{over } t_0 \leq t \leq t_1,$$

and

$$u_2'z_2'(x_2^*(t)) - \overline{p}_2\lambda = 0 \quad \text{over } t_1 < t \leq t_h,$$

so that

$$\lambda = \frac{u_1'z_1'(t)}{\overline{p}_1} = \frac{u_2'z_2'(t)}{\overline{p}_2} \quad \text{over } t_0 \leq t \leq t_h.^8 \tag{8.14}$$

With respect to consumption activity timing,

$$u_1(z_1(x_1(t_1^*))) - u_2(z_2(x_2(t_1^*))) - \lambda(\overline{p}_1x_1(t_1^*) - \overline{p}_2x_2(t_1^*)) = 0 \quad \text{at } t_1^*;$$

so

$$\lambda = \frac{u_1(t_1^*) - u_2(t_1^*)}{\overline{p}_1x_1(t_1^*) - \overline{p}_2x_2(t_1^*)}. \tag{8.15}$$

Finally, with respect to the timing of work and consumption,

$$u_2(z_2(x_2(t_h^*))) - \lambda(\overline{p}_2x_2(t_h^*) + \overline{w}) = 0 \quad \text{at } t_h^*,$$

so that

$$\lambda = \frac{u_2(z_2(x_2(t_h^*)))}{\overline{p}_2x_2(t_h^*) + \overline{w}} = \frac{u_2(t_h^*)}{c_2(t_h^*)}, \tag{8.16}$$

where the flow of goods and labor costs of any activity i at time t is

$$c_i(t) = \overline{p}_ix_i(t) + \overline{w}. \tag{8.17}$$

Equation (8.14) describes the optimal use of purchased consumption goods and labor: The marginal contribution to the flow of utility per dollar must be the same for all goods over all consumption activities at all times because goods inputs can be costlessly moved about over T. The numerator in (8.14) describes the "marginal utility product" of a consumption good. This is defined as the increment to the rate of utility flow $u_i(z_i(x_i))$ from an incremental increase in the rate of goods use, x_i. It is fully analogous to the marginal revenue product of an input used by a firm that sells in imperfect product markets – as does the household in producing for its own consumption.[9]

As the production environment, $E(t)$, changes throughout the day, T, changing the relative efficiencies of production of the various activities, goods will be shuffled about to maintain (8.14) at all times. This temporal mobility of goods, it has been noted, is a fundamental difference between the labor and income aspects of the constraint (8.12). So the efficient use of consumption goods, $x_i^*(t)$, is always time-specific in response to the rhythmically changing production environment. Finally, the familiar rules for optimal input allocations become, in this time-specific setting, (a) that a consumption good must yield the same marginal utility product in all its uses and at all times, (b) that different inputs must be used in the same activity in such proportions that their (flow) marginal products are proportional to their prices, and (c) that different inputs must be used in different activities in such proportions that their marginal utility products are proportional to their prices.

The first-order condition in equation (8.15) describes the optimal time of day, t^*, to stop doing activity 1 and start doing activity 2. It embodies the fact – absent from standard analysis – that under the time constraint a moment more of doing activity 1 is a moment less of doing activity 2; so the optimal switching time between them depends on the flows of utility and costs in both activities. These, in turn, depend on the changing production environment. Although (8.15) suggests this in requiring that the ratio of differences – of utility flow to expenditure flow – be equated to the value of the constraint, it is clearer in the slightly different form

$$u_1(z_1(x_1^*(t_1^*))) - \lambda \bar{p}_1 x_1^*(t_1^*) = u_2(z_2(x_2^*(t_1^*))) - \lambda \bar{p}_2 x_2^*(t_1^*), \quad (8.18)$$

so that after substituting from (8.14) and simplifying the notation, at the optimal switching time,

$$u_1(t_1^*) - u_1' z_1'(t) x_1^*(t_1^*) = u_2(t_1^*) - u_2' z_2'(t) x_2^*(t_1^*). \quad (8.19)$$

Each side of (8.19) describes what will be defined later as a "net utility flow" at time t_i^* – the rate of flow of utility yielded by a moment of doing the activity less the reduction in utility over the rest of the consumption period consequent on its using up $x(t_i^*)$ of consumption goods. At an optimal switching moment, these net utility flows will be equal for the two activities.

Finally, the condition of equation (8.16) describes the optimal moment, t_h^*, to switch from consumption activities to work. So it defines the optimal allocation of the household's fixed labor services between household production and market labor: Of the $L = L_w + L_h$ available man-hours, $L_w^* = t_T - t_h^*$ are optimally sold on the labor market, and $L_h^* = (t_i^* - t_0^*) + (t_h^* - t_i^*)$ are used in household production. It will become clear later that this standard, atemporal result involves a good deal more than is usually recognized.

One further comment on these static first-order conditions is called for before turning to look more closely at the optimal choice process. The usual interpretation of a Lagrange multiplier as the marginal utility of the constraint holds, of course, for this analysis. But because both labor services and income are constrained, λ incorporates the marginal utility of the wage rate and the marginal utilities of the components of the endowment. The full-income constraint (8.9) makes this clear. Maximum daily utility is a function of the constraint, S,

$$U^* = g(S),$$

and the marginal utility of that constraint is

$$\partial U^* / \partial S = \partial g / \partial S = \lambda.$$

But because

$$S = S(Y_p, \bar{w}, L) = Y_p + \bar{w}L$$

and

$$U^* = g(S(Y_p, \bar{w}, L)),$$

three separate marginal utilities are implied by this: the marginal utility of unearned, or full, income,

$$\partial U^* / \partial Y_p = (\partial g / \partial S)(\partial S / \partial Y_p) = \lambda, \tag{8.20}$$

the marginal utility of the wage rate,

$$\partial U^* / \partial \bar{w} = (\partial g / \partial S)(\partial S / \partial \bar{w}) = \lambda L = \lambda T, \tag{8.21}$$

and the marginal utility of labor,

$$\partial U^*/\partial L = (\partial g/\partial S)(\partial S/\partial L) = \lambda\bar{w}. \tag{8.22}$$

In the first-order conditions, λ reflects all three of these characteristics. The intensity of consumption activities – the expenditure on consumption goods in (8.14) that determines their marginal utility products – depends on income. The duration of consumption activities – the flow rate of utility and costs in (8.15) and (8.16) – depends on labor directly used in consumption. Both function in a time context. Once again, as in Part II, optimality requires simultaneous adjustment on both duration and intensity margins. When the first-order conditions are satisfied, the intensities of consumption activities are optimally adjusted to available income, and consumption activities, alone and in combination, are optimally extended in time until, on both margins simultaneously, a moment makes the same contribution to daily utility whether it is spent in doing activity 1 or activity 2 or in earning the income that allows the use of consumption goods inputs in activities 1 and 2. These aspects of the process are far clearer in a time-specific model.

8.5 The value of time in consumption and work

So far, these are much the same as the results got from the standard household production model. But the time-specific model also forces attention to the process of household choice – its anatomy.

The first-order conditions just derived are static; they describe conditions at t_1^* and t_h^* and say something quite general about optimal conditions at other times. But they reveal little about the household's optimal behavior over time – about how it reaches t_1^* and t_h^*. In a time-specific context, the optimal moments for changing activities should emerge from optimal choice rules that the household can follow all the time. And they do. Although these rules are especially simple when activities are assumed, as they are here, to be independent in both production and consumption, they have a number of useful implications, nonetheless.

Consumption activities

The condition defining the optimal moment to switch from one consumption activity to another was expressed, in equation (8.19), in terms of the "net utility flow" of each of the two activities. The first-order condition showed that at the optimal switching moment,

t_1^*, the two relevant net utility flows had to be equal. Now we can employ a deeper significance of that net utility flow.

Analogous to the static first-order condition (8.19), define for each activity i at each moment t of the day T its net utility flow:

$$\mu_i(t) = u_i(t) - \lambda \bar{p}_i x_i(t), \quad i = 1, \ldots, m, \, t_0 \leq t \leq t_T. \tag{8.23}$$

$\mu_i(t)$ is the value of time spent in activity i at moment t. Because (8.14) is necessary for the efficient production of consumption activities, (8.23) is assumed to satisfy it at all times of the day and for all activities.

Of course, every possible consumption activity, $i = 1, \ldots, m$, at every moment t of T has a defined $\mu_i(t)$ describing the net utility flow that that activity would generate at that moment, if it were undertaken then. The values of time spent in different consumption activities at any given moment will typically be different because goods prices, production functions, and utility flows differ among commodities, and their productions are differently affected by the environment. The value of time spent in any one consumption activity will change over the day, because the efficiency of its production changes with the changing environment, changing either its speed of output, $z_i(t)$, and therefore its satisfactions, $u_i(t)$, or its goods costs, $\bar{p}_i x_i(t)$, or both.

At any moment, the optimal choice rule for the household is simply to do what will maximize the net flow of utility, $\mu_i(t)$ – in other words, to spend time, always, in the activity in which time has the most value. From the m possible activities that could be done at any moment, only one is chosen.

The choice rule implies that an activity, i, will be done if $\mu_i(t)$ is the largest available, that it will be continued so long as $\mu_i(t)$ is greater than that of any other activity, and that it will be replaced as soon as the new activity becomes a better way to spend time. That defines t_1^*. At the optimal moment of switching, t_1^*, (8.19) implies that time has the same value in both activities,

$$\mu_1(t_1^*) = \mu_2(t_1^*). \tag{8.24}$$

The household following this choice rule maximizes accumulated daily utility. A mild qualification is implied by the second-order conditions – that at t_1^* it is necessary that in the ordered sequence the value of time in the first activity be increasing less (or decreasing more) than the value of time in the next,

$$\mu_1'(t_1^*) < \mu_2'(t_1^*). \tag{8.25}$$

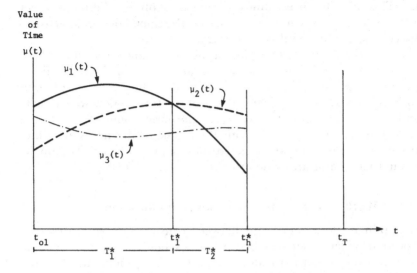

Figure 8.2. The value of time in consumption: net utility flows and activity choice.

Values of $\mu_i(t)$ for the consumption period of the three-activity case are illustrated in Figure 8.2. Consumption activities 1 and 2 are optimal for their respective periods because they generate the largest net utility flow. At the optimal switching time t_1^*, they are equally appealing. Another activity, 3, with a net utility $\mu_3(t)$, like the dot-dash line, would remain a possible choice throughout T, but, *ceteris paribus*, it would not be chosen because there is always a better way – activity 1 or 2 – to spend the time.

Work

Under the myopic hedonism implicit in maximizing the net utility flow from consumption at each moment of the day, it would appear that that same choice rule could never lead the household to choose work activity with its presumed absence (at best) of direct satisfactions. But although in this chapter we will assume, as is traditional, that $u_w = 0$ in direct utility flow from working, work nonetheless yields indirect satisfactions through the increased intensity of consumption activities made possible by the goods that money will buy. In tier I, marketed work time yields a vicarious utility by altering the composition of the real resource constraint on consumption activities. This, like the direct utility of consumption, is reflected in a net utility flow; so work can be governed by the same household activity-choice rule as that regulating consumption activity choice.

But although work activity will fit the same activity tracking rule, it needs some additional qualifications, and through them the time-specific model serves to reveal more about the character of both work and consumption. The discussion of this section will initially ignore those complications, drawing the basic connection between work and consumption rules but then making the necessary time-specific distinction between the duration of work activity and its timing that complicates (and enriches) the analysis.

8.6   Work and consumption: timing and duration

The optimal allocation of time between consumption and work – the allocation of labor services between household production and the labor market – implicit in the optimal switching moment, t_h^*, is defined in equation (8.16) by

$$\lambda = u_2(t_h^*)/c_2(t_h^*),$$

so that

$$u_2(t_h^*) - \lambda \bar{p}_2 x_2(t_h^*) = \lambda \bar{w}. \tag{8.26}$$

In terms of the value of time, μ, the optimal moment to switch from activity 2 to work, is when

$$\mu_2(t_h) = \lambda \bar{w}. \tag{8.27}$$

On the time margin that defines the optimal allocation of time between work and consumption, then, the net utility flow of the consumption activity is equal to the marginal utility of labor or time-as-money-only from equation (8.22). From this, the choice rule that maximizes net utility flows can be extended to include work activity by defining the net utility flow of work at time t as, generally,

$$\mu_w(t) = u_w(t) + \lambda(\bar{w} - \bar{p}_u x_w(t)), \tag{8.28}$$

where u_w is any direct satisfaction (positive or negative) from work and x_w is any goods inputs necessary to the household's production of work activity. So long as both of these continue to be assumed to be zero, the net utility flow of work – the value of time spent working – reduces to

$$\mu_w(t) = \lambda \bar{w}. \tag{8.29}$$

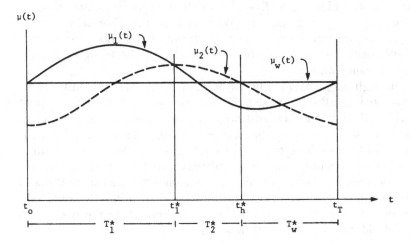

Figure 8.3. The value of time: net utility flows in work and consumption.

Now the same optimal household activity-choice rule applies at all times over T to all activities; the household should choose that activity that yields the highest net utility flow, $\mu_i(t)$, $i = 1, \ldots m,w$, at each moment t.

In the two-consumption-activity example, $\mu_1(t)$ is the largest value of μ from t_0 to t_1^*; at the optimal switching time from consumption activity 1 to activity 2, $\mu_1(t_1^*) = \mu_2(t_1^*)$, satisfying (8.15); $\mu_2(t)$ is the largest available μ from t_1^* to t_h^*; at the optimal time to switch from consumption to work, $\mu_2(t_h^*) = \mu_w(t_h^*)$, satisfying (8.16); finally, $\mu_w(t)$ is the largest available value of μ from t_h^* to the end of the day, t_T. Over the whole period and over all activities, all values of $\mu_i(t)$ satisfy (8.14); so all first-order conditions are met by this tracking rule – the activity schedule it generates maximizes daily utility. In Figure 8.3, the stuff of Figure 8.2 is extended over the whole of T to include both consumption and work activities.

Optimal durations of work and consumption

Now for the qualifications. They derive from two facts: First, the utility flow of work activity depends on vicarious satisfactions (and nothing else if $u_w = 0$) derived from its contribution to consumption satisfactions at (by necessity) another time of day; second, the utility flow from work activities depends on how much work is done in the day – its duration, $L_w = T_w$ – not (at all under present assumptions) on its timing during the day. Work transforms labor services into money income and money income into purchased goods inputs that complement and increase the productivity of the labor used indirectly in consumption.

Through λ, μ_w is mainly duration-specific. The net utility flow from work at 10:03 a.m. depends on how much time will be spent working during the day, and hence the marginal utility product of goods inputs to consumption; it does not depend on what is happening at 10:03 a.m. The reason, of course, is that the marginal utility product of consumption goods decreases as their rate of flow increases, meeting both diminishing marginal product in household production ($z'' < 0$) and diminishing marginal utility in household consumption ($u'' < 0$). This is important enough in the process of household choice to warrant defining

$$\Gamma_c(x_c) = \partial(u'_c z'_c)/\partial x_c = u'_c z''_c + z'^2_c u''_c < 0$$

$$= u'_c z'_c \left[\frac{z''_c}{z'_c} + z'_c \frac{u''_c}{u'_c} \right] < 0 \qquad (8.30)$$

as the "marginal utility product of consumption."

In consumption, μ_i is mainly time-specific. The net utility flow in consumption depends mainly on the efficiency of the momentary production environment, $E(t)$. So, for instance, the relative attractions of sleep at 3:00 a.m. are more influenced by the cool, dark, quiet environment of 3:00 a.m. than by the marginal value of goods inputs determined by the income generated during the day.

The result is that both μ_i in consumption and μ_w in work must be specified as functions of both time of day, t, and the amount of labor sold on the market, L_w – so $\mu_i(t,L_w)$ and $\mu_w(t,L_w)$.

So time allocation to work has two separate aspects: the optimal division of labor between market and household production activities, L_w^* and L_h^*, and its optimal timing, t_h^* to t_0^*. Because in a Becker model that deals only with accumulated flows, $L_w^* = T_w^* = T - T_h^*$, these two aspects of the work–leisure choice usually are not obvious. The timing values, t, in this model are not endogenous to the analysis; they describe specific times of day, such as when the sun comes up or when school starts or when a plane leaves for Washington, that define the external environment in which the household makes its activity decisions. The convention that specifies some arbitrary moment as t_0 (= t_T from the day before) so that t_h^* is neither more nor less than $T_w^* = T - t_h^*$ is simply not enough for time-specific analysis;

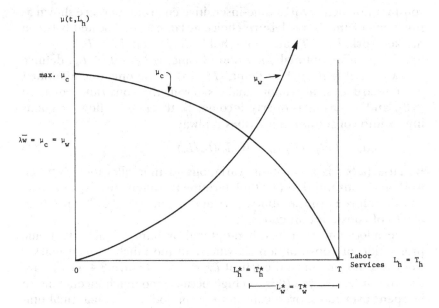

Figure 8.4. "Time allocation" and the value of time spent in work and consumption.

t_h^* is when market work optimally starts; $T_w^* = L_w^*$ is its optimal duration as a fraction of the day.

The way the model is now specified, no aspect of work has been described as time-sensitive – the wage rate w is assumed constant over the day, work satisfactions u_w are assumed zero, and there is no requirement of goods inputs to work activity, x_w. So the value of time in work is wholly duration-specific – it depends only on the division of labor between market and home production, not at all on when it is done. Significantly, as we shall see, this does not imply household indifference to when to work. But under present assumptions, for any given labor allocation, L_w, the utility flow from work is a constant, regardless of the time of day, t. Figure 8.3 reflects this constancy for a given work duration, L_w^*, in $\mu_w(t,L_w^*)$. A change in $L_w = T_w$ would shift the constant $\mu_w(t,L_w)$ and, to a lesser extent, the curves $\mu_1(t,L_w)$ and $\mu_2(t,L_w)$. These shifts determine the optimal allocation of the household's fixed labor supply between market work and household production – the optimal work–leisure decision. This is easier to see in the different representation of Figure 8.4.

In Figure 8.4, the net utility flow for work and an average net utility flow for consumption (most simply, one generated by a single consumption activity in a time-insensitive environment) are shown as functions of the work–leisure choice as labor is reallocated between market work, $L_w = T_w$, and household production, $L_h = T_h$. $T_h^* = T - T_w^*$, the familiar optimal allocation of time, is $L_h^* = L - L_w^*$, defined by $w\lambda = \mu_w(t) = \mu_c(t)$. This point, $(T_h^*, \bar{w}\lambda)$, is the only one identified by standard time-allocation analysis. From the constraint equation (8.8), and ignoring property income, Y_p, the rate of flow of goods inputs into consumption activities is always

$$x_c(t) = (\bar{w}/\bar{p}_c)(T_w/T_h) = (\bar{w}/\bar{p}_c)(L_w/L_h). \tag{8.31}$$

Because $(\bar{w}/\bar{p}_c)$ is a constant, variations in time allocation between work and consumption (T_w/T_h) determine the intensity of goods flows and therefore both the utility, $u_c(t)$, and the marginal utility product, $u'z'(t)$, of consumption goods.

The allocation of a less-than-optimal amount of labor to home production of consumption activities and too much to paid market work is a movement to the left of $L_h^* = T_h^*$ in Figure 8.4. Goods are used too intensively; $x_c(t)$ is too high because too much income has to be spent over too short a consumption period. So the marginal utility product of goods is less than optimal, directly reducing the value of time spent in work, $\mu_w(t)$. In addition, although there is an increase in the flow of utility in consumption, $u_c(t)$, both the diminishing marginal product of $x_c(t)$ and the diminishing marginal utility of consumption activities serve eventually to limit that increase to some maximum value, max $\mu_c(t)$. As consumption time approaches zero, so L_w approaches T, the flow rate of goods use x_c necessarily becomes infinite, and the net utility flow of consumption $\mu_c(t)$ reaches its maximum. All work and no play leaves Jack with consumption goods that yield a zero marginal utility flow.

Departure from an optimal allocation of labor in the opposite direction has the household spending a more-than-optimal amount of time in consumption and hence too little in earning consumption goods inputs to combine with labor in consumption. The rate of goods flow, $x_c(t)$, is suboptimal. Too little income, $\bar{w}L_w$, is earned when $L_w < T_w^*$, and the daily income that is earned is spread out over a too-long consumption period, diluting its flow rate. As a consequence, with such a goods-starved time allocation, the marginal utility product of goods rises, and with it the value of time spent working; $\mu_w(t)$ becomes infinite as L_w approaches zero. The net utility flow of a moment of consumption, in contrast, is deprived of the goods that complement the labor input; so the value of time in consumption falls until, as L_w approaches zero, $\mu_c(t)$ approaches zero.

The optimal allocation of labor between home production and earning income is optimal because it balances the use of household labor in its two quite different employments: as an input to household production of activities that generate consumption utility and as a tradable commodity that can secure the consumption goods inputs that increase the productivity of labor used in consumption. When the values of household labor in these two employments are equal, $\mu_c(t) = \mu_w(t)$, the allocation of labor is optimal.[10]

Optimal timing of work and consumption

Having established the optimal duration of work, we can now deal with its optimal timing within the day. It is worth reiterating that to this point, the net utility flow of work – the value of time spent working – is not time-specific; so given a duration choice, L_h, the value of time spent working is the same at any time of day; the flat $\mu_w(t,L_h)$ curve in Figure 8.3 will shift up and down with changes in L_h, but it will always be flat. Later we will consider more realistic cases where time-specific characteristics of work itself can enter the household's judgment of when it should be done, but at this stage it is useful to continue to assume that work is itself temporally neutral.

But even when work can be done equally well at any time of the day, the activity-choice rule – maximize $\mu_i(t,L_h)$ – requires that the household schedule its work at those times when time spent in consumption activities is least valuable. Work is a leftover. This was embodied in Figure 8.3, where work was shown to take place precisely between t_h^* and t_T, even though its own net utility flow was no different before than after t_h^*.

This is an important result of considerable relevance to the time-shape of economic activities. Even if work activity yields the same net utility at all times of the day, the household still will not be indifferent to when work is scheduled. Because working in the labor market means not consuming, the household has a clear incentive to consume when that is the best way to spend time and to work when it is not. Work activity is scheduled by default; it is a temporally residual activity. Because activity choice involves the comparison of alternatives at each moment, it is not necessary that all of them be time-specific in order for a time-specific utility-maximizing activity schedule to emerge.

The time-shaped environment, then, even though it affects only the efficiency of household production and affects neither its enjoyment nor the efficiency of market work activities, is enough to de-

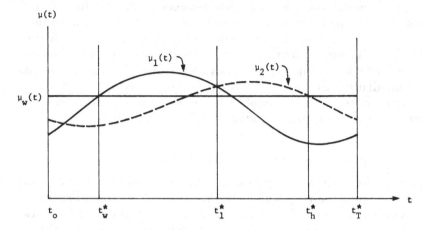

Figure 8.5. Net utility flows in unit time T.

fine a utility-maximizing time of day, t_h^*, to stop consumption and start working. Later, when additional reasons are considered for why a particular work schedule may be optimal, it will be important to remember that optimal household schedules do not depend solely on those factors.

The last main point to be made on the optimal timing of activities was implied earlier. In time-specific analysis it is necessary to specify marginal conditions for the switch from consumption to work, t_h, and for the switch from work to consumption, t_0; t_0 cannot be defined arbitrarily as the moment when work stops and consumption starts, leaving only a single margin to consider; t_0 has to be linked explicitly to the world outside the household, because changes in t are changes in real time, t, defining the external environment to which the household adjusts. Analytically, this means only that the conditions derived for optimality on the consumption–work margin, t_h, must be applied, too, to the work–consumption margin, t_0; both must satisfy condition (8.16). This is reflected in Figure 8.5 by making the start of the "day," t_0, exogenous to the household choice problem and different from its optimal switching times; so

$$\mu_2(t_h^*, L_h^*) \;=\; \mu_w(t_h^*, L_h^*) \;=\; \mu_w(t_w^*, L_h^*) \;=\; \mu_1(t_w^*, L_h^*).$$

8.7   Implications of the model

This section addresses the orthodox questions put to household time-allocation models: the effects of a change in wage rate on the allocation of time (labor services) between leisure (household production) and work (marketed labor); its effects on the choice of consumption activities, the Becker-Linder issue of secular changes in consumption and work activities induced by rising wages; and, finally, income elasticities of goods demand. All are revealed in a rather different light and a more detailed anatomy by the time-specific model.

A change in wage rate: income effects

The effects of wage rate and goods price changes are revealed with clarity in the flow-duration framework of the time-specific model. The appropriate signs of income and substitution effects appear in changes in net utility flows, and the specific incentives that induce them are revealed in the process.

A change in wage rate, of course, affects the household's optimal allocation of labor between work and consumption. The income effect depends on the intensity of goods use in consumption activities; the substitution effect depends on the differential value of wages in the net utility flows of work and consumption. Net utilities prove remarkably useful in sorting out these two effects. Consider the pure income effect first.

A pure increase in income, Y_p, is a relaxation of the budget constraint, S. An increase in S will increase daily utility by λ because more income allows an increased rate of flow of consumption goods and services, $x(t)$, and that, *ceteris paribus*, will add to the rate of flow of utility an amount $\lambda = u'z'(x(t))$. Initially, we will again consider a single consumption activity, z_c.

An income effect will always induce a reallocation of time from work to consumption because the increased intensity of goods use in consumption increases the value of time spent there, μ_c, and reduces it in work, μ_w. This is intuitively appealing. It is clear in comparing, again, net utility flows at an optimum where $\mu_w(t_j^*, L_h^*) = \mu_c(t_j^*, L_h^*)$; $j = w,h$, and so the equality holds when switching from consumption to work and from work to consumption. Then an increase in unearned income, $dY_p = dS$, will increase the net utility flow in consumption at t_j^* by

$$\partial\mu_c/\partial S = -\bar{p}x(t_j^*)\frac{\partial\lambda}{\partial S} > 0, \tag{8.32}$$

while reducing the net utility flow of work by

$$\partial\mu_w/\partial S = \bar{w}\frac{\partial\lambda}{\partial S} < 0. \tag{8.33}$$

The signs are unambiguous, because

$$\frac{\partial\lambda}{\partial S} = \lambda\frac{\partial x(t)}{\partial S}\left[\frac{z''}{z'} + z'\frac{u''}{u'}\right] < 0 \tag{8.34}$$

as a result of the diminishing marginal product of goods flows, $z'' < 0$, and the diminishing marginal utility of consumption activities, $u'' < 0$. That $\partial x(t)/\partial S$ is positive is clear in the simple case of one consumption activity with a constant rate of goods flow, because

$$x(t) = (S - \bar{w}T_h)/\bar{p}T_h; \tag{8.35}$$

so

$$\frac{\partial x(t)}{\partial S} = 1/\bar{p}T_h. \tag{8.36}$$

The income effect is positive. An increase in income makes it optimal to increase the allocation of labor to consumption at the expense of work: The greater intensity of consumption-goods use with a higher income reduces the value of time spent working, μ_w, on the time margin, whereas it increases the value of time in consumption, μ_c.

A change in wage rate: substitution effect

The sign of the pure substitution effect of a compensated wage rate change is also straightforward; the substitution effect appears as an unambiguous change in the net utility flows of work and consumption at t_j^* that alters the incentive to work. The concern for the moment is with duration, not timing; so let $T_h = t_h - t_0$. Then, because $u_w = 0$, accumulated daily utility,

$$U = \int_{t_0}^{t_h} u(t)\,dt = \int^{T_h} u(t)\,dt,$$

which remains constant with a compensated wage rate change; so

$$dU/d\bar{w} = 0 = T_h\frac{du(t)}{d\bar{w}} + u(t)\frac{dT_h}{d\bar{w}}. \tag{8.37}$$

At an optimal allocation of $T_h^* = L_h^*$ hours to consumption,

$$\mu_c(t_j^*,L_h^*) = u_c(t_j^*) - \lambda\bar{p}x(t_j^*) = \lambda\bar{w} = \mu_w(t_j^*,L_h^*)$$

at t_j^*. Then an increase in the wage rate, $d\bar{w}$, will, *ceteris paribus*, increase $\mu_w(t_j^*,L_h^*)$ by $\lambda d\bar{w}$ while leaving $\mu_c(t_j^*,L_h^*)$ unchanged. For T_h^* – without any time-allocation response to these altered net utility flows – the whole increase in wage earnings has to be offset by an equal decrease in income if daily utility is to remain constant; so

$$-dS = d\bar{w}L_w^* = d\bar{w}(T - T_h^*). \tag{8.38}$$

With T_h^* constant, any expenditure increase – if it were allowed – would increase $x(t)$, hence $u(t)$, hence U. With $x(t)$ constant, λ is unchanged; so the substitution effect of the compensated wage rate change is simply

$$\partial\mu_w(t_j^*,L_h^*)/\partial\bar{w} = \lambda > \partial\mu_c(t_j^*,L_h^*)/\partial\bar{w} = 0. \tag{8.39}$$

This unambiguously increases the incentive to allocate labor to earning.

As the household responds to these changes in net utility flows by increasing work time, the reduction in consumption time, $dT_h/d\bar{w}$, allows an increased $u(t)$ flow rate by (8.37), and hence increased goods intensities in consumption. Because $\partial\lambda/\partial x < 0$ and $\partial\mu_c/\partial x = -\bar{p}x(\partial\lambda/\partial x) > 0$,

$$\partial\mu_c/\partial x > \partial\mu_w/\partial x, \tag{8.40}$$

and the reallocation of time from consumption to work reduces the incentive for further reallocation. The pure substitution effect has reached its full extent when $\mu_w = \mu_c$; it is induced by the differential effects on μ_c and μ_w of the wage rate change and extinguished by the effect of increased goods intensities.[11]

8.8   The Becker-Linder effect: the mix of activities

A closely related issue concerns the different effects that a change in wage rate has on different consumption activities and hence on the composition of demand for consumption goods and its timing. Becker (1965) suggested that a wage increase always increases the allocation of time to goods-intensive consumption commodities at the expense of time-intensive ones; indeed, he saw the reallocation of time from work to consumption with a rising wage rate as a special case of that general phenomenon where marketed work activity is the ultimate time-intensive "commodity," so that an increased wage rate implies less demand for work time. Staffan Linder (1970) elevated the relationship to a warning to rich societies that increasing wage rates must relentlessly bias consumption choices toward goods-intensive activities and away from the wholesome, leisurely pursuits that take much time but few goods. So both applied their analyses to long-run secular trends, and both appear to have reached a plausible but quite incomplete conclusion.

If an increase in the wage rate is to alter the allocation of time between consumption activities 1 and 2, given the total time spent in consumption, it must change $\mu_1(t^*)$ or $\mu_2(t^*)$ or both. Starting from an initial equilibrium at t^*, more time will be allocated to activity 1 with an increased wage rate only if

$$\partial\mu_1(t_1^*)/\partial\overline{w} > \partial\mu_2(t_1^*)/\partial\overline{w}. \tag{8.41}$$

Because

$$\partial\mu_1(t_1^*)/\partial\overline{w} = -\overline{p}_i x_i(t_i^*)\frac{\partial\lambda}{\partial\overline{w}} > 0 \quad \text{for } i = 1,2,$$

canceling $\partial\lambda/\partial\overline{w}$ and adding $\overline{w}$ to both sides reduces (8.41) to the condition

$$c_1(t^*) > c_2(t_1^*). \tag{8.42}$$

This leads to the Becker-Linder conclusion. Becker described the time intensity of a consumption commodity as

$$\alpha_i = \frac{\overline{w}T_i}{\overline{p}_i X_i + \overline{w}T_i}$$

and its complement, the goods intensity of a commodity, as

$$\gamma_i = \frac{\overline{p}_i X_i}{\overline{p}_i X_i + \overline{w}T_i} = 1 - \alpha_i.$$

Because his analysis assumed fixed production coefficients, X_i/T_i, the time and goods intensities can be expressed in pure flow time-specific form, with recognition that they are themselves time-specific, as

$$\alpha_i(t) = \frac{\overline{w}}{\overline{p}_i x_i(t) + \overline{w}} = \frac{\overline{w}}{c_i(t)} = 1 - \gamma_i(t). \tag{8.43}$$

Then, from (8.42), a wage increase will increase the allocation of time to activity 1 only if

$$\alpha_i(t_1^*) < \alpha_2(t_1^*). \tag{8.44}$$

This can be stated more generally: An incremental increase in the wage rate will increase the allocation of time to relatively goods-intensive activities at the expense of relatively time-intensive ones. This is what Becker generalized to explain the long-run dominance of the income effect in the work–leisure choice and what Linder extrapolated to a vision of the frantic, time-obsessed, high-wage "leisure class."

The difficulty with this conclusion is that it holds only for small changes in wage rates; yet the interesting issues – to which both authors applied it – involve very large changes. The missing element is that the effect on optimal activity choice of sustained changes in wage rates must include changes in the relative intensities of goods use in different consumption activities, because these will be induced by the rising wage.

We know that before and after a wage change, goods flow intensities in all activities must adjust so that efficiency condition (8.14) is satisfied. But *some consumption activities will be able to absorb an increase in the rate of goods flows more effectively than others, and efficiency requires that those are the activities that get a disproportionate share of the increased goods flow from the higher wage rate.* What determines this characteristic of an activity – its "goods-absorptive capacity" – is the sensitivity of its marginal utility product, $u_i' z_i'(x_i(t))$, to increased goods flows. Earlier, in equation (8.30), we defined this response for a single consumption good as $\Gamma_c(x_c)$. Now, recognizing that each consumption activity, i, has its own goods-absorption capacity, define

$$\Gamma_i(x_i) = \partial(u_i' z_i')/\partial x_i = u_i' z_i'' + z_i'^2 u_i''$$

$$= u' z' \left[\frac{z_i''}{z_i'} + z_i' \frac{u_i''}{u_i'} \right] < 0. \tag{8.45}$$

With both diminishing marginal product of x_i and diminishing marginal utility of z_i, $\Gamma_i(xi)$ must be negative for all activities. But an activity for which $\Gamma_i(x_i)$ is close to zero has a greater capacity to absorb an increased goods input flow than one for which it is large and negative. This is illustrated in Figure 8.6, where a household's flow production and utility functions are pictured for activities 1 and 2; for simplicity, the same good, x, is assumed to be used as an input to both. Activity 2 clearly has a greater ability to absorb increased goods intensities than activity 1, because of both production and utility functions.

Consider the case of two consumption activities further. From an equilibrium in which $u_1' z_1'/\overline{p}_1 = u_2' z_2'/\overline{p}_2 = \lambda$, as required by (8.14) for

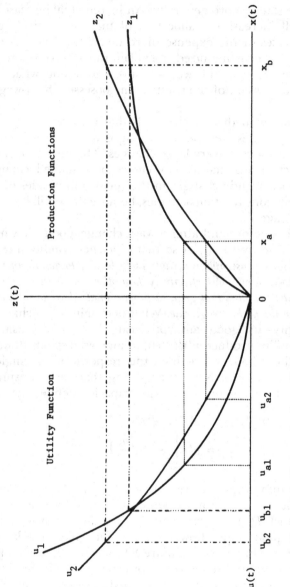

Figure 8.6. The goods-absorptive capacity of activities z_1 and z_2.

allocative efficiency, introduce a change in the wage rate. For simplicity, let $\bar{p}_1 = \bar{p}_2$. Then maintenance of condition (8.14) requires that

$$\partial(u_1'z_1')/\partial\bar{w} = \partial(u_2'z_2')/\partial\bar{w} = \partial\lambda/\partial\bar{w};$$

so

$$\Gamma_1\partial x_1/\partial\bar{w} = \Gamma_2\partial x_2/\partial\bar{w}. \tag{8.46}$$

If activity 2 has a very large absorptive capacity, so that Γ_2 is nearly zero while activity 1 suffers rapidly diminishing returns and rapidly diminishing marginal utility so that Γ_1 is large and negative, then the increased flow of goods inputs allocated to activity 2, $\partial x_2/\partial\bar{w}$, will be very much greater than that allocated to activity 1, $\partial x_1/\partial\bar{w}$. The increased goods intensity induced by a wage increase is not evenly distributed among consumption activities; instead, incremental increases in goods flows are disproportionately allocated to those activities that production and utility functions make best able to incorporate increased goods flows in the production of utility-bearing activities. In general, from (8.14), with n activities,

$$\frac{\partial x_i(t)}{\partial\bar{w}} = \frac{\bar{p}_i}{\bar{p}_j}\frac{\Gamma_j}{\Gamma_i}\frac{\partial x_j(t)}{\partial\bar{w}} \quad \text{for all } j \neq i. \tag{8.47}$$

Activities cannot – contra Becker and Linder – be classified generally as time-intensive or goods-intensive, because their absorption of goods depends on how production and utility functions optimally distribute goods among activities.

For small changes in the wage rate, the Becker-Linder results are acceptable; the effects of absorptive capacities and their differences between activities cancel out in comparing the responses of two net utility flows to the incremental wage change, simply because the comparison reduces to $-x_1\Gamma_1(\partial x_1/\partial\bar{w}) \gtreqless -x_2\Gamma_2(\partial x_2/\partial\bar{w})$, and all that remains when the optimal $\partial x_1/\partial\bar{w}$ is substituted is $\bar{p}_1x_1$ and $\bar{p}_2x_2$; any differences in Γ_1 and Γ_2 induce offsetting differences in $\partial x_1/\partial\bar{w}$ and $\partial x_2/\partial\bar{w}$. Together, they cancel out. And that leaves the Becker-Linder variables, $\bar{p}_1x_1$ relative to $\bar{p}_2x_2$ – or α_1 relative to α_2 – as an adequate first-order approximation of the effect on net utility flows of an incremental change in wage rate.

But for the more-than-incremental wage changes that are central to their applications of the analysis, it is necessary to include the effect on the goods flows, x_i, of accumulated wage rate changes, $\partial x_i/\partial\bar{w}$. A large $\partial x_i/\partial\bar{w}$ for an activity cancels out for incremental change, but it will, with continued wage increases, lead to a large x_i, regardless of its initial level. The $\partial x_i/\partial \bar{w}$, in other words, determine the values of α_i, and hence the effects of incremental wage changes on net utility flows when large secular changes are involved. And the $\partial x_i/\partial \bar{w}$ depend on relative goods prices and relative Γ_i. So the relative goods-absorptive capacity of an activity Γ_i determines its relative α_i,

$$
\begin{aligned}
d\alpha_i/d\bar{w} &= \frac{p_i x_i}{c_i^2}\left[1 - \frac{\bar{w}}{x_i}\frac{dx_i}{d\bar{w}} \right] \\
&= \frac{p_i x_i}{c_i^2}\left[1 - \frac{\bar{w}}{x_i}\frac{p_i}{p_j}\frac{\Gamma_j}{\Gamma_i}\frac{dx_j}{d\bar{w}} \right] \\
&\gtreqless 0.
\end{aligned}
\tag{8.48}
$$

The eventual time or goods intensity of an activity, therefore, depends not at all on present time or goods intensity but on its relative goods-absorptive capacity.

Of course, this is appealing – the relative abilities of consumption activities to employ increased goods flows in the production of utility determine the α_i, which in turn determine optimal goods and time allocations. Becker and Linder, in taking α_i as an immutable characteristic of the ith activity, missed the essential part of the process of adjustment to secularly rising wage rates. In attributing to a single technical characteristic of an activity what in fact depends on other technical and utility characteristics, they reached the wrong conclusions; it is impossible either to generalize the role of inherent "time intensity" and "goods intensity" of activities, as did Becker, or to construct a relentless machine of utility maximization that leads to frustration, as did Linder.

The consumption activities that will get increased time and goods with rising incomes are those, quite simply, that we continue to like the most with rising incomes; they are as likely to be currently leisurely and contemplative activities as the harried, frantic ones Linder set out for us. Walking in the woods may be a very time-intensive activity at a low wage rate – an afternoon, adequate shoes, and a bus ticket to the edge of town – yet it becomes a very goods-intensive activity at a high wage rate when the woods are located in the Alps and the hotel bill and air fare from one's empty Los Angeles house are both at peak-season rates. It is clear – contra Linder – that contemplative and leisurely activities need not have large and negative values of Γ_i; they may survive rising incomes handsomely.

The final extension of this analysis deals with income elasticities.

Because both durations and intensities of goods flows are increased for activities with the largest absorptive capacities, the goods they use will be "superior" – expenditures on them will increase more than in proportion to income increases. Activities with small absorptive capacities (large negative Γ_i's) will use inferior goods; expenditure flow increases will be more than offset by reductions in activity duration. The intensity of goods use in consumption activities will never fall with increases in income. But the duration of an activity will increase or decrease depending on its relative absorptive capacity, as shown in (8.47). Intensity and duration, together, determine demand for X_i per unit time T.

The income elasticity of demand for the goods input per T to activity i is

$$\varepsilon_i = \frac{dX_i}{dS} \frac{S}{X_i},$$

or, considering only wage income and constant flow rates for simplicity,

$$\varepsilon_i = \frac{dx_i T_i}{d(\bar{w}T_w)} \frac{\bar{w}T_w}{x_i T_i}$$

$$= \frac{\bar{w}}{T_i} \frac{dT_i}{d\bar{w}} + \frac{\bar{w}}{x_i} \frac{dx_i}{d\bar{w}}. \tag{8.49}$$

So the usual income elasticity over T is the sum of two terms – an elasticity of duration and an elasticity of intensity. Because the income elasticity of duration,

$$\frac{\bar{w}}{T_i} \frac{dT_i}{d\bar{w}} \gtrless 0, \tag{8.50}$$

whereas the income elasticity of intensity,

$$\frac{\bar{w}}{x_i} \frac{dx_i}{d\bar{w}} \geq 0, \tag{8.51}$$

superior goods are those whose strong positive intensity elasticities coincide with a positive duration response, normal goods are those whose intensity elasticity is strong enough to offset any reduction in demand from a negative duration elasticity, and inferior goods are those whose negative duration elasticities dominate. Once again, it is clear that duration and intensity, together, determine goods demand and that the relative absorptive capacity of an activity, by determining the intensity response in (8.47), plays a central role. It should, perhaps, be emphasized that these sources of income elasticities would be supplemented by others if the utility function were differently specified.

8.9   Summary and conclusions

This chapter has developed a simple model of a household's optimal adjustment to an environment of days and nights and winters and summers that continuously alters, over the unit time T, the efficiency of its various consumption activities. Its purposes are two: (a) to derive the optimal timing of consumption and work activities from household utility maximization in order to describe the effects of when things are done during the day (or year) – the time-shape of work and consumption – and (b) to lay out and examine the anatomy of the process of household consumption choice that must implicitly underlie standard household production or "time-allocation" models, even though they deal explicitly only in accumulated summary variables.

The household does things more or less easily at different times in large part because it exists in an environment that is different at different times. At any given moment, the household does some consumption activities better than others. The efficiency with which it does many things changes repetitively, rhythmically over the day with changes in the household's environment: Stores open and close; trains leave; children get home from school and friends from work; the sun comes up, bringing cheap light and the inputs for a suntan. These environmental changes, given endowments, preferences, prices, and production functions, determine the household's utility-maximizing schedule of activities. The particular elements of the environment that are incorporated into this analysis are those entirely repetitive, rhythmic, and hence fully anticipated changes that occur in equilibrium day after day or week after week or year after year. It is, of course, a rhythmic equilibrium because it reflects adjustment to a rhythmic environment. And because that environment is exogenous, the household is linked irrevocably to the real time of the world outside it.

The solution to the model generates an optimal schedule of household activities over the day. Because the only environmental elements considered in this model are repetitive, there is only a single optimal schedule for any one kind of unit time, T. It describes in real clock time when each activity should start, when it should stop, what activities precede and follow it, and the optimal flows of goods and service inputs and intensity with which the activity is done. So all the usual stuff of standard household time-allocation models can be got from this one by throwing away information on the timing and intensity of activities, leaving only summary data on durations and implicit average intensities.

Yet it is just that time-specific information that serves to reveal the process that underlies the summary variables of standard consumption models, the nature of the information their temporal abstraction loses. Examination of the anatomy of conventional consumption analysis was well begun in this chapter. There are important differences between the characteristics of money and labor constraints and their behaviors over the unit time that the full-income constraint, in collapsing them into one, obscures. Furthermore, orthodox models of household time allocation do not describe the allocation of time but, instead, the allocation of a household's fixed endowment of labor services; homogeneous labor services can always be measured in time units, like the constant flow of anything, but that does not make them into time. When labor services are identified as labor services, time can once again be the context within which the consumption process takes place, not a "thing" that is divided up as a factor input to household production. Rescued from mislabeling, time plays the same role in household production that it plays in production by the firm. This rather important mis-specification in the standard analysis explains its simultaneous power and limitations – that it analyzes the allocation of labor, which is something that is both scarce and important to the household, but says nothing about the value of time, except as that time is spent at work earning income; the time-specific representation overcomes that shortcoming.

CHAPTER 9

The anatomy of household activities: goal and process; work and home production; capital and self-control

The last chapter developed a time-specific model of household work and consumption behavior; this one extends and complicates that simple adaptive model. The complications are of two sorts. The first come from a fuller description of the preferences, activities, and inputs that are the building blocks of the simple model. The second arise in considering aspects of household timing that are omitted from that essentially passive description of behavior. Some of these complications are suggested by the model itself and the opportunities that a time-specific analysis gives for a richer description of household behavior; some are suggested by the time-specific analysis of production of Part II and its implications for household production modeling. All of these complications share the common characteristic that their identification is important to a number of aspects of household economic behavior but that they can be seen clearly, if at all, only through the lens of a time-specific analysis.

It is useful to summarize what is to come. The by-now-familiar procedure – by which time-specific analysis breaks down an accumulated flow from standard theory into its components of flow rates and duration – is applied, in Section 9.1, to household preferences. The result is a unique and useful way to distinguish between household satisfactions that come from the doing of an activity and those that come from its having been done. These two quite different sources of satisfaction were implicit in the utility flows of the simple model, as they are in standard utility theory. Much is gained by making them distinct and explicit. The next section employs this distinction in carrying out the promise, implicit in analyzing the value of time spent at work in Chapter 8, explicitly to consider the pleasures or pains of working, along with the recognized pleasures derived from earning an income that buys goods inputs for consumption. A most useful result is to blur even further the arbitrary line between work and consumption activities; here, the same sorts of people can be seen to make the same sorts of decisions on the same sorts of criteria in both their work and consumption activities. In Section 9.3, the richer descriptions of consumption and work

192

activities that come from the first two sections are used to examine the activity characteristics that influence a household's choice to do a consumption activity at home with its own resources or hire it done on the market – the economic determinants of the rise and fall of consumption markets, an economics of do-it-yourself.

The next two sections return to the earlier part of the book to bring a key element from the time-specific analysis of production into the time-specific model of household activity. Section 9.4 reconsiders the nature of the "goods and service inputs," $x_i(t)$, in the household production model – in both time-specific and standard models – in light of the input characteristics first identified in Chapter 3. Especially important is the fact that it matters very much if some of those goods and services are derived from capital owned by the household, because the price of services from owned capital stocks is duration-specific, sensitive to utilization – to activity duration in the household – and that makes it dependent on the household's activity choice. And vice versa. Linder's conclusions about wealthy societies, discussed in the last chapter, are shown in Section 9.5 to be highly sensitive to this more careful, accurate representation of the nature of the goods and services used by households. Veblen fares better under time-specific examination than does Linder.

The last section of this chapter includes two complications that fit into the simple model smoothly – different calendar time units, T, and adjustment costs between activities – and one complication that does not – the effect on the timing of household activities if preference or production efficiency is affected by activity duration. This suggests the value of a time-specific household model for analyzing the conflicts of dynamic utility maximization and time preferences that have long intrigued economists as well as the issues of addiction and self-control that have only recently attracted their analytical attention.

9.1   Process utility and goal utility

Some things are enjoyable to do; some things are enjoyable to have done. This distinction goes back at least to Aristotle's *Nicomachean Ethics* (1973), but it describes a difference among household activities that is not easy to represent in the standard analysis, despite its often central role in household behavior. Pollak and Wachter (1975) searched for the "value of time" implied in the Becker model (when a household chooses to cook its own meals because cooking is fun, but hires someone to clean the house because cleaning is not). Gronau (1977) tried more generally to modify the Becker model so that it could sort out what determines whether a household will produce a consumption commodity at home or hire someone on the market to do it. The fact of different sources of utility is central to these as well as to other important aspects of consumer-demand behavior.

When household behavior is analyzed in specific time, it is natural to make a distinction among utility sources. Define *process utility*, $u(z_i(t))$, as the flow of *satisfactions from doing* activity i at intensity z_i at time t, and define *goal utility*, $u(Z_i)$, as the *satisfaction from having done* activity i (at average intensity z_i for a period T_i). In the vocabulary of the last chapter, process utility is derived from activities, z_i, and goal utility from commodities, Z_i.[1]

Once the distinction between them is established, it can best be blurred in a full-information equilibrium by expressing them in equivalent flow terms: The average flow equivalent of an activity's goal utility, $u(Z_i)$, is simply

$$u(z_i) = u(Z_i)/T_i$$

over the period during which the activity lasts, T_i. This expresses those satisfactions that come only with completion of Z_i of an activity in the flow terms that have been used in the time-specific structure; it does not change the nature of the satisfactions described, but only their representation. And it makes usefully explicit that the utility flow implied by a goal-utility activity depends on how long it takes; *ceteris paribus*, the quicker the better for a goal activity.

Because goal utility can be expressed as a flow equivalent, the two different sources of utility for an activity can be added together to consider more realistic cases of activity preferences that would have something of both – where either or both the doing and the accomplishment of an activity would enter the household's utility function. So, most generally, the rate of total utility flow at t from any activity i done at an intensity z_i for a period T_i is the sum of its process utility and the flow-rate equivalent of its goal utility:

$$u_i(t) = u(z_i(t)) + u(Z_i)/T_i. \tag{9.1}$$

This makes explicit the two sources of utility that were only implicit in the flow utility, $u_i(t)$, of the last chapter.

What is most useful about (9.1) is that it not only identifies two quite different underlying characteristics of preferences and integrates them but also can represent a wide variety of activities with different mixtures of these characteristics. Goal and process utilities can, each of them, be positive, negative, or zero. Thomas Schelling

Table 9.1. *Goal and process utilities*

Process $u(z_i)$	Goal $u(Z_i)$		
	+	0	−
+	+ +	+ 0	+ −
0	0 +	0 0	0 −
−	− +	− 0	− −

ιas written that he runs for physical fitness but does not like running at all; it terms of process and goal, he finds running to be an activity with a negative process utility offset (because he does run) by a sufficiently strong positive goal utility to make its total utility flow (9.1) positive and even make it a preferred activity for some part of the day. The dichotomy of goal and process utilities becomes – with the possibility of utility, disutility, and indifferences for each – a very fruitful way to represent household tastes for consumption activities. And it is fully integrated into the time-specific household model.

Despite the generally chilling effect of taxonomies, the one generated by these possibilities is interesting. It is represented in Table 9.1. Of the nine combinations of characteristics, five are not especially interesting in discussing consumption activities, because they describe activities that are either too good or too bad. The one that gives both positive goal utility and process utility (+ +) lacks character;[2] the one that gives negative goal and process utilities (− −) is wholly offensive. And the four that combine disutility and indifference in various ways would never, with positive prices and no other attributes, be relevant as household consumption activities, although when this analysis is applied to work activities, these possibilities become highly relevant.

But the remaining four are interesting. In Chapter 8, as noted earlier, there was no differentiation between sources of utilities, and because all were represented as flows, they might as well have been pure process utilities (the cell +0) that feel good while being done but for which there is no additional satisfaction at having done them – no pleasure in accomplishment. A pure process activity is highly existential: Absent a thrill of conquest (goal utility), love-making appears usually to have mostly process utility. At the other extreme is a pure goal activity (0+) that is an indifferent experience in the doing, but satisfying to have got done, or to have someone else do for you. All that matters for a pure goal activity is its completion, Z_i.

In the other two types of activities there is an evident conflict; the things that are recommended by goal utilities and by process utilities are not the same. One kind of activity $(-+)$ is no fun at all to do because it has process disutility, but it is satisfying to have done (and have done with) because it has goal utility. This is Schelling's running and Pollak and Wachter's housecleaning, and it is identified by Gronau as the kind of household activity that will induce the formation of external markets that sell substitutes for household production. Although the discussion of Section 9.3 shows that there is more to it than that, such activities do create an incentive for markets to develop, because in this case the household will want both to avoid doing i and to get the pleasures consequent on its having been done. Gronau argued that people surveyed in time-diary studies implicitly identify "home production" – as against "leisure" – by this criterion.

But if negative process utility and positive goal utility tend to induce the formation of markets to replace production by the household, an activity with the opposite characteristics – positive process utility and negative goal utility – creates the need for self-control and perhaps the formation of markets to assist in exercising it (Winston, 1980; Ainslie, 1975; Elster, 1977). These $+-$ activities create temptations in the pleasures of their doing but punishment in their having been done. Even a full-information equilibrium – though it may assure choices that maximize daily utility – often will not remove the conflict that exists when the consumer wants to do what he knows he will regret. Harvey Leibenstein said of television that "the worst thing about it is that it's just interesting enough to keep you watching but not interesting enough that you're glad you did." Watching TV is a $+-$ activity in his preferences. These are matters central to household conflict, self-control, and compulsion in consumption.

So the simple utility function of standard consumption analysis is seen in a time-specific representation to harbor satisfactions of two quite different sorts, process and goal utilities, that will combine in different degrees with different signs in different activities for different households. The resulting characterization of household preferences can be incorporated in the flows of the simple model of the last chapter to yield a complex and realistic description of household preferences over consumption activities. Some implications of this richer conception of preferences are developed in the next two sections. The first expands the earlier time-specific analysis of work activities, and the next examines consumption markets, identifying the characteristics of an activity that determine whether it will be produced at home or purchased on the market.

9.2   Work: money income, job satisfaction, and goods

In the last chapter, the net utility flow from work activity was defined broadly, in (8.28), as

$$\mu_w = u_w + \lambda(\overline{w} - \overline{p}_w x_w(t)).$$

But then, in the interest of both simplicity and orthodoxy, u_w and $x_w(t)$ were promptly assumed to be zero. So, on the one hand, any direct utility from work was assumed away, leaving only the indirect satisfactions of earning money that derive solely from the consumption pleasures it enhances. On the other hand, any goods costs required by work activity were assumed away, leaving all money income available to buy inputs to consumption. It is now useful to incorporate both of these aspects into the analysis: first, the fact that work activity itself – not just its income – affects household utility.

Work has both direct and indirect utility, as in (8.28). In addition, work can be enjoyable or painful to do, and it can bring satisfaction or dissatisfaction in having been done; the flow of direct satisfactions from work, like the direct satisfactions from consumption, can include both process utility, $u(l_w)$, and goal utility, $u(L_w)$. Then the value of time spent working becomes

$$\mu_w = u(l_w) + u(L_w)/T_w + \lambda(\overline{w} - \overline{p}_w x_w(t)). \tag{9.2}$$

I want to retain, but play down, the goal–process distinction in the direct utility of work for now, in order to emphasize the more basic characteristic of work evident in (9.2). It is that the value of time spent working depends in part on the direct utility of working (process), in part on the direct utility of having worked (goal), and in part on indirect utility from the consumption goods that the earnings from work will buy; the value of time spent working is the sum of these. Whereas the indirect consumption satisfactions that money buys will be nonnegative, the direct goal and process satisfactions of work can, either or both of them, take on any value: The household can get disutility or be indifferent or get positive pleasure from either the process or the goal of its employment.

So although the only essential difference between work and consumption activities is that work pays a money wage and consumption does not, it is a difference that is crucial, because that wage gives work indirect utility that can offset any direct disutility, justifying its choice as the preferred activity, even when it is unpleasant. It is not difficult to find examples of unpleasant consumption activities, of course, but if consumption has no source of offsetting indirect utility, such activities will simply be avoided by the people who judge them distasteful.[3] But because the wage yields positive indirect utility, work can represent the best way to spend time, even though it is hard, disagreeable, exhausting, and destructive. Equation (9.2) incorporates separate, explicit "psychic" and money income components, both of which contribute to the incentive to work.

Households behave the same in their activity choices whether they choose consumption activities or work; the same criterion applies to both: Do the thing that maximizes the value of time. All activities have the same essential characteristics, excepting only that work pays a positive wage rate and consumption does not. No arbitrary distinction among activities is necessary.

The second element reintroduced into the analysis of work in this section is the fact that work activity often requires goods inputs, reducing the wage that is available to buy consumption inputs. This is a useful complication that generates no analytical problems. The distinction must be made between a gross wage rate, $\bar{w}_g$, paid by employers and the net wage rate, $\bar{w}$, left to the household after it has paid the costs of those goods inputs to work activity, $\bar{p}_w x_w$. The net wage,

$$\bar{w} = \bar{w}_g - \bar{p}_w x_w, \tag{9.3}$$

is what counts both as the rate of income in the value of time at work and as the opportunity cost of time spent in consumption, c_i. Chapter 10 considers the further refinement that time-sensitive goods inputs often contribute to generating a time-sensitive net wage rate.

So the conclusions of the last chapter on the effects of a change in wage rate persist when goods inputs to work are included, but now that change can come from a change either in the gross wage rate or in the costs of goods inputs: For a given household, an increase in commuting costs, for instance, will have the same effects as a decrease in gross wage of the same magnitude. Between employments, of course, the magnitude of any particular work input change will depend on the relative weight of that input in the goods costs of a particular kind of work – *ceteris paribus*, salesmen who travel by car obviously suffer a greater net wage reduction with an increase in gasoline prices than do college professors who walk to their jobs. Systematic regional differences appear for similar reasons.

Incorporation of direct utility or disutility from work modifies the analysis of Chapter 8 in interesting and not wholly obvious ways. In that analysis, Figure 8.4 described the optimal allocation of house-

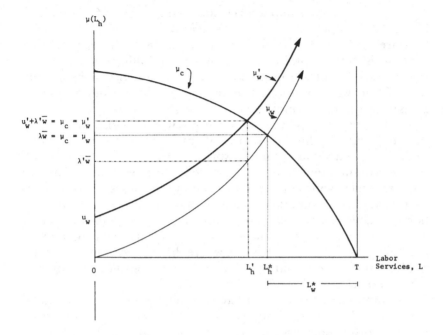

Figure 9.1. Labor allocation when work has positive utility.

hold labor between consumption (in general) and work activities as a function of the values of time in those two activities. As the allocation of labor between them was altered, the value of time in each, μ_c and μ_w, was changed; that labor allocation was optimal when the values of time in both were the same. Departing from an optimal allocation, too much work raised the value of time spent in consumption but reduced the value of time at work: Too much income was concentrated in a too short consumption period, increasing the rate of flow of consumption satisfactions while reducing the marginal utility of income, λ. On the other side of an optimal allocation, too little work reduced the value of time in consumption and increased it in work: Too little income was spread over too long a consumption period, reducing the rate of flow of consumption satisfactions while increasing the marginal utility of income.

That same analysis is useful when work is no longer an indifferent activity but instead carries positive or negative direct utility. Figure 9.1 reproduces the earlier Figure 8.4, including the curves μ_w and μ_c. It shows the optimal allocation of labor with indifferent work, $u_w =$

0, as L_h^* hours in consumption activities and $L_w^* = T - L_h^*$ in market labor. At the optimum, $\mu_w = \mu_c = \lambda\overline{w}$. But if work brings direct pleasures of its own, $u_w' > 0$, then with an unchanged wage rate the curve μ_w is shifted upward by u_w' to μ_w'. The resulting optimal allocation of household labor brings $L_h' < L_h^*$ in consumption activities and $L_w' > L_w^*$ to work; sensibly, it is optimal to allocate more time to pleasant work than to indifferent work at the same wage.

But Figure 9.1 implies more about positive job satisfactions than that. In increasing the allocation of labor to market work in response to the increased value of time at work, $\mu_w' > \mu_w = \mu_c(l_h^*)$, the value of time in consumption must increase, too. More work at a constant wage rate means more income that buys more goods that are used over a shorter consumption period. So the rate of flow of consumption satisfactions increases, and the marginal utility product of goods and the marginal utility of income, λ, fall. The optimal allocation of L_w' of labor to a pleasing job is one where the indirect utility of work, $\lambda\overline{w}$, has fallen to $\lambda'\overline{w}$, and the value of time in consumption, μ_c', has risen, so that $\mu_w' = \mu_c' = u_w' + \lambda'\overline{w}$.

It is interesting, I think, that having a job that brings sheer enjoyment in one's work – without any increase in wage rate, change in preference function, or other changes – generates the symptoms of harriedness that Linder blamed solely on rising wage rates. The results of an enjoyable job are the following: an increased goods intensity of consumption; the need to reallocate time incrementally from less to more goods-absorptive activities; reduction in the total time available for enjoyment of consumption; a decline in the relative value of money income per se. These harried individuals suffer because, damn it, life is too much fun, and they face the constant agony of making choices among highly desirable alternatives. That agony may be real, but it can be expected to engender a lower order of sympathy than that in which Linder clothed his victims. I suspect that the existence of this sort of harriedness is more fundamental in explaining the appeal of Linder's hypothesis to successful, excited, and deeply committed academics and members of the Swedish Parliament than is the real wage effect Linder's analysis relied on.

Quite a different story is described by Figure 9.2, where the same questions are asked concerning those whose jobs bring them direct pain or distaste. The indifferent work equilibrium of Figure 8.4 is again pictured for reference as $\mu_c = \mu_w = \lambda\overline{w}$ and L_h^*. The value of time in work when work is painful is represented by the curve μ_w'', which is shifted downward from μ_w by the direct disutility of work, $u_w'' < 0$. The predictable reduction in the optimal allocation of labor

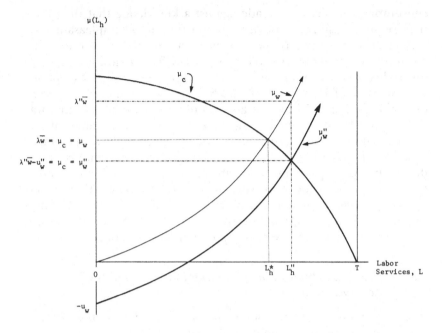

Figure 9.2. Labor allocation when work has negative utility.

to work and consequent increase in time spent in home consumption is indicated by L_w''. Compared with an indifferent job, unpleasant work reduces the optimal allocation to work and increases consumption time until the consequently reduced income is spread so thinly over the consequently extended consumption period that the value of time in consumption, μ_c, falls to equality with the now-low value of time in work, μ_w''. The marginal utility of income, λ, must be driven high enough, λ'', by this reduced market labor to offset the disutility inherent in its acquisition.

Unpleasant work leads to too much time in consumption – the antithesis of harriedness, a desultory search for something to do – and a reallocation of time away from activities with high goods requirements and toward those that retain their pleasures relatively best as goods are withdrawn and time is substituted for them. It is interesting, I think, that with nothing changed but direct work satisfaction, optimizing behavior changes the same household from harried suburbanite right out of Linder to a lazy, indolent loafer, searching out simple, time-intensive pleasures like fishing, aware that a penny saved is a bit of unpleasant work avoided.[4] With distasteful work, consumption choices are made against a knowledge that the goods they require require, in turn, spending time in an unpleasant way.

A clear implication is that too little attention may routinely be given in economic analysis to direct job satisfaction and too much to the indirect satisfactions of income, despite occasional exceptions like the work of Hirsch (1976) and Sen (1975). An important recent exception is Tibor Scitovsky's analysis of work satisfactions that was derived not from economics but from a careful examination of evidence from modern physiological psychology and the development of its economic implications. He presented persuasive empirical evidence – based in part on Michigan Survey Research Center data – that people who enjoy their work also work long hours, that L_w^* and u_w are positively related (Scitovsky, 1976, pp. 90–100). He also found – in further support of the preceding analysis – that those who enjoy their jobs more also enjoy their leisure more.

9.3   Home production or the market: an economics of do-it-yourself

What is it about a consumption commodity that determines whether it will be produced at home by the household or will induce the development of a market where it can be produced commercially? Two of the most pointed criticisms of standard household production analysis held that that analysis is inadequate to illuminate this central question. I noted earlier that in trying to sort out the value of time to the household, Pollak and Wachter contrasted an activity the household would want to do itself with another activity that it wants to hire someone else to do – that contrast motivated the process-utility/goal-utility distinction developed earlier. Later, Gronau devised a simple theory of the choice between home production and market purchase in order to make sense out of empirical time-diary studies that defied explanation in the standard time-allocation model. In this section, the time-specific household model – with the additions developed in the last two sections – will be shown to imply a rich and highly suggestive model of the activity characteristics that determine that choice. The choice itself is implicit in the structure of the model of Chapter 8. Once again, this neoclassical time-specific household model carries the same implications – despite its stodgy and developed orthodoxy – that Scitovsky got from the very different tradition of physiological psychology; this complementarity, I think, lends strength and plausibility to both.

This question of home or market production is not, it should be said, a mildly entertaining bit of economic trivia that deals with weekend carpenters, amateur auto mechanics, and homemade jam. It is an issue that is quite central to economic theory and economic history; it deals with why consumption goods and service markets develop and why they change. It seeks to identify the characteristics of household consumption activities that induce the formation of markets and those that discourage it and to describe the way those activity characteristics shape the household's response to changing level, composition, and distribution of income, to both home and commercial production technologies, to job satisfaction, and to changing tastes.[5] Obviously, a full-blown theory of market formation is a good deal more than I can develop here, but its structure follows quite naturally from what has already been done; so much can be done even without extensive further development.

To keep things simple, it is useful to focus on a household consumption activity, i, that is the preferred activity over a period T_i on the basis of the usual criterion that μ_i is greater then than any other μ. So there is no question about whether or not i should be done during T_i, but only by whom and how. And we ignore specific time of day, for now, to deal only with duration. The alternatives to be considered are (a) home production of i or (b) hiring someone, an "outsider," to do it for the household, that is, buying T_i of z_i, hence Z_i, on the market. Assume, like Becker, fixed production coefficients; so Z_i fixes T_i, X_i, and x_i.

If the household does i itself, the value of its time during T_i will be

$$\mu_i = u_i - \lambda \bar{p}_i x_i$$
$$= u(z_i) + u(Z_i)/T_i - \lambda \bar{p}_i x_i, \tag{9.4}$$

recognizing process and goal sources of utility.

If, on the other hand, the household hires an outsider to do i, then the value of its time during T_i will be

$$\mu_{mi} = u_w + u(Z_i)/T_i - \lambda(\bar{p}_{mi} x_{mi}^e + \bar{p}_{li}^e - \bar{w}). \tag{9.5}$$

This needs some explaining. First, (9.5) shows the net utility flow to the household if it hires someone else to do activity i and spends T_i at work instead. The only comparison we will consider is between the household's doing i itself, on the one hand, or working while someone else does i, on the other. Either way, the household gets its Z_i at the end of T_i, and either way, the whole production of Z_i costs the household L_i of its labor.[6]

Second, it is important that the time period that is relevant to the household's choice between buying i and doing-it-yourself is the household's own time, T_i, that Z_i would take if it were done at home. It does not matter how much or how little time the hired outsider takes to do i (assuming always that the quality of Z_i is the same); all that matters is its provision and its costs to the household. So (9.5) includes the following variations on previously defined variables:

$\bar{p}_{mi}$: the prices of goods and nonlabor service inputs used by the outsider to produce Z_i; they may be greater or less than the prices, $\bar{p}_i$, that the household pays.

x^e_{mi}: the effective goods and nonlabor input flows used by the outsider to make Z_i; it is not the actual time rate of flow of inputs – because the actual duration of the hired production process is irrelevant to the household – but simply X_{mi}, the total goods and nonlabor services used by the outsider in producing Z_i, divided by the time, T_i, it would take the household to produce Z_i itself: $x^e_{mi} = X_{mi}/T_i$.

$\bar{p}^e_{li}$: the effective price of the hired labor services of the outsider comparable to the household's wage rate; again, if the actual wage paid to the outsider is $\bar{p}_{li}$ and it takes him T_{li} to do the job, Z_i, then the outsider's effective wage rate is $\bar{p}^e_{li} = \bar{p}_{li}T_{li}/T_i$, because that is what is relevant to the household's choice.

Now the criterion familiar from the last chapter can identify the characteristics of consumption activities that determine whether they will be produced at home or purchased. That choice depends, simply, on whether the household's time is better spent doing i or working while hiring on the market someone else to do i. So the criterion for optimally doing-it-yourself is $\mu_i > \mu_{mi}$, and the household will maximize utility by producing i at home only if, combining (9.4) and (9.5) and rearranging,

$$[u(z_i) - u_w] - \lambda(\bar{p}_i x_i - \bar{p}_{mi} x^e_{mi}) > \lambda(\bar{w} - \bar{p}^e_{li}). \tag{9.6}$$

This nicely structures the essential elements of the decision between home production and purchase. The first term in (9.6) describes the pleasures of doing i relative to working – the greater the joys of i or the less enjoyable is work, the more likely it is that i will be done at home. The second term describes the relative costs of goods and service inputs needed by the do-it-yourselfer and the outsider – the greater the cost saving from doing-it-yourself (the less the cost penalty), the more likely it is that that will be the best way for the household to spend its time. Finally, the right-hand side describes the cost of hiring the outsider relative to what the household can earn – the greater the outsider's effective wage relative to the household's, the more likely it is that it will pay the household to produce i itself.

It is worth special note, I think, that in the choice between do-it-yourself and buying i on the market, the total satisfactions of activity i are irrelevant. All that matters is its process satisfaction, the pleasure or displeasure of doing i. This is so because the goal satisfactions of Z_i are the same whether it is bought or done; so they cancel out of the comparison (9.6). You may, for instance, desperately want a reliable and smoothly functioning automobile, but that has nothing to do with whether you fix it yourself or take it to a garage.[7]

Not only are the quite different reasons for a household to choose to produce i at home made explicit in (9.6), but also it shows that the particular mix of those motivations that brings an activity into home production importantly shapes the household's response to changes in income or wage rates or other parameters.

Gronau's model showed that any rise in unearned income, Y_p, would induce less home production. But this conclusion can be seen to rest crucially on why an activity is done at home in the first place. If the reason is that the cost savings of its home production are so large that they offset a distaste for doing i, then higher income does reduce home production. But an increment in unearned income can affect (9.6) only by reducing the marginal utility of income, λ. Rearranging (9.6),

$$\frac{1}{\lambda}[u(z_i) - u_w] - (\bar{p}_i x_i - \bar{p}_{mi} x^e_{mi}) > (\bar{w} - \bar{p}^e_{li}). \tag{9.7}$$

If unearned income is to have any effect, it must depend on the existence of different preferences for work and doing activity i. If i is done at home only because it is cheaper – it is neither more nor less satisfying than working – then Y_p is simply irrelevant. If the household is indifferent between doing i and working and it finds home production of i more economical at low levels of unearned income, it will find home production more economical at high levels of unearned income, too. So Gronau's conclusions can be turned around: Equation (9.7) shows that if i is not done at home, despite the fact that it is more fun than working, then an increase in Y_p will increase, not decrease, its home production – it is not the poor who hand-loom their own fabrics or develop their own photographic film. So persuasive though Gronau's theory is for cleaning bathrooms, it is surely too narrow a view to describe home production and the economic determinants of consumption markets.

Equation (9.6) reflects the influence on the location of production –

in home or market – of a quite wide range of household economic circumstances. A *rise in general wage rates* will affect household and outsider wage rates, $\bar{w}$ and p_{li}, proportionately, but will lower the marginal utility of money, λ, making direct preferences relatively more important in the household's production decisions and goods cost differentials relatively less: With increasing incomes, pleasant activities will move into home production and unpleasant activities into the market. A *change in the composition of household income* through unearned income, Y_p, will generate the preference-sensitive response described earlier. A *change in income distribution* that reduces wage differentials between employing households and hired workers, $\bar{w}$ and $\bar{p}_{li}$, will encourage home production – as has been lamented at many Scarsdale dinner parties of the past three decades and in Gronau's comparisons of U.S. and Israeli employment of maids. A *change in production technology* that increases the relative efficiency of commercial (home) production will reduce (increase) the relative goods and/or labor costs of market production, reducing the amount of home (market) production. The *development of market institutions*, such as consumer-equipment rental firms that provide households with task-specialized capital equipment, will have similar effects, because they make available to households goods and (especially) services at prices closer to those paid by the outsider.[8] Finally, the *relative direct utilities of household production and work* enter in the obvious way: The increasing popularity of chopping wood or gourmet cooking will increase home production, whereas an increase in the enjoyment of work – for instance, by women – will reduce it, even with no change in the wage rates.

Each of these issues deserves a much fuller treatment; none will get it here.

9.4   Household capital and the economics of utilization

It was, of course, of central importance to the analysis of production in Part II that not all goods and services are the same, that they differ in their economic characteristics, with important effects on economic efficiency. This fact is of considerable importance, too, for optimal household activity choice and timing. The only kind of nonlabor input considered in the household production analysis in Chapter 8 was a storable good, like a six-pack of beer or a pound of flour, that could be used by the household at the same time-invariant price, $\bar{p}_i$, at any time of day. So the characterization of purchased goods inputs there departed from that of orthodox household production models only (if importantly) in their being described as time-specific, with explicit rates of flow and durations. But whereas it is typical in household production theory to consider only that one sort of goods input, this is at sharp variance with the basic time-specific analysis of production developed in the early chapters of this study, where different input characteristics were shown to generate different *price* behaviors that significantly influence optimal choice. So what was essential to the time-specific analysis of Part II has disappeared entirely in Part IV. It is time to remedy that.

The relevant economic characteristics of goods and service inputs are, in one dimension, whether they are storable ("goods") or perishable ("services") and, if they are services, whether the household or an outside agent owns the sources from which those services come.[9] Together, these delineate three distinct kinds of what are imprecisely called "goods and service inputs to household production, x_i." They are the following:

1. *Purchased goods, x_i:* storable inputs like ground coffee and gasoline and laundry soap that are purchased by the household and held at negligible cost until they are used. Their price to the household, $\bar{p}_i$, is time-invariant; they are temporally footloose. These have been assumed until now to be representative of all household goods and service inputs.

2. *Purchased services, x_{si}:* perishable inputs like electricity, long-distance telephone service, lawn-mowing services, or taxis that are purchased by the household as a service, per se. Because they cannot be stored at low cost, they are bought when they are used. Their prices can therefore be time-sensitive, $p_i(t)$, and often are; electric power and long-distance telephone calls often are peak-load-priced, as are the services of rental cars on weekends and Vermont ski cabins in January.

3. Owned capital services, x_{ki}: input services from the refrigerator or house or automobile or camera owned by the household. The prices of capital services in the household, like those in the firm, depend inversely on capital utilization, on the duration of the household activities in which those capital services are used.

The first of these has been considered extensively, if implicitly, in the last chapter and in this one. The second is no different from the first unless prices are time-sensitive, and even that adds little to our previous analyses of time-specific costs, because, in general, what was said about the flow rate of costs when input flow rates are time-specific, $c_i(t) = p_i x_i(t)$, also applies to the flow rate of costs when prices, too, are time-specific, $c_i(t) = p_i(t)x_i(t)$. In the next chapter, more will be said about the determinants of time-sensitive input prices. So this section examines the significance of the third kind of input – services from household capital whose prices are duration-specific.

Owned capital services used in household production are, of course, different from other household inputs because their prices are duration-specific but they are not time-specific: Household capital service prices depend on the duration of the activity i in which they are used, T_i, but not on when it is done, t_i. Both of these characteristics affect the demand for household capital.

The price of a unit of capital service flow, x_{ki}, from a household-owned capital stock used in the production of activity i is, by the obvious adaptation of (3.12) from the analysis of production,

$$p_{ki} = p_{ki}(P_{ki}, T_i) = P_{ki}/T_i, \qquad (9.8)$$

where the cost of owning a unit of the capital stock $\bar{K}_i$ for calendar period T is, again from (3.11),

$$P_{ki} = \bar{P}_{mi}(r_T + \delta_T).$$

This owner cost per T (or rental rate) of a unit of capital stock depends on its purchase price per unit, $\bar{P}_{mi}$, and the interest, r_T, and depreciation, δ_T, rates per calendar period T.

With a yearly owner cost of $1,000, one hour of capital services from the family car will cost $2.75 if the car is used for an hour each day, but more than $83.00 if the car is instead used only an hour each month. A $75,000 summer house used for two weeks of the year costs over $530 per day (if real interest and depreciation add up to 10% per year); used all year round, it will cost $21 per day. Without multiplying examples, it is evident that the potential effect the household's capital utilization has on the price of its capital services is not trivial. And, in fact, households often leave expensive capital stocks – cameras, seasonal sporting equipment, specialized tools, etc. – idle for months and years on end. Aside from housing capital, the variability of utilization of households' capital stocks would surely seem greater than that of producers' capital, if only because of greater specialization of functions by firms.

So if household activity i uses capital service inputs, the longer is its duration T_i per unit time T, the lower is the price of its capital services. A number of implications follow from this quite fundamental time-specific fact.

First, capital that is versatile enough to provide service inputs to a number of household activities will carry a lower capital service price in each of them, because the utilization rate that determines prices is the sum of durations of the activities in which it is used,

$$p_{kj} = P_{kj}/\sum_{j=1}^{n} T_j, = 1, \ldots, n. \tag{9.9}$$

So the cost of housing services is typically quite low because housing services are used as an input to the production of so many household activities. Highly specialized capital, in contrast, may be cheap to own, yet yield only very high-priced services. With the same sort of calculation as before, when it is used as a full-time residence, the hourly cost of the services of that $75,000 house is a bit less than a dollar, whereas the hourly cost of services from a $30 electric drill that is used once a year for an hour comes to $3.00.

Second, anything that affects the length of time the household spends in a capital-using activity will affect the price it pays for those capital services. So the utilization effect on capital service prices amplifies any differences between households due to preferences, environment, or knowledge of household technology. For activities that include owned capital services as inputs, observed differences in consumption behavior will be the result both of underlying preference or environmental or technological differences and of the capital price effect (or "utilization effect") that amplifies them. Passions affect prices, and so do environmental differences and knowledge of consumption technology. An enthusiastic amateur potter pays less to use his expensive kiln than does a more disinterested hobbyist; the prices of capital services from a boat or a motorcycle are lower in Florida than in Massachusetts, but the prices of ski services are greater.[10] This capital price effect will amplify differences most strongly for the most capital-intensive activities, defined by

$$\kappa_i = \frac{p_{ki}x_{ki}}{c_i(t)}. \tag{9.10}$$

The pure role of preferences in explaining differences in observed household purchases, which is already sharply curtailed by household production analysis, is further reduced for both household capital and complementary inputs by recognition of amplification from the capital price or utilization effect.

Third, whether or not a household should purchase a particular household capital good – the demand for household capital – also involves the relationship between capital service price and activity duration. Ownership of a piece of household capital, *ceteris paribus*, will always increase the allocation of time to the activities that use that capital. The cost of the flow of services, x_{ki}, from owned capital is zero on the duration margin, T_i (neglecting use-depreciation); so in

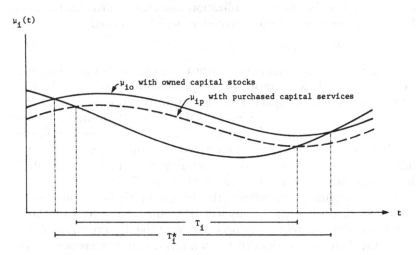

Figure 9.3. Activity duration with owned or purchased household capital services.

an optimal schedule, the duration of activity i must be extended until increases in other, noncapital costs or the increasing μ_j of the next activity make it optimal to switch; the resulting optimal duration, T_i^*, will always be greater if the capital stock is owned than if identical capital services had been bought on the market at the same average price.[11] The effect of ownership on the optimal amount of time spent doing activity i will be greater the greater is its capital intensity, κ_i.[12] In Figure 9.3, a portion of the graph of changing activity time values over the day – that was introduced in Chapter 8 – is used to illustrate the difference in the value of time in activity i according to whether it uses purchased capital services, μ_{ip}, or those from its own capital stock, μ_{io}.

Timing is often important in the markets where capital services are traded, and timing will influence purchase incentives. Unless the household absorbs the costs of variable utilization – as it does with yearly leases of houses or cars – the prices of purchased capital services are likely to be time-sensitive, because many of the households in a market experience the same rhythmic environment and respond in much the same ways. So demands for capital services are frequently rhythmic, and rhythmic price patterns emerge, forcing the household to pay more for capital services just when it wants them the most. That combination of shared environmental rhythms and shared responses induces time-sensitive prices for the purchase of a

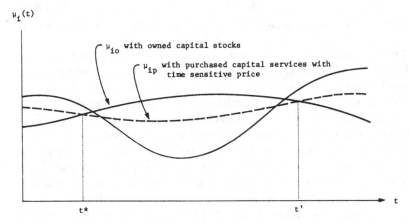

$\mu_i(t)$

μ_{io} with owned capital stocks

μ_{ip} with purchased capital services with time sensitive price

t*

t'

t

Figure 9.4. Time-sensitive purchased capital services versus owned household capital stocks.

host of capital services from hotel rooms to airline tickets to vacation cottages and motion-picture seats. If prices are time-invariant, time-specific quantity rationing – queuing – often takes its place.

Faced with time-sensitive prices for purchased capital services, it becomes important to the household that the prices of its owned capital services are not sensitive to time of day. Use of services from owned capital can be shifted about in the day to produce the activity in which they are used at the most effective time; owned capital services are temporally footloose, like storable goods inputs and un-like household labor and purchased capital services, with their po-tentially time-sensitive prices.

So, in making its decision to buy capital stocks, a household must compare the time-specific price of purchased services with a time-invariant (but duration-specific) price of services from its own capital stocks *during the period of optimal production of that activity.* The fact that purchased services may be available at other times at lower prices is simply irrelevant. Owning its own capital allows the house-hold not only to get x_{ki} of services for T_i of the day but also to get those services during the most effective T_i hours. This "convenience factor" is often attributed vaguely to additional utility, but it is clear that it is simply a matter of productive efficiency – the services of a car on the weekend at reduced rates do not substitute for the ser-vices of a car to get the children to school on time on Tuesday morning. In Figure 9.4, buying the capital services to produce i is shown to be cheaper than getting them from owned capital stocks, both before t^* and after t'. But because that is not a time when time is best spent doing activity i, ownership remains the cheaper way to produce i when it matters, roughly between t^* and t'.

Finally, two related matters involve household purchases of capital services in much these same ways, but they affect capital that is owned outside the household rather than within it. Both are the result of the diversity of activities undertaken by households, as compared with the relative specialization of activities in firms. One concerns the capital equipment rental market noted earlier in discussion of households' decisions to produce an activity at home or purchase it on the market. Household-equipment rental firms make a specialized capital stock available – from punch bowls and party tables to carpet cleaners, trailers, and axle pullers – that, although it increases home productivity mightily, is so rarely needed that its capital service price would be very high if it were owned by an individual household. By renting such equipment to a number of households, these firms increase its utilization and thereby lower the price of its capital services. Each user shares in those price reductions made possible by them all.[13] The second, a related aspect, suggests that the outsider discussed earlier who provides marketed services to the household that substitute for home production is often little more than an itinerant capitalist in the most literal sense whose main economic function is like that of the rental firms, to buy expensive and specialized capital equipment that is then made available to the household at lower capital service prices that reflect the economies of utilization that such "professional" specialization allows. The labor component of such services may be negligible, but the cost savings to the household through increased capital utilization are very real.

9.5   Rising incomes, household capital, and the logic of the Linder hypothesis

Increasing incomes – through higher wage rates or unearned incomes – lead to an increased goods intensity of consumption activities. This is the standard result of standard Becker time-allocation analysis and also – though with the important qualifications of Chapter 8 – of the time-specific model. It was the source of Linder's concern that rich societies become increasingly harried as they use abundant goods inputs to save scarce time.

But with the identification of important differences in the types of goods inputs used in household production, even this limited result can be seen to be correct only if goods prices, p_i, are exogenous to households. Once households have some control over the prices they pay for goods inputs, what must increase with increasing incomes is the value of goods inputs, $p_i x_i$, in the simplest case, and not necessarily their quantities, x_i. The "goods inputs" of the Becker-Linder argument must, of course, include as an essential component the inputs of services from households' own capital stocks.

Then an important source of increased value of goods inputs to household production with increasing incomes is, simply, the rising capital service prices that come from owning capital goods that are utilized on the average less of the time. The household's consequent measure of discretion over goods input prices is, not recognized in conventional theory; yet precisely through that control the household can increase the value of goods inputs to its consumption activities without effort or end simply by increasing its stock of household capital while reducing its utilization. There is persuasive evidence that that is precisely what has happened in wealthy societies.

This appears devastating to the logic of Linder's hypothesis that the need to absorb increasing quantities of goods must lead to ever more frantic consumption activity. In concentrating on "goods" inputs, per se, he conjured up the persuasive picture of a consumer who, if he is to obey the utilitarian imperative of increasing goods relative to time inputs, confronts an ever greater flow of things that he must do something with. That is surely an unnerving prospect. Small wonder Linder was able to convey so clear a sense of horror — with increasing income, the consumer becomes a Sorcerer's Apprentice who must try as he will to get rid of that incessantly increasing flow of things. He is inundated by the logic of his own optimal consumption. Implicit was Linder's assumption that to use goods must take time — he neglected the truly leisurely use of goods that derives from their idleness.

When we see that "goods inputs" include, along with those purchased things, services from the household's own capital stocks, and when it is seen that the price of those capital services depends on utilization, then a very different picture of the affluent consumer emerges — one much more familiar both to us and to Veblen.

Rather than Linder's harried victim, the utilization effect on capital prices takes the analysis back to Veblen's man of leisure (1953). With capital services as important goods inputs, we see the wealthy consumer as he sips his imported beer from a rarely used crystal pilsner glass while sitting on the porch of the Lyford Quay house in which he spends one week a year, trying to decide whether to go scuba diving (using the new equipment in his closet) or take a nap on the cabin cruiser lying at anchor in the bay or give it all up and head back to New York and his empty apartment in time for a weekend of gourmet cooking, the opera, and perhaps even making leisurely love with his beautiful Swedish wife in the expensively decorated spare room.

So long as households can increase the value of goods inputs used in their consumption activities by accumulating rarely used household capital stocks, there need be nothing frantic about their consumption activities with rising incomes. Indeed, the existence of household capital services and the nature of their pricing turn Linder's argument on its head. It is the relaxed, leisurely, and hedonistic consumer, unmoved by any of Linder's Puritan compulsion to use his accumulated stock of household capital, who (*ceteris paribus*) will achieve the greatest value of goods flow in consumption.

9.6   Adjustment costs, duration, and timing

This final section expands on the time-specific household analysis by introducing three sorts of useful complications: consideration of different calendar time periods, T; the possibility of adjustment costs in switching between activities; the effects on utility and on productive efficiency of how long an activity has lasted and how long since it last was done. The first two of these fit neatly into the simple model. The last takes the time-specific analysis beyond the simplest passive-adaptive behavior considered up until now to suggest the sort of internal dynamics of household consumption behavior considered by Strotz (1955–6) in his important paper on dynamic utility maximization. This has long been of explicit concern to empirical psychologists, whose findings have recently been introduced to economists through the pioneering work of Tibor Scitovsky (1976).

These latter extensions of the analysis are not fully developed. They are included both because they link the time-specific model to issues of conflict and self-control that are of recent concern and because they help to define the boundaries of applicability of the simple adaptive model; like any theory, this one is more useful the more clarity there is about what it does and what it does not do. It does describe optimal adjustment to a rhythmically changing exogenous environment; it does not describe a richly complex dynamic of internal response.

The year and other time units, T

Whereas the exposition of the household model has, with only occasional lapses, represented the calendar time unit, T, as the 24-hour day, it is obvious that the model also works when T is a week or a year. To change the calendar time unit, it is necessary only to respecify appropriately the elements of the rhythmic environment to which the household activities optimally adapt – whether they consist of daily light and dark periods or weekly church and work events or seasonal blizzards and picnics. Nor is there any reason why only a single calendar time unit should be considered; day–night environmental changes can be nested within weekly changes that are set, in turn, in a yearly context of seasonal change.

The only significant analytical difference among time periods – from the day to the year – is the burden each puts on the model's assumption that the household adjusts to a full-information equilibrium. One of the considerable strengths of the model when applied to daily rhythms is that it represents those aspects of economic behavior that, because they are frequently repeated, can reasonably be modeled in full-information equilibrium. This key role of repetitive behavior is extended in Chapter 12 to become an important aspect of neoclassical analysis. But as the analytical calendar time unit becomes longer, the assumption of full information becomes increasingly tenuous. Only the more obtrusive seasonal rhythms, for instance, are certain to be remembered from one year to the next; so potentially optimal adjustments to yearly change may well be missed simply because each year there remains something for the household to learn (remember) about the way its preferences and production opportunities fit with the seasonally changing environment the last time around. But despite the likelihood that the household may forget from one year to the next when to dig up the tulip bulbs – greater than the likelihood that it will forget from one day to the next when to leave home to get to work on time – a cautious extension of the calendar time unit seems entirely permissible and fruitful.

Adjustment costs of changing activities

The second tractable complication recognizes that often there are adjustment costs in switching activities. These have appeared frequently in models of joint production – as "interruption costs" in an early version of the optimal shift-working model of Part II (Winston, 1974a), as "switching costs" in Ferguson's joint production model

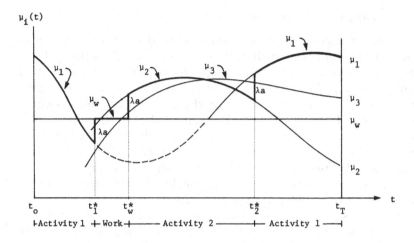

Figure 9.5. Adjustment costs of switching activities.

(1969), and most recently in Peter Lloyd's model (1980) of "length of the production run." Costs incurred in changing activities can be incorporated into the model most simply by altering the optimal switching criterion (8.24) to include a fixed element, λa, representing the value of the flow of money costs of changing activities. It shows up as a discontinuity in the graph (Figure 9.5) of net utility flows over the day. With adjustment costs of a, μ_j must exceed μ_i by λa in order to induce switching from i to j.

A more precise use of the time-specific representation might differentiate adjustment costs by activity pairs and direction of switch – so a_{ij} could describe the cost of switching from i to j, with $a_{in} \neq a_{ij} \neq a_{ji}$. It would also make the flow equivalent of a lump-sum adjustment cost, a_{ij}, depend on the duration of the next activity. Any such adjustment cost Δ_{ij}, is less of a deterrent to switching to j the longer j will last: $a_{ij} = \Delta_{ij}/T_j$. With any adjustment costs, a desirable activity like Activity 3 in Figure 9.5 may never be done, because even though it represents the best way to spend time during part of the day, it is too expensive to get to. Careful specification of these costs and their behavior would be essential to analyses of commuting costs or discretionary work timing or, especially, sex-role differentiation within households. It would be necessary, too, to include time costs of adjustment. The money and time costs of activity switching sharply restrict the things a mother of young children can do with her "spare" time and significantly affect the way she spends her time.

Durations

A more drastic amendment of the simple adaptive model is implicit in the fact that both preferences for and production efficiency of a household activity may be influenced by how long it has been going on and by the length of time since the activity was last done. It has been assumed that both production and utility functions were invariant with respect to time per se – that z_i responded only to changes in the exogenous environment, whereas u_i responded, in turn, only to z_i. A more realistic modeling of household activity choice and timing would have to deal with activities for which the flow of enjoyment and the efficiency of production were influenced by how long the activity had been going on or how long since it was last done or both. Most physiological satisfactions are affected by these durations. Love-making is not the only obvious case where the pleasure of a household activity is predictably influenced by how long it has been going on, and the flow of satisfactions anticipated in starting it again is predictably affected by how long it has been since it last was done.

Scitovsky (1976) examined a rich – and, to economists, largely alien – empirical literature in physiological psychology for insights into consumption behavior and incorporated them in his *The Joyless Economy*. The evidence from those empirical studies indicates that much of consumption behavior is affected by timing and duration, and Scitovsky presented evidence that a regular pattern of increase, climax, and decline in enjoyment is typical of many activities.

It is unnecessary (and unwise) to reject Pollak's warning (1978) that making nice separations of unobservable utility functions from unobservable household production functions often may be an unproductive exercise, but it is useful, I think, to see the implications of the changes in utility and household production functions that these considerations introduce. The original flow utility function (8.3) would be respecified as

$$u(t) = u_i(z_i(t), t - t_{i-1}), \quad \text{for } t_{i-1} < t < t_i, \tag{9.11}$$

to reflect the effect on satisfaction at time t of the time since activity i was started, $t - t_{i-1}$, and

$$u(t) = u_i(z_i(t), t - t_i), \quad \text{for } t_i < t < t_{i-1}, \tag{9.12}$$

to describe the effect of the period since i was last done, $t - t_i$. The original instantaneous production function (8.2) would similarly become

$$z_i(t) = z_i(x_i(t), t - t_{i-1}; t), \quad \text{for } t_{i-1} < t < t_i, \tag{9.13}$$

while i is being done and

$$z_i(t) = z_i(x_i(t), t - t_i; t), \quad \text{for } t_i < t < t_{i-1}, \tag{9.14}$$

while it is not.

Then, in place of the assumptions that the utility function was unaffected by time and that changes in production efficiency were due only to exogenous environmental changes, the responses of these four functions to the two sorts of duration effects would represent:

excitement $\qquad\qquad\qquad \partial u_i(t)/\partial(t - t_{i-1}) > 0$

boredom $\qquad\qquad\qquad\quad \partial u_i(t)/\partial(t - t_{i-1}) < 0$ $\qquad$ for $t_{i-1} < t < t_i$

hunger or appealing novelty $\quad \partial u_i(t)/\partial(t - t_i) \quad > 0$

forgotten pleasures $\qquad\qquad \partial u_i(t)/\partial(t - t_i) \quad < 0$ $\qquad$ for $t_i < t < t_{i-1}$

warming up $\qquad\qquad\qquad \partial z_i(t)/\partial(t - t_{i-1}) > 0$

fatigue $\qquad\qquad\qquad\qquad \partial z_i(t)/\partial(t - t_{i-1}) < 0$ $\qquad$ for $t_{i-1} < t < t_i$

rest and rejuvenation $\qquad\quad \partial z_i(t)/\partial(t - t_i) \quad > 0$

atrophy of skills from disuse $\;\; \partial z_i(t)/\partial(t - t_i) \quad < 0$ $\qquad$ for $t_i < t < t_{i-1}$

Duration effects and optimal activity timing

An important implication of all this for the present analysis is that if these durations affect productive efficiency of an activity or its enjoyment, then they will also affect the optimal timing of activities. To the extent that duration matters to an activity's production and utility, the household's optimal schedule will no longer be simply a matter of passively adapting the timing of its consumption activities to the exogenous rhythmic changes in environment. When efficiency or enjoyment is also affected by the activity's duration, the simple hedonistic choice rule, "Do whatever has the highest μ_i" will no longer necessarily maximize daily utility. The changing environment alters the conditions of production over the day, but the duration of an activity also alters its production or enjoyment. So it is not always optimal for the household to start doing something, i, as soon as it becomes the most valuable way to spend time. The enjoyment of i may last only for a limited time; so it may be best to schedule it when it is most efficiently done, not when it is first efficiently done. Scitovsky's (approving) illustration was (European) children who learn not to eat sandwiches or croissants at 5:00 p.m., even though that is the most satisfying thing to do then; to do so will reduce the satisfactions to be got from the well-prepared dinner served at 7:00 p.m. In

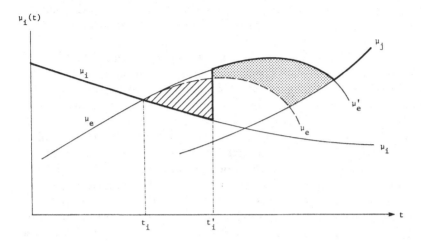

Figure 9.6. Delayed gratification, conflict, and self-control: the timing of a duration-sensitive activity.

psychology and philosophy, this is posed as a question of delayed gratification (Mischel, 1974; Maital, 1978) or willpower and self-control (Elster, 1977; Ainslie, 1975).

The graph of net utility flows again proves useful, this time in describing delayed gratification, the incentives to self-control, and the need for it, all at once. It is clear in Figure 9.6 why duration complicates the simple optimal adaptive activity schedule pictured earlier. It shows three consumption activities available to an individual. All of these, i, j, and e, are affected by changes in the external environment. But the value of time in activity e (say, eating) is affected, too, by its duration. So at whatever time it starts, the subsequent patterns of rise and fall of μ_e will be the same. But e is more efficiently produced at different times of day. In these circumstances, the household's previously simple choice is complicated. Before t_i, activity i is clearly the best thing to do. At t_i, eating, e, becomes the most valuable way to spend time. But if the individual responds to that incentive and starts to eat at t_i, he will follow the dash-line net utility curve, μ_e. Alternatively, he can continue to do i even after t_i, despite the fact that $\mu_e > \mu_i$. If he does, the potential efficiency or enjoyment of e will increase with the changing environment. If he waits and switches to e only at t_i', he will then follow the higher μ_e' curve. To make this more concrete, say that the consumer can eat, e, alone at t_i, or wait until t_i', when there will be the greater pleasure μ_e'

of eating with convivial company. If he waits until t_i', he will maximize daily utility; if he eats at t_i, he will maximize immediate net utility flow.

The increase in daily utility from delaying e until t_i' is evident in Figure 9.6 in the relative positions of curves μ_e and μ_e'. So is the conflict the individual suffers during the period from t_i to t_i' while he continues to do activity i, even though the flow of satisfaction is greater in doing e. This is the conflict in preferences essential to all models of self-control, from the classic analysis of dynamic utility maximization by Strotz onward (Winston, 1979a). The solution Strotz proposed in that early article also appears in Figure 9.6 – it was to internalize the "long-run" or daily utility-maximizing behavior through repeated experience so that the curve μ_e would simply progressively deform until it conveniently followed the solid-line optimal path to μ_e', including coincidence with μ_i over t_i to t_i' and the discontinuity at t_i'. This ultrarationalist solution to the problem eliminates conflict by bending momentary preferences in service of their higher daily objectives. It should be noted before leaving this question that if one assumed that Strotz's solution always applied to repetitive behavior, all the complications introduced by consideration of durations would dissolve, because momentary preferences could always be assumed to have adapted fully to maximization of daily utility. Some such assumptions must be made in any theory that denies the prevalence of conflicting preferences. But this is the stuff of another discussion (Winston, 1980).

The sequence of activities

Finally, it should be noted that the sequence of activities generated by the simple model is solely the result of adaptation to the rhythmically changing environment. If breakfast is eaten before the household goes to work, it is only because breakfast production is more efficiently done at 7:00 than at 9:30. With the discussion earlier in this section, this may be reinforced by the fact that adjustment costs prevent cooking breakfast at work or costlessly getting back home at 9:30. But the implicit assumption of independence of activities through the day ignores important elements of interaction whereby what the household does at one moment often affects the efficiency with which other things are done or the enjoyment they generate subsequently. A household's wage rate probably is affected by whether it regularly consumes its five daily martinis before or after work; to a professor, it sometimes matters whether a lecture is prepared before or after it is presented. Activity sequence may often be important.

The question of sequence can – like the complications of the preceding section – be assumed away simply by defining "an activity" as including all the temporarily related component activities it requires. Again, the time-specific context makes that sleight of hand especially dubious. A more useful alternative is to model activities – following Stigler and Becker (1977) – as having explicit utility and investment aspects. Because both can be positive or negative, an activity done at time t can yield pain or pleasure at t and either increase or decrease the efficiency of production of future activities. Although this will not be pursued further here, it is central to the structure of the addiction model discussed in Chapter 12.

9.7   Summary

A time-specific representation of the household not only describes the household functioning in time, giving insights into the scheduling of household consumption and work activities, but also, and more important, gives unique insights into the process of choice in consumption and work that is the standard stuff of standard models of consumption and labor supply. The distinction between process and goal sources of utility that is inherent in the time-specific perspective distinguishes among activities in an optimization model in ways that often are important and opens the way – because it is possible to represent more than a single dimension of utility – to identifying inherent conflicts in the household's behavior. It is not necessary to pretend that the household choices of consumption theory are always simple trade-offs; instead, they may involve the household's wanting to have its cake (goal utility) and eat it too (process utility). Important economic problems and markets can be understood only if such conflicts can explicitly be modeled. With the distinctions developed in this chapter, that becomes possible. So do other refinements of work and consumption theory.

Work activity is represented in the next part of the chapter as having, in all but one essential respect, the same characteristics as consumption, and the household is represented as making its activity decisions on exactly the same criteria between work and consumption and among consumption activities. The only difference between work and consumption needed to generate the full range of household behaviors in this analysis is that work pays a money wage and consumption does not. That difference is powerful, however, because it allows work to be the preferred activity even when it carries clear and persistent disutility. Work can be no fun, but it can also be a source of direct satisfaction. Incorporation of these possibilities into the simple formal model allows consideration of work as potentially unpleasant, indifferent, or directly rewarding, and those variations can be considered as they modify the optimal activity schedules described in Chapter 8. Pleasant work will, relative to indifferent work, increase the time spent at work; unpleasant work will reduce it. This is predictable. But these direct pleasures or pains of work – independent of its income generation – also induce household optimizing behavior patterns like those associated with seeming unrelated characteristics such as "responsibility," "harriedness," or "reliability." The conventional view of causality gets reversed – restriction of the household to a distasteful job causes indolent and irresponsible behavior, not the other way around.

This analysis of work, together with the earlier delineation of utility in consumption, generates a very neat and simple way of describing the household's decision on whether to produce a consumption commodity at home or buy it on the market. It is an economics of do-it-yourself that helps to explain the emergence and disappearance of commercial markets for consumer goods and services. The choice between home and commercial production here is consistent with the early important work of Gronau, but because it is derived from a more inclusive model that relies directly on the characteristics of the activities themselves, the time-specific model goes a good deal beyond his representation. It includes the effects on the household's make–buy decision of the level and distribution of wages between the household and the outsiders who provide commercial substitute services, of the relative satisfactions of home production and work, of the differences in home and commercial technologies, and of the availability of rental markets in specialized home capital.

Capital services are – for the household, as for the firm of Part II – fundamentally different from other inputs to household production simply because their price depends directly on capital utilization, on the duration of relevant household activities. This modifies the analysis of optimal activity choice and scheduling based on the usual assumption that all nonlabor inputs are the same. Incentives to own household capital are influenced by, and influence in turn, the household's activity choices and their timing. Differences between households in their activity choices will be amplified by this utilization effect when capital is an input to activities. And the utilization effect on capital service price further weakens the logic of the

Linder hypothesis, apparently fatally, because households can increase without limit or effort or harriedness the input of goods to their consumption activities when those goods are the services of mostly idle household capital.

Finally, in the last section, time units other than the day are considered – the year, the week – along with adjustment costs between activities. There is little need to modify the model on either account. But more fundamentally, this last section also introduces complications of optimal activity choice because of the fact that the duration of an activity often affects the efficiency of its production or its ability to provide satisfaction. So does the length of time since an activity was last done. Aside from the interesting list of consumer reactions generated when these are fitted into the time-specific household production model – including growing excitement, boredom, warm-up, and fatigue – its effect on the household's optimal activity timing requires the household to exercise self-control – to delay gratification – in order to achieve maximum daily utility.

PART V

Time-specific markets

CHAPTER 10

A theory of time-specific markets: generalized peak loads

The firms of Part II and the households of Part III are recognized in this chapter as economic actors who use similar watches and look at the same calendars. They meet in a number of markets, where they trade goods and services at specific times. The most important of these is undoubtedly that for labor services, but time-specific markets for perishable consumer and producer goods and services are significant, too. A theory of time-shaped markets is based on the incentives previously described for firms and households to specify and adhere to their own optimal activity schedules. When confronting each other in market transactions, they interact to modify these optimal schedules as they create the need for time-specific price or quantity rationing. "Peak-load" and seasonal pricing and night and weekend wage differentials emerge from this interaction. So do idle factories, closed offices and stores, and all-night gasoline stations and a host of other familiar evidences of the working of time-specific markets.

Section 10.1 briefly describes a framework that can bring the time-specific behaviors of the firms and households previously analyzed into the context of markets. Sections 10.2 and 10.3 use that analysis to describe labor markets and time-specific consumer goods markets, respectively, and Section 10.4 takes a step toward a time-specific general equilibrium of markets through an analysis of producers' goods markets that illustrate both the potential complexity of a time-specific general equilibrium and aspects of economies that constrain that complexity. In the next chapter, the implications of these descriptions for a set of illustrative problems are developed.

10.1 A graphic representation of time-shaped markets

No major innovation is needed to represent firms and households trading in a single market, but modification of both orthodox market analysis and the earlier representation of events in time proves useful. The analysis of time-specific markets can be largely graphic, because it embodies the more formal descriptions of earlier chapters.

In a time-specific market, supply and demand functions have to be represented as time-sensitive; each will shift as t changes over the unit time T. As usual, only regular, repetitive, and therefore predictable changes will be considered initially; so attention can still be focused on one representative period, T. Supply and demand curves, $s(t)$ and $d(t)$, in price-quantity space, describe the rates of flow of a good or service $q(t)$ supplied or demanded at time t as functions of price at t, $p(t)$. Such supply and demand functions are both instantaneous – in showing the demand for or supply of an instantaneous flow rate of product or service – and time-specific – in being defined for a specific and explicit moment, t, during the unit time T. Together, instantaneous supply and demand define an equilibrium price and rate of flow of output at moment t.

Although a single instant is easy to represent in elementary supply-demand terms, over the whole unit time, T, instantaneous supply and demand functions may shift about, reflecting rhythmic changes embedded in the optimal schedules of buyers and sellers. So supply and demand are both time-shaped over T. Consider demand first. In the quadrant at the top of Figure 10.1, household demand (for electric power, by way of illustration) is shown as it shifts from $d(t_n)$ to $d(t_d)$ between its low off-peak level (say 4:00 a.m.) and its peak level (say 3:00 p.m.). Over the day, T, the instantaneous demand curve $d(t)$ shifts, sweeping out all the area between. That pattern of movement of the demand function over T can be made explicit by combining a shifting instantaneous demand function with a graph, in $q(t),t$ space, of the implicit time-shape of those shifts. The result is a familiar time-shaped function like the load curves of Chapter 5 or the activity net utility flow profiles of Chapters 8 and 9 or the output time-shapes of Chapter 3. Simply extending the price axis of Figure 10.1 downward to become a time axis does this. Then the upper quadrant is instantaneous price-quantity space, and the lower quadrant is quantity-time space, in which the time-shape of demand is drawn: The load curve of Figure 5.1 is stood on end to be combined with its underlying and now-explicit shifting instantaneous demand functions.

Figure 10.1 is easy to read: With a given time-invariant price, $\bar{p}$, a smoothly shifting demand curve in the upper price-quantity quadrant will trace out, as a time-specific quantity demanded at price $\bar{p}$, a demand flow profile, $q_d(t,\bar{p})$, in the lower time-quantity quadrant. The horizontal distance to $q_d(t,\bar{p})$ represents the quantity demanded at price $\bar{p}$ at time t. But it will be more readable – despite the disconcerting need for upward-sloping demand curves – if the whole diagram is rotated by 90° as in Figure 10.2.

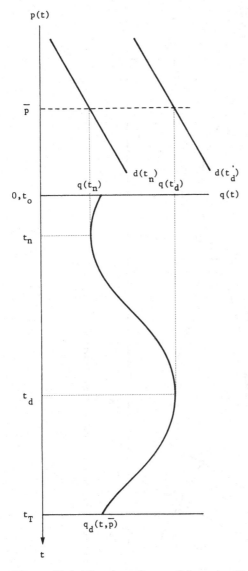

Figure 10.1. The time-shape of time-specific demand.

Time-specific supply is represented in the same way as demand: It is added in Figure 10.2. The instantaneous supply curve moves from $s(t_0)$ to $s(t_2)$ and back over T, tracing out the supply profile, $q_s(t,\bar{p})$ as the time-shape of quantity supplied at time-invariant price $\bar{p}$; dis-

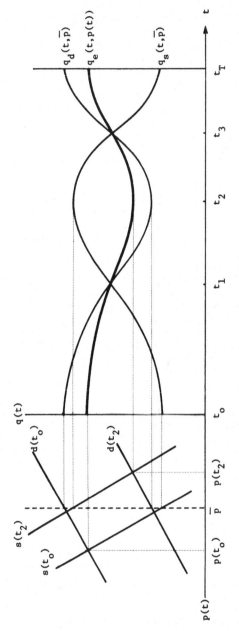

Figure 10.2. Time-specific market clearing.

tance from the t axis again represents the quantity flow rate at price $\bar{p}$ at time t – now quantity supplied.

The distance between demand and supply profiles at any time measures the excess supply or demand flow that would result under time-invariant price, $\bar{p}$. So in Figure 10.2, price $\bar{p}$ generates excess supply from t_1 to t_3 and excess demand from t_3 to t_1 (in the next period T).

If price can vary freely over T, time-specific prices – peak-load prices – $p(t)$, can eliminate excess supply and demand by equilibrating the flow of quantity bought and sold at each moment over T. This price-equilibrated flow is represented as an equilibrium quantity profile, $q_e(t,p(t))$, the heavy curve, in the quantity-time space of Figure 10.2. The time-specific price pattern – $p(t)$ over T – that maintains that equilibrium is only implicit in these figures, although its maximum and minimum values can always be made explicit in the supply-demand quadrant, as $p(t_0)$ and $p(t_2)$ in Figure 10.2.

Two further comments will be helpful before this framework is applied to analysis of labor and product markets: One involves aggregation in these markets of the firms and households of Parts II and IV and the other the ubiquitousness of corner solutions in the analysis of time-specific markets.

Earlier chapters modeled the time-specific behavior of individual firms and households. Here an aspect of that behavior is aggregated into the time-specific market supply and demand functions. So they incorporate both the responses of individual firms and households and the changing composition of the firms and households that make up the market at specific times as firms shut down or start up production and households initiate or drop activities. In any market, the firms are assumed to be roughly similar, but not identical; so although they make a given product or use a given labor supply, they do it with somewhat different technologies. The same rough similarity is assumed for the households in a market: Although affected by much the same environmental rhythms, they will have somewhat different preference and production functions. In each case, optimal activity schedules, taken together, will generate pronounced patterns but rarely uniformity of time-specific market behavior. This heterogeneity of firms and households is an important source of efficiency in time-specific markets.

The other useful preliminary observation is that corner solutions are bound to be more common in time-specific markets than in those we usually deal with. In the orthodox time context of accumulated daily or yearly purchase and sale, markets cannot long survive with corner solutions; in a time-specific context, they can and do. All that a time-specific corner solution implies is that there are periods during T in which the market is inactive; a corner solution occurs at any moment when there is no price that will simultaneously induce positive supply and positive demand. Indeed, it will be apparent by the end of the chapter that "standard and normal hours of operation" describe intermittent, rhythmic corner solutions in markets that are highly time-specific. In the stylized market of Figure 10.3, for instance, demand is time-invariant, d, but supply is $s(t_2)$ between t_2 and t_1 and then shifts to $s(t_1)$ from t_1 to t_2. Given demand and supply, there is no price that will bring an equilibrium at a positive rate of output from t_2 to t_1. The market will simply close down at t_2 to reopen at t_1 the next "day."

10.2   The time-specific market for labor services

The labor market is certainly the most important of time-specific markets; it involves virtually all households and firms in the exchange of a perishable service. In Chapter 4, household "preferences" for scheduling their work during normal daytime hours were given as the reason for time-specific wage rates – for a nighttime wage premium. They, in turn, were taken as the major illustration of the rhythmic prices that can induce firms optimally to schedule their daily operations intermittently, shutting down regularly despite the increased capital costs that incurs. In Part IV, the household's utility-maximizing response to a rhythmically changing household production environment generated an optimal activity schedule, even with time-invariant production and preference functions.[1] Now these are joined in an analysis of the labor market both to reveal the way market mechanisms work to coordinate the timing of activities of cost-minimizing firms and utility-maximizing households and to reveal something of the efficiency of that coordination. So in the analysis of this section, optimal household schedules confront optimal production schedules; different actors with different incentives generate market forces that reconcile and coordinate those schedules.

Time-specific disequilibrium

When both are faced with a time-invariant wage rate, the optimal schedule on which households will want to sell their labor is not the same as the optimal schedule on which firms will want to buy it. It was established in Chapters 3 and 4 that firms producing storable

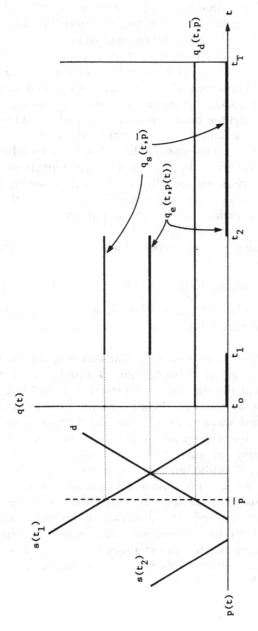

Figure 10.3. Intermittent markets: time-specific corner solutions.

products while paying a time-invariant wage rage, $\bar{w}$, will optimally produce output and use labor at a constant rate over the whole of T. Aggregating over all such firms, the optimal labor service demand profile is constant, $l_d(t,\bar{w})$, a horizontal line in Figure 10.4. It was established in Chapter 8 that the household's optimal time to work while earning a time-invariant wage rate, $\bar{w}$, is when consumption activities are least attractive; that means, for most households, working during normal, daytime hours on normal weekdays.[2] Then, aggregating over all households in a community,[3] the time-specific labor supply derived from those optimal household activity schedules will be concentrated during the day under a time-invariant wage rate. Some labor services will be offered at other hours by those whose preferred activities make that schedule optimal, but the daytime concentration remains and is reflected in the optimal labor service supply profile, $l_s(t,\bar{w})$ of Figure 10.4.

The actual quantities of labor services traded at $\bar{w}$ – actual employment – will be limited to

$$l_e(t,\bar{w}) = \min[l_s(t,\bar{w}),l_d(t,\bar{w})], \tag{10.1}$$

shown by the hatched line of Figure 10.4. So at time-invariant wage $\bar{w}$, there is excess demand for labor at night and unemployment during the day.

With a time-specific wage rate $w(t)$ that can respond to time-specific market disequilibria, reconciliation of supply and demand for labor services over the day can be achieved and the labor market cleared moment by moment. Relative to the time-invariant $\bar{w}$, time-specific nighttime wage rates will rise and daytime wage rates will fall, inducing changes in optimal activity schedules of firms and households that serve in turn to equate supply and demand throughout the day, T. Although these responses follow from the earlier time-specific analysis of firms and households in a straightforward way, it is useful to review their logic here, because those earlier models imply not only the direction of response but also something useful about its composition – what sorts of firms and households are responsible for the changes in schedule that yield aggregate time-specific adjustments of quantities supplied and demanded. Consider the firm first.

Firms' labor demands

The optimal duration of a firm's production, and hence its use of labor during the day, has been shown to depend, *inter alia*, on the

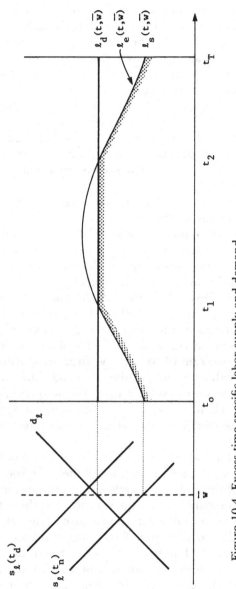

Figure 10.4. Excess time-specific labor supply and demand.

amplitude of the wage rhythm over the unit time – $\beta(t)$ in Chapter 4. Twenty-four-hour-per-day operation is necessarily optimal only if the amplitude of the wage rate over the day is zero, the time-invariant wage, $\bar{w}$. Time-specific wage rates, $w(t)$, discourage 24-hour/day operation of some plants. Whenever during the day wage rates rise, some firms will be induced to shut down then and concentrate their production during periods of low wages. As those firms stop producing, their labor demand at that time of day is subtracted from the aggregate time-specific labor demand. So the fact that a higher time-specific wage rate at t discourages firms' utilization generates, in the aggregate, a downward-sloping instantaneous labor demand curve at t (as usually drawn).

That utilization response to time-specific wage rates is reinforced by the factor use response of those firms that do continue to operate at t, as they will reduce optimal crew size then – factor flow proportions – because of the higher average wage rates. The magnitude of that response will depend, of course, on elasticities of factor service substitution inherent in the firms' technologies.[4]

Both the shutting down of firms and the changing of optimal factor flows in those firms that continue to operate in high-wage periods are incorporated in the negative wage response of the instantaneous labor demand curve, d_l. There is only one such curve in Figure 10.4. For a collection of competitive firms producing storable products, there is nothing to make labor demand time-sensitive; so for them, d_l would be time-invariant over T – the quantity of labor services demanded changes, of course, but only in response to changes in the time-specific wage rate. The labor demand curve does not shift.

Familiar observations about the efficiency of price-induced demand adjustments have their analogue in the time-specific labor demand response of firms. Higher nighttime wage rates induced by time-specific excess demand induce the shutdown of those firms that use the largest amounts of labor services relative to capital and those whose technical ability to alter that factor use in response to time-specific prices is slightest. The firms that do not shut down despite higher night wages are those with the largest concentrations of capital per worker and those induced by time-specific wage rates to reduce their use of labor services during operation at night. So time-sensitive wage rates assure that society's scarce and insensate capital stocks are utilized, in the aggregate, more than its time-sensitive and opinionated labor.

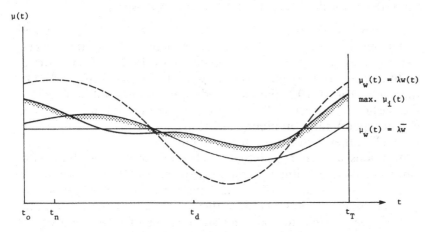

Figure 10.5. The value of time in work and consumption with time-invariant, $\bar{w}$, or time-specific, $w(t)$, wage rate.

Households' labor supplies

Household response to time-specific wage rates is equally useful in clearing the labor market moment by moment, and doing so efficiently. Underlying the shifting instantaneous household labor supply functions that generate excess supply during the day and excess demand at night is the fact that for most households the value of time – net utility flow – in consumption activities is greater, relative to that of work, during evenings, nights, and weekends, so that their optimal schedules call for working during the day. With a time-invariant wage rate, $\bar{w}$, the typical household will have a net utility flow profile from work like the straight line $\mu_w(t) = \lambda\bar{w}$ in Figure 10.5. But at that wage, the maximum net utility flow from consumption activities, the shaded line, max $\mu_i(t)$, varies over T. With $\bar{w}$, work is the preferred activity at a moment like t_d in Figure 10.5, because $\mu_w(t_d) > \mu_i(t_d)$ for the most attractive consumption activity. Aggregation over largely similar optimal household schedules generated the supply curves $s_l(t)$ and the labor schedule profile $l_s(t,\bar{w})$ of Figure 10.4.

A time-specific wage rate $w(t)$ alters the value of time spent at work relative to the value of time spent in consumption at any moment. In addition, a time-specific wage rate alters those relative values in different degrees and directions at different times during T. Without necessarily changing the profile of consumption satisfactions, the net utility flow of work becomes time-specific,

$$\mu_w(t) = \lambda w(t).\tag{10.2}$$

A higher night wage rate, then, in response to nighttime excess demand makes it relatively more attractive for households to work at night as $\mu_w(t_n)$ rises relative to max $\mu_i(t_n)$. For some households, like the one in Figure 10.5, the increased nighttime net utility of work – the dashed line $\mu_w(t)$ – will cause work to become the most valuable way to spend time at night, and those households will optimally reschedule their work from day to night.

Additions and subtractions of such households' contributions to labor supply at any time t in response to increases or decreases in the wage rate at t assure that the instantaneous quantity of labor supplied at t is a positive function of the wage rate at that moment, $w(t)$.

Note that these additions and subtractions of labor services at t involve rescheduling of work activity during the day. So the positive wage response in any instantaneous labor supply curve, like those in Figure 10.4, is compatible with a backward-bending aggregate labor supply curve, as usually conceived, defined on total accumulated hours, ΣL_w, supplied per unit time, T. With appropriate restrictions on $w(t)$, the labor supply response can be seen as solely a matter of work schedule, with $w(t)$ leaving consumption net utilities entirely unaffected by leaving λ unchanged. Because the slope of the labor supply depends on rescheduling of work, changes in relative values of work and consumption at night, t_n, are no less important than changes in those relative values in daytime, t_d – the effect on utility of rescheduling work from one period to another depends on relative net utilities at both times of day.

Again, the characteristics of those particular units that respond to time-specific wage rates at any time have clear efficiency implications, for households as for firms. But for households, equity enters, too. Not all households will, or need to, reschedule their activities in response to a time-specific wage rate. Those who find that a given change in time-specific wage rates alters their optimal schedule are those for whom an original inequality,

$$\mu_w(t) = \lambda w(t) \gtrless \max[u_i(t) - \lambda p_i x_i(t)] = \max \mu_i(t),$$

is reversed for night, t_n, and day, t_d. Those who will be induced by time-specific wages to work at night are (a) those with relatively the most attractive daytime consumption activities, max $\mu_i(t_d)$, (b) those with relatively the least attractive evening and nighttime consumption activities, max $\mu_i(t_n)$, (c) those whose occupations yield the greatest nighttime wage differentials, $w(t_n) - w(t_d)$, and (d) those for whom money income has the greatest value, λ. These appear frequently as central characteristics in empirical surveys of night workers – the ardent golfer (a), the misanthrope or estranged family man (b), the jazz musician (c), and the young, the poor, and the indebted (d) (Mott et al., 1965; Great Britain, 1970). It is they whose relative willingness to work at night helps eliminate excess nighttime labor demand. In Chapter 11 the welfare implications of this selective process of time-specific adjustment will be examined further.

10.3 The time-specific product market: peak-load pricing and "the capacity problem"

Firms and households trade in product markets, too, with results that are in many ways the same as those of the labor market. But both the mechanisms of adjustment and the market populations differ. The output of only some firms generates time-specific markets. Despite the fact that households use purchased consumption goods and services at repetitively specific times, those that can be stored cheaply over the day (year) are the temporally footloose goods inputs of Chapter 8. Even with considerable similarity in environment, production technologies, and tastes, household inventories will damp any tendency for market demand for such products to be strongly time-specific.

But perishable consumption services must be purchased when they are used in household production. For them, time patterns of demand are based on optimal household activity schedules that rest, in turn, on environmental rhythms, $E(t)$, given tastes, technology, and prices. Electric power is again both an important and a representative example, a perishable input to household activities that are time-specific, creating a highly time-specific demand pattern for electricity over the day (and week and year).

An analysis of time-specific product markets involves not only adjustment to market-clearing or peak-load prices but also "the capacity problem," the determination of the optimal capital stock (hence, presumably, productive capacity) to install in the production of a product with a rhythmically varying demand. So this section will first lay out the dimensions of the temporal mismatch generated by time-invariant prices and then look at the cost structure of firms producing to rhythmic demand, at the optimal adjustments by both firms and households, and finally at the process of their adjustments of time-specific prices.

As in the time-specific analysis of marginal costs in Chapter 5, it becomes clear in the course of the discussion, I think, that the subject of peak-load pricing and optimal capacity in time-specific markets has proved elusive in the literature because it involves a highly complex set of interactions between actors and time. In Chapter 5, that complexity was stressed in the enumeration of the components of marginal cost of a time-shaped output with the two quite different available methods of tracking that output; in this discussion, much of that complexity is avoided in order to show, instead, the nature of the time-specific market adjustment process and the complexity of a time-shaped optimality. So complexity in multiple tracking methods is suppressed here by considering only utilization tracking in order that complexity in the firm's optimal adjustment can be explored. Combining them both would, at this stage of development of time-specific analysis, appear fully to justify Frisch's concern with intractable complications.[5]

Time-shaped disequilibria

At a time-invariant price, $\bar{p}$, the optimal schedules of demand and supply conflict for perishable consumption services as they did for labor services. For the firm as supplier, it is optimal still to produce all output at a constant rate over the 24 hours if (as is assumed in this section) it faces no rhythmic input prices. This is embodied in the fixed supply curve, s_i, of the ith consumption service pictured in Figure 10.6. For the household as consumer, it is optimal to buy a perishable consumption service at the moment when the activity in which it is used is most valuable. This is reflected in time-specific shifts of the demand curve, $d_i(t)$, in Figure 10.6. So with product price, $\bar{p}$, constant over T, the producers' optimal profile of supply will be constant at $q_s(t,\bar{p})$, whereas the households' optimal demand profile will be time-specific, $q_d(t,\bar{p})$. I have again drawn, in Figure 10.6, an electric-power daily demand load curve for concreteness, but any other time-specific pattern of demand would do as well for illustration – transportation or restaurant services, for instance. As in the labor service market, a time-invariant price over the day (year) creates time-specific excess supply during part of the day (night and early morning if t_T = midnight in Figure 10.6) and excess demand during the rest.

The issues to be addressed initially are two: (a) How much of a given demand load will the firm optimally produce? In other words, what is the time-specific equivalent of the firm's optimal output decision from familiar price theory? (b) What optimal capital stock or "capacity" does that decision imply? In a time-specific market, even a price-taking firm cannot be assumed to make an optimal output

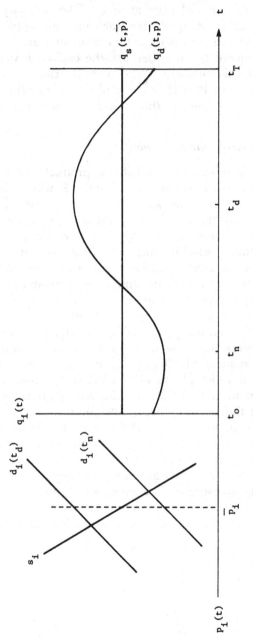

Figure 10.6. The time-specific product market.

decision simply on the basis of price at time t. The difficulty is that although the familiar price-equals-marginal-cost rule applies at a moment of time, and although price at that moment is given, marginal costs at that moment are not, because the capital service price brings duration of production into that cost. At the risk of repeating some of the arguments of Part II, it is useful to look carefully at the firm's optimal output decision at time t and over the unit time T.

The costs of time-specific production

The analysis of firms producing a perishable product with a rhythmic demand pattern was developed in Chapter 5, where the firm was assumed to use owned capital and a footloose variable input, $v(t)$ (called "fuel" there), whose price, $\bar{p}_v$, was time-invariant over T. The emphasis there was on the nature of costs and technology and their variations as the firm adjusted its output flow rate, $q(t)$, at different times of day to track a known rhythmic pattern of demand, "the load curve." It is this cost-output-adjustment relationship that is central to the price-output-capacity relationship of interest here.

By seeing the various output levels as strata of an output profile or load curve – each stratum produced by a different capital or "plant" – the problem of least-cost tracking of output variations was converted, in the analysis of Chapter 5, into a problem of the optimal utilization of those plants so that the cost-technology-utilization relationships of time-specific production could be brought to bear. Stratifying the output rate profile for the firm made explicit the difference in duration of the different rates of output over the day, and it clarified the cost concepts relevant to the decision on optimal rate of output and capacity.

Figure 5.3 made explicit the stratification of output rates on the demand load profile. Because each stratum of the output flow rate, $\dot{q}_j(t)$, is viewed as produced by a separate plant, any given rate of output at time t, $q_r(t)$, is the vertical sum of contributions of a number of plants:

$$q_r(t) = \sum_{j=1}^{r} \dot{q}_j(t). \tag{10.3}$$

When $q_r(t)$ is the rate of output, any capital stratum that produces for a higher rate of output, say $\dot{q}_m(t)$, where $q_m(t) > q_r(t)$, is shut down at t. So, given a demand profile, each output stratum has associated with it a capital stock and a utilization rate. In Figure 5.3, $\dot{q}_b(t)$ is produced throughout the day; so that stratum of output has a duration of $T_{pb} = T$ and a utilization rate of $T_{pb}/T = 1$. But $q_i(t)$, in contrast, is produced only part of the day; so stratum $\dot{q}_i(t)$ has a duration $T_{pi} < T$. This would be conveyed graphically by a stratified version of the load duration curve, Figure 5.4.

Production costs are specific to output rate strata and depend on input prices (fuel price and owner cost of capital), the utilization of that stratum, and the technology used to produce it. It is the fact that costs depend on utilization – that capital prices are duration-specific – that makes them specific, too, to a particular stratum of output, and that complicates the analysis in general.

Familiar cost concepts fit here with the now-familiar decomposition into an instantaneous, time-specific representation. The long-run marginal cost of producing a given rate of output flow, $q_r(t)$, at time t is the cost of producing the marginal stratum, $\dot{q}_r(t)$ – the sum of variable input, $\bar{p}_v v_r(t)$, and capital service cost flows, $p_k(T_{pr})k_r(t)$, of that marginal stratum. Variable input costs at t depend only on the rate of flow of the variable input used then, $v_r(t)$, because its price, $\bar{p}_v$, is time-invariant. The flow of capital service costs depends on capital use, $k_r(t)$, and its utilization-sensitive price, $p_k(T_{pr})$. Because duration of use of the marginal stratum, T_{pr}, declines with increasing output rates, capital service price rises and marginal costs are positively related to the rate of output flow. Denote marginal costs at time t for the jth output stratum $\dot{q}_j(t)$ as

$$\dot{c}_j(t,T_{pj}) = p_k(T_{pj})k_j(t) + \bar{p}_v v_j(t). \qquad (10.4)$$

Then average costs of producing at rate $q_r(t)$ at a moment of time, t, are

$$c_r(t) = \sum_{j=1}^{r} \dot{c}_j(t,T_{pj}) \Big/ \sum_{j=1}^{r} \dot{q}_j(t), \qquad (10.5)$$

and average daily unit costs are

$$C/Q = \int_{t_0}^{t_T} \left[\sum_{j=1}^{r} \dot{q}_j(t) \right] c_r(t) \, dt \Big/ \int_{t_0}^{t_T} q(t) \, dt. \qquad (10.6)$$

Technical substitution – the use of different factor proportions to produce different strata of output in response to the different factor flow prices inherent in their different levels of utilization – clearly affects the cost structure, as described in Chapter 5, and hence the output rate associated with a given marginal cost. If the production technology has no scope for factor substitution, the production of different strata of output rates over the day will all use the same technology and input flow proportions. Then marginal costs of increasing output rates must rise with output rates, because higher capital service prices are not at all offset by substitution out of capital and into the variable input. At a moment t, unit costs will increase with increasing rates of output and over the day; unit costs will increase with increasing variability of output rates. If the production technology allows substitution, the impact of quantity variations on costs is moderated in each of these respects, because relative factor flows can be adjusted to the relative factor flow prices of different strata. More capital-service-intensive technologies will be used for a base stratum than for a peak-output stratum, with consequent reduction in the increase in marginal costs, in unit costs at t, and in unit costs over the day. But only if the elasticity of flow substitution is infinite can marginal costs be constant over increasing output rates or can the output rate be varied over the day without cost penalty.

Optimal output flow rates and optimal capacity

With the sort of cost structure just described, the optimal level of output, $q^*(t)$, at time t for a price-taking, profit-maximizing firm faced with an exogenously determined demand profile for its perishable product is simple to specify. *Ceteris paribus*, daily profits will be maximized if instantaneous marginal costs equal price at each moment of the day.

But in a time-specific product market, this deceptively familiar statement is a far cry from its equivalent in orthodox production analysis; *"ceteris paribus"* here bears a very heavy weight at t, requiring that nothing change – demand, price, supply, duration of production – at any other moment in T. To specify optimal output at t, it is necessary in general to know optimal output at all other times of T. This, once again, is the result of utilization's role in determining costs.

Optimal output, can, however, be approached by stages with useful insights, starting with the simplest case of a time-invariant price and the firm's optimal adjustment to it.

Given (a) an exogenous product price, $\bar{p}$, (b) that is time-invariant, (c) a demand profile, $q_d(t,\bar{p})$, and (d) no load-shedding adjustments of demand in response to supply decisions, the firm's optimal production decision yields a time-specific market situation like that of Figure 10.7. The firm will extend production rate, $q(t)$, until $mc(t) = \bar{p}$ at

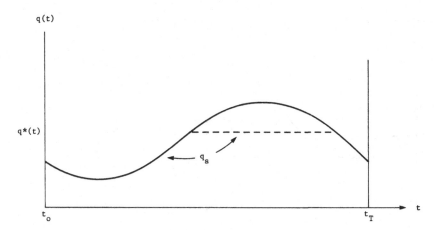

Figure 10.7. Optimal quantity rationing of time-shaped demand.

every time of day, subject to time-specific demand limitations. Given the demand profile, and hence determinateness of utilization rates by strata, marginal cost determines a unique optimal output flow rate, $q^*(t)$, as that for which $mc(q^*(t)) = \bar{p}$. There is a positive relationship, therefore, between price and optimal output rate; a higher product price covers higher marginal costs that are unambiguously associated with higher output rates.

Optimal capacity is derived simply from this, because the maximum optimal rate of output, $q^*(t)$, given the capital stocks implied by the technologies of production of all the strata that contribute to that rate, determines the total amount of capital capacity needed to produce it. If max $q^*(t) = q_r(t)$, the optimal capacity is

$$\bar{K}_r^* = \sum_{j=1}^{r} k_j(\dot{q}_j(t)). \tag{10.7}$$

What makes the determination of optimal output and capacity straightforward in this case, of course, is that the duration of potential production of each stratum of output is determined solely by the demand profile; so marginal costs are defined apart from the producer's output decisions. His output decisions do not return to haunt him by altering strata durations and hence marginal costs, either as those decisions affect his own changing strata utilization or, because we assume no load shedding, as they might feed back through alterations in the consumers' demand profile.[6]

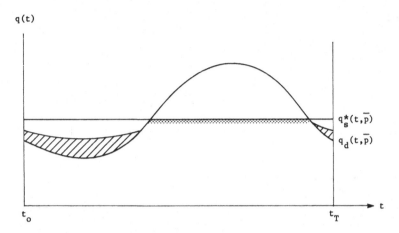

Figure 10.8. Load shedding with quantity rationing: capital costs unaffected.

Quantity rationing and load shedding

The firm's profit-maximizing output decision under a time-invariant price slices the top off the households' demand profile, leaving unsatisfied demand at that price – quantity rationing – in the peak demand period.[7] If the household responds to that quantity rationing by increasing demand at another time – by "load shedding" – that may, in turn, alter the firm's costs, changing its optimal output decision.[8]

Whether load shedding does or does not alter optimal output depends simply on where the load is shed to. If the demand sliced off the peak reappears as an addition to base-load demand – Figure 10.8 – it will lower unit costs both at each t and over T, raising profits, but it will not affect marginal costs of the optimal stratum of output; so it will not affect the optimal output and capacity decision. If, on the other hand, the truncated demand reappears to extend the duration of production around optimal output level – Figure 10.9 – that will lower marginal costs of those strata, making a higher rate of output optimal, $q_s^*(t,\bar{p})$. So to predict the effect of a change in $\bar{p}$ on $q^*(t)$ and $\bar{K}^*$ would require a knowledge of intertemporal quantity adjustments – a cross-time quantity elasticity.[9]

Time-specific, peak-load pricing

When product price, $p(t)$, is time-specific, varying over the day in response to the excess supply and demand generated by $\bar{p}$, both

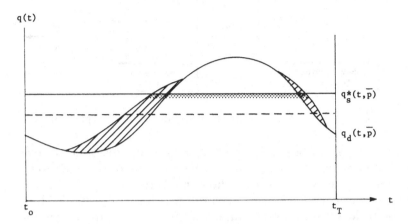

Figure 10.9. Load shedding with quantity rationing: capital costs reduced.

firms and households can be shown to adjust appropriately. Again, both the direction of adjustment and the characteristics of the specific firms and households that do the adjusting within the aggregate are relevant.

Firms will respond to higher time-specific prices during periods of high demand by increasing optimal output rates then; higher time-specific prices cover the higher marginal costs of higher output rates. Two aspects of the firms' response are efficient. Those firms and technologies that respond to a given price increase at any time t will be those with the lowest marginal costs of producing that stratum of output. And the optimal output response (the supply elasticity at t) will be greater the longer the period over which that level of output will be demanded; the effect of reduced utilization on marginal costs militates against satisfying transient peaks in demand.

In off-peak periods, lower time-specific product prices discourage firms from producing then—they will optimally shut down the most costly strata during those periods as low prices fail to cover the marginal costs of those levels of output. And again, those specific firms and technologies that will reduce $q(t)$ during off-peak periods are those with relatively the highest costs of production.

So the producers' supply profile, $q_s^*(t, p(t))$, is reshaped by time-specific prices toward conformity with time-specific demand.

Household adjustment, too, brings product demand into time-specific conformity with supply in the manner described before: High (low) prices of goods inputs x_i at t both encourage substitution

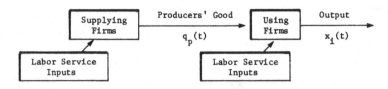

Figure 10.10. Structure of a time-specific producers' good market.

out of (into) x_i in doing activity i and reduce (increase) the relative net utility flow from activity i then, making it less (more) likely to be the preferred activity.[10] So those households responsible for the aggregate time-specific adjustments are those with the greatest technical ability to substitute other inputs in producing activity i and/or those with the most attractive alternatives to doing i then.

The predictable complication in this process, of course, is the feedback of these demand adjustments on the firm's demand load curve, and hence strata utilization rates, marginal costs, and optimal output and capacity decisions. The pattern of time-specific prices that equilibrates the market moment by moment will embody this interaction; to estimate it would require intertemporal cross-price elasticities of both time-specific supply and demand. The maximum optimal $q^*(t)$ that emerges from this process of mutual adjustment of supply and demand determines, as in equation (10.7), the optimal capital capacity, $\bar{K}^*$.

10.4   Producers' good market: toward a time-specific general equilibrium

Even a brief examination of markets for perishable producers' goods indicates the rapidly increasing complexity of time-specific interactions among firms and between firm and household sectors as the analysis is extended from a partial toward a general compass. I will only suggest that complexity now, but even that suggestion is useful.

Two industries and at least three other markets influence the time-specific pattern of output in a single producers' good market: Trade involves the supplying firms and using firms, the labor service markets into both, and the output market of the using firm. And this representation ignores joint outputs and all but the most elementary jointness of inputs. The resulting flow, in simple schematic, is shown in Figure 10.10. With time-invariant prices for labor inputs to both sectors and a time-invariant price for the output of the using sector, instantaneous supply and demand curves would not shift over the day; so the resulting supply and demand profiles for the producers' good market would be flat and, with a market-clearing price, superimposed as in Figure 10.11. Nothing would be differentiated by time of day.

But introduction of even the simplest and most indirect time-specific influence will alter this. When supplying firms face the usual rhythmic wage rate, paying a higher wage rate at night than during the day, the instantaneous supply curve in the producers' good market will shift left at night to $s(t_n)$, as in Figure 10.12, and the supply profile of producers' goods at the time-invariant price, $q_s(t,\bar{p})$ will be less at night than during the day, where t_n and t_d in Figure 10.12 again represent typical moments during the night and day. The instantaneous supply curve shifts from $s(t_n)$ to $s(t_d)$, of course, because marginal costs of producing any given output rate in the supplying industry are higher at night. Whereas all markets except that for suppliers' labor services remain time-invariant, the producers' good market will have become time-sensitive; to avoid excess supply during the day and excess demand during the night, producers' good prices then must become time-specific $-p(t_n)$ at night and $p(t_d)$ in the day. These changes in price of the producers' good induce more supplying firms to operate at night in the familiar way, despite the cost penalty of doing so. This rhythm in the producers' good market, it should be noted, comes from the households' time-specific optimal work schedules, transmitted through suppliers' costs.

Of course, nothing assures that there will be a positive flow of output and purchases $q_e(t,p(t))$ at all moments over the day, despite time-specific producers' good price—the equilibrium may involve a corner solution in instantaneous supply and demand and therefore the shutdown of both supplying and using firms during the night. Then production will be intermittent, as in Figure 10.13, where the night wage premium has made it optimal for all suppliers to shut down at night, because users are not willing to pay enough to offset the higher nighttime labor costs.

If both supplying and using firms in the producers' good market pay rhythmic wage rates, the tendency toward such corner solutions, and hence intermittent production flows, is increased by mutually reinforcing shifts in supply and demand by time of day. In Figure 10.14, the night wage premium is shown to shift both the suppliers' instantaneous supply curve to $s(t_n)$ at night and the users' nighttime demand curve to $d(t_n)$: Using firms' demand for the producers' good

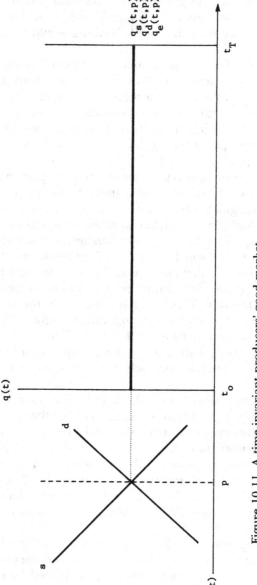

Figure 10.11. A time-invariant producers' good market.

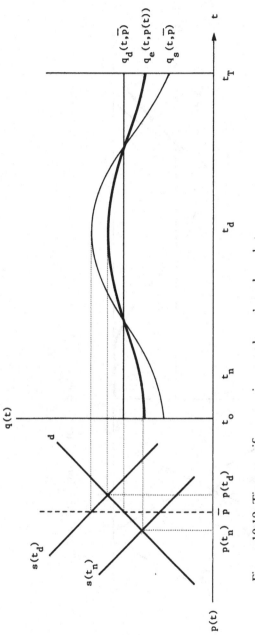

Figure 10.12. Time-specific wages in a producers' good market.

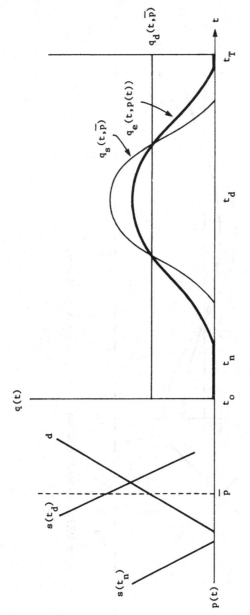

Figure 10.13. Intermittent supply.

declines at night as some of them shut down to avoid higher night-time labor costs. As they are represented in Figure 10.14, one or the other of these effects of nighttime wage premiums, taken alone, would only reduce the nighttime trade in the producers' good market; together, they eliminate it.

The jointly optimal intermittent production schedule that emerges in this case is significant because it describes the time-pattern of operation that is considered "normal"; these highly time-specific "normal hours of operation" emerge because of the importance of labor costs (hence their ability significantly to shift instantaneous supply and demand in the producers' good market) and because of their ubiquitousness (hence their influence in discouraging both $s(t_n)$ and $d(t_n)$ at the same time). So an important and widely used input to firms' production that has a strong time-specific supply induces adaptation of other markets to its time-pattern, and that pattern becomes the standard of "normalcy."

Implicit in this is all that was identified earlier as influencing firms' optimal production schedules. So the degree of influence the time-specific labor market will have on the producers' good market depends on relative factor prices and factor intensities and the elasticities of factor service substitution in the two industries. Low elasticities of substitution, high wage rates, and low capital intensities in both sectors will lead to the extreme intermittence of production of Figure 10.14. Use of very little, very cheap labor services that are very easily substituted for by capital will encourage constant output flows over the 24 hours.

But even in so greatly simplified a producers' good market as this, consideration must finally be given to the time-pattern of demand for the output of the using industry, $x_i(t)$. If that output is storable, of course, nothing more need be said, because the economies of production timing alone will determine the optimal schedule. But if $x_i(t)$, too, is a perishable product, then the time-shaped pattern of its demand will amplify or damp the rhythm of the producers' good market generated by its inputs. When $x_i(t)$ is a consumption service, the households' rhythmic optimal activity schedule will once again impinge on the timing of a producers' good market; this time the household is in its role as consumer.

Demand timing from the household's optimal activity schedule influences the firms' production schedules in the manner described earlier: Households bid up the price of a perishable service at the time of day that they want it and bid down the price when they do not. If their instantaneous demand is sufficiently price-inelastic over

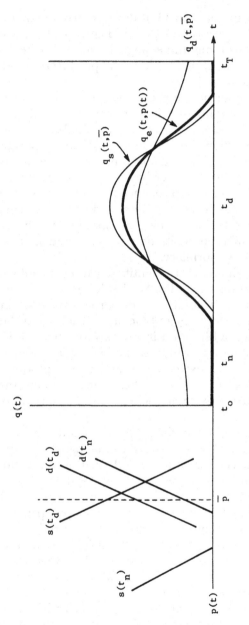

Figure 10.14. Intermittent supply and demand.

those time patterns, the time-specific prices will induce firms to schedule their production in conformity with the household schedule by altering their own optimal schedules. So if sufficiently strong demand for a firm's perishable product comes during a high-labor-cost period, that is when the firm will produce. This is evident, of course, in industries like transporation and entertainment that produce leisure-complementary services.

Figure 10.15 traces that household demand influence one step back into the producers' good market. The supply pattern is shown again in instantaneous supply curves, $s(t_d)$ and $s(t_n)$, reflecting the influence of higher nighttime wage rates on supplying firms. Were price constant, suppliers would deliver $q_s(t,\bar{p})$ at a higher rate in the daytime than at night – costs would dominate. But in the instantaneous demand curves $d(t_d)$ and $d(t_n)$, demand for the producers' good is shown to be even more strongly concentrated in the daytime than is supply. The reason, let us presume, is that $x_i(t)$ has a pronounced daytime demand and a relatively meager demand at night. So in this case the demand profile, $q_d(t,\bar{p})$, reinforces the time-pattern of supply, and the resulting market-clearing quantities traded, $q_e(t,p(t))$, are even more concentrated during the day than when supply is considered alone.

But consider, in contrast, the time-pattern of output in the producers' good market when the demand for the final output of the using firms, $x_i(t)$, is strongly rhythmic but in the opposite phase – nighttime demand is strong and daytime demand is weak (the entertainment industry, hotel rooms, etc.). This can be pictured in Figure 10.15 simply by exchanging the labels on the instantaneous day and night demand curves so that $d(t_d)$ becomes $d'(t_n)$ and $d(t_n)$ becomes $d'(t_d)$. Then the demand profile over the day is $q_d'(t)$ in the producers' good market; demand is concentrated at night and is meager during the day. The resulting market-clearing output profile, $q_e'(t,p(t))$, is dominated by the demand rhythm in this case – the supply rhythm is more than offset by a stronger demand time pattern, induced, we assume, by strongly time-specific demand for final output $q_i(t)$.

Of course, these simple examples of time-patterns could be multiplied endlessly. The point – explicitly to incorporate the effect on producers' goods markets of derived demand rhythms from consumption-goods markets – has been adequately served.

It should be clear that an increasingly complex set of harmonics is generated as the compass of the analysis moves from partial to general equilibrium. In a time-specific general equilibrium, firms will adjust to time-patterns of input supply and output demand directly

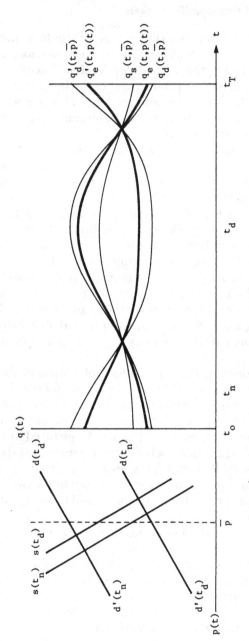

Figure 10.15. Reinforcing and damping rhythms from the product market.

from households as well as indirectly through other firms. So any direct rhythmic influence of the household is complicated by indirect rhythms reflected in trade with other firms. In addition, the periodicities of these rhythms are different as daily, weekly, monthly, and seasonal patterns occur simultaneously and interact. Each of the household's rhythms is passed through the technical and economic parameters of the firms and sectors that amplify or damp those time-specific patterns.

Two aspects of this potentially chaotic interaction of firms and households in multiple rhythms tend to bring more order than this description implies; both work, paradoxically, by making the system more predictably and pronouncedly time-specific. One of those moderating facts is that the household rhythm is ubiquitous in its influence over the economy and dominant over the day–night and weekly periods. So working during weekdays in the daytime and concentrating consumption during evenings and on weekends is so much the dominant preferred household schedule that most industries and firms are affected in the same way – therefore the "normalcy" of normal hours of work. The other moderating force that gives order to potential chaos is, simply, that much of the trade between firms and from firm to household involves storable goods that are therefore temporally footloose, breaking the necessary simultaneity on which the time specificity of markets rests. A significant number of markets, therefore, can be highly time-specific, operating only during those very intermittent "normal" hours, because they supply a storable good. Indeed, harmonic reverberations in the system would be minimized if all activities were simultaneously time-specific even though that would mean highly intermittent, pulsed, economic activity.

CHAPTER 11

Welfare and distortions in time-specific exchange

The last chapter concentrated on polite and well-behaved rhythmic markets and their tendency to work toward time-specific equilibria with nicely adaptive time-specific prices and evident appeal to welfare and efficiency. This chapter concentrates on distortions, disaggregation, and mismatched rhythmic behavior in time-specific markets. The first part more closely examines the welfare and efficiency implications of time-specific pricing that were introduced in rather glowing terms in the last chapter. This discussion focuses on the alternatives to time-specific pricing and on the winners and losers hidden under the general welfare improvement such markets must create. The second part deals with the electric-power market in the United States and Sweden (among others), with a government-enforced policy of time-invariant prices in a time-specific market. It looks at the nature of the disequilibrium that this policy maintains, and it looks at the scope for incorporation of unconventional power sources implied in time-specific market analysis. In the last part, three illustrative time-specific labor market distortions are shown to have repercussions for orthodox economic concerns; they are the investment strategies of poor countries, the history of capital productivity growth in the United States, and the effect of income taxation at high marginal rates.

11.1   Efficiency and welfare with time-specific pricing

Any discussion of the welfare and efficiency implications of alternative market strategies must rest on the fact that time-specific markets are time-specific – that, in fact, they trade a perishable product produced or demanded at specific times. That fact cannot usefully be assumed away. This means that in such a market there must be either (a) time-specific *price rationing* over the unit period T or (b) time-specific *quantity rationing* over the unit period T in the form of either time-specific *excess supply* or time-specific *excess demand*, or (c) all of the above. It may devoutly be wished that all of these rhythmic changes within the unit time could be ignored as they are in conventional price theory, but they cannot be. So the evaluation of markets depends on how the time-specific price or quantity adjustments are made – which firms and which households bear how much cost of adjustment. It is the considerable virtue of time-specific analytical perspective, I think, that it focuses disagreements over alternative market organizations on the right questions.

The best time-invariant price

It is useful to begin by examining the alternative of an optimal time-invariant price that was mentioned briefly in the last chapter: If price were adjustable but time-invariant, a unique and stable time-invariant price, $\bar{p}^*$, would emerge from competitive exchange that would bring a sort of equilibrium to the time-specific market. This "equilibrium" is pictured as the solid lines in the profiles of Figure 11.1. In Chapter 10, $\bar{p}^*$ was called a stable disequilibrium price because it produces universal disequilibria – at virtually no moment over T is the market other than in excess demand or excess supply – but it achieves price stability by a balanced pattern of offsetting quantity disequilibria over T. Any other time-invariant price would shift the burden of time-specific adjustment more toward suppliers or more toward demanders. For instance, $\bar{p}_1$ in Figure 11.1 is high enough to eliminate excess demand entirely, but only at the cost of putting all adjustment over T onto suppliers in the form of excess supply; in contrast, $\bar{p}_2$ is low enough to eliminate excess supply by putting all adjustment costs on demanders in the form of quantity rationing and excess demand; $\bar{p}^*$ is a stable time-invariant price precisely because it distributes those disequilibrium adjustments between the two sides of the market.

At any time t, the actual quantity traded at $\bar{p}^*$ will, of course, be $\min[q_s(t,\bar{p}^*), q_d(t,\bar{p}^*)]$ – the shaded line in Figure 11.1 – so there will persistently be one or the other form of quantity rationing: excess supply or excess demand. What this reveals about conventional supply and demand representation over unit time T is informative – and again emphasizes that events of importance to conventional economic analysis are hidden under conventional unit time. In Figure 11.2, conventional daily supply and demand functions, S and D, have been got from the supply and demand profiles of Figure 11.1 simply by integrating the area under the supply and demand profiles over T at various time-invariant prices, $\bar{p}$.

The fact that the "equilibrium" quantity supplied and demanded, Q^*, at $\bar{p}^*$, in a time-specific market is less than either daily demand or

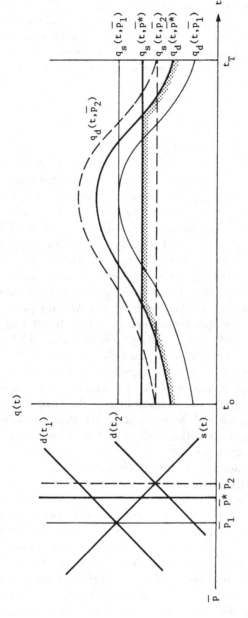

Figure 11.1. Flexible time-invariant pricing.

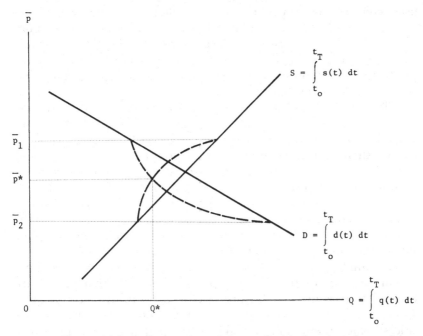

Figure 11.2. Daily supply and demand with time-invariant pricing.

daily supply at that price reflects, of course, the underlying periods of time-specific excess supply and excess demand. So use of orthodox analysis with its gross unit time, T, and its time-invariant price to describe a time-specific market will inevitably mask disequilibria.

The time-specific price

The enthusiasm of the last chapter for use of time-specific pricing in time-specific markets – in place of even the best of time-invariant prices – arose from the fact that price changes during periods of excess demand and excess supply in T induce efficient adjustment of optimal activity schedules on both sides of the market. The directions of adjustment are appropriate to clear the market moment by moment, and the incidences of adjustment are such that markets respond efficiently – the right firms and the right households do the adjusting.

A higher time-specific price for a good or service at t will induce buyers, whether firms or households, to alter their activities then, either by abandoning the activity in which that good or service is used (consumption or production) or by altering the mix of inputs to that activity so that less of the higher-priced input is used then. Those buyers who adjust the most are those for whom adjustment is the least costly: those with the greatest elasticities of substitution in production and those with the least relative advantage of doing that particular activity at that particular time.

Sellers will respond to a higher time-specific price, whether they are firms or households, by increasing the flow of supply then: households because the higher wage rate makes work relatively more attractive then, and firms because higher product prices allow them to cover higher marginal costs then. Those sellers who respond the most will be the households that give up the least utility in rescheduling their work and consumption activities and those firms that can produce increased output rates at the lowest marginal cost. Lower prices of inputs and product have symmetric effects on the other side of the time-specific adjustment.

What underlies the efficiency of these adjustments of a time-specific market to time-specific prices is, simply, that sellers are enabled to pass on, and buyers are forced to incur, the real time-specific costs of supply – of labor and products. Time-invariant prices delude the users into making their privately optimal scheduling decisions on the assumption that costs are the same over all the unit time, when in fact they are not.[1] It should not need further repetition, but time-specific costs are clearly social costs – society's resources have time-varying costs, and society's members have time-varying demands, because society exists in a pervasive rhythmic environment.

The sources of efficiency

It is useful to be more explicit about the underlying sources of welfare and efficiency gain from using time-specific pricing in time-specific markets. The relevant comparison is with the alternative of the best time-invariant price over the unit period T, $\bar{p}^*$. Then the time-specific prices, $p(t)$, that keep the market clear over T will (a) substitute price rationing for quantity rationing and (b) increase the productivity of the society's given stocks of resources – capital and labor in our two-factor context.

In the product market, time-specific prices lower peak demand and raise base demand, reducing the amount of capital and increasing its utilization. With a flatter output curve, there is less waste in the form of idle capital over the unit time. This results in lower production costs and hence, in a competitive economy, lower average prices to consumers. Those are production economies. Also in the product market, households benefit directly from the increased availability of time-specific goods at the prevailing price with the elimination of quantity rationing. To be sure, peak-period prices may be higher than the time-invariant price, $\bar{p}^*$, but they are real prices, in the sense that they carry with them information about the actual availability of the goods then, whereas $\bar{p}^*$ does not. It is not much help to have low-priced electricity on a hot afternoon if a power outage has shut off the air conditioner.

The labor market reflects the same efficiency effects of time-specific pricing: elimination of quantity rationing and reductions in cost and price made possible by optimal utilization of productive resources. In the labor market with a time-invariant wage, quantity rationing takes the form of unemployment of labor during the day and excess productive capacity during the night. Both are eliminated as time-specific wage rates induce optimal rescheduling of labor to night work and rescheduling of production to days. Again, both of these changes describe increased, and optimal, flows of services (hence product) from given capital and labor resources.[2]

Welfare gains and losses of individual households

But there remain questions about the distribution of those gains among households, both as they respond to time-specific prices and as they respond to time-specific wage rates. Only in the convenient, if unlikely, event that the induced productivity increases were so large that time-specific pricing increased all wage rates at all times of day and reduced all prices at all times of day would each household clearly gain from time-specific pricing – only then would a move from time-invariant to time-specific pricing be uncompensated Pareto-optimal. Absent assurance that that will happen, it is useful to look at the individual household as it is affected by time-specific prices and wage rates.

Nice, neat statements about the effects on household welfare of a change from time-invariant to time-specific pricing do not emerge. The reason is simple: The typical household has to pay more for a consumption service x_i under time-specific pricing just when the activity in which it is used is most attractive. So the net utility flow of that activity at that time falls with time-specific pricing. Whether or not that decline is compensated by the off-peak increase in net utility flow from the activity – which is allowed by the lower off-peak price and lower average price over the day – depends on the relative effi-

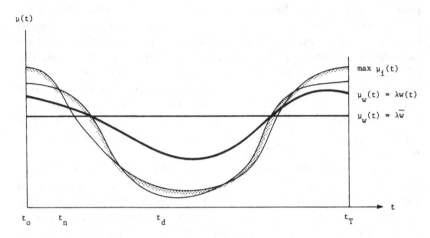

Figure 11.3. Optimal work timing unchanged by time-specific wage rate.

ciencies of production both among activities at any time and for that particular activity over the unit time, T: The household that is discouraged from going sailing in the summer by a high time-specific price may not feel adequately compensated by much lower prices for sailing in the dead of winter.

Similar considerations affect the individual household's response to the time-specific wage rate; again, only if all wage rates of all households were increased at all times of day would the welfare effects of time-specific wage rates on the individual households be unambiguous – only then could it be claimed (as is often the implicit requirement of reformers) that everyone is always made better off by time-specific wages and their resulting increase in social product.

The incidence of work-schedule adjustments

The effects of a time-specific wage pattern on different sorts of households are made explicit in Figures 11.3 and 11.4. In both, the change in wage rate from time-invariant pattern, $\bar{w}$, to a rhythmic pattern, $w(t)$, induces the same change in the value of time spent working – from $\lambda\bar{w}$ with a constant wage to $\lambda w(t)$ with a time-sensitive wage. The time-specific wage rate does not alter the optimal schedule for the household of Figure 11.3, but it does for the household of Figure 11.4; the first still works days, but the second optimally reschedules work from day to night.

μ(t)

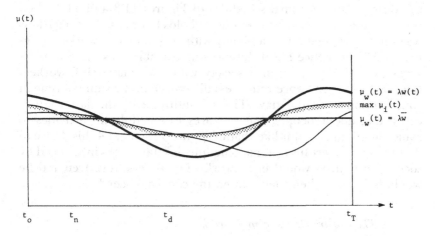

$\mu_w(t) = \lambda w(t)$
max $\mu_i(t)$
$\mu_w(t) = \lambda \bar{w}$

t_o t_n t_d t_T

t

Figure 11.4. Optimal work timing altered by time-specific wage rate.

The difference between these households that leads to their different responses to the same time-specific wage rate is reflected in the variability of their maximum net utility flows, max $\mu_i(t)$, over the day, the variability of the value of their time spent in consumption over T. For the more flexible household of Figure 11.4, the relative rewards of consumption done during the day and night are much the same – max $\mu_i(t)$ is relatively flat – so that household responds to the higher wage that can be got by working at night. The more time-bound household of Figure 11.3, on the other hand, finds daytime consumption much less appealing than consumption at night – max $\mu_i(t)$ changes markedly over the unit time – so that household optimally adheres to daytime work, despite the wage inducements to work at night. Among households, therefore, those who are induced by a given time-sensitive wage rate to alter their work schedules are those who are the least averse to it because they have the least to lose in daily utility; they have the least difference in the value of their consumption time over the day.

Surveys of workers have shown less professed dislike of shift-working in those households situated in "shift-working communities," where a large part of the population works during nonnormal hours (Winston, 1971b); the availability of friends and of services is among the time-specific environmental characteristics that rhythmically alter household production efficiency and shape the household's optimal activity schedule. This can be represented simply as the difference in optimal schedules of Figures 11.3 and 11.4 when they represent not two different households but the same gregarious household living either in a society with very few shift-workers (Figure 11.3), and hence big differences in available consumption pleasures over the day, or in a society with very many shift-workers (Figure 11.4), and hence much less difference in the value of time in consumption over the day. The misanthrope of the last chapter cares, too, about people, but he cares to schedule his activities to avoid them – in a graph like that of Figure 11.3 or 11.4, his desire to do so would invert his optimal schedule, insofar as it is influenced by society, so that he would be at work while others were free and he would be asleep when they wanted the convivial beer.[3]

The welfare effects of night work

Two related implications of this discussion are relevant to much-debated issues of the welfare effects of night work on households. First is the fact that night work can have seriously damaging physiological effects on some workers. This would be reflected in the present analysis, because it affects the shape of the household's net utility flow profile from consumption, max $\mu_i(t)$. Consumption is the time-complement of work. A household that can work at night or in the day with little or no physiological difference would have, given preferences, prices, and environment, a relatively flat net utility profile when compared with a household that suffers physiologically from nonnormal work hours. Physiological time-sensitivity enters the household's optimal schedule through the sensitivity of its activity production functions to the time-specific environment – again, Figure 11.3 compared with Figure 11.4. The worker, for instance, who cannot produce sleep of reasonable quality except under conditions of a very dark, quiet, and cool environment will show ill-effects of night work as compared with the worker who can sleep anywhere and any time: Studies of U.S. shift-workers have concluded that "the central problem of working shifts is getting adequate sleep" (Mott et al., 1965, p. 235). The net utility profile of such an environment-sensitive worker (Figure 10.3) would markedly differentiate between day and night consumption – hence day and night work – whereas that of the insensitive worker would not (Figure 10.4).

   That leads to the second related issue: the nearly total irrelevance of evidence of the physiological effects of night working based on data describing average workers' responses. What matters, because self-selection is an integral part of the response to time-specific wage rates, is the effect of night work on those who work nights, not on the average citizen or average worker.[4] It is important, therefore, that the social costs of any level of time-specific labor supply be minimized by maximizing opportunities for self-selection among workers. Empirical evidence, once again (Winston, 1977b; Baily, 1974; Farooq and Winston, 1978), strongly suggests that the absence of mobility and self-selection among work-timing patterns contributes to significantly lower nighttime labor productivity in less developed countries and consequent waste of scarce capital stocks. This is an issue to which we will return in Section 11.3.

The costs of time-specific pricing

It would be misleading to leave the subject of time-specific welfare and efficiency without taking note of the potential costs of time-specific pricing. Time-specific metering costs are clearly important, but the efficiency of time-specific markets is affected, too, by switching costs that make activity durations important, by coincidence and sequencing of activities where temporal priority is characteristic of a production process, like the gathering of news before the time-specific production of a daily newspaper.

Metering costs may make it socially optimal to retain time-invariant pricing even in time-shaped markets that trade perishable products. The productivity advantages of time-specific pricing can be more than offset by metering costs – the transactions costs of collecting time-specific sales data and the subsequent complexities of accounting with time-specific prices. In that case, time-invariant prices will be optimal – society will incur high production costs in order to avoid even higher transactions costs. It simply is not worth it to price time-specifically under those conditions.

It should be noted, however, that in any specific case that conclusion rests on a difference between (a) production cost savings of time-specific pricing and (b) the costs of time-specific metering and accounting, and both of those costs are subject to considerable change. Recent advances in electronics technology have radically altered the technologies and costs of timekeeping, recording, and accounting – the central aspects of time-specific metering costs – at the same time that changes in relative input costs like those of energy products have markedly increased the cost savings to be got from time-specific pricing in some important time-specific markets. On both counts, therefore, markets that once were rationally allocated with time-invariant prices may now call for time-specific pricing. The notable case in point, of course, is the U.S. electric-power market, to which we will turn in a moment.

The meshing of durations of jobs and employment has been assumed to be a matter of indifference in time-specific markets, but often it is not. It usually matters to both buyers and sellers of services – especially labor – how long an employment event will last without interruption. The same can be true for products. Workers often incur commuting and interruption costs in going to work, costs that are independent of the wage rate. Employers in many production processes pay similar start-up costs for switching workers each time a new crew member comes along and has to settle into the job. Frequently there are minimal work durations set by workers who are willing to "come in" only for a minimum number of hours or by employers who will hire only full-time workers for many jobs. Any shorter work period will be quantity-rationed. To be sure, a set of wage rates denominated by time of day but further adjusted for work-period duration can evolve – as they have in markets like some of those for part-time labor – but they fit awkwardly into the simple models we have dealt with. So they count as a qualification. However, extensive empirical work by Fred Best on the timing of work activities has left little doubt that the durations of work and leisure – their distribution within different unit times T – significantly affect the value of time in such activities to the household (Best, 1980). Demonstration of the sensitivity of women's labor-force participation to daily job duration has reinforced this finding (Cogan, 1977). Although these complications could be incorporated into the model with suitable respecification of units time and the addition of fixed event-specific wage components, they would take the analysis well beyond its present aims.

11.2   Time-specific distortions and mismatch: the electric-power market

The electric-power market, as I have frequently noted earlier, is a nearly ideal illustration of a time-specific market in which a nonstorable product is subjected to strong and well-known daily (and weekly and seasonal) demand rhythms and one that uses production technologies that seek to reduce the costs of tracking those demand variations. So it is a useful context in which to exemplify the time-specific market analysis. This section does that briefly with discussions of two aspects of U.S. electric-power markets: a stylized time-specific representation of existing U.S. regulatory strategy and an application of time-specific analysis to the incorporation of nonconventional power sources. Both are illustrative; neither pretends to completeness.

A time-specific view of U.S. regulatory policy

In a number of countries – notably the United States and Sweden – public regulatory policy has discouraged the time-specific pricing of electric power that has been represented earlier as most efficient. Instead of letting peak-load prices induce time-specific conformity of supply and demand over the day, regulators have simultaneously presented households with time-invariant prices and presented producers with legal imperatives to supply whatever pattern of demand emerges with those prices and, furthermore, to set those prices on the basis of average costs rather than marginal costs. So regulatory policy has departed from the time-specific pricing ideal through three decrees to the power industry:

Decree No. 1 requires that the industry use only time-invariant prices. That policy maximizes the amplitude of the demand rhythm. The average cost of production of any given accumulated daily output is therefore higher, *ceteris paribus*, than it would be with a time-specific pricing policy, because a greater part of that daily output must be produced with relatively lower levels of capital utilization and higher fuel costs; technological substitution of fuel for capital over the load curve can go far, but only so far, toward offsetting the higher capital service costs that are inherent in the lower utilization that is in turn inherent in the higher demand amplitude. And if relative fuel costs rise, the cost impact of this maximized demand amplitude rises too.

Left to their own devices, less thoroughly regulated firms that nonetheless were required to charge a time-invariant price would choose the optimal time-invariant price, $\bar{p}^*$, which would truncate the demand load curve, slicing demand off the top as in Figure 10.10 by refusing to supply the sporadic and high-cost peak levels of output. So there would be quantity rationing, with excess demand during peak demand periods. But consider decree No. 2:

Decree No. 2 requires that there be no excess demand at any time, no quantity rationing to power customers. In a time-shaped market, this policy assures that there will be a maximum amount of excess supply. In terms of the load curve of Figure 11.5, whatever demand profile emerges in consequence of the time-invariant price in the industry, the supply profile is required to lie above it at all points.

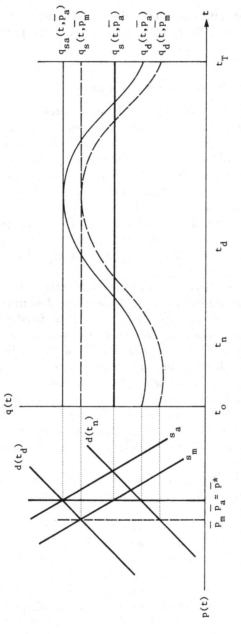

Figure 11.5. The U.S electric-power market.

Other than sheer, willfully legislated waste, this combination of policies – a time-invariant price that brings forth maximum consumer-demand variability over T and a rule that whatever $q(t)$ they demand must be supplied – assures a maximum of excess capacity in the industry. Supply is, at all but the most fleeting moment of peak demand, quantity-rationed; demand variation is unfettered.

Left to their own devices with these two admonitions, producers would price at their marginal cost, producing output at a maximum rate of $q_s(t,\bar{p}_m)$ at a price, $\bar{p}_m$, that covered the marginal costs associated with the highest rate of demand $q_p(t)$ that becomes, by mandate, the highest rate of output. But that would leave the producers not only in a position of natural monopolies, where all this regulation started, but also in a position of making time-specific Ricardian rents – suppliers would set the necessarily time-invariant price of all output rates equal to the time-specific marginal costs of the most expensive output rate at the same time that consumers were encouraged by the time-invariant price to stay ignorant of those time-specific costs of peak output.[5] (This enforced ignorance is clearly reminiscent of Shephard's Production Office in Chapter 6.) That could justify decree No. 3:

Decree No. 3 requires firms to price output at less than marginal cost, indeed, at average cost, like $\bar{p}_a$ in Figure 11.5. This final decree has three effects. First, in establishing a lower time-invariant price, $\bar{p}_a$, than the marginal cost price, it increases the demand for electric power, shifting the whole demand profile up to $q_d(t,\bar{p}_a)$. Second, it thereby increases the necessary installed capacity, so that producing firms can adhere to decree No. 2 and meet all peak-load demand, max $q_{sa}(t,\bar{p}_a)$. So this policy, in effect, alters the firm's supply curve from one based on marginal costs, s_m, to one based on average costs, s_a, in Figure 11.5. Third, although it brings the price down toward (and indistinguishable from) the "best" time-invariant price, $\bar{p}^*$, it does not thereby alter the underlying waste inherent in perpetual excess supply as does $\bar{p}^*$, nor does it alter the distribution of disequilibria. Average cost pricing, therefore, maintains maximum excess capacity; so although $\bar{p}_a$ is in the same neighborhood as $\bar{p}^*$, the latter implies quantity rationing of demand, and hence lower production costs and higher resource utilization and productivity. Finally, in light of the developments of the past decade, it should be noted that rising fuel costs increase the cost of a time-invariant pricing policy by increasing the costs of pure supply adjustment.[6]

Two sorts of departures from these policies are currently under consideration, and the time-specific analysis makes their comparison usefully clear. One, predictably, simply abandons time-invariant prices and substitutes time-specific, peak-load prices instead. The other abandons the imperative that power suppliers must satisfy all time-specific demand generated by time-invariant prices and substitutes quantity rationing instead. Both reduce output fluctuations, and hence costs over the unit time, flattening the output curve; peak-load pricing does it by flattening the demand load profile, and "load management" does it by authorizing selective quantity rationing of an unchanged demand profile.

The strengths of peak-load pricing have been adequately celebrated in the earlier discussion. Its weakness is the weakness of any price rationing: Its heavy dependence on existing income distribution. Those households that are discouraged from peak-load consumption by higher time-specific prices have been shown earlier to be either (a) those with relatively attractive alternative inputs or consumption activities then or (b) those with low incomes that force them to value those increased costs very highly. In terms of Chapter 8, a large marginal utility of income, λ, implies a large value of goods inputs $\lambda p_i(t_p) x_i(t_p)$ at the peak period t_p, and hence a large reduction in net utility flow, $\mu_i(t_p)$, with peak-load pricing quite aside from preferences or alternative activities.

The administrative fiat of "load management" that allows firms to quantity-ration power during peak periods has, of course, the opposite strengths and weaknesses: It can specify as trivial and expendable a specific set of peak uses of power without regard to household preferences or incomes. In a major experiment in southern California, for instance, swimming-pool pumps are summarily denied power during peak periods, thus avoiding socially obnoxious income-distribution effects by using use-specific quantity rationing. But it does so by substituting the judgments of government regulators for those of the households, and that is likely to become increasingly arbitrary – and certainly inefficient by our usual criteria – as load management cuts increasingly deeply into peak demand.[7]

Time-specific pricing to utilize nonconventional power sources

A different aspect of the electric-power market is also nicely captured by time-specific analysis, because that description of the market pictures nonconventional sources of electric power – particularly wind and tidal power – in a way that implies a useful if nonconventional policy toward them.

The reason these power sources are not now included as "conventional" is, simply, their timing. Their output does not come at the right time relative to the demand pattern – it is either unpredictable ("unreliable"), like the wind, or predictable but on a rhythmic pattern that is out of phase with the rhythm of demand, like the tides. Or both. Technology and costs of production are not problems (McMullan et al., 1976); only timing is. So the conventional wisdom about nonconventional power sources is that they will become feasible parts of our energy resources only when low-cost electric-power storage technology is sufficiently developed that their unreliable and inappropriately timed supplies can be carried over until they can be absorbed by the far more predictable time-shaped demand. This view, of course, is quite in keeping with the extreme demand-domination implicit in the foregoing description of U.S. power policy.

But an alternative policy is suggested by the time-specific market model, which would allow the utilization of these power sources, at least in a limited way, even without cheap storage.

The last three chapters have examined in some detail the theoretical foundations of a household's response to time-specific prices; a time-specific price increase induces substitution out of that input in the production of activities and/or the abandonment of those activities in which that product is used. Although what was considered in that analysis was the household's response to a price that changed on a predictable rhythmic pattern, rhythmic predictability is not a necessary condition; some response to time-specific price change can undoubtedly be induced by less regular price changes. What is necessary and sufficient, given our usual assumptions about consumer motivation, is (a) that the household know the price at each moment of time and (b) that the household have the ability to change the input mix or activities or both.

Consider information first, how the household knows of the price at time t. The method implicit in the earlier discussion – the method most appropriate to the rhythmic price patterns over T that we have concentrated on – is simply that $p_i(t)$ is defined by a time-specific price schedule plus, importantly, a clock or calendar. The household reads t from the clock and calendar and then reads $p_i(t)$ from the time-conditional price schedule. But clearly there are other ways to transmit price information: In a simple enough power system, for instance, the fact that the wind was blowing outside could crudely indicate to households a lower electric-power price; so could, with more regularity and predictability, a price schedule augmented with a tide table. But the functions of schedule and timekeeping device can be combined, and, most simply, an explicit direct signal can transmit current prices to the household, moment by moment. The California experiment with peak-quantity rationing of power to swimming-pool pumps, mentioned earlier, uses a simple device on the pump to sense a signal sent through the power lines from the central power station to turn the pump off and on over the peak period; an only slightly more complicated signal would convey time-specific prices, moment by moment.

The advantage of instantaneous time-specific price information is that it can adapt to changes in supply or demand as they occur; its disadvantage is its unpredictability, which reduces the household's ability to adjust to price change.

In terms of the now very familiar time-specific supply and demand profiles – any one of them – that describe time-shaped markets, the unpredictable upward shifts in supply at time t that would come, for instance, with increased availability of wind power or the predictable but badly timed upward shifts that would come from tidal power would both lower the equilibrium price, $p(t)$, at time t. The households' incentive to respond to that lower time-specific price would be the same as before, and to the extent that they were able, they would alter the input mix or change activities.

It could not be expected that households (or industries) would be able or willing to respond to unpredictable and inconveniently timed variations in price in exactly the same manner and to the same extent that they would respond to the regular, predictable rhythmic price patterns we have previously discussed (indeed, to assert that they would would subvert much of the point of this study of rhythmic events). The suggestion, instead, is that there would be some response to even these nonsystematic or awkwardly systematic price changes, so that some incorporation of ill-timed alternative power sources is feasible even without waiting for the evolution of cheap storage technologies: Prices can be expected to induce some adaptation of demand to supply even when the supply variations are nonrhythmic.[8]

11.3   Time-specific distortions and mismatch: the labor market

The descriptions of efficient labor markets in the last chapter and the beginning of this one assumed that the time-specific labor service flows and the time-specific wage rates that emerged to clear the market would be the same for both households and firms – that what firms paid out for labor, households would get, and what households sold, firms would buy. But in important cases there will be a wedge driven between the wage paid by the firm, on which its production decisions are based, and that received by the household, on which its work-timing decisions are based – or a wedge between labor services sold and bought. And that wedge itself may be time-specific. This section briefly examines three important cases in which labor market distortions are time-specific, so that they have different impacts on household production decisions at different times of day. In one, distortion affects the productivity of labor; in the second, it affects the cost of goods inputs to work activity; in the third, it affects the after-tax wage of labor.

Nighttime labor productivity in less developed countries: time-specific "unlimited supplies of labor"

Studies in advanced countries have failed to establish that labor productivity is different between night and day (Vroom, 1968). But for less developed countries (LDCs), there is little doubt that labor productivity is markedly lower at night than during the day and that this low nighttime productivity acts like a higher wage rate, inducing some firms to shut down at night, with consequent reduction in capital productivity and employment: This is in countries with a shortage of capital and the need for expanded employment (Baily, 1974; Winston, 1977*b*).

Figure 11.6 is a time-specific representation of the industrial sector in an LDC under the usual assumptions that the industrial wage rate is high enough (for whatever reason) to create "an unlimited supply of labor." So over the day, *T,* there is permanent excess supply, despite the households' dominant optimal daytime work schedules reflected in the familiar time-shape of the labor-supply profile, $l_s(t,\bar{w})$. This has been described, less precisely if no less accurately, in the fact that workers under conditions of unlimited supplies of labor do not have the market power to impose their work-timing preferences on the labor market (Farooq and Winston, 1978). The other aspect of the industrial labor market that is clear in the figure is that the wage rate is so high at $\bar{w}$ that the only pressure to make it time-specific comes from the supply side and that some sort of Lewis-type restriction is assumed to prevent effective bidding down of the wage rate day or night. So the wage rate remains both high and time-invariant. But, of course, the market itself is not time-invariant.[9]

The implication of Figure 11.6 is that because there are no effective

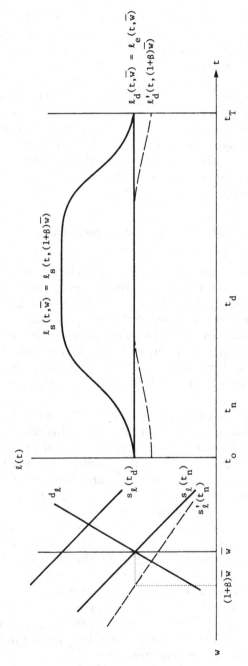

Figure 11.6. Reduced nighttime productivity with unlimited supplies of labor.

time-differentiated wage rates, the response of firms will increase the utilization of capital. An advantage of this sort of "unlimited supply of labor" disequilibrium, our analysis to this point suggests, should be the inducement to all firms making storable products to utilize their scarce productive capital at maximum levels, because they do not have the usual advanced-country disincentive to high utilization in the form of a night wage premium. But at this point, day–night labor productivity differentials become highly relevant.

At night, lower productivity forces firms to pay $(1 + \beta)\bar{w}$ to get the same quantity of productive labor service flow that they get for $\bar{w}$ during the day. There is a difference between what households sell as labor services and what firms get as labor services – the wedge between the two sides of the market. It can be expressed in quantity or price terms, but prices – the effective wage rate paid by the firm and received by the household for an efficiency unit of labor – most clearly describe the time-specific incentives that affect the firm. If average nighttime labor productivity is only a fraction, y $(0 \leq y \leq 1)$, of daytime productivity, then the implicit nighttime wage premium paid by the firm is β, where $\beta = (1/y) - 1$. So in Figure 11.6, the effective labor-supply curve facing firms at night becomes $s_l'(t_n)$, which is shifted from $s_l(t_n)$ by $\beta\bar{w}$. In consequence of the higher effective nighttime wage rate, employment is reduced to $l_d'(t, (1 + \beta)\bar{w})$, because some firms find it optimal to shut down at night rather than pay the higher labor costs to operate then.

From the workers' perspective, of course, the wage rate is the same both night and day. Those who have jobs at night see no increased wage rate, and those who do not have jobs but would be willing to work then are genuinely unemployed in the sense that they offer labor at the prevailing wage rate but find no work. The result of the nighttime productivity differential is unemployment of labor, idle capital, and reduced output from the given (and limited) capital stocks. That suggests a closer look at its causes.

This idleness of capital stocks at night, it should be emphasized, has quite different welfare significance from that in the advanced countries discussed early in the chapter, even though it may look much the same to firms' managers. In an advanced country, the higher time-specific wage rate is a payment by firms to workers to induce them to choose to work at a time of day they would not choose under a time-invariant wage rate. Given preferences, environment, resources, and technologies of both firm and household production, idleness of firms' capital in a smoothly functioning economy is fully Pareto-optimal – it is simply the cost to society of its scheduling work and consumption when it wants to. This is not the case for an LDC. If lower nighttime labor productivity were somehow inherent in poor countries, one might want to note that in the presence of nighttime unemployment a lower nighttime wage rate would appear both socially optimal and individually preferable to the alternative of unemployment.[10] But the cause of the time-specific productivity change appears to be less mysterious and less inexorable than that. And it carries more direct implications for economic understanding and policy.

The much lower levels of household capital stock used by workers in LDCs appear to be a primary cause of the differences in time-specific productivity between advanced and underdeveloped countries. The literature on the physiology of shift-working suggests not only that sleep quality is of great importance but also that – put in terms of the time-specific household model – the production of sleep at nonnormal times of day is a highly capital-intensive household activity. The environmental changes over night and day sharply alter the efficiency with which sleep is done. But that strong environmental rhythm can be offset by increased use of household capital services.

An advanced-country worker comes home from working the night shift at 8:00 in the morning to an air-conditioned bedroom with window shades and screens that cut out daylight and insects and a door and windows that reduce the noises of the rest of the family and neighborhood as they go about their daytime activities. So that worker arrives at work at midnight the next night relatively well rested. And that shows up in his relatively high productivity. The worker on the same schedule in a poor country, in sharp contrast, comes home from the night shift at 8:00 in the morning to an open, one-room house in which he tries to sleep in a single bed, fully exposed to the noise, heat, and light of conflicting rhythms and conflicting activities of family, neighborhood, environment, and bugs.[11] He arrives at work at midnight without adequate rest, and consequently his productivity is low. Given their meager household capital stocks, the only way workers in poor countries can avoid disruptive characteristics of geophysical and social rhythms during sleep is by conforming to the "normal" activity rhythms of their neighborhoods and families – by working days.

A potential misallocation of capital stocks between industrial and household sectors is clearly implied: Socially scarce capital is involved both in creating the households' low nighttime labor productivity and in the firms' response to it. Inadequate household capital stocks lead to low nighttime labor productivity, which results in lower utilization of industrial capital stocks. Any action, including direct investment in worker-housing capital, that would reduce the decline in nighttime productivity would increase the flow of industrial capital services from unchanged capital stocks. In Figure 11.6, the labor-supply curve facing firms would thereby be shifted back from $s'(t_n)$ toward $s(t_n)$, inducing increased utilization, employment, output, and capital productivity as a consequence of increased time-specific labor productivity.[12]

Complementing such an investment allocation policy would be one that encouraged intertemporal mobility of workers to maximize their chances for self-selection among work schedules. The evidence is that the wrong people, in terms of household characteristics, often work shifts in poor countries, largely because meager employment opportunities block mobility. So part of the productivity problem is due to having so many ill-adapted people – those of Figure 11.3 – working shifts, even though they find that schedule injurious to their health and productivity (Farooq and Winston, 1978).

Economies of scale in time-specific work costs

A different sort of time-specific wedge in the labor market is created by the costs of goods inputs to work activities. Since Murray Foss's 1963 study of the changing patterns of capital utilization in U.S. industry, it has been apparent that something unusual happened to shift-working behavior during World War II. Before that, night working increased at a slow rate. During the war, it increased markedly. Although that discontinuity might be explained by a number of war-related changes – patriotic zeal, high prices, high wages, cost-plus contracts, etc. – what remains puzzling is that after the war, when these stimuli were gone, shift-working failed to drop toward prewar levels.[13] The long-run trend toward increased utilization and shift-working continued, but it did so on top of the discontinuity of the war.

The explanation for this anomaly appears to lie mainly in a change in the goods costs of work activities.[14] This is a part of the earlier model of work activities that was explicitly dismissed in the analysis of time-specific labor markets both in the last chapter and so far in this one. But from equation (9.3), if goods costs are incurred in work activity, $p_w(t)x_w(t)$, they drive a wedge between the gross wage rate paid by employers and the net wage rate received by workers.

Although goods costs of work were considered in Chapter 9, that discussion neglected timing, implying that goods costs would be the same at any time of day. But it is clear that the costs of goods inputs to work activities often are themselves highly time-specific: Commuting or getting a meal during work or a beer after work carry very different costs at different times. So it is necessary to distinguish, if only crudely, between goods costs for work done by time of day: $p_w(t_d)x_w(t_d)$ and $p_w(t_n)x_w(t_n)$.

Then what happened in the United States appears to have been this: In most communities, shift-working was uncommon enough before World War II that nighttime provision of services to shift-workers was done on a small scale, with consequently high costs. The war-induced increase in night work brought economies of scale to that nighttime provision of work-related services, permanently altering the relative costs of night work and day work, thus permanently altering the trend in shift-working and capital utilization.

Figure 11.7 shows the prewar time-specific labor market, with firms' demand for labor, d_l, as a time-invariant function of the wage rate, $w(t)$, and households' supply of labor as a function shifting from $s_l(t_d)$ during more generally optimal daytime work hours to $s_l(t_n)$ at night. If there were no difference in the goods costs of work activities over the day and night, the night labor supply would simply shift by $\beta w(t_d)$, because the wage rate for any given quantity of labor service flow had to be $\beta w(t_d)$ higher at night to induce work at that nonpreferred time. That higher nighttime wage rate would have the familiar effects of inducing some firms to shut down, demanding less labor at night, and inducing some households to reschedule their work from day to night in response to the higher nighttime wage rate.

But if the goods costs of work are

$$c_w(t) = p_w(t)x_w(t),$$

and night work carries higher time-specific goods input costs, then the cost difference between night and day is

$$dc_w(t_n) = p_w(t_n)x_w(t_n) - p_w(t_d)x_w(t_d) > 0, \tag{11.1}$$

and the nighttime labor-supply curve is further shifted from $s_l(t_n)$ to $s_l'(t_n)$ by $dc_w(t_n)$ for each rate of labor service flow. The gross wage rate paid by the firms for nighttime labor is

$$w_g(t_n) = (1 + \beta)w_n(t_d) + p_w(t_n)x_w(t_n). \tag{11.2}$$

But although firms pay out $w_g(t_n)$ for a unit of labor services at night, workers get, after paying the higher time-specific goods costs, only the net wage rate $w_n(t_n)$:[15] Although $s_l(t_n)$ is the nighttime labor-supply curve, $s_l'(t_n)$ is the nighttime labor supply that faces the firms; the

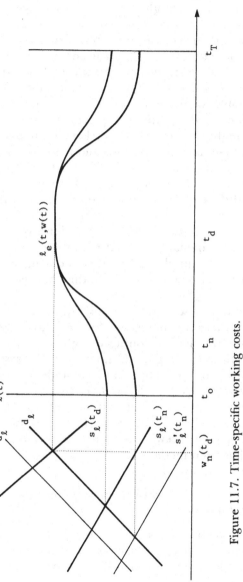

Figure 11.7. Time-specific working costs.

difference is $dc_w(t_n)$, the higher costs of night working. Firms are discouraged from operating at night by high gross wage rates, and workers are discouraged from working at night by low net wage rates. So $l_e'(t,w(t))$ is a time-specific equilibrium labor profile for the prewar market. It reflects the high gross night wage and little shift-working.

With the advent of the war, high prices, favorable contracts, and patriotic feelings increased firms' (time-invariant) labor demand to d_l', making it profitable for more firms to schedule nighttime operation. Because the increased nighttime employment increased the derived demand for nighttime services to workers, economies of scale (time-specific, of course) reduced the costs and prices of those inputs to work activity, reducing $dc_w(t_n)$ and shifting $s_l'(t_n)$ to the right in Figure 11.7. Scale economies might completely eliminate any day–night goods price differentials, making $dc_w(t_n) = 0$; if so, the nighttime labor-supply curve $s_l'(t_n)$ would shift all the way back to $s_l(t_n)$. So the increase in profitability of nighttime operation that initially increased nighttime labor demand lowered nighttime goods costs, increasing nighttime labor supply and further inducing night work. Both firms and workers were induced by the scale economies to schedule more work at night.

At the conclusion of this scenario, once nighttime scale economies had been achieved, there was no reason for them to be reversed – the high goods costs that had discouraged nighttime operation before the war were no longer high, and nothing in the system need change them back again. In Figure 11.7, labor demand can shift after the war back to the prewar level, d_l, but still keep nighttime employment at the wartime level that first induced scale economies of goods inputs to night work. As drawn in $l_e'(t,w(t))$, postwar daytime employment is the same as prewar daytime employment, but nighttime employment has been increased.[16]

Progressive income taxes that become time-specific with high marginal rates

The final case of distortion to be considered in the labor market describes the time-specific effect of progressive income taxes. It is no less important for following in a straightforward way from the preceding analysis.

If workers' incomes are taxed, the time-specific supply of labor may be shifted; to induce a given quantity of labor at nonpreferred times, a higher pretax wage rate is required. The issue, it is important to note, is the effect of income taxes on when people choose to work – and its implications – not the traditional issue of the effect of taxes on how much they work.

If workers' incomes are subjected to a sufficiently high marginal income tax rate, the distortion in work timing can be large and its effects on resource productivity potentially serious. In Sweden, the average industrial worker faces a 65% marginal income tax rate. The marginal tax rate, of course, reduces any nighttime wage premium, β, received by a worker: A 30% wage premium for night work is reduced to 10% by the Swedish marginal tax rate. Nighttime labor supply can be expected to respond to such drastically reduced incentives to work at night. Firms will respond, too, because they pay the gross pretax nighttime wage rate – a full $\beta w(t)$ – so they will determine their optimal utilization on the basis of that much higher wage. The result must be lower capital utilization and lower productivity of capital resources. This is a uniquely time-specific effect of personal income taxes on the productivity of capital.

11.4   Summary and conclusions

This chapter has served to expand and apply the basic analysis of time-shaped markets developed in the preceding one. It has moved from that initial discussion in two directions: It has focused on the welfare and efficiency implications unique to time-specific markets, and it has used the time-shaped market model to examine the kinds of uniquely time-specific distortions that can arise in those markets.

Efficiency has unusual dimensions in a time-specific market. There exists a "best" time-invariant price that will bring a stable disequilibrium to that market, but it does so by distributing disequilibria about between buyers and sellers in a stable way. In orthodox theory, that price would appear to be an equilibrium price, but in fact it is only stable; the quantity traded over the unit time would mysteriously be less than either the quantity supplied or the quantity demanded at that price. A time-specific price is a more efficient alternative than the best time-invariant price because it increases the productivity of fixed resources – bringing their utilization in line with the timing preferences of their owners – and it distributes their product in line with the preferences of users. The potential disadvantage of time-specific pricing is its efficient service of preferences that are weighted, as usual, by incomes. Considered alone, the household was shown to be a potential winner or loser with time-specific pricing, because prices rise just when the typical household most wants to use a service.

Time-specific pricing in the labor market induces adjustments that relate directly to the household characteristics spelled out in the time-specific theory of household behavior, including, usefully, the accommodation of households' physiological characteristics that play so large a role in social assessment of the effects of shift-working. It is clear in this analysis that much of the social concern with shift-working is misdirected to the average worker rather than to the worker who will – with considerable incentive for self-selection among work schedules – actually work during "nonnormal" hours. Finally, brief consideration was given to the costs of time-specific pricing – metering costs, fixed "set-up" costs that restrict variations in the duration of work or consumption, especially work – and the often changing relationships of those costs to the potential gains of time-specific pricing.

Looking at the electric-power market as an archetypical time-specific product market revealed the degree of departure from time-specific efficiency embodied in current U.S. electric-power regulatory policies and, more optimistically, the theoretical rationale and promise of those changes in policy currently under most active consideration: peak-load price-rationing of demand and quantity-rationing of demand through "load management." In a brief and rather different illustration of the value of time-specific modeling in the electric-power market, it was shown that incorporating some nonconventional power sources appears possible without waiting, as is assumed necessary, for the development of low-cost storage technologies.

Finally, the labor market presented three cases that illustrate the implications of time-specific market analysis for questions of traditional economic concern. A radically different investment policy in underdeveloped countries is implied by an examination of the effects on the utilization of installed capital of reduced nighttime labor productivity in poor countries and the likelihood that the time-shape of productivity – so different from that of rich countries – is due in large part to underinvestment in household capital stocks. In the context of recent U.S. economic history, the time-specific model suggests that economies of scale in the provision of services to night workers may have played a role in the discontinuous increase in shift-working, and hence industrial capital utilization, during World War II. In the last illustration, high marginal income tax rates were shown to have the effect of reducing workers' incentives to work at night and firms' incentives to utilize their productive capital at night – both of which reduce measured real productivity.

PART VI

Postscript

Time-specific analysis of nonrhythmic events: relational exchange and the role of repetition

This postscript is added to suggest how time-specific analysis applies to nonrhythmic economic events within calendar time units and to endogenous time units defined by economic function and to draw some of their broader implications for economic theory. The basic structure of time-specific analysis was set out in Chapter 2, and it is unchanged in these extensions – what happens within a conventional unit time is still revealed by using two nested time units – but in one case the rhythmic predictability of events within T is modified, and in the other the calendar unit time is replaced by an endogenous time unit. These are discussed in the first two sections. A third section considers the repetitiveness of economic events, per se, suggesting that its degree, with wholly rhythmic events at one end of a continuum and wholly unique events at the other, is crucial in establishing the relevance of familiar analytical techniques: Neoclassical models of economic behavior appear to be highly appropriate to the analysis of repetitive, rhythmic events; at the same time, they are rather silly in the analysis of nonrepetitive, unique events.

12.1 The illusion of constancy: nonrhythmic events within calendar unit time

Through the previous chapters we have considered (with some lapses) only economic events that are repetitive – events that occur at the same time, t, in each calendar unit time, T – so together they generate regula₁ rhythmic change over a series of such calendar time units: lunch every day at noon; running the plant Monday through Friday every week; closing the golf course every fall. These strictly rhythmic economic events are simple conceptually; they have been shown to have important implications for economic theory and understanding, and they provided the simplest and most persuasive context for the introduction of time-specific analysis. But this section and the next will show that they are not the only useful application of that time-specific perspective.

Randomly timed events within the unit time

The simplest departure from a strictly rhythmic determinism considers events whose timing within the unit time, T, is random but has a known, anticipated, and constant frequency in every unit time. Much of the relevance of input and output characteristics introduced in Part II survives this limited introduction of stochastic behavior: Capital services still have duration-specific prices; other inputs have time-specific and time-invariant prices; the scheduling incentive remains to avoid high costs by altering time-specific activity choice – production or idleness, work or consumption, consumption activity z_1 or z_2 – in response to time-specific prices.

Such a simple stable but nonconstant time-specific model has been used to derive the implications of nonrigid preferences (Winston, 1980), a model in which the individual alternates randomly – flip-flops – between two preference sets, never knowing which will prevail at any given moment during T. It is a model of inconsistency and personal conflict, a model of people wanting to lose weight or quit smoking or stick to a self-imposed work schedule, but finding it difficult to do. Any such nonconstancy of preferences, of course, is masked if the analytical unit time t is also a long calendar period T; similarly, the underlying nonconstancy is masked by using expected values under stochastic preferences. So the underlying state of perpetual change is, in the now-familiar pattern, represented analytically as changeless, because that ceaseless oscillation has the same time-shape (now stochastic) in each unit time. To the extent that preference variability affects rational behavior, the analysis of expected values will lose essential information: Constancy is still not the same thing as regularity of change.

Just how essential that lost information is is apparent when that flip-flop model describes compulsive consumption. Because they have stable but nonconstant preferences, rational utility-maximizing consumers can suffer addictive compulsion, racked by internal conflict – "being of two minds" – and in need of self-control in a manner quite familiar in people if not in consumption theory. "Antimarket" institutions – like consumer credit counselors and alcoholic treatment centers and SmokEnders – develop in this model that charge consumers a fee to help them to *not* consume particular goods. Tricks and devices evolve, including self-deception – Schelling's "egonomics or the art of self-management" – to help that rational consumer to behave optimally. There is such a thing as too much self-control – utility can sometimes be maximized by a myopic hedonism in which the rational consumer does not maximize expected utility but, instead, does what feels good at each moment over T. All of these forms of all-too-human economic behavior emerge from an orthodox utility-maximizing model of the consumer, once stable but nonconstant preferences are introduced. None of this, of course, is implied by orthodox modeling:[1] As Schelling observed, such need for self-management – lest "consumers [get] negative satisfaction out of something they spend a lot of money to consume" – is an anomaly in conventional consumer theory (1978a, p. 293). It is not an anomaly in a time-specific consumer theory.

Mismatched rhythms

Time units and the periodic activities they denominate often nest nicely with each other – hours into days into weeks into months into years. But sometimes they do not, as in the case of lunar and diurnal periods. So the timing of the tidal rhythms that can generate cheap electric power is deterministic, and so is the timing of the diurnal rhythms that determine the time-shape of electric-power demand, but they do not match. From the perspective of either periodicity, events that are rhythmic in the other are not rhythmic events. This, of course, is the basis of the real economic problem of utilization of cheap tidal power discussed in Chapter 11. Tides cannot be counted on to provide electric power when, within the daily unit time, T, it is needed; viewed from the other side, the daily load curve cannot be counted on to absorb electric power when, within the lunar unit time, T, it is available. This inherent rhythmic mismatch requires either the conventional solution of cheap storage to make electric power temporally footloose or quantity rationing or the unconventional solution of time-of-supply pricing discussed earlier.

12.2 An endogenous unit time: the case of relational exchange

A time-specific analysis in which the unit time T becomes an endogenous measure is nicely illustrated by the theory of "relational exchange." It demonstrates, in an analysis of market transactions, the now-familiar way that the choice of T can obscure elements of behavior that are crucial to understanding an economic process. Relational exchange analysis describes a function of legal contracts. It was developed – by Williamson (1979) for labor markets and by Goldberg (1980) for general markets – not as a time-specific model

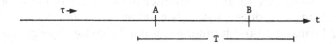

Figure 12.1. Unit time and relational exchange.

but as a description of the neglected market phenomenon of small numbers transactions.[2] When relational exchange is set in a time-specific perspective, it becomes apparent that a conventional unit time once again inadvertently loses important temporal information – in this case, information about the temporal sequence of the specific events that make up a transaction and systematically alter transactors' incentives over time.

We need to resurrect the idea of "perspective time" in order to describe relational exchange. Perspective time was introduced in Chapter 2 as that use of time in economic analysis (and behavior) in which it is important how events appear from the time perspective, τ, of economic actors – how their knowledge, opportunities, or behavior change as they move through time. Perspective time was distinguished from "analytical time" on the one hand and "commodity time" on the other. But as soon as it was introduced, the idea of perspective time was set aside on the grounds that the fully rhythmic and repetitive economic events on which this study was going to concentrate justified to a remarkable degree the assumption of perfect information and foresight by all actors, and that, in turn, eliminated the relevance of the distinction between perspective time and analytical time: If everyone knew everything over all time, one's temporal perspective would not alter his behavior. But in this chapter, nonrhythmic events are considered within a different sort of nonrepetitive unit time; so perspective time returns.

From the time perspective, τ, of the (two) participants in a market transaction, they move through time – along the time line in Figure 12.1 – through a sequence of transactions events, like A and B, that change their opportunity sets systematically. Those changes are the subject of relational exchange analysis. "A transaction" encompassed by the endogenous unit time T is decomposed, as in any time-specific analysis, into the temporally ordered set of events seen by the two economic actors as they move through time; the transaction between them is made up of ordered events that change their individual opportunities and constraints. The two participants are assumed, as usual, to be motivated by self-interest. In the simplest transaction there are only two events: a payment event and a goods-

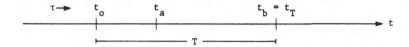

Figure 12.2. Perspective time and relational exchange.

delivery event. If these are not simultaneous, their sequencing changes the opportunities open to the two parties as they move through time. So "the transaction" does not look the same – and individually optimal behaviors are not the same – when viewed (a) over the whole transaction as a collection of unordered events as it does when viewed (b) as an ordered series of events in time. Because orthodox theory views the whole of a transaction as a lump – a single event like A-and-B in T – time-specific and relational exchange analyses identify something that is usually obscured, in the familiar way, by the abstraction implicit in choice of T.

In the simplest transaction, buyer V makes a money payment to seller O (event A) in exchange for O's delivery of goods to V (event B). If events A and B are not simultaneous, then the self-interest of each trader, along with the sequencing of these two transactions elements, creates the problem analyzed by relational exchange. If t_0 is the moment the decision is made to undertake the transaction,[3] and if payment, A, comes before delivery of the goods, B, so that $t_0 < t_a < t_b = t_T$, then Figure 12.2 describes the time-shape of events over which τ moves; τ, of course, has to be the same for both transactors V and O.

The opportunities of self-interested actors change systematically over T ($= t_T - t_0$): They are different before event A (V's payment to O: $\tau < t_a$), between that payment and event B (O's delivery of the goods to V: $t_a < \tau < t_b$), and after event B ($t_T < \tau$). During $\tau < t_a$, which includes the moment of decision to enter the transaction, t_0, voluntary exchange assures that each party expects to gain from the complete transaction on the familiar ground that underlies the gains from trade. During $t_a < \tau < t_b$, however, things change. O's self-interest requires that he take the money and run. During this time, he has V's money and has not yet reached the moment t_b of his own compensating transaction event, B, delivery of the goods. In an isolated two-person transaction, if O fails to exploit his time-specific advantage over V, he cannot be acting in his assumed self-interest.

Of course, identifying the reasons why he typically does not abscond with V's money is a primary point of this analysis. (Williamson called the temptation to do so "small group opportunism.") So a naive V might get this far, but most of us V's are not naive and will put ourselves in this potentially vulnerable position of $t_a < \tau < t_b$ only when we have "protection of reliance," in the legal jargon Goldberg used – some way of keeping O from taking off with our money. An enforceable contract is one such way (Goldberg, 1980); justifiable trust is another (Arrow, 1974; Bok, 1978; Schelling, 1978b); the time-specific formulation suggests, additionally, altering event timing as a third; repetition as a fourth.

The particular transactions event sequence of this illustration – payment-then-delivery – is not central, of course, to the issue of relational exchange. If event A were, instead, the delivery of the goods and event B were the payment for them (ordinary trade credit or charge accounts), then the vulnerable transactor, V, would simply become the seller and the potential opportunist, O, the buyer; all the rest of the simple case remains, including, crucially, O's incentive during $t_a < \tau < t_b$ to run – this time with V's goods instead of his money.[4]

Two or three quite useful implications follow from analysis of even this minimal transaction. One is that the alternative to protecting V's interests somehow during his period of vulnerability is simply not to trade at all, and that is clearly Pareto-inefficient; it denies to both V and O the potential gains from trade. Arrow's functional justification of the role of codified behavior, including trust, is, of course, much to this point (Arrow, 1974). The next implication is that if transactions events A and B actually occurred simultaneously, so that $t_a = t_b$, then the temporal situation, $t_a < \tau < t_b$, that causes the problem could not exist, and there would be no period of vulnerability of either party to the transaction. Simultaneity simply eliminates the problems described by relational exchange; so, of course, does the illusion of simultaneity got by thinking in terms of a too-large analytical unit time, t.[5] Finally, the asymmetry between the opportunities open to O and V that comes with time as they move from $\tau < t_a$ to $t_a < \tau < t_b$ joins with the requirement that each act in his own self-interest to cause the problem of relational exchange.

So the underlying relational exchange problem would be eliminated

1. if there were no trade
2. if all transactions elements were in fact simultaneous
3. if O's self-interest could be attenuated (a) by an altered objective function (trustworthiness), (b) by external legal authority

(enforceable contracts), or (c) by O's hope for future – repetitive – transactions with V that would link control of his present opportunism to potential future gains from trade.

More complicated relational transactions have the same basic structure and these same general elements in their control.[6]

12.3   Repetitiveness, neoclassical theory, and opportunism

The dimension of repetitiveness of economic events has an analytical status that appears to have been too little appreciated. Indeed, there is a striking parallel between large numbers of transactions in market space and large numbers of transactions in time – between competitiveness and repetitiveness in transactions.[7] And although an extensive development of this theme is more appropriate to the beginning of a book than the end of one, it seems appropriate to conclude a study that has concentrated on the careful temporal analysis of rhythmic, repetitive events with an explicit if preliminary and partial consideration of repetitiveness per se. The degree of repetitiveness of economic events is a characteristic that (a) determines the appropriateness of even the most textbookish of orthodox neoclassical market analysis and (b) when applied to transactions, modifies the incentives that transactor O has to exploit his sequential advantage over V.

Neoclassical theory

The most extreme version of orthodox neoclassical market analysis includes assumptions of (a) perfect information, (b) rationality as optimization, and (c) an unchanged decision environment. It seems clear that these are not unreasonable assumptions when applied to highly repetitive events. They certainly can be unreasonable when applied to other (often important) economic events that occur with less regularity. But that fact suggests a greater sensitivity among analysts to the repetitiveness of particular economic events as a variable that determines the appropriateness of their orthodox analysis rather than the wholesale rejection of that analysis, because it can be inappropriately applied.[8]

Take as illustrative an economic activity that occurs regularly in conjunction with a rhythmic geophysical unit time like the day – say the decision on how to get to work:

1. Repetition ensures cognition and learning in the dullest economic actor; so even "perfect knowledge" may not be an outra-

geous description of the conditions of decision: Information about repetitive events is cheap and easy to process (Stigler, 1961).[9]

2. Repetition allows the nice adjustments explicitly needed for optimization. It is likely that all potential global, and not just local, optima will eventually have been considered in deciding how to get to work (Alchian, 1950).

3. Repetition suggests that the event will occur many times without significant change in the decision environment, including tastes, prices, technologies, expectations, etc. Simon's observation (1959) is relevant: that relative rates of change in environment and adaptive ability determine the appropriateness of equilibrium analysis.

4. Repetition makes expectations a reasonable guide to the future, because they are firmly based on a large amount of relatively accurate past information, including successful previous forecasts.

In the extreme, even a purely static equilibrium model will tell much about repetitive economic behavior. It can be argued that the economic decision is not made about an individual event in repetitive cases – how to get to work next Tuesday morning – but about a class of events – getting to work.[10] Then the decision cost component of each transaction is small because it is spread over a large number of transactions events.

So, the most uncomfortable assumptions of orthodox market analysis are plausible – even realistic – when applied to repetitive transactions, and it seems necessary to reject the relevance of highly abstract analyses (Lachmann, 1976; Shackle, 1958; Kornai, 1971) that start with the fact that the future is unknowable as a first principle and then derive the implication that therefore nothing can be known. Unless those analyses recognize crucial differences in the repetitiveness of economic events, their criticism is as limited as the scope of their target; it makes sense to underscore the deep existential uncertainty that surrounds unique decisions about unique events, but it is pretentious and inappropriate to extend it to repetitive events. And if neoclassical economics were seen only as an economics of repetitive events, it would nonetheless remain a powerful tool of social analysis.

Repetitive transactions attenuating opportunism

Now turn back to the relational transactions problem described earlier. At its base, those problems are caused by the time sequence of transactions events that alters the relative opportunities of the transactors, *seriatim;* so their assumed self-interest creates conflicts – temptations and vulnerabilities. Repetitive transactions change that. If a transaction of the simple type AB is expected to be repeated over and over again, the self-interest of O is no longer clearly served by taking advantage of V during the period $t_a < \tau < t_b$. Against O's temptation to opportunism is set his self-interest in the gains from trade of further transactions. With potentially repetitive transactions, $t_a < t_b$, and at the same time, $t_b < t_a$. O may have an incentive under strict myopia to take advantage of V in $t_a < \tau < t_b$, but a longer time horizon reveals the gains from possible future trade with V that such opportunism will jeopardize, and the myopic incentive may not survive. As in the flip-flop model discussed in Section 12.1, given repetition and awareness of events *in* time, t, O's analytical unit time T will determine his optimal behavior – the more encompassing is T, the less relevant may be his myopic judgment with its consequent opportunism.

Repetition, to be sure, is not sufficient to establish symmetry between V and O in even a long series of repetitive transactions. V, in the simplest case, is always vulnerable to O's opportunism during $t_a < \tau < t_b$, whereas O has no equivalent period of vulnerability to V. Yet both stand to lose the gains from trade if either should break off the potentially repetitive series of transactions. But even if an incomplete symmetry is established, the raw unrestricted drive of O's opportunism that appears in a one-shot transaction (a used car, a set of encyclopedias) is tempered by the prospect of the future gains from trade that O forsakes if he indulges his myopic self-interest. Honesty, as Arrow argued, may pay; control of momentary self-interest, given repetitive transactions, may lead to a longer-run self-interest.[11]

12.4 Two notes on repetitiveness: reputations and liars as free riders in time and space

The number of transactions in time and the number of transactors in market space often interact. Even if O engages in unique, nonrepetitive transactions in which his trading partners are different in each transaction $(V_1, V_2, ..., V_n)$, his temptations to opportunism in any $t_a < \tau < t_b$ of any one transaction may be reduced if information about his transaction behavior flows at low cost from current buyer (V_1) to potential future buyers (the V_i). This information flow is most likely, of course, where there is a relatively small number of potential buyers and they are known to each other – they have established information channels. Then, even without the discipline of the prospect of repetitive transactions with V_1, the potential loss of reputation with the other potential transactors will act in much the same way to protect all the V_i during any period of vulnerability with O. O's calculation, again, weighs the gain of fleecing V_1 against the loss of gains from future trade with V_2, V_3, etc., consequent on his damaged reputation. People are more honest in small towns, except when they deal with tourists.[12]

Finally, note the striking parallel between the opportunistic traders in these time-specific analyses of market transactions and the familiar free riders of public goods and cartel theories. One is a free rider in a time context; the other is a free rider in social or market space. Both are liars (Bok, 1978).

In social space, the free rider is one who misrepresents his own preferences or behavior in order to profit from the actions of others. He lies about his preferences for public goods, intending that others will represent their preferences more honestly and that he will get the public goods for free. Or he is the chiseler in a cartel who deceives his fellow cartel members into thinking he is going along with colluded pricing, while he secretly shades price to increase his own sales. And so on. The problem is familiar.[13]

Over time, the free rider of relational exchange is the opportunistic liar, O. In the time sequence of transactions, decisions made at t_0 affect the choice set of the actors when they move on to other events – like the vulnerability of V during $t_a < \tau < t_b$. The liar, O, induces others, V, to make decisions at t_0 on the basis of false information so that those decisions will advantage the liar.[14] O induces V to make his payment, event A, only by convincing him that the goods will later be delivered, event B. If O had not lied, either he would have told the truth that he would not deliver the goods – so V would not have made the payment and thereby not have become vulnerable – or, alternatively, he would have told the truth that he would deliver the goods – so again V would not be vulnerable during any part of the transaction. In neither case does the problem of temporal change in opportunity affect behavior – honesty eliminates it by adding an additional objective to modify the pure self-interest of transactors. Douglass North (1981), Melvin Reder (1979), Mike McPherson (1981), and Kenneth Arrow (1974) have recently turned to this crucial dimension of market behavior.

Repetition protects V in much the same way as honesty. In order for there to be a transaction, V has to accept the truth of O's commitment to B before t_a, and V is not likely to do so if he has been burned by O before – or if he knows by reputation of others who have. Legally enforceable contracts are also a way of guarding against liars for unique transactions, just as the legally mandated taxes are a way of guarding against liars for public goods in face of the same individual incentives to cheat.

Notes

1. Introduction

1 In correspondence.

2 There is a strong parallel between recent developments in the pure theory of international trade and these time-specific models. Both consider more complete descriptions than have been customary of the characteristics of goods and services – their mobility of specificity between sectors or moments of time or countries – and what they mean for efficient production and exchange.

3 The discrete-time model has been absorbed into the subsequent shift-work literature by Baily (1974) and Betancourt and Clague (1975), among others.

2. Timing, information loss, and unit time in economic analysis

1 Anyone wanting the larger challenge of asking "What is time?" should look at Whitrow's accessible little book *The Nature of Time* (1972) or Fraser's *Time as Conflict* (1978). Martin Gardner has described some of the latest philosophical propositions on time in *Scientific American* (1979), and among the most thorough and informed surveys is that of Georgescu (1971).

2 Martin Gardner's description of "the familiar subject of time's relativity" is useful in both describing and justifying this parochially human conception of time: "Newton believed the universe was pervaded by a single absolute time that could be symbolized by an imaginary clock off somewhere in space (perhaps outside the cosmos). By means of this clock the rates of all the events in the universe could be measured. The notion works well within a single inertial frame of reference such as the surface of the earth, but it does not work for inertial systems moving in relation to each other at high speeds" (1979, p. 21). Because most human economic activity is clearly confined to the single inertial frame of reference on the surface of the earth – none of it involves inertial systems moving in relation to each other at high speeds – it seems wholly justifiable to stick to something akin to the Newtonian conception. I will.

3 This sort of separation of characteristics of time is certainly not original. Indeed, the distinction between the order of events and their perception

by human observers as past-present-future is central to many analyses of time by philosophers and economists. But, once made, they put it to markedly different uses: McTaggert used it to argue that time is not real; see Georgescu (1971) for an excellent summary of McTaggert's influential if unbelievable argument. Shackle argued that only the present "moment-in-being" is real and that all else is illusion. Georgescu and Hicks are closest in spirit to the analysis of this book – having been most influential – Hicks seeing both temporal order and perception as important to economic understanding, but perception as having been given short shrift in the dominant "equilibrist" analyses of the day (1976), whereas Georgescu argued that perception lies at the base of all time (1971, p. 133), that temporal order is derived from man's perception of it.

4 This is a favorite theme of science fiction writers, who often endow their extraterrestrial characters with the ability to act like economists; see Vonnegut's Tramfalmadorians in *Sirens of Titan* (1959), for instance.

5 This scarcity is generally accepted as obvious. But Georgescu-Roegen took Robbins to task for having asserted that time is scarce because "there are only twenty-four hours in the day," asking "would the fact that there are one million microns in one meter make space (land) plentiful?" Clearly, Robbins (and Becker and my discussion in Part IV of this book) asserted a scarcity of time relative to the amount typically desired at zero price.

6 Strictly, commodity time can no longer be held to be an analytical category when it is recognized – as it is in Chapter 8 – that limited labor services and not a reified Time are what is involved in commodity-time ("time-allocation") models like Robbins's and mine and Becker's. But the idea that "time is scarce" and that therefore it matters how we "spend it" is so deeply and usefully ingrained in both economic and common usage that it seems fruitless and even petulant to try to purge vocabulary of commodity-time concepts.

7 These two are frequently recognized: Phelps and Pollak (1968) decomposed time preference into two components analogous to analytical time and perspective time; the conflicts of "myopic" judgments in Strotz's well-known analysis (1955) of dynamic utility maximization depend on simultaneous awareness of perspective "Now" and analytical "planning period." But frequently they are not recognized.

8 The abstracting role of the unit time is explicit, within my reading, only at a very abstract level in Georgescu-Roegen's *Entropy Law* (1971) in his discussion of analytical boundries (p. 66ff). He also considered lower limits to the size of the elementary time unit – "the texture of time" – and reviewed the question of durationless instants that concerned some twentieth-century philosophers like Whitehead. Hood's analysis came close, but his use of the Marshallian long run as an illustration suggests that he wanted to make a different point (1948, p. 456). The most familiar consideration is undoubtedly Hicks's choice of the length of his

analytical "week" in *Value and Capital* (1946) as a period during which nothing of analytical importance changes. Fraser (1978) has discussed the smallest time unit that will fully describe physical phenomena.

It should be noted that this problem of temporal abstraction persists in continuous time, where it appears formally as mis-specification of the relevant functions. Conceptually, however, it comes to the same thing in either discrete or continuous time: the sin of abstracting from ceaseless oscillations without first determining whether or not they are relevant to an understanding of the problem.

9 Kornai's analysis of the process of production and exchange (1971) relies implicitly on a smaller than usual unit time to reveal the discontinuities in what is usually taken to be a smooth and continuous flow from production through inventories to sales. It is worth noting, too, that economists often are quite scrupulous about the distinction between discrete and continuous analysis. But when the choice between them is not made simply on the pragmatic ground of mathematical convenience, it appears to be made on the length of the unit time relative to the analytical horizon – with a large number of units time within the analytical horizon, the specification of continuous variables is deemed acceptable. This is quite the opposite criterion from one based on examination of the underlying time-specific pattern of events, yet the continuity or discontinuity of events that is revealed by an appropriate choice of the unit time would appear to be a far more reliable basis for the choice between discrete and continuous modes of analysis.

10 But it need not be. Scitovsky (1976) warned – appropriately, I think – against too much novelty. So despite my considerable sympathy with those who are seeking other modifications to or even abandonment of neoclassical theory, this analysis is almost stridently neoclassical. It is, though, a legitimate part of what Leibenstein (1979) has called "micro-micro theory," in probing, as did Nelson and Winter (1980), March (1978), Simon (1959), and Williamson et al. (1975), the interior of the analytical units we ordinarily use: In this analysis the units are time units; in those they were decision or organizational units. One day it will prove of considerable value to join their disaggregation and mine.

11 Robin Marris's (1964) was not, but it was not easy to see how his analysis of multiple-shift operation in the United Kingdom, with its quite unorthodox theory, could be merged with our conventional representation of the production process; indeed, it was to achieve that merger that I first developed the time-specific models of optimal shift-working and utilization (Winston, 1970).

12 This is taken largely from McWhorter (1976).

13 The nine display digits are made up of eight diodes each. All numerals can be represented as decompositions of a figure 8 made with seven small straight line segments. One additional tiny diode is needed for a decimal point: $9(7 + 1) = 72$.

14 It is interesting that this sort of *seriatim* assignment has been suggested as a way of reconciling conflicting management aims (Cyert and March, 1963) and as a way of achieving Adam Smith's famous economies of specialization without a larger market (because a single pin maker can specialize tasks *seriatim* the same way a larger number of pin makers can specialize among themselves at a moment of time) (Marglin, 1971).

15 This, $(33 + 6)9$, does not add up to 429, because two additional scan lines (what I have called phases) in an 11-scan-line cycle are used to monitor and control the process sequence, leaving nine scan lines to differentiate the nine display digits: $(33 + 6)11 = 429$.

16 It seems likely that the most sophisticated analyses and uses of time and timing in production are found in the design of electronic circuitry. The principle of "multiplex" – of *seriatim* task assignment to a single unit of capital equipment – is ubiquitous. Other homely examples of multiplex technology are FM stereophonic broadcasting and multiple utilization of long-distance telephone lines (the appeal to the industry of fiber optics and laser message transmission is simply that they allow tighter time scheduling of multiplex signals).

17 The keystroke-read-display cycle I have described is the longest of a number of different cycles used simultaneously in the calculator – all based on the rhythm of the main clock signal. Memory registers and the adder, for instance, work on nested and shifting cycles of 3 and 39 oscillations of the main clock. This is why a six-cycle unit time would not be fine enough, as implied by the description only of the read-display functions in the text.

18 Refining of the unit time is currently leading to a radical change in our understanding of endocrinology. It has been discovered that hormonal secretions that were believed to be roughly constant throughout the day are, in fact, emitted in sharp peaks, followed by long periods of quiescence. Until a revision of ideas about the appropriate analytical time unit justified the development of devices that could monitor hormone concentrations constantly, it was impossible to discover that fact (Weitzman, 1976). Indeed, it now appears that daylight directly alters concentrations of the hormone melatonin, which in turn influences mood, efficiency, fertility, and health (therefore certainly utility and household production functions) (*New York Times*, June 23, 1981, C1).

3. Modeling the time-shape of processes, technology, and prices

1 It might seem that selection of an ETU sufficiently small relative to T would assure satisfactory choice of the ETU without undue effort in examining its content. But that is not the case. Betancourt and Clague (1981) have shown that a firm's optimal shift-working schedule within a day depends on the seasonal schedule of its production – the optimal

schedule of production on October 15th depends on the number of days per year the production process will operate.

2 I wish I could suggest that the increasing popularity of what are called "instantaneous production functions" in recent economic theory implies that more authors have considered what they mean by an "instant" and whether or not changes within it are relevant to their analysis. But "instantaneous" rarely means either more or less than flow "per unit time." The nature of the processes within that unit time and therefore the nature of the "instantaneousness" of the function they evoke are rarely considered; these production functions can be (3.1) or (3.4); usually they seem to be the latter.

3 It will provide a useful sense of bearings if I relate this model to the literature, although most production functions one encounters simply cannot be unambiguously classified by their use of stock or flow variables and assumptions about the time period or nature of variables and operations because of the following considerations: (a) When flows are specified "per unit time" it is not clear if that means a unit of time of continuous or interrupted operation. For instance, see the work of Stigler (1952) and Friedman (1962). (b) A "stock" relationship described at a moment in time like Solow's (1962) "a machine . . . must be operated by a crew of fixed size" implies an instantaneous time rate of flow of services, but without more information it is unclear whether the fixed-size crew works a 24-hour day, the machine works only eight hours at "full capacity" (and if so, why), so only ⅓ (¼?) of the "crew of fixed size" is actually found tending the machine at any one time in order that the others can be resting to run the machine later. (c) Most usually, authors use charmingly imprecise phrases like "K is capital; L is labor," or Varian's K, which is "some kind of machine which we will vaguely refer to as capital" (1978, p. 4).

4 The complications this eliminates are not very serious, but they would make it necessary to juggle two sorts of utilization and idleness of capital at the same time – one that differentiates among machines at any t and the other that differentiates for all machines among times t during T. Because the second is the novel element being introduced here, the first will be ignored for now, but it has not been in applied studies (Winston, 1977; Hughes et al., 1976).

5 So t_T of one unit period T is the same as t_0 of the next – or adjacent to it, depending on how seriously one wants to take the problems of durationless instants versus instants of infinitesimal duration.

6 It is assumed that there are no startup or shutdown costs in T; so production is costlessly switched on or off at t_0 and t_p. See Winston (1974a) for the formal incorporation of "interruption costs," and see Lloyd (1980) for a nice analysis of setup costs and optimal length of a production run.

7 As in note 4, in those applications, this strictly time-based measure of

capital utilization has been tempered by consideration of how much of the capital stock is in use at each time t within T_p.

8 Assuming that the instantaneous production function is both time-additive and time-invariant is a reasonable place to start, but as the analyses of household production in Chapter 8 and of markets in Chapter 10 make amply clear, it means that we must ignore for now important sources of economic time specificity. And, of course, it is assumed that there are no lags in production response, even though the function is instantaneous; this is another useful simplifying assumption for now.

9 "The difference between flow [of materials] and [flow of] services is so fundamental that it separates even the dimensionalities of the two concepts . . . The amount of a [materials] flow is expressed in units appropriate to substances (in the broad sense) – say pounds, quarts, feet, etc. The rate of flow, on the other hand, has a mixed dimensionality (substance)/(time). The situation is entirely reversed in the case of services. The amount of service has a mixed dimensionality in which time enters as a factor, (substance) × (time). If a plant uses one hundred workers during a working day (eight hours), the total of the service employed is eight hundred *man* × *hours*. If by analogy with the rate of [materials] flow we would like to determine the rate of service for the same situation, by simple algebra the answer is that this rate is one hundred *men*, period. The rate of service is simply the size of the fund that provides the service and consequently is expressed in elementary units in which the time factor does not intervene" (Georgescu-Roegen, 1971, pp. 227–8).

10 The typical "machine" is easy to visualize as either yielding its capital services to production or not – it is on or off. Other forms of productive physical capital usually can be similarly classified at a moment of time, t, as either doing for production what they are intended to do or not. So a warehouse is yielding its capital services at t if it is storing and protecting goods; it is idle at t if it is empty. A factory building is yielding its capital services when it is protecting goods and machines and workers, and it is idle when it is empty. Ambiguities inevitably can be conjured up (whether or not a painting is yielding capital services when no one is looking at it depends on its function as aesthetic object, as store of wealth, as document of record), but the utilization/idleness dichotomy is still useful.

11 For one concrete and dramatic illustration, it has been estimated that during the rapid output growth of the decade of the 1960s, fully one-half of South Korea's growth in capital service flow came from increased utilization of capital stocks – increased utilization was exactly as important as capital investment in that case (Kim and Kwon, 1977). In a recent study of U.S. manufacturing, Foss's figures (1981) suggest that over the 47 years from 1929 to 1976, 18% of the total growth in capital services came from increased utilization.

12 The need for active maintenance time can be seen as capital's equivalent need for "rest." In any careful empirical use of time-specific analysis in production, it is essential to acknowledge the need for such maintenance time; this was done in the studies previously cited. But its magnitude is so slight compared with the human need and preference to allocate more than 75% of our total time to nonwork activities that it seems permissible to ignore active maintenance time and treat capital as constantly available.

13 The way these familiar concepts mislead is instructive. It hinges, again, on the "temporal hyperopia" that afflicts standard methods of economic analysis – its concentration on what happens in extensive time, over a series of T's, to the virtually complete disregard of what happens in intensive time, within the typical T. If extensive time is all one sees, "fixed costs" means that costs per T are fixed for some period into the future (the short run). Variable costs can be varied "now" or at least within the short run. But in the long run (by definition), fixed costs can be varied, too – so the very familiar phrase "fixed costs become variable costs in the long run." By inference, therefore, any distinction between factor inputs on this basis of "fixed" and "variable" costs can only be a short-run distinction; in the long run we (like others, e.g., Shephard) can ignore the difference between capital and labor costs in production.

But, of course, that logic is valid only under the strict hyperopia that sees only extensive time. Within any unit time, T, the distinction between the behavior of capital costs and that of labor costs remains whether T happens to occur in the short-run period or the long-run period. So long as capital is used in production, it will be durable over any unit period T and will be paid for per unit time T.

So whether we are in a short run or long run in extensive time, the fundamental difference in the cost characteristics of capital and labor inputs in production remains, and it is never true that this difference between "fixed" and "variable" costs disappears. What changes between the short run and the long run is only that the cost of capital per unit time T cannot be varied in the short run, whereas it can be in the long run; but its cost behavior within unit time is the same. In the vocabulary of this section, the value of the owner cost, $P_k\overline{K}$ cannot be changed in the short run, but it can be changed in the long run by changing $\overline{K}$. But the fact is that $p_k(T_p)\overline{K} = P_k\overline{K}/T_p$ remains true, whatever the value of $P_k\overline{K}$ or whatever the extensive time horizon in which T is set.

14 Or household (Chapter 9).

15 When depreciation increases with use, so that $\delta_T = \delta(u)$, where $u = T_p/T$, the necesary condition for the price of capital service to fall with increasing utilization is

$$\frac{u}{\delta_T} \frac{\partial \delta}{\partial u} < \frac{r_T}{\delta_T} + 1.$$

With a 5% interest rate and 10% rate of depreciation at $u = 1$, depreciation could be quite sensitive to utilization – having an elasticity of almost 1.5 – and still the capital service price would fall with increasing duration of production. Interviews with managers in a number of companies and countries have suggested that it is highly unlikely that going from one- to two-shift operation, for instance, would even double the depreciation rate (elasticity = 1), especially with adequate time for maintenance. To push the issue to its logical end, even if $(u'/\delta_T)(\partial\delta_T/\partial u) < (r/\delta_T + 1)$ for some $u' < 1$, the price of capital service would still fall with increasing utilization over $0 \leqslant u \leqslant u'$, and that is enough to maintain the sense of the analysis.

16 Capital-in-finance is very different from capital-in-production (Harcourt, 1969, p. 372). As a financial asset, capital – even physical capital like a machine – yields (costs) an amount per unit time T. It is always P_k that is relevant to alternative financial assets, the owner cost of capital or the rental rate, but not to production or consumption, where the relevant price is that of the capital service flow, $p_k(T_p)$.

17 Although much of this analysis uses the wage rate – in our dominant two-factor tradition – as the illustration of a time-specific, rhythmic input price, the widespread existence of such price behavior is certainly beyond doubt, despite the propensity to abstract from time patterns in economic analysis and data: "Nothing is more normal for a statistical bureau than to orient its data collection according to the inventory of the tool box of the analytical social scientist" (Georgescu, 1971, p. 246). In many economies, electric power is cheaper in off-peak periods; transportation, recreational, agricultural, and other production often depends on inputs (sunlight, warm air, ice, water, snow) that are literally free at some times of the year but quite expensive at others; processes that use agricultural inputs usually face prices that vary seasonally. Rhythmic prices appear to be ubiquitous (Nerlove, 1972; Hutchings, 1971; Stigler and Kindahl, 1970).

18 The time-specific wage rate $w(t)$, therefore, does not reflect "overtime" wage rates. Overtime usually depends not on when (t) but on how much (T_w) a worker works in the calendar unit time; so overtime wage rates are not time-specific but (like capital, but with opposite sign) duration-specific. To keep the analysis focused on essentials of time-specific behavior, overtime wage rates will be ignored. The time-specific perspective is amenable to their analysis, but they are simply less important than the other price and cost patterns in time on which we will concentrate.

19 One might adopt other conventions, but they would still have to reflect the underlying reality of the factor characteristics described earlier and their effects on costs and optimal production scheduling in T.

4.   Time-shaped costs: optimal scheduling of storable production

1 Although it might escape notice at this point, by Chapter 9 it will become clear that I have restricted the realism of this analysis of firms by making production functions always time-invariant. So the only temporal influence on the firm I have allowed comes through the input markets (here) or output market (Chapter 5); production itself is not affected by seasons, by congestion, by the rhythmically varying availability of free inputs like light and dark and warmth and cold. This is easy to defend on grounds of maintaining a tractable analysis, but it should be kept in mind that a significant source of rhythmicity in any economy is thereby left out of these production models.

2 This wage rate has a sawtooth shape over a series of units time. More realism and generality are implicit in the wage rate function of Appendix A.

3 $d(ac(T_p,t))/dt_p = 0$ when $c'_k(T_p) = -c'_l(t)$.

4 It is worth being careful about these phrases. The *ex ante/ex post* dichotomy is very much the same in production theory as the long-run/short-run dichotomy – both describe the variability of the capital stock or lack of it. They differ only in their implicit time perspectives. The *ex ante/ex post* distinction (in either micro or macro usage) is set in perspective time; the long-run/short-run distinction is set in analytical time. So for an actor at τ_1 in Figure 4.10, A is an *ex ante* event. But later, from τ_2, it is past; so he sees A as an *ex post* event. If A is an investment event and the capital stock has a durability of T_A, then in analytical time "the short run" is simply the period from t_A to $t_A + T_A$, and "the long run" is any longer period such as $t_B - t_A$. As Hood (1948) noted, the short-run/long-run measure is endogenous to the production process, defined by the durability of the capital stock. Viewed from the perspective of τ_2, the actor will be "in the short run" for decisions about production until $t_A + T_A$. So I will use "*ex ante*" and "long run" interchangeably to mean that the size of the capital stock can be varied and "*ex post*" or "short run" to mean that it cannot. Within the unit time, of course, the capital stock cannot be varied in size in either the short run or the long run.

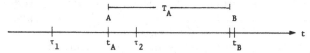

Figure 4.10.

5 Minimizing $c(t) = p_k(T_p)k(t) + w(t)l(t)$ with respect to $k(t)$ and $l(t)$ subject to $f(k(t),l(t)) - q(t) = 0$ yields the first-order conditions

$$p_k(T_p) - \lambda \partial f/\partial k(t) = 0$$
$$w(t) - \lambda \partial f/\partial l(t) = 0$$

so that

$$\frac{\partial f/\partial l(t)}{\partial f/\partial k(t)} = \frac{w(t)}{p_k(T_p)}.$$

6 The separation of technological and economic influences in this context is not obvious. Shephard's (1970) conception of *ex ante* elasticity of substitution describes technological substitution possibilities over an unconstrained production set. The *ex post* restriction placed on that set describes the restricted alternatives available after some input levels have been fixed by, for example, the investment event. The *ex post* elasticities of substitution describe substitution possibilities within given subsets that have some fixed values. An *ex post* elasticity, too, is a strictly technical description of technical options. But the particular set over which those *ex post* technological elasticities are described can be the result of an economic decision resting, *inter alia*, on the costs of investment. Strictly, an economic decision (not to blow up the capital stock and start over again) restricts the technological alternatives over which any *ex post* elasticity of substitution, as a purely technological measure, is then defined. Absent the economic incentive to keep the fixed capital and not toss it out, the producer would always face the full and rich *ex ante* set of options – only an economic choice prevents his taking advantage of them, imposing *ex post* restrictions. The *ex die* elasticity is much the same in this sense in that economic and not solely technological influences will determine which variables are fixed over the unit time and which can vary. But the *ex die* elasticity, given some specified list of fixed inputs, is a purely technological relationship. So capital stocks are fixed over T by their technological characteristic of durability; labor inputs may be fixed over T_p by the high costs of inducing workers to work for only part of a shift. But both the resulting fixed capital service and labor service flows will define the *ex die* elasticity of substitution.

7 Apparently this engineering evidence on the effect on depreciation of the speed of output, $q(t)$, was misinterpreted in Taubman and Wilkinson's model (1970), where it was applied to optimal utilization, T_p^*/T.

8 Three quite different explanations have been proffered for why the firm might optimally leave its capital stock idle part of the time, T. The effect of time-specific input prices like the wage rate derived from household work and consumption timing preferences is, of course, central in this study. Deardorff and Stafford (1976) presented a production model in which workers' preferences for a given length workday, T_w^*, require compensating wage premiums to induce them to work either a longer or a shorter workday. With s discrete shifts of operation, unit labor costs will therefore rise with increasing T_p ($= sT_w$, $s = 1,...,n$). These two aspects

of wage behavior are entirely compatible. This study models a wage premium that induces work at nonpreferred *times;* Deardorff and Stafford modeled an overtime wage premium that induces a nonpreferred *duration* of work, a nonoptimal work–leisure choice. [See Boulding's original discussion of this (1955, p. 800).] But the time-specific behavior of this study, of course, applies equally to rhythmically priced nonlabor inputs, too. The third explanation for $T_p^* < T$, finally, is Taubman-Wilkinson's increasing capital depreciation, which, as noted in the preceding note 6, appears to rest on a misinterpretation of the engineering evidence on depreciation, speed, and duration of production (1970).

9 In two excellent analyses of industry in Kenya, Mary Ann Baily (1974) analyzed these possibilities for what I have called *ex die* substitution, and Howard Pack's earlier empirical studies (1976) revealed a number of examples of such partial adjustment within the day. In Sweden, there is considerable interest in developing technologies with high *ex die* substitution so that an "automated" plant can be run by a minimal crew during nights and weekends. Walter Oi (1981) identified such substitution as a key aspect of variable utilization.

Appendix A: The formal model of time-specific production

1 Because $y(t)$ is an instantaneous capital-labor ratio, it describes both the relationship between factor service flow rates and, during operation, the relationship between factor stocks. Sen (1964) called it "the degree of mechanization."

2 Although this is compatible with the assumption of a zero *ex post* flow elasticity of substitution and a nonzero *ex ante* flow elasticity, it is not the same thing as the familiar putty-clay assumption of neoclassical growth theory. We use factor service (flow) elasticities; putty-clay models use elasticities defined on capital *stock* (investment). These are not at all the same thing.

3 Capital price variables are as defined in Chapter 3. In light of the unusual specification of the price of capital services, it is reassuring that given any level of utilization, the cost of capital per unit time T is the same whether calculated in terms of flows (capital service flow, $T_p k$, times capital service flow price, p_k) or in terms of stocks (size of the capital stock, $\overline{K}$, times the daily cost of owning a unit of capital, P_k), because

$$p_k[T_p k] = [p_k T_p]k = P_k k = P_k \overline{K}.$$

4 Nadiri and Rosen (1969) used a model that appears deceptively similar to this one both formally and in deriving optimal capital utilization in their target level of factor demand. In fact, however, theirs is very different (a) in being used primarily – with fixed hiring cost and overtime wages per worker – to derive an optimal average workday per worker, not optimal capital utilization, (b) in independently determining an opti-

mal level of capital utilization solely as a function of an assumed increase in depreciation rate with use, and, finally, (c) in using a Cobb-Douglas production function following Taubman and Wilkinson (1970).

5 It can be shown that an optimal solution exists with utilization less than 1 ($T_p^* < 1$) if the wage rate rises sufficiently rapidly over the unit time (i.e., if W''' is sufficiently large).

6 These first-order conditions (A.12) and (A.13) have a useful economic interpretation in time-specific analysis. Because the effective instantaneous wage rate paid by the firm for a worker, l, is, with $\sigma_T = 0$,

$$\bar{w}(T_p) = W/T_p$$

– because l is fixed over the period of operation – (A.12) becomes

$$\frac{\bar{w}(T_p)}{p_k(T_p)} = \frac{\partial F/\partial l}{\partial F/\partial k},$$

which is the familiar condition that for factor (flow) proportions to be optimal, the ratio of their (flow) prices must equal the ratio of their marginal products. Equation (A.13) can be written as

$$\frac{k}{l} = -\frac{d\bar{w}(T_p)/dT_p}{dp_k(T_p)/dT_p}.$$

So, cross-multiplying at the optimal level of utilization, the marginal cost of capital services with respect to utilization must equal the marginal cost of labor services with respect to utilization.

7 This can be illustrated simply, because an instantaneous Cobb-Douglas production function

$$q = k^a l^{1-a}$$

can be solved explicitly for optimal utilization, T_p^*, using the wage function (A.6). The result is

$$T_p^* = \frac{\beta B}{(1 - a)\beta B' - a}.$$

Factor prices, P_k and w_0, have dropped out, leaving optimal utilization dependent solely on capital's share, a, and on the marginal (with respect to T_p) and average amplitudes of the wage rhythm, $\beta B'$ and βB.

8 The "optimal productivity" of a capital stock is the obverse of the "desired capital stock" of investment-demand analysis. As an explicit statement of desired capital stock, (A.25) is

$$\bar{K}^* = Q_0 y_0 / T_p^* f(y_0).$$

Then the desired capital stock depends, as in Hickman's analysis (1964), on relative factor prices P_k/w_0 negatively and on target daily output Q_0 positively (and "technology").

5.   Time-shaped output: least-cost production of perishable peak-load products

1 $q^*(t)$, strictly speaking, is optimal only for $T_p = T$. When $T_p < T$ in utilization tracking, another speed may (or may not) be optimal; so $q^*(t)$ will be derived from T_p. For purposes of present exposition, this can best be ignored.

2 Because this is a deterministic model, there need be no standby capacity for unexpected changes in either demand or supply; but see Winston (1979b).

3 Again, the fully predictable, deterministic nature of the time-shape of output considered here is necessary to this statement.

4 Apparently unaware that the effect of utilization on capital service price had been spelled out earlier by Winston (1970) and Winston and McCoy (1974), Wenders proposed a model of electric-power technology along very much these lines (Wenders, 1976).

5 And this assumes that the generator is as efficient for 1 hour as for 1 of 24 – that $q_i^*(t)/k_i$ is constant with respect to utilization.

6 My insistence on relating this analysis to electric-power generation to keep it from being too abstract encounters a terminological problem here: Speed, as revolutions per minute of an alternating-current generator, cannot be varied, because speed in that sense determines the cycles per second of the current alternations – 50 cps in Europe and 60 cps in the United States. But in a more basic and more relevant sense, the speed of flow of electric power from a given generator is variable, because the number of watts of output flow varies with the amount of energy applied to the generator. So in electric-power generation, more "speed" means more $q(t)$ got from a generator that is turning at the same "speed."

7 Panzar's neoclassical model of peak loads is quite similar to this one.

8 Although they would be in a full three-dimensional representation like that of Figure 3.3.

9 Nicholls wrote his Ph.D. thesis on the evidence of stochastic variations of this sort in the meat-packing industry, but no one, to my knowledge, has applied it to deterministic time-shaped output.

10 Although it is not very interesting analytically, the current period of sharply reduced $p_k/\bar{p}_v$ for energy-related inputs is significant in altering the optimal investment policies in industries like electric-power generation.

11 The principle of choice is simple so long as it is kept nicely general and vague – that a change in rate of output should be met by changing utilization rather than the rate of output of a given capital stock whenever the former costs less than the latter. Unfortunately, anything more concrete gets messy, because whereas the *ex ante* cost of an increment to output through an increase in the stratified capital stock, to be utilized only part of the time, is easy to specify (as $c_i(q^*)$ with the appropriate

capital service price), that for an increment to output through adjustment of output rate is not, because it works through adjustment of the
size of the capital stock.

12 It should be noted, too, that this discussion has neglected two important
aspects of actual time-shaped production in that (a) it has been assumed
that there are no scale economies in the technologies used in either
utilization or speed tracking and (b) in working with deterministic predictable time-shaped output it has ignored the importance of producing
for unexpected variations in output, and so it has ignored those cost
characteristics of technologies uniquely designed for fast response as an
additional dimension in assessment of marginal cost; see Winston
(1979a).

13 We assume that they, like the generalized variable input $v(t)$ used
throughout this chapter, have a time-invariant price, $\bar{p}_v$, over T and not a
rhythmic wage rate like that of Chapter 4.

6.   Shephard's dilemma: duality and the process of production

1 This chapter deals only with the production of output – bicycles or
frozen foods – that is storable over the analytical unit time so that it can
be scheduled to minimize costs over that period – the stuff of Chapter 4.
The production of perishable and time-shaped output analyzed in
Chapter 5 – electric power or transportation services – is even less appropriate to mathematical duality theory; it violates the requirement of cost
minimization over the unit time, because it is produced under the additional constraint of a time-shaped demand.

2 See Fuss and McFadden's Preface (1978) for a summary of the duality
literature that was brought to textbook accessibility by Dixit (1976) and
Varian (1978).

3 The genuinely instantaneous production function of preceding chapters,

$$q(t) = f(k(t), l(t)), \tag{a}$$

uses factor service flows at rates $k(t)$ and $l(t)$ to produce a rate of flow of
output, $q(t)$, where t is an elementary or nondivisible moment of time. If
they are either off or on at a constant rate, those flows accumulate to K
$= T_p k(t)$, $L = T_p l(t)$, and $Q = T_p q(t)$ per unit time T when the production
process is operated $T_p \leq T$ of the unit time. Accumulated flows per unit
time can be incorporated directly in a time-divisible production function
of the sort Shephard used,

$$Q = F(K, L) = F(T_p k(t), T_p l(t)) = T_p f(k(t), l(t)), \tag{b}$$

if (a) is linear homogeneous with respect to duration of production. So
under gentle restrictions, these representations of technology are
equivalent. But the prices of their arguments are not, because T_p and t

are determined by the firm's cost-minimizing production schedule within T.

4 Georgescu-Roegen's important analytical distinction (1971, Chapter V) between historical and mechanical clock time is appropriate, with a change in context, to this central point: Within the unit time, the wage rate depends on pure historical time or moment, the price of capital services on pure duration.

5 Which would be $P_k/[(1 - \theta)T]$ in Shephard's context.

6 The large literature despairing of price-induced inefficiencies in mis-planned developing countries, starting with Despres and Kindleberger (1952), is obviously relevant.

7 "We hold the view that there is an intimate, symbiotic relationship be-tween theory and econometrics, and that development of a fully success-ful economic analysis of production requires an integration of theoreti-cal and econometric ideas in a unified approach" [Fuss and McFadden, 1978, p. viii].

8 Cost and production data with sufficient time-specific detail to be used in even the most simplified two-factor duality models of production exist only for the approximately 1,200 establishments – spread over 73 sectors in Malaysia, the Philippines, Colombia, and Israel – of the World Bank's Capital Utilization Study (Hughes et al., 1976) and for 44 establishments in an ILO study of utilization in Nigerian manufacturing (Winston, 1977b). The UNIDO data in Betancourt and Clague's study (1981) of capital utilization has some of the information appropriate to two-factor modeling. For U.S. production, few data are available, even at that level of simplification: The Census Bureau's reports on shift-working (U.S. Department of Commerce, 1976) – collected only since 1975 – include crude production timing data for 20 two-digit industries in the form of average shifts worked per day, but with no information about the other major sources of variable utilization – days of operation per week or weeks operated per year. Electric-power production data report utiliza-tion as "load duration," but information on timing – the "load curve" – is not widely available outside the load dispatchers' offices of the firms. In addition, electric-power production is almost always constrained by time-specific demand, and therefore – under such quantity rationing – output rates are almost never cost-minimizing (Wenders, 1976; Winston, 1979b).

7.   Factor intensities, capacity, and the Leontief paradox

1 Sections 7.1 and 7.2 of this chapter follow closely my "On Measuring Factor Proportions" in *The Economic Journal* (Winston, 1979c), and Sec-tion 7.3 follows "Capacity: An Integrated Micro and Macro Analysis" in *The American Economic Review* (Winston, 1977a).

2 The same danger obviously afflicts "supply-side policies" in advanced countries when they hope to achieve greater investment by lowering capital prices (Winston, 1981).

3 Ignoring the important issues of how to measure "machines" – by current value, replacement cost, historical cost – and the vagaries of capital pricing that must underlie any aggregation by capital values.

4 "The . . . omission [of] the length of the working day from neoclassical production analysis vitiates also the familiar comparisons of the capital-output and capital-labor ratios" (Georgescu-Roegen, 1970, p. 9).

It can be argued – and has been by Lars E. O. Svensson since I published the *Economic Journal* article on which the discussion of the Leontief paradox in the next section is based – that for analyses of an economy's general equilibrium, and hence for optimal patterns of trade, the correct measure is indeed the industry's relative employment of the economy's factor endowments, which means the capital-per-employee ratio. Svensson's argument is cogent; a more detailed 3 × 2 general-equilibrium analysis by Jones and Easton (1981) implies the same thing. The ambiguity of two common measures of factor intensities remains, however, and what might better be called "the relative factor absorption" – what is measured by an industry's capital–employee ratio – is clearly the result of a far more complicated interplay of technology, work-timing preferences, and factor endowments than has thus far been suggested. It is hardly a technological parameter of the industry. Preliminary application of the Jones-Easton general-equilibrium model to an economy with multiple shift-working amply supports this.

5 In contrast, Lary's measurement of factor proportions as value added per employee, although it conjures up a host of problems of its own (with its extreme reliance on perfectly competitive equilibrium) (Lary, 1968, Chapter 2), avoids the error to which this is addressed when it is used to measure physical plus human capital input per unit of raw labor. Excellent summaries of the literature are to be found in the work of Bhagwati (1969) and Baldwin (1971) and, on the role of human capital, in the work of Branson and Monoyios (1977).

6 The elasticity of factor service substitution plays no role in this context, and I have ignored the effects of scale.

7 The U.S. Bureau of the Census reported the distribution of employees among shift schedules for 20 two-digit SIC industries for 1975. These data were used to generate timing correction factors that were used, in turn, to derive estimates of instantaneous factor proportions from the Branson-Monoyios figures for labor and human capital. Even in these very aggregated data, the correction factors generated by shift differences among sectors cover most of the theoretically possible range. The rest of the data used to reestimate the Branson-Monoyios (1977) results are theirs, including those for 90 SITC sectors, net exports, physical capital, shipments, human capital, and raw labor. Their data cover both

1963 and 1967. Details of the data and corrections have been reported (Winston, 1978).

8 Unfortunately, noneconomic (maximum or engineering) capacity is sometimes, apparently unintentionally, transformed into economic capacity when it is defined with the proviso that output is at a "technical" maximum "under standard and normal hours of operation" (as, for instance, by Leif Johansen). But this can hardly be an engineering concept of capacity when those "standard and normal hours of operation" are, themselves, the result of an economic decision. Nor is the error entirely innocent. It represents as a technical fact of life what may well be the result of dubious economic policy – as when poor countries induce low utilization of their capital stocks by their factor price policies or by legislated nighttime wage differentials.

9 Of course, an economy's "maximum available resources" – which define maximum aggregate output – will always be less than the maximum possible flow of resources that could be got from its factor stocks and its population. This distinction is clearest for labor where we typically accept, as a different though economic question, the factor owners' (households') decisions on how much resource flow (labor service) they choose to make available from their factor stocks (population) and how much they choose to withhold (take as leisure). War and other passions may induce changes in work preferences that would change the available labor resources from a given population, and hence aggregate capacity, but that is beside the present point.

10 The survey of 44 firms in Nigeria involved an economy with a very high level of aggregate demand. As predicted, a number of firms reported that they were operating well beyond their capacity levels – some at as much as 150%. They said they were doing so because product prices were high, but they also said that they had explicit plans for investment that would allow them to reduce utilization back to the levels they considered to be least-cost – back to economic capacity operation with more capital stock and the larger output. This is clearly consistent with Hickman's useful idea of capacity as the lower boundary of the investment-inducing level of sustained output (Hickman, 1964).

11 The third and "most eclectic of the indexes" of capacity (Perry, 1973, p. 707) – the Federal Reserve's – is an amalgam of the McGraw-Hill index, capital stock estimates, and assumptions about optimal capital productivity that defies simple classification in a model of the firm.

8. Modeling the time-shape of work and consumption: the optimal household schedule and the value of time

1 Becker (1965), Michael and Becker (1973), Lancaster (1966), Linder (1970).

2 My borrowing the vocabulary of Sanyal and Jones's "Trade in Middle Products" model (1979) is not accidental – there are clear parallels in structure, only a few of which are developed here.

3 A timeless environmental parameter, E, is included in later (Michael and Becker, 1973, p. 382) versions of the standard time-allocation model, but it serves no explicit analytical purpose. Here it is both time-specific and central to the analysis.

4 Goods prices, $\bar{p}_i$, and the wage rate, $\bar{w}$, can be made time-sensitive, and they will be in the next chapter. For now, they are assumed constant over T.

5 This is an extreme assumption that eliminates some of the more interesting questions of household activity timing. The less formal discussion of the next chapter considers them. In the meantime, it is useful to see how much can be said even with all time sensitivity confined to the production tier.

6 Lifetime allocation over a series of unit times involves extensive time or macro-time and therefore does not risk confusion with timing within the unit time T.

7 And the labor supply of an l-person household is fixed at $L = lT$ per period T.

8 If labor services had been left explicit in the production function, (8.14) would also imply $(\partial u/\partial z)(\partial z/\partial l) = \bar{w}\lambda$ at all times and for all activities.

9 Yet the fact that the household's production unit adopts the household's utility function as its objective function – resisting the temptation to exploit its monopolistic position – yields the usual welfare result that marginal costs equal marginal utility for each activity (at each moment of time). This is inherent in the adjustment via (8.14) to optimal activity intensity.

10 Without further restrictions, the analysis of this chapter says that with an optimal duration of work, L_w^*, the household will go to work any time the value of time in consumption falls below $\mu_w(t,L_h^*)$. Because nothing assures nicely monotonic behavior of consumption efficiency over T, the implication is that the household might start and stop working over and over again throughout the day, each time $\mu_c(t,L_h^*)$ fell below the constant $\mu_w(t,L_h^*)$; the only restriction is that the total amount of such time must add up to T_h^*. This is useful. It suggests (a) that adjustment ("commuting") costs between consumption and work often intervene to prevent costless activity switching, (b) that there are significant differences among occupations (and sexes) in the ease of switching from consumption to work activities (the author versus the lathe operator), (c) that there would, *ceteris paribus*, be greater daily utility from costless switching than from difficult switching, and (d) that the duration of the unit time, T, determines many such costs, differentiating, for instance, between commuting and migration costs. These are, I suspect, interesting issues, but we shall not pursue them now.

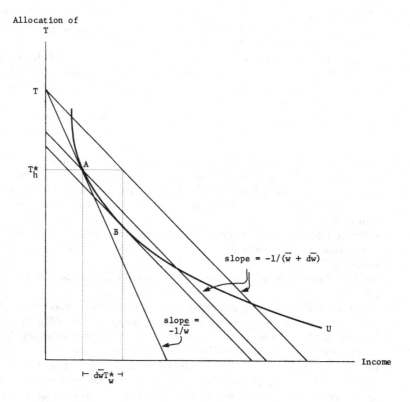

Figure 8.7.

11 This sequence is implicit in descriptions of the substitution effect in the usual graph of (daily) time allocation. From an original equilibrium A with T_h^* of leisure and wage $\bar{w}$, the increase in wage rate to $\bar{w} + d\bar{w}$ is offset by a compensating increase in taxes of $-dS = -d\bar{w}T_w^*$ with an unchanged allocation of time. The now-relevant budget line has a slope of $-1/(\bar{w} + d\bar{w})$. But at A, that budget line shows that the marginal incentive to work is greater than that to consume. So the household increases time working. Movement to the southeast of A, along U, however, requires further taxation to offset the potential utility-increasing effects of the higher income that comes with working more. Those movements along U raise the relative value of consumption by reducing the time spent consuming, until, at point B, which defines the limit of the substitution effect of $d\bar{w}$, the relative values of consumption time and income are in (compensated) equilibrium once again.

9.   **The anatomy of household activities: goal and process; work and home production; capital and self-control**

1 Were I to conform more to the vocabulary of Chapter 8 and less to common usage, $u(z_i)$ would be "activity utility" and $u(Z_i)$ "commodity utility." "Process" and "goal" seem more to the point.

2 Although it was described with a suspiciously precise numerical estimate, the Cunard steamship advertising slogan reflects this in "Getting there is half the fun."

3 An investment aspect of a consumption activity can give it an indirect utility that can then make it a preferred activity even if it has negative direct utility. This was suggested by Stigler and Becker (1977) and was developed elsewhere (Winston, 1980).

4 Along with being unambitious and unreliable if L_w can be reduced only by sporadic attention within a "full-time" unpleasant job. The effect on behavior of unpleasant work is, of course, a recurrent theme in classical and radical economics; see Adam Smith, *Wealth of Nations* (1937), or Marx's *Grundrisse* (1973).

5 In examining home versus commercial production, the underlying structure of the household production perspective may itself evaporate: Z_i becomes indistinguishable from X_i when there is no required complementary input of labor or capital services from the household. Both Z_i and X_i, then, can be purchased on the market, and $Z_i = X_i$ is the production function for the household's production of Z_i. This usefully points up an aspect of the make-or-buy decision I shall not pursue now – that instead of the single, fixed flow coefficient home production relationship I deal with in this section, there is often a continuum of technologies describing the degree of processing of the goods and service inputs in the household production: The greater the degree of processing, the less the need for complementary inputs of household labor and/or capital services to produce Z_i. So, for instance, if Z_i were a meal of given quality, it could be made from scratch by the devoted cook using a flow of inputs x_i at prices $\bar{p}_i$ and a good deal of time and labor, L_i. Or it could be done with more reliance on prepared foods – bakery bread and cake mixes and horseradish out of the jar – hence more expensive and different x_i' but with less L_i in consequence. Or – ignoring the TV dinner as violating our quality assumptions – Z_i could be a catered meal, delivered hot by the local restaurant with a very large $\bar{p}_i'' x_i''$ and negligible household input of labor in its preparation, L_i''. So what I am discussing in this section is only two points on such a continuum – the single, fixed flow coefficient technology of starting from scratch and the caterer as outsider who plunks the completed meal down before the waiting household.

6 What are not considered in this simple case – though it would certainly appear interesting to do so – are more complicated alternatives in which

the household compares i to j and j to work. This is relevant to the questions of the value of time raised in the last chapter and to more-than-one-person households, where sex roles and division of activities within the household become important. For now, however, things seem complicated enough in even the simplest case.

7 It becomes clear that in assuming "quality" constant in any Z_i, I have assumed no special role for the pride of personal accomplishment – a smooth-running engine is a smooth-running engine no matter who tuned it. Specification of a further type of goal utility could capture this, but I will ignore it.

8 It is tempting to say that these firms "make a technology available" to households, but that is not so. Such technology usually is available through ordinary commercial channels, but at very high capital service prices because of the household's low utilization: A household can buy a $50,000 automatic car-wash machine if it wants to. This is clearly the capital service pricing phenomenon that played a central role in the production theory of Part II. It is introduced into the household production model in the next section.

9 As discussed earlier, the basic issue – for which there is no established vocabulary – is not who owns the capital stocks, although I initially thought that was it, but rather who absorbs the costs of varying utilization rates – of idleness. So, long-term rental that covers calendar periods that include both use and idleness – such as a yearly lease of an apartment or a car – brings with it the same dependence of capital service price on utilization as does ownership. The hourly rental of carpet cleaning equipment or a car over the weekend does not. Although even these examples suggest an obvious continuum – often the car is idle much of the weekend – I shall stick to the two extremes for simplicity. The issue was – because of the assumed specialization in firms' production – easier to ignore in production theory than in the household, where a wider variety of activities appear.

10 Sweden's very skewed allocation of $\bar{K}$ in summer houses and boats is a case in point.

11 The fact that the marginal cost of extended utilization of owned capital stocks is zero makes capital ownership an effective self-control device for the household. It can affect its future behavior, encouraging a particular "better" course of action by buying those capital stocks relevant to the production of "good" activities (Elster, 1977). The consequent zero marginal duration costs will then increase the time spent in those "good" activities. Such binding strategies are part of what Schelling (1978a) called "the art of self-management."

12 This is easily incorporated in a modified version of the formal model. If activity i uses inputs from owned capital stocks, the daily full-income constraint (8.9) is changed only to recognize separate purchased and

owned sources of goods and service inputs,

$$\ldots \int_{t_{i-1}}^{t_i} (p_i x_i(t) + p_{ki} x_{ki}(t))\, dt + \int_{t_i}^{t_j} p_j x_j(t)\, dt + \ldots.$$

Then, in solving for t_i^*, the optimal time to switch from activity i to activity j – the basis for (8.15) and therefore for defining $\mu_i(t)$ in (8.23) – the only relevant goods and services cost will be the cost of purchased goods, $p_i x_i(t)$. Despite the use of inputs from owned capital stocks with an average cost $p_{ki} x_{ki}(t)$, the net utility flow in activity i will be affected only by purchased input costs,

$$\mu_i(t) = u_i(t_i) - \lambda p_i x_i(t_i).$$

Capital service flows will be constant – for reasons rehearsed in Chapter 3 – and the partial derivative of the owned capital component of the costs of activity i with respect to duration will be

$$\partial \left[\int_{t_{i-1}}^{t_i} p_{ki} x_{ki}(t)\, dt \right] \Big/ \partial t_i = p_{ki} x_{ki}(t) + T_i x_{ki} \frac{\partial p_{ki}}{\partial t_i} = 0,$$

assuring that only purchased goods and service inputs are relevant to the value of time in activity i on the time margin.

Although the costs of an activity's capital services from owned capital stocks are subject to the daily cost constraint, they are costless in the household's optimal activity choice. The value of time spent in activity i is determined as if capital services were free – as indeed they are for the purposes of the decision to do i or j at time t. So to the extent that owned capital services enter the production function of an activity, the value of time spent in that activity, $\mu_i(t)$, will be increased by these "free" resources; t_i^* will be extended in time until a changing environment that decreases purchased goods productivity in activity i or increases it in activity j brings $\mu_i(t)$ down to $\mu_j(t)$. The result is an increase in the duration of activity i.

13 This is less comfortably set in a discussion of daily repetitive patterns than it would be over a yearly T, where it could describe the annual rental of a special garden sprayer or a trailer to get the children's belongings to and from college.

10. A theory of time-specific markets: generalized peak loads

1 Two uses of "preferences" meet in this context: preferences as household utility functions and preferences for working during the day as the optimal schedule. Because the second has been shown to be the result of

the first and much else besides, there is room for confusion. Rather than coin a new phrase, however, or use awkward quotation marks around the second and more casual use of the word, I will not distinguish between them unless it matters.

2 If this statement needs any defense, to the obvious regularities in which we all live can be added the frequently encountered assertion that daytime is the time when people should work – an assertion built into protective labor legislation in a number of countries. It is well reflected in the work of Carpentier and Cazamian (1977).

3 "Community" defines time-specific labor markets, because larger regional movements of workers take large amounts of time relative to daily work time – it is one thing to consider large areas in migration studies where the movement is for whole days at a time, at least, but daily time-specific markets deal with repetitive behavior over a short unit time and therefore require a narrow regional compass. Commuting, not migration, is at issue. This ties to the problems of labor market timing in less developed countries discussed in the next chapter and the length of T in the last.

4 Their *ex die* elasticities.

5 "However, in adopting such an entirely general point of view [of time-shaped production], the relationships become so complicated that it is difficult to formulate conclusions that are generally valid and at the same time easy to apply" (Frisch, 1965, p. 29).

6 It is worth noting that the level of output with the given demand profile generated by time-invariant price $\bar{p}$ is different from (and always less than) the level of output discussed earlier that the firm would optimally supply at $\bar{p}$, $q_s(t,\bar{p})$, the supply profile. In the present case, the marginal costs of the $q_i(t)$ are determined within the duration constraint of the demand load curve; in that earlier description of $q_s(t,\bar{p})$, they are not. So marginal costs are higher for each stratum of output rate (above $q_b(t)$) when duration is constrained by demand than when it is not.

7 A time-invariant price, $\bar{p}$, might, of course, be high enough – and the demand profile at that price flat enough – that excess supply would prevail at all times. This is not irrelevant in regulated industries.

8 Because it assumes that utility and production functions are time-insensitive, the model of Chapter 8 cannot describe such quantity-induced load shedding: If x_i is not available at time t, that fact will not alter household demand at $t + a$ when it is available. Activities were assumed there to be temporally independent. So demand for x_i at $t + a$, off peak, could depend only on conditions at $t + a$, not whether or not demand has been frustrated at some other time t. This is similar to the problem of consumption timing discussed at the end of Chapter 9.

9 Like $(dq_d(t')/d\bar{q}(t))/(\bar{q}(t)/q_d(t'))$, where $d\bar{q}(t)$ is quantity rationing at t and $dq_d(t')$ is the consequent increase in demand.

10 So the Chapter 8 model accommodates household load shedding in

response to time-differentiated prices – it has trouble only with the quantity rationing response.

11.   Welfare and distortions in time-specific exchange

1 The implication is that this is a nearly classic case of using prices to internalize an external cost. That is valid. Time-invariant prices over time-specific markets block information about real costs; the difference between this and the usual case of externalities is only that these are time-specific costs rather than product- or process-specific costs.
2 It is worth emphasizing that in both markets the increased utilization of capital and labor stocks is a movement to an optimum utilization, as judged by the owners of those resources and by society, if markets fully clear. This does not rest simply on an assertion that increased utilization, per se, is always welfare-improving. It is not. The time-invariant price makes 24-hour-per-day utilization optimal for the firm, but its actual utilization is constrained by the fact that actual nighttime labor supply, $l_s(t,\bar{w})$, does not permit that optimal schedule. So the firm's actual utilization is far below its optimum with the time-invariant price and therefore with quantity rationing of labor. The time-specific price that rises at night therefore (a) reduces the firms' optimal utilization, reducing their demand for labor at night, but (b) increases the firms' actual utilization by making more labor supply available at night. The optimum is reached by both adjustments.

   For labor, the time-specific price induces rescheduling of labor from the redundant period of unemployment during the day to the period during the night when there is excess demand. Of course, that reduction might be induced, too, by quantity rationing: Those who cannot get jobs during the day take jobs at night because they are available then, despite the continued optimality of a day work schedule at the time-invariant wage rate. The welfare effects of this depend on the methods of quantity rationing that assign workers to day or night work. Empirical evidence strongly suggests that this selection is quite a serious problem in underdeveloped countries that rely far more on quantity rationing than on prices to distribute workers over day and night work (Farooq and Winston, 1978). See Section 11.3.
3 The social effects on optimal household schedules of coincidence of schedules in a community would be reinforced by the economic effects of scale economies discussed in Section 11.3.
4 Emphasis on the average worker is pervasive in Swedish studies of shift-working, and it supports a quite widespread conviction there that shift-working is, per se, bad for people. The conclusion is that it should be banned, or at least made very rare and difficult to institute. At a recent meeting in Stockholm dominated by Swedes of that persuasion, but

Swedes who also share a reverence for their national sports heroes, it was suggested that the fact is also established, beyond much doubt, that it is terribly damaging for the average person to hurl himself down the side of an ice-and-snow-covered mountain at speeds up to 65 miles per hour – indeed, that activity is certainly fatal to many middle-aged matrons. From this fact, consistent application of the logic of Swedish social policy requires, of course, that Ingmar Stenmark, the premier national sports hero, should be barred by a protective government from competing in (and winning) the Winter Olympics. Economists' attention to the margin, stressing that there are many activities – including many time-specific ones – for which average responses are highly irrelevant, continues to unnerve noneconomists.

5 The Ricardian analogy is the familiar one where the price of all corn in the city is determined by the costs of production on the marginal land, and rents are earned on all lands that can produce and deliver corn to the city more cheaply. The crucial welfare difference in time-specific rents is that corn from all sources is perfectly substitutable in use; so its source-invariant price is most efficient. In a time-specific product like electricity, there is no necessary substitutability in use between different times over T; so it is not optimal to force a time-invariant price on all uses at all times. Absent time specificity in use, a time-invariant price would naturally emerge from the market; but the time-shape of demand makes only a time-specific price efficient.

6 With either speed or utilization tracking.

7 An intermediate pricing scheme is often available to industrial users in which they give up reliability of power – they volunteer to be quantity-rationed during peak-load periods – in exchange for lower if still time-invariant prices. So they face quantity rationing with price inducements to accept it.

8 Simple technology is available to make some of that unpredictable response automatic with devices set to sense and respond to the magnitude of prices transmitted via power line to the household – like a swimming-pool pump that goes on only when the price of electric power falls below a preset level. This clearly suggests that some damping of price variations from pure instantaneous response might be desirable.

9 In my early efforts to make sense out of low levels of capital utilization in poor countries, I introduced this model in crude form, only to be reminded by all and sundry that nighttime wage premiums were rarely paid in LDCs; so it was difficult to use high nighttime wages to explain low levels of utilization (Winston, 1968, 1971a). Although I took refuge in the fact that wage rates of labor were not the only rhythmic input cost faced by firms in poor countries and that basic capital price distortions were a real culprit in low utilization – against any rhythmic input cost – it became clear later that that was a needlessly weak reed. Productivity differentials that have the same effect on firms' utilization decisions as

do nighttime wage premiums are far more fundamental. They were first noted by Baily (1974).

10 What little direct empirical evidence we have comes from a survey of unemployed (and employed) industrial shift-workers in Pakistan, 96% of whom, rather than have no job at all, were quite explicit in their preference for day work over night work but continued to work at night (Farooq and Winston, 1978, pp. 238–9).

11 The data of the Farooq-Winston study in Pakistan speak for themselves: 83% of the day workers reported no sleeping problems, whereas 19% of the shift-workers did; 10% of the day workers reported problems sleeping in the heat, whereas 70% of the shift-workers did; 3% of the day workers had problems sleeping with noise, whereas 15% of the shift-workers did; finally, 7% of the day workers reported problems with insects while they slept, whereas 12% of the shift-workers did (Farooq and Winston, 1978, Table 1).

12 Some figures from the Nigerian survey of capital utilization give a suggestion of the magnitudes that might be involved. Because the average industrial capital stock per crew member (i.e., worker while working) in Nigerian industry was about $50,000, the social value of a housing capital investment that completely eliminated the nighttime productivity differential for one worker would be the same $50,000; allocation of that amount to such housing would, under highly simplified, if useful, assumptions, provide a worker at no premium wage rate to operate $50,000 worth of capital on a night shift. Although that estimate seems awfully high, that rests partly on my use of the corrected measure of capital-per-worker, which removes the understatement typical of most empirical estimates, as described in Chapter 7.

The eagerness to show compassion for night-shift-workers in LDCs that has been manifested in legally imposed night-shift wage premiums (Colombia, India, and others) might far better have taken the form of improved housing for night workers that would increase the utilization of that industrial capital stock.

13 Foss wrote: "The World War II experience must have constituted a powerful stimulus to multiple shifting and it is reasonable to assume that the experience acquired during the war with two- and three-shift operations was carried over into the postwar years of high-level demand. In fact, some of the illustrations used in this article suggest that the major change in relative equipment utilization took place during and immediately after World War II, and that changes since then (aside from cyclical movements) have been relatively small" (Foss, 1963, p. 8).

14 Although the strongest effect would appear to be the time-specific scale economies described here, it is likely that their impact was augmented by increased nighttime labor productivity, that after a decade of low levels of employment, lower nighttime labor productivity – caused both by restricted self-selection of night workers and by lower levels of household

capital – had discouraged shift-working so that the increased wealth and mobility of the war removed that deterrent to higher utilization. And certainly a pure learning effect, as implied by Foss's quotation (Note 13), must have played a role.

15 I am knowingly using subscript n for net wage in $w_n(t)$ and for nighttime in t_n. This is the only place these two meet, in time-specific work activity costs; it seemed not sufficiently confusing to warrant using less straightforward symbols in all that preceded this encounter.

16 An implication for less developed countries trying to increase the utilization of scarce capital stocks by increasing night-shift-work (or weekend or other "nonnormal" operating times) is that they concentrate their night shifts within communities, because that allows the exploitation of the economies of time-specific scale – the markets over which such scale economies can be achieved are geographically limited. The interviews with Pakistan workers that formed the basis for the Farooq-Winston study were rich with illustrations of workers' perceptions of higher nighttime work costs. The scale economy of agglomeration of night work reinforces the household preference effect described in the first part of this chapter.

12. Time-specific analysis of nonrhythmic events: relational exchange and the role of repetition

1 Although Sen's metapreference analysis (1977) and Strotz's consistent planning model (1955–6) offer different – complementary – explanations; see Winston (1978) and Elster (1979).

2 Two previous analyses deserve mention: Macneil is the source in the legal literature of Goldberg's emphasis on the relational nature of these contracts, and Hobbes's *Leviathan*, Chapter 14 (1962), has a remarkably explicit discussion of the temporal vulnerability of the partners to a covenant, as well as recognition of the problems created by the absence of an explicit contract enforcement mechanism.

3 Kornai's analysis of transactions includes a much richer event sequence, starting before t_0. But his are different purposes (Kornai, 1971).

4 One might pursue the interesting fact that to the extent that B is expected to happen, even with probability less than 1, during $t_a < \tau < t_b$ the incomplete transaction is itself an asset to V as an account receivable.

5 Harvey Leibenstein pointed to transactions with kidnappers as ones that are especially freighted with distrust, and hence often elaborately contrived for simultaneity. The U.S.-Iranian hostage transaction of 1981 was an international example of such requisite simultaneity.

6 So Goldberg's analysis emphasizes the role of contracts in, for instance, the installation of expensive, durable, and customer-specific capital. The seller, then, is vulnerable to the buyer's opportunism after the plant is built but before all goods deliveries have been made.

7 Winston (1978).
8 Kornai and Shackle are two of the most effective critics who seem to have advocated that posture.
9 Even the classic motive for self-induced misinformation – the reduction of cognitive dissonance – is less likely to survive repetitive events as repetition multiplies the costs of self-deception.
10 That decision has much of the character of a stock in a static model, rather than a flow; its representation as human capital is apt.
11 This can be put more formally with useful insights. Stick to the simple case of an AB transaction between O and V. Then, in terms of the purest self-interest, O's incentive to fleece V during $t_a < \tau < t_b$ is P_v, the price paid by V for the goods B. (This formulation is general and does not depend on the sequence of transactions that makes V vulnerable – whether V is buyer or seller – so long as the value of the goods is not dependent on this transaction. Then if O runs off with the goods instead of the money, they have the same value, P_v.) O's gain at τ from treating V honestly – his loss from not fleecing V – is, assuming that V will only be taken advantage of once,

$$H_0(\tau) = \sum_{i=1}^{n} \frac{G_i(t_i)}{(1 + r)^{t_i - \tau}},$$ (12.1)

where n is the number of such (expected) future transactions between O and V, G_i is the net gain from trade accruing to O, in money terms, of an ith completed transaction in the future, t_i is the timing of that ith transaction, and r is O's discount rate. Then the purest of self-interest will prevent O from taking advantage of V so long as

$$H_0(\tau) > P_r(\tau).$$ (12.2)

Ignoring any differences among the n future transactions, honest behavior will be recommended to the most crassly self-interested opportunist by the following:

1. $G_i/P_v(\tau)$, the advantage of his future gains from trade relative to the advantage of current opportunism,
2. n, the number of future transactions O expects to have with V,
3. t_i, the time distribution of those transactions, and hence the present value of the gains of honest behavior – the more proximate in time, the greater the incentive to behave honestly – and
4. r, O's discount rate or – in psychological/sociological jargon – inability to delay gratification: the lower, the more honest.

12 The equation in Note 11 can be modified to describe the opportunist's reputation by making the gains from future transactions stochastic, with the probability of any future transaction dependent on O's prior "honest" behavior and the cost of information flows between the V_i. Then a

demographic change like urbanization that increases the costs of information flow among the V_i will appear to reduce the honesty of transactions – because it would increase the frequency with which O's would exploit V's – but in fact it will be only the consequence of altered self-interest. Indeed, people might well have a heightened preference for honest behavior (if, for instance, more were stung and hence became more appreciative of the social value of honesty), but the "objective data" would reveal less of honest behavior.

13 It is interesting to reflect on the fact that economic theory has judged it obvious that free-rider incentives will dominate behavior in public goods and cartel contexts – to do otherwise is deemed naive, even in the so-called voluntary-exchange theories of taxation (Musgrave, 1959, Chapter 4) – but paradoxically it is judged equally obvious that all private transactors will be honest in their dealings with each other. Hirshleifer is characteristically clear on this (1976, Chapter 18). So Williamson, Wachter, and Harris believed they had to conjure up "a deeper variety of self interest . . . than is ordinarily assumed in economics" (Williamson et al., 1975, p. 258) in order to justify opportunism. But it was only a deeper self-interest than is ordinarily assumed in market analyses, not in tax analyses. See Hirschman (1980).

14 Bok's *Lying* (1978). Bartlett's *Positive Theory of Government* analyzed provision of subsidized biased information to the same end.

References

Ainslie, George. 1975. "Specious Reward: A Behavioral Theory of Impulsiveness and Impulse Control." *Psychological Bulletin* 82:463–96.

Alchian, Armen A. 1950. "Uncertainty, Evolution, and Economic Theory." *Journal of Political Economy* 57:211–21.

Aristotle. 1973. "Nicomachean Ethics," 7, 1–10. In *Aristotle's Ethics*, edited by J. L. Ackrill, pp. 129–46. New York: Humanities Press.

Arrow, Kenneth J. 1974. *The Limits of Organization*. New York: W. W. Norton.

———. 1978. "The Future and Present in Economic Life." *Economic Inquiry* 16:157–69.

Arrow, Kenneth J., and Kurz, Mordecai. 1970. "Optimal Growth with Irreversible Investment in a Ramsey Model." *Econometrica* 38:331–44.

Bach, Johann Sebastian. 1975. Bach Suite No. 1. In *Eisenberg's Bach: Six Suites for Solo Violoncello*. Neptune: Paganiniana Publications.

Baily, Mary Ann. 1974. "Capital Utilization in Kenya Manufacturing Industry." Ph.D. dissertation, Massachusetts Institute of Technology.

Baldwin, Robert E. 1971. "Determinants of the Commodity Structure of U.S. Trade." *American Economic Review* 61:126–46.

Bartlett, Randall. 1973. *Economic Foundations of Political Power*. New York: Free Press.

Barzel, Yoram. 1980. "Measurement Cost and the Organization of Markets." University of Washington (mimeograph).

Becker, Gary S. 1965. "A Theory of the Allocation of Time." *Economic Journal* 75:493–517.

———. 1976. *The Economic Approach to Human Behavior*. Chicago: University of Chicago Press.

Best, Fred. 1980. *Flexible Life Scheduling: Breaking the Education-Work-Retirement Lockstep*. New York: Praeger.

Betancourt, Roger R., and Clague, Christopher K. 1975. "An Economic Analysis of Capital Utilization." *Southern Economic Journal* 42:69–78.

———. 1981. *Capital Utilization: A Theoretical and Empirical Analysis*. Cambridge University Press.

Bhagwati, Jagdish. 1969. *International Trade, Selected Readings*. Harmondsworth: Penguin.

Böhm-Bawerk, Eugen V. 1891. *The Positive Theory of Capital*. London: Macmillan.

Bok, Sissela. 1978. *Lying: Moral Choice in Public and Private Life*. New York: Pantheon.

Boulding, Kenneth E. 1955. *Economic Analysis*, 3rd ed. New York: Harper & Bros.

Branson, William H., and Monoyios, Nikolaos. 1977. "Factor Inputs in U.S. Trade." *Journal of International Economics* 7:111–31.

California Energy Commission. 1979. *California Load Management Research, 1978: California Electric Utilities Demonstration Project.*

Carpentier, J., and Cazamian, P. 1977. *Night Work*. Geneva: International Labour Office.

Cassels, J. M. 1937. "Excess Capacity and Monopolistic Competition." *Quarterly Journal of Economics* 51:426–43.

Clark, J. Maurice. 1923. *Studies in the Economics of Overhead Costs*. Chicago: University of Chicago Press.

Cogan, John F. 1977. "Labor Supply with Time and Money Costs of Participation." R-2044-HEW. Santa Monica, Calif.: Rand Corporation.

Cyert, Richard M., and March, James G. 1963. *A Behavioral Theory of the Firm*. Englewood Cliffs, N.J.: Prentice-Hall.

Dalton, Hugh. 1932. *Principles of Public Finance*, 7th ed. London: G. Routledge.

Deardorff, Alan V., and Stafford, Frank P. 1976. "Compensation of Cooperating Factors." *Econometrica* 44:671–84.

de Leeuw, Frank. 1962. "The Concept of Capacity." *Journal of the American Statistical Association* 57:826–40.

Denison, Edward F. 1962. *The Sources of Economic Growth in the United States and the Alternatives Before Us*. New York: Committee for Economic Development.

  1980. "The Contribution of Capital to Economic Growth." *American Economic Review* 70:220–4.

Despres, Emile, and Kindleberger, C. P. 1952. "The Mechanism for Adjustment in International Payments – the Lessons of Postwar Experience." *American Economic Review* 42:332–44.

Dixit, A. K. 1976. *Optimization in Economic Theory*. Oxford: Oxford University Press.

Eary, Donald F., and Johnson, Gerald E. 1962. *Process Engineering for Manufacturing*. Englewood Cliffs, N.J.: Prentice-Hall.

Eels, F. R. 1956. "The Economics of Shift Working." *Journal of Industrial Economics* 5:51–62.

Elster, Jon. 1977. "Ulysses and the Sirens: A Theory of Imperfect Rationality." *Social Science Information* 16:469–526.

  1979. *Ulysses and the Sirens: Studies in Rationality and Irrationality*. Cambridge University Press.

Farooq, Ghazi M., and Winston, Gordon C. 1978. "Shift Working, Employment, and Economic Development: A Study of Industrial Workers in Pakistan." *Economic Development and Cultural Change* 26:227–44.

Felix, David. 1978. "De Gustibus Disputandum Est: Changing Consumer Preferences in Economic Growth." Washington University (mimeograph).

Ferguson, C. E. 1969. *The Neoclassical Theory of Production and Distribution*. Cambridge University Press.

Festinger, Leon. 1964. *Conflict, Decision and Dissonance*. Stanford: Stanford University Press.

Fisher, Irving. 1930. *The Theory of Interest*. New York: Macmillan.

Foss, Murray F. 1963. "The Utilization of Capital Equipment: Postwar Compared With Prewar." *Survey of Current Business* 43:8–16.

  1981. *Changes in the Workweek of Fixed Capital: U.S. Manufacturing, 1929 to 1976*. Washington, D.C.: American Enterprise Institute for Public Policy Research.

Fraser, J. T. 1978. *Time as Conflict: A Scientific and Humanistic Study*. Basel: Birkhauser Verlag. ·

Fraser, J. T., Haber, F. C., and Muller, G. H. (editors). 1972. *The Study of Time: Proceedings of the First Conference of the International Society for the Study of Time, Oberwolfach (Black Forest) – West Germany*. New York: Springer-Verlag.

Friedman, Milton. 1962. *Price Theory: A Provisional Text*, rev. ed. Chicago: Aldine.

Frisch, Ragnar. 1965. *Theory of Production*. Dordrecht: D. Reidel.

Fuss, Melvyn, and McFadden, Daniel (editors). 1978. *Production Economics: A Dual Approach to Theory and Applications.* Amsterdam: North-Holland.

Gardner, Martin. 1979. "On Altering the Past, Delaying the Future and Other Ways of Tampering with Time." *Scientific American* 240:21–30.

Georgescu-Roegen, Nicholas. 1970. "The Economics of Production." *American Economic Review* 60:1–9.

——— 1971. *The Entropy Law and the Economic Process.* Cambridge: Harvard University Press.

——— 1976. "Chamberlin's New Economics and the Unit of Production." In *Monopolistic Competition Theory: Studies in Impact: Essays in Honor of Edward H. Chamberlin,* edited by Robert E. Kuenne, pp. 31–62. New York: John Wiley.

Geweke, John. 1978. "Temporal Aggregation in the Multiple Regression Model." *Econometrica* 46:643–61.

Glass, Philip. 1979. *Einstein on the Beach.* New York: Tomato.

Goldberg, Victor P. 1980. "Relational Exchange: Economics and Complex Contracts." *American Behavioral Scientist* 23:337–52.

Goppers, Karlis. 1972. "Causes of Planned and Unplanned Excess Capacity in Capital Equipment: An Investment Decision Approach." Massachusetts Institute of Technology (mimeograph).

Great Britain, National Board for Prices and Incomes. 1970. *Hours of Work, Overtime and Shiftworking.* Report No. 161. London: Her Majesty's Stationery Office.

Gronau, Reuben. 1977. "Leisure, Home Production and Work – The Theory of the Allocation of Time Revisited." *Journal of Political Economy* 85:1099–123.

Hahn, F. H. 1973. *On the Notion of Equilibrium in Economics: An Inaugural Lecture.* Cambridge University Press.

Harcourt, G. C. 1969. "Some Cambridge Controversies in the Theory of Capital." *Journal of Economic Literature* 7:369–405.

Hickman, Bert G. 1964. "On a New Method of Capacity Estimation." *Journal of the American Statistical Association* 59:529–49.

Hicks, J. R. 1946. *Value and Capital: An Inquiry into Some Fundamental Principles of Economic Theory,* 2nd ed. Oxford: Oxford University Press.

——— 1976. "Some Questions of Time in Economics." In *Evolution, Welfare, and Time in Economics: Essays in Honor of Nicholas Georgescu-Roegen,* edited by Anthony Tang, Fred M. Westfield, and James S. Worley, pp. 135–52. Lexington, Mass.: D. C. Heath.

——— 1979. *Causality in Economics.* New York: Basic Books.

Hirsch, Fred. 1976. *Social Limits to Growth.* Cambridge: Harvard University Press.

Hirschman, Albert O. 1980. *Morality and the Social Sciences: A Durable Tension.* Memphis: P. K. Seidman Foundation.

Hirshleifer, Jack. 1976. *Price Theory and Applications.* Englewood Cliffs, N.J.: Prentice-Hall.

Hobbes, Thomas. 1962. *Leviathan or the Matter, Forme and Power of a Commonwealth Ecclesiasticall and Civil.* New York: Collier.

Hood, William C. 1948. "Some Aspects of the Treatment of Time in Economic Theory." *Canadian Journal of Economics and Political Science* 14:453–68.

Houthakker, H. S. 1951. "Electricity Tariffs in Theory and Practice." *Economic Journal* 61:1–25.

Hufbauer, G. C. 1970. "The Impact of National Characteristics and Technology of the Commodity Composition of Trade in Manufactured Goods." In *The Technology Factor in International Trade,* edited by Raymond Vernon, pp. 145–231. New York: Columbia University Press for the National Bureau of Economic Research.

330   References

Hughes, Helen; Bautista, Romeo; Lim, David; Morawatz, David; and Thoumi, Francisco. 1976. "Capital Utilization in Manufacturing in Developing Countries." World Bank staff working paper No. 242.

Hutchings, R. 1971. *Seasonal Influences on Soviet Industry.* New York: Oxford University Press.

Hutt, W. H. 1939. *The Theory of Idle Resources.* London: Jonathan Cape.

Jameson, Kenneth P. 1980. "Supply Side Economics: Growth versus Income Distribution." *Challenge* 23:26–31.

Jevons, W. Stanley. 1888. *The Theory of Political Economy.* London: Macmillan.

Johansen, Leif. 1968. "Production Functions and the Concept of Capacity." Recherches Récentes sur la Fonction de Production. Collection Economie Mathematique et Econometrie, No. 2. Namur: Ceruna.

Jones, Ronald W. 1980. "Comparative and Absolute Advantage." *Schweizerische Zeitschrift für Volkswirtschaft und Statistik,* pp. 308–24.

Jones, Ronald W., and Easton, Stephen T. 1981. "Factor Intensities and Factor Substitution in General Equilibrium." Discussion paper 81-1, University of Rochester.

Jorgenson, D. W., and Griliches, Z. 1967. "The Explanation of Productivity Change." *Review of Economic Studies* 34:249–83.

Keynes, John Maynard. 1935. *The General Theory of Employment, Interest and Money.* New York: Harcourt, Brace.

Kim, Young Chin, and Kwon, Jene K. 1977. "The Utilization of Capital and the Growth of Output in a Developing Economy: The Case of South Korean Manufacturing." *Journal of Development Economics* 4:265–78.

Klein, L. R. 1960. "Some Theoretical Issues in the Measurement of Capacity." *Econometrica* 23:272–86.

Klein, Lawrence R., and Long, Virginia. 1973. "Capacity Utilization: Concept, Measurement and Recent Estimates." *Brookings Papers on Economic Activity* 3:743–56.

Koopmans, Tjalling C. 1957. *Three Essays on the State of Economic Science.* New York: McGraw-Hill.

Kornai, Janos. 1971. *Anti-Equilibrium: On Economic Systems Theory and the Tasks of Research.* Amsterdam: North-Holland.

Lachmann, Ludwig M. 1976. "From Mises to Shackle: An Essay on Austrian Economics and the Kaleidic Society." *Journal of Economic Literature* 16:54–62.

Lancaster, Kelvin. 1966. "Change and Innovation in the Technology of Consumption." *American Economic Review* 56:14–42.

Lary, Hal B. 1968. *Imports of Manufactures from Less Developed Countries.* New York: Columbia University Press for the National Bureau of Economic Research.

Leibenstein, Harvey J. 1976. *Beyond Economic Man: A New Foundation for Microeconomics.* Cambridge: Harvard University Press.

———. 1979. "A Branch of Economics Is Missing: Micro-Micro Theory." *Journal of Economic Literature* 17:477–502.

Leontief, Wassily. 1954. "Domestic Production and Foreign Trade: The American Capital Position Re-examined." *Economia Internationale* 6:3–32.

———. 1966. *Input-Output Economics.* New York: Oxford University Press.

Linder, Staffan Burenstam. 1970. *The Harried Leisure Class.* New York: Columbia University Press.

Lloyd, Peter J. 1980. "Economies of Scale Due to the Length of Production Runs." Seminar paper No. 145, Institute for International Economic Studies.

Macneil, I. R. 1974. "The Many Futures of Contracts." *Southern California Law Review* 47:691–816.

Maital, Shlomo, and Maital, Sharone. 1978. "Is Discounting the Future Irrational? Origins and Nature of the Time Preference Controversy." Princeton University (mimeograph).

March, James G. 1978. "Bounded Rationality, Ambiguity, and the Engineering of Choice." *Bell Journal of Economics* 9:587–608.

Marglin, Stephen A. 1971. "What Do Bosses Do?" Harvard University (mimeograph).

Marris, Robin. 1964. *The Economics of Capital Utilization: A Report on Multiple-Shift Work.* Cambridge University Press.

Marshall, Alfred. 1961. *Principles of Economics,* 9th ed. London: Macmillan for the Royal Economic Society.

Marx, Karl. 1973. *Grundrisse: Foundations of the Critique of Political Economy.* New York: Vantage.

McMullan, J. T., Morgon, R., and Murray, R. B. 1976. *Energy Resources and Supply.* Chichester: John Wiley.

McPherson, Michael S. 1978. "Liberty and the Higher Pleasures: In Defense of Mill." Williams College (mimeograph).

1980. "Want Formation, Morality, and the Interpretive Dimension of Economic Inquiry." Research paper No. 33, Williams College.

1981. "Morality and the Useful Economist." Williams College (mimeograph).

McWhorter, Eugene W. 1976. "The Small Electronic Calculator." *Scientific American* 234:88–98.

Michael, Robert T., and Becker, Gary S. 1973. "On the Theory of Consumer Behavior." *Swedish Journal of Economics* 75:378–96.

Mischel, Walter. 1974. "Processes in Delay of Gratification." *Advances in Experimental Social Psychology* 7:249–92.

Mises, Ludwig von 1949. *Human Action: A Treatise on Economics.* New Haven: Yale University Press.

Mitchell, Bridger M., Manning, Willard G., Jr., and Acton, Jan Paul. 1978. *Peak-Load Pricing: European Lessons for U.S. Energy Policy.* Philadelphia: J. B. Lippincott.

Mott, Paul E., Mann, Floyd C., McLoughlin, Quin, and Warwick, Donald P. 1965. *Shift Work: The Social, Psychological and Physical Consequences.* Ann Arbor: University of Michigan Press.

Musgrave, Richard A. 1959. *The Theory of Public Finance: A Study in Public Economy.* New York: McGraw-Hill.

Nadiri, M. Ishaq, and Rosen, Sherwin. 1969. "Interrelated Factor Demand Functions." *American Economic Review* 59:457–71.

Nelson, Richard R., and Winter, Sidney G. 1980. "Firm and Industry Response to Changed Market Conditions; An Evolutionary Approach." *Economic Inquiry* 18:179–202.

Nerlove, M. 1972. "On the Structure of Serial Dependence in Some U.S. Price Series." In *The Econometrics of Price Determination Conference,* pp. 60–112. October 30–31, 1970. Washington, D.C.: Board of Governors of the Federal Reserve System and Social Science Research Council.

Nicholls, William H. 1948. *Labor Productivity Functions in Meat Packing.* Chicago: University of Chicago Press.

North, Douglass C. 1981. *Structure and Change in Economic History.* New York: W. W. Norton.

Oi, Walter Y. 1962. "Labor as a Quasi-fixed Factor." *Journal of Political Economy* 70:538–55.

1981. "Slack Capacity: Productive or Wasteful." *American Economic Review* 71:64–9.

332   References

Pack, Howard. 1976. "The Substitution of Labour for Capital in Kenyan Manufacturing." *Economic Journal* 86:45–58.

Panzar, John, C. 1976. "A Neoclassical Approach to Peak Loan Pricing." *Bell Journal of Economics* 7:521–30.

Perry, George L. 1973. "Capacity in Manufacturing." *Brookings Papers on Economic Activity* 3:701–42.

Phan-Thuy, N., Betancourt, Roger R., Winston, Gordon C., and Kabaj, Mieczyslaw. 1981. *Industrial Capacity and Employment Promotion: Case Studies of Sri Lanka, Nigeria, Morocco and an Overall Survey of Other Developing Countries*. Farnborough, Hants: Gower for the International Labour Office.

Phelps, E. S., and Pollak, R. A. 1983. "On Second-Best National Saving and Game-Equilibrium Growth." *Review of Economic Studies* 35:185–99.

Pollak, R. A. 1968. "Consistent Planning." *Review of Economic Studies* 35:201–8.

⸻ 1978. "Endogenous Tastes in Demand and Welfare Analysis." *American Economic Review* 68:374–9.

Pollak, Robert A., and Wachter, Michael L. 1975. "The Relevance of the Household Production Function and Its Implications for the Allocation of Time." *Journal of Political Economy* 83:255–77.

Reder, M. W. 1979. "The Place of Ethics in the Theory of Production." In *Economics and Human Welfare: Essays in Honor of Tibor Scitovsky*, edited by M. Boskin, pp. 133–46. New York: Academic.

Riley, Terry. 1964. *Terry Riley in C*. New York: Columbia Records.

Robbins, Lionel. 1930. "On the Elasticity of Demand for Income in Terms of Effort." *Economica* 10:123–9.

Robinson, Joan. 1953–4. "The Production Function and the Theory of Capital." *Review of Economic Studies* 21:81–106.

Rosenstein-Rodan, P. N. 1934. "The Role of Time in Economic Theory." *Economica* 1:77–97.

Samuelson, Paul Anthony. 1947. *Foundations of Economic Analysis*. Cambridge: Harvard University Press.

⸻ 1976. "Speeding up of Time with Age in Recognition of Life as Fleeting." In *Evolution, Welfare, and Time in Economics: Essays in Honor of Nicholas Georgescu-Roegen*, edited by Anthony M. Tang, Fred M. Westfield, and James S. Worley, pp. 153–70. Lexington, Mass.: D. C. Heath.

Sanyal, Kalyan K., and Jones, Ronald W. 1979. "The Theory of Trade in Middle Products." University of Rochester (mimeograph).

Schelling, T. C. 1978a. "Egonomics, or the Art of Self-Management." *American Economic Review* 68:290–4.

⸻ 1978b. *Micromotives and Macrobehavior*. New York: W. W. Norton.

Scitovsky, Tibor. 1976. *The Joyless Economy: An Inquiry into Human Satisfaction*. New York: Oxford University Press.

Sen, Amartya Kumar. 1964. "Choice of Techniques of Production with Special Reference to East Asia." In *Economic Development with Special Reference to East Asia*, edited by Kenneth Berrill, pp. 386–98. New York: St. Martin's Press.

⸻ 1975. *Employment, Technology and Development*. Oxford: Clarendon Press.

⸻ 1977. "Rational Fools: A Critique of the Behavioral Foundations of Economic Theory." *Philosophy and Public Affairs* 6:317–44.

Shackle, G. L. S. 1958. *Time in Economics*. Amsterdam: North-Holland.

⸻ 1972. *Epistemics and Economics: A Critique of Economic Doctrines*. Cambridge University Press.

1973. "Keynes and Today's Establishment in Economic Theory: A View." *Journal of Economic Literature* 11:516–19.

Shephard, R. 1953. *Cost and Production Functions*. Princeton: Princeton University Press.

1970. *Theory of Cost and Production Functions*. Princeton: Princeton University Press.

Simon, Herbert A. 1959. "Theories of Decision-Making in Economics and Behavioral Sciences." *American Economic Review* 49:253.

1978*a*. "On How to Decide What to Do." *Bell Journal of Economics* 9:494–507.

1978*b*. "Rationality as Process and as Product of Thought." *American Economic Review* 68:1–16.

Smith, Adam. 1937. *An Inquiry into the Nature and Causes of the Wealth of Nations*. New York: Random House.

Solow, Robert M. 1962. "Substitution and Fixed Proportions in the Theory of Capital." *Review of Economic Studies* 29:207–18.

Stigler, George J. 1952. *The Theory of Price*, rev. ed. New York: Macmillan.

Stigler, George J., and Becker, Gary S. 1977. "De Gustibus Non Est Disputandum." *American Economic Review* 67:76–90.

1961. "The Economics of Information." *Journal of Political Economy* 69:213–25.

Stigler, G. J., and Kindahl, J. K. 1970. *The Behavior of Industrial Prices*. New York: National Bureau of Economic Research.

Strotz, R. H. 1955–6. "Myopia and Inconsistency in Dynamic Utility Maximization." *Review of Economic Studies* 23:165–80.

Taubman, Paul, and Wilkinson, Maurice. 1970. "User Cost, Capital Utilization and Investment Theory." *International Economic Review* 11:209–15.

Theil, H. 1954. *Linear Aggregation of Economic Relations*. Amsterdam: North-Holland.

Tversky, Amos, and Kahneman, Daniel. 1974. "Judgement under Uncertainty: Heuristics and Biases." *Science* 185:1124–31.

U.S. Department of Commerce, Bureau of the Census. 1976. *Survey of Plant Capacity, 1975*. MQ-C1(75)-1. Current Industrial Reports Series.

Varian, Hal R. 1978. *Microeconomic Analysis*. New York: W. W. Norton.

Veblen, Thorstein. 1953. *The Theory of the Leisure Class*. New York: New American Library.

Vonnegut, Kurt, Jr. 1959. *The Sirens of Titan*. New York: Dell.

Vroom, Victor H. 1968. "Industrial Psychology." In *The Handbook of Social Psychology, Vol. 5: Applied Social Psychology*, 2nd ed., edited by Gardner Lindzey and Elliot Aronsen, pp. 196–268. Reading, Mass.: Addison-Wesley.

Weitzman, Elliot D. 1976. "Circadian Rhythms and Episodic Hormone Secretion in Man." *Annual Review of Medicine* 27:225.

Wenders, John T. 1976. "Peak Load Pricing in the Electric Utility Industry." *Bell Journal of Economics* 7:232–41.

Whitrow, G. J. 1972. *The Nature of Time*. New York: Holt, Rinehart & Winston.

Williamson, Jeffrey G. 1971. "Capital Accumulation, Labor Saving, and Labor Absorption Once More." *Quarterly Journal of Economics* 85:40–65.

Williamson, Oliver E. 1975. *Markets and Hierarchies: Analysis and Antitrust Implications: A Study in the Economics of Internal Organization*. New York: Free Press.

1979. "Transaction-Cost Economics: The Governance of Contractual Relations." *Journal of Law and Economics* 22:233–61.

Williamson, Oliver E., Wachter, Michael L., and Harris, Jeffrey E. 1975. "Understanding the Employment Relation: The Analysis of Idiosyncratic Exchange." *Bell Journal of Economics* 6:80–97.

Winston, Gordon C. 1963. "Income and the Allocation of Effort: An International Comparison." Ph.D. dissertation, Stanford University.

1968. "Excess Capacity in Underdeveloped Countries: The Case of Pakistan." Research memorandum No. 25, Williams College.

1970. "The Optimal Utilization of Capital." Karachi, Pakistan (mimeograph).

1971a. "Capital Utilization in Economic Development." *Economic Journal* 81:36–60.

1971b. "Capital Utilization: Physiological Costs and Preferences for Shift Work." Research memorandum No. 42, Williams College.

1974a. "Capital Utilization and Optimal Shift Work." *Bangladesh Economic Review* 2:515–58.

1974b. "Factor Substitution, *ExAnte* and *ExPost.*" *Journal of Development Economics* 1:145–63.

1974c. "The Theory of Capital Utilization and Idleness." *Journal of Economic Literature* 12:1301–20.

1977a. "Capacity: An Integrated Micro and Macro Analysis." *American Economic Review* 67:418–23.

1977b. "Increasing Manufacturing Employment Through Fuller Utilization of Capacity in Nigeria." World Employment Programme research working paper WEP 2-24/W.P.7, International Labour Office.

1978. "On Measuring Factor Proportions in Industries with Different Seasonal and Shift Patterns or Did the Leontief Paradox Ever Exist?" Research memorandum No. 71, Williams College.

1979a. "Being of Two Minds – Economic Decision-Making under Inconsistency." Institute for Advanced Study (mimeograph).

1979b. "The Effects of Demand Load Timing on Investment and Technology of Electric Power Generation: A Time Specific Analysis." For Economic Dynamics Inc. project "Analysis of Decision Methodology Relative to Adoption of New Technology, Phase II," under contract RFP 1298-2 for the Electric Power Research Institute.

1979c. "On Measuring Factor Proportions in Industries with Different Seasonal and Shift Patterns or Did the Leontief Paradox Ever Exist?" *Economic Journal* 89:879–904.

1980. "Addiction and Backsliding: A Theory of Compulsive Consumption." *Journal of Economic Behavior and Organization* 1:295–324.

1981. "Capital Investment versus Capital Utilization: Productivity and the Timing of Production." Williams College (mimeograph).

Winston, Gordon C., and McCoy, Thomas O. 1974. "Investment and the Optimal Idleness of Capital." *Review of Economic Studies* 41:419–28.

Index

accelerator, 143
accumulated flows, 41–7, 130–4, 158,
177, 312; of costs, 59; of inputs, 45,
46; of output, *see* output flows, accumulated; of utility, 161
accumulated wage payment, 82
activities: capital intensive, 209; characteristics of, 192–7, 202; composition
of, 183–9; duration of, 162, 189–93,
225; goods intensities of, *see* goods-
intensive activities; intensity of, 190;
interaction of, 221; investment aspects
of, 221; sequence of, 168, 220–1
activity: adjustment costs, 214–16;
choice, optimal, 161, 171–9, 198, 206,
225; preferences, 194–7; switching
costs, 215; timing, 190, 218–22, 231–
4, 261–5
addiction, 193, 221
adjustment: aggregate, time-specific,
248; costs, 214–16; to environment,
190; mechanisms of, 238, 262; technological, 103
aggregation, 231, 236, 237, 246
Ainslie, George, 196, 218
Alchian, Armen A., 294
analytical: range, 22; time, 16–18, 26,
37, 290, 299; unit time, *see* time units,
analytical
Aristotle, 193
Arrow, Kenneth J., xii, 4, 16, 292, 295, 296
Austrian theory, 9–10

Bach, Johann Sebastian, 26–8
Baily, Mary Ann, 89, 141, 267, 275, 298,
308, 322
Baldwin, Robert E., 144, 145, 313
Bartlett, Randall, 326
Barzel, Yoram, xii
base-load, 106, 108, 124, 243, 262; tech-
nology, 107–10, 242–4
Bautista, Romeo, xv
Becker, Gary S., 7–8, 15, 16, 157–65,
177, 181, 183–90, 193, 203, 212, 221,
299, 314, 315, 317

behavior: inconsistent, 288; optimal pat-
tern of, 25; repetitive, 215, 220; time-
shaped, 167; *see also* activities
being of two minds, 288
Best, Fred, 268
Betancourt, Roger R., 89, 141, 153, 298,
301, 312
Bhagwati, Jagdish, 313
Blomqvist, Ake, xv
Böhm-Bawerk, Eugen V., 9, 17
Bok, Sissela, 292, 296, 326
boredom, 218
Boulding, Kenneth E., 307
Branson, William H., 146, 313
Bridge Problem, 123–5
business cycle, 149

Cage, John, 26
calendar time, 9, 11, 37, 39, 40–2
capacity: economic, 149–51, 244–7, 314;
engineering, 149–51, 314; excess,
135, 153, 263, 271, 272; macroeconomic, 148–9, 151–4; microeconomic,
148, 149–54; optimal, 244–6; the
problem, 238–48; productive, 25, 105,
121, 148–54, 248; social, 153; time-
specific model of, 151–4
capacity utilization, *see* utilization of capacity
capital: costs, 69, 73, 82, 110, 121, 122,
124, 133; per crew member, 141, 142;
per employee, 142; in finance, 305;
intensity, 143, 145, 210, 243; price effect, 209; prices of, 54–6, 86, 135,
308; rental, 53, 211; stratum, 105–10,
243
capital-labor ratio, 93, 145, *see also* factor
proportions
capital price effect, 209, 213, *see also*
utilization effect on prices
capital service, 5, 42–8, 54, 62, 68, 91,
96, 100, 107, 110, 129, 130, 132, 207,
209, 222, 303, 305; price of, 55–6,
103, 108, 130, 212, 222, 240, 243,
298, 304, 318, *see also* prices, dura-

capital service (*cont.*)
    tion-specific; productivity, 48; pur-
    chased, 207–13
capital stocks, 27, 31, 42, 48–50, 53–4,
    68, 96, 100, 103, 133, 243, 300; de-
    sired, 309; divisible, 103–6; durable
    over T, 68, 77, 307; household, *see*
    household capital, stocks; human, 142,
    146, 314; idle, 25, 31, 75, 109, 135,
    262; insensate, 237; misallocation of,
    278, 323; optimal size of, 113, 122,
    124, 239, 240; owner cost of, 54–6,
    80, 208, 243, 304, 305; ownership of,
    318; productivity of, 25, 38, 96, 275,
    283; purchase price of, 41, 56; vint-
    age, 98
capital utilization (*see also utilization*): em-
    pirical studies of, 141–4, 279–82;
    household, *see* household, capital util-
    ization of
Carpentier, J., 320
cartel, 296, 326
Cassels, J. M., 149
Cazamian, P., 320
Clague, Christopher K., 89, 141, 153,
    298, 301, 312
Clark, J. M., 7, 8
clock time, 22, 39
Cogan, John F., 268
cognitive dissonance, 325
Colombia, 323
commodities, 162, 193
commodity time, 15–16, 290, 299
commuting, 268, 280, 316, 320
comparative static analysis, 14
composition, fallacy of, 151
conflict, 196, 214, 219, 221, 288–9; in
    preferences, 196, 214, 220
consumer demand, 193, 208–12, 246
consumer goods markets, time-specific,
    227
consumption: compulsion in, 196, 288;
    optimal timing of, 161, 162, 174, 178,
    190
consumption activities, 157–61, 171–3,
    181, 190–2, 221; characteristics, 185–
    90, 202; goods intensities of, 177,
    183–5, 212, *see also* marginal utility
    product; mix, 183–90; time intensities
    of, 184
consumption and work, 171–80; optimal
    duration of, 175–9; optimal timing of,
    179–80
continuous time analysis, 89, 91, 300
contracts, 292, 296

corner solution, rhythmic, 231, 249
cost contours, 86
cost data, 312
cost function, 64, 69–72, 136
cost surfaces, 60, 82–6, 103, 109
costs: adjustment, 103, 193, 214–18,
    220–2, 261, 262, 267, 316; average,
    69, 72, 73, 78–83, 109–11, 149, 243,
    246; capital service, 71, 75, 243; fixed,
    53, 69, 304; interruption, 215, 268,
    302; long-run, 73; marginal, *see* mar-
    ginal costs; metering, 57, 267; migra-
    tion, 316; peak and off-peak, 123–5;
    pseudo-, 137; short-run, 73; social,
    262; storage, 57; time-shaped, 59–65,
    67–90, 262, *see also* work costs; vari-
    able, 53, 121–4, 243, 304
Cyert, Richard M., 300

Dalton, Hugh, 33
data, time-specific, 140–1
Day, Richard, xiv
Deardorff, Alan V., 307
deLeeuw, Frank, 149
demand: excess, 228, 234–40, 246, 249,
    259, 261, 268, 269; intertemporal
    elasticities of, 248; peaks, 246, 262;
    profile, 228, 244–7, 249–57; time-
    shaped, 8, 101, 239, 240, 248, 252,
    255
demand functions, instantaneous, 227,
    228, 248, 252
demand rhythm, *see* demand, time-
    shaped
depreciation, 81, 304, 307, 308
Despres, Emile, 312
discrete analysis, 300, *see also* shift work-
    ing
disequilibrium, time-specific, 233, 240,
    258
Dixit, A. K., 311
do-it-yourself, 8, 192, 202–7, 222
duality theory, xi, 45, 129–39, 138, 139
duration: elasticity of, 189; of jobs ver-
    sus employment, 268; of production,
    17, 23, 38–42, 49, 68–76, 103, 107,
    109, 113, 132, 194, 216–18, *see also*
    utilization; of work, 175–9, 307
duration effects, 218–20
duration-specific: costs, 75, *see also* costs,
    capital service; prices, 75, 86, 176,
    177, 243, *see also* capital service, price
    of
duration-weights, 113
dynamic analysis, 14, 26

Easton, Stephen T., 313
econometrics, 21, 312
economic growth, 25, 183–9, 212–14
economic rhythms, 24–6, see repetitive and time-shaped
economies of scale, 38, 52, 55, 279, 311; time-specific, 282, 323, 324
Eels, F. R., 6, 8
efficiency, 70–90, 233–8, 246, 258–85
effort prices, 165
Einstein, Albert, 12
electric power, 6, 100, 107, 108, 119, 227, 239, 240, 258, 262, 268–74, 289, 310, 312, 322; time-of-supply pricing of, 272–4; unconventional sources of, 258, 268, 272–4, 289
electric power plants, nuclear, 108
electronics, 26, 27–33
elementary unit time (ETU), see time units, elementary analytical
Elster, Jon, xii, 196, 218, 318, 324
employment, 50, 56, 275
endocrinology, 300
endowments, household, 164–7
environment: exogenous, 177, 180, 190, 219; household production, 26, 90, 157–80, 190, 209, 231, 239, 265
equilibrium: full-information, 26, 159, 193, 196, 215; general, 151, 227, 248–57, 313; partial, 255; profile, 231; pseudo, 190, 231, 258–9; time-specific, 190, 231, 258
events: nonrhythmic, 287–97; randomly timed, 288–9; repetitive, 288, unique, 9, 287
ex ante, ex post, 307
exchange, see markets, relational exchange
excitement, 218
expectations, 294

factor: markets, 52–4; ownership, 52–4; prices, 54–66, 75, 77, 81, 94, 96, 103, 108, 113, 115–7, see also capital, capital service and labor; utilization, 47–54, 62
factor characteristics, see input characteristics
factor flow: proportions, 72–80, 86–8, 103, 140–54, 169, 236, 243, see also specific factor services; rates, 76–81, 89, 141, 167, see also intensity
factor proportions: measures of, 141; two meanings of, 141–4
Farooq, Ghazi M., 267, 275, 279, 321, 323, 324

fatigue, 50, 218
Federal Reserve index of capacity, 314
Ferguson, C. E., 215
firms: and households, 231; partitioned, 136–9; regulated, 119, 268–74; worker-controlled, 89
flow rates, 13, 17, 41, 47, 134, see also intensity; instantaneous, 23, 158; per unit time, 26
flows, 13, 17, 41, 47 (see also accumulated flows); relationship with stocks, 48–51; sources of, 48–51
Foss, Murray F., 279, 303, 323, 324
Fraser, Julius T, xv, 4, 299
free disposal, property of, 135–6
free riders, 295, 296, 326
Frisch, Ragnar, xi, 4, 5, 7, 37, 135, 137, 240, 320
full effort constraint, 165
full income constraint, 165, 170, 190
functional time unit, 22
Fuss, Melvyn, 311, 312

gains from trade, 263, 292, 295
Gardner, Martin, 298
Georgescu-Roegen, Nicholas, xii, xv, 4, 7, 47, 298, 299, 303, 305, 312, 313
Geweke, John, 21
GIGO, xiii
Glass, Phillip, 26
goal utility, see utility
Goldberg, Victor P., xii, xiv, 15, 290, 292, 324
goods: inferior, normal, and superior, 188–9; perishable, see perishability
goods-absorptive capacity, 185, 200
goods input flows, 47, 162, 198; intensity of, 178–85
goods inputs: marginal utility product of, 176; time-sensitive prices of, 280, 282, 315; to work, 197–202, 279, 280
goods-intensive activities, 181–9
Goppers, Karlis, 89
Grabois, Miriam, xvi
Grabois, Neil, xv
gratification, delayed, 218, 222
Great Britain, 238
Greenspan, Alan, 148
Griliches, Zvi, 5, 7, 52, 54, 129
Gronau, Reuben, 8, 193, 196, 202, 205, 206, 222

Hahn, F.H., 159
harmonics, 255
harriedness, 200, 201, 212, 213, 222

Harris, Jeffrey E., 326
Hickman, Bert G., 309, 314
Hicks, John R., xiii, 3, 4, 7, 14, 16, 19, 22, 299
Hirsch, Fred, 202
Hirschleifer, Jack, 326
Hirschman, Albert, xiv
Hobbes, Thomas, 324
Hollister, Robinson, xv
honesty, 295–6, 325
Hood, William C., 4, 7, 14, 22, 299, 307
household activities, 155–80, *see also* consumption activities, household production, *and* work activities
household activity schedule: optimal, 5, 8, 57, 158, 167, 190, 227, 233, 237, 239, 252, 257, 319
household behavior, time-shaped, 157, 163, 167, 171
household capital, 206–14; demand for, 208–12; ownership of, 209, 211; rental market, 211; services, 213; stocks, 192, 206–12, 278, 318; utilization of, 206–12, 318
household demand, 171, 227; time profile, 246
household inventories, 239
household labor: as time, 162–7; supply, 167, 170, 198, 237; *see also* household activities, time-allocation, work
household preferences, 193–7
household production: models, 157, 160–2, 192; technology, 209, 318; time-shaped, 158–90, 196, 317
household resource endowments, 159, 160–7, 174
household response to time-specific prices, *see* prices, time-specific
household time-allocation, *see* household activity schedule, labor as time
household welfare, 159, 238, 258–68
Houthakker, H. S., 8
Hufbauer, G. C., 144, 145
Hughes, Helen, 141, 142, 143, 302, 312
Hutchings, R., 305
Hutt, William H., 7

idleness of capital stocks, optimal, 43, 53, 59, 72, 73, 213, 318
income: and substitution effects, 181–3; changes in, 205, 212; distribution, 202, 206, 272; elasticities, 181–2; full, 165, 170, 190; marginal taxes on, 282; marginal utility of, 170, 198, 201, 205; psychic, 197–202, *see also* job satisfac-

tion, work utility; taxes, time-specific, 282; unearned, 164, 170
India, 323
information, 3, 14, 25, 31, 159, 290, 293; loss of, 7, 18, 19, 45
input: characteristics, 47–53, 102, 129, 131, 138, 192, 206; flows, 47–52; stocks, 47–51
input prices, 54–60, 75, 77, 113, 133, *see also* factor, prices; duration-specific, 54–9, 60–6, 134; time-invariant, 54–9, 60–2; time-marginal, 64; time-specific, 54–9, 60–6, 134, 307
inputs, 5, 75, 135, 162 (*see also* factor), footloose, storable, 50–2, 71, 100, 206–7, 130, 239, 279; perishable, 50–2, 206, 207
instantaneous: demand and supply, 244–7, 249–57; flow rate, 23, 38–41, 42, 59, 69, 132, 302; production function, 41–6, 60, 68–9
intensity, 67–8, 80, 160–8, 185, 194, *see also* flow rates
intermittent normal hours, 257, *see also* corner solution, rhythmic
International Labour Office, 141
international trade: patterns of, 143–8, 313; theory, 164–7
investment, 90, 93, 98, 148, 151, 274–8
isocost: curve, 60–5; surface, 60, 64
isoquant: instantaneous, 41–4, 46, 86, 113; surface, 46

Jevons, W. Stanley, 16
Jha, Raghbendra, xv
job assignment, *seriatim*, 27, 300
job satisfaction, 197–202, *see also* utility from work
Johansen, Leif, 314
Jones, Ronald, xv, 313, 315
Jorgenson, D. W., 5, 7, 52, 54, 129

Kahneman, Daniel, xi
Kenya, 141
Kim, Young Chin, 303
Kindleberger, C. P., 312
Klein, Lawrence, 149, 151, 152
knowledge, perfect, 9, 26, 62, 293–6
Kornai, Janos, 15, 22, 294, 300, 324, 325
Kunreuther, Howard, xv
Kwon, Jene K., 303

labor: marginal utility of, 170, 174; market, 232–9, 274–83; marketed, *see*

work activities; optimal allocation of,
178, 181, *see also* time-allocation, household activities; productivity, 80, 277;
stocks, 48–50; as time, 162–4; time-
sensitive demand for, 236; utilization
of, 53, 56, *see also* household activities,
time-allocation, work-leisure choice
labor force participation, 268
labor input, alternative measures of, 47–
51
labor services: accumulated, 49, 50; demand, 234–6; endowment of, 190;
flows, 5, 42, 44, 48–51, 53, 54, 56, 64,
72, 77, 92, 129–30, 133, 159, 161,
163–4, 167, 240, 249; hired by household, 204; prices, 54–7, *see also* wage
rate
labor supply: household, 163, 177, 237–
8; instantaneous, 15, 163, 238; profile,
135, 232–9, 274–83; time-specific, 11,
232–9; unlimited, 275
Lachmann, Ludwig, 9, 16, 294
lags, 216–8, 303
Lamb, Mary, xiv, xvi
Lancaster, Kelvin, 157, 314
Lary, Hal B., 313
learning, 25, 293
Leibenstein, Harvey J., xi, xiv, 196, 300,
324
Leiserson, Mark, xv
leisure, 181, 185, 314
Leontief: paradox, 144–8, 313; production function, 67, 69, 76
Leontief, Wassily, 67, 145
less developed countries, 153, 275, 323
Lewis, Stephen R., xv
liars, 295, 296
Lindbeck, Assar, xv
Linder, Staffan B., 8, 15–16, 157, 181,
183–90, 192–3, 200, 201, 212, 214,
314
Linder hypothesis, 212–4, 222
Lloyd, Peter J., 215, 302
load: base, 101; management, 117, 272;
peak, 100, 101, 108, 124; shedding,
244, 246, 320
load curve, 101, 110–17, 228, 240, 242,
289, 312, 320; stratified, 106, 239–44
load duration curve, 107
long run, 14, 73, 76, 78, 299, 304, 307

McCoy, Thomas, xii, xv, 7, 90, 310, 312
McFadden, Daniel, 311
McMullan, J. T., 272
Macneil, I. R., 324

McPherson, Michael S., xii, xiv, xv, 15,
296
macro-time, 4, 304
maintenance time, 303
Maital, Sharone, 17, 219
Maital, Shlomo, 17, 219
make-or-buy decision, 317
March, James G., xi, 26, 300
marginal costs, 7, 109, 110, 111, 113,
115, 116, 117, 118, 119–26, 271, 320,
see also time-shaped output
marginal output stratum, 106, 243
marginal product, 78, 82, 113, 309;
diminishing, 110, 178, 181, 185–90
marginal utility, 181, 185–90
marginal utility product, 168, 176, 178,
185
Marglin, Stephen, 300
market, labor, *see* labor, market
market disequilibria, time-specific, 234,
259–61
market institutions, 206, 259
markets, 18, 52, 206, 222; formation of,
196, 202; producer goods, 227, 248–
57; relational exchange, 15, 289–92;
rental, 53, 211; time-shaped, 11, 101,
227–57, 258, 262
Marris, Robin, xv, 6, 7, 73, 300
Marshall, Alfred, 3, 137
Marx, Karl, 317
mechanization, degree of, 141, 308
metapreferences, 324
Michael, Robert T., 16, 163, 314, 315
Michigan Survey Research Center, 202
micro-time, 5, 7
migration, 320
Mischel, Walter, 218
Mises, Ludwig von, 9, 16
money income, 190, 197–202, 206, 221
Monoyios, Nikolaos, 146, 313, 314
Morawetz, David, xv
Musgrave, Richard A., 326

Nadiri, M. Ishaq, 308
Nelson, Richard R., xii, 300
neoclassical analysis, 7, 24–5, 76, 110,
215, 287, 293–6, 313; limits of, xiii,
293–5
Newton, Sir Isaac, 298
Nicholls, William H., 310
Nigeria, 141–3, 153, 314, 323
night work, welfare effects of, 265–7
nighttime labor productivity, 267, 274–
7, 323
nighttime labor supply, 283

North, Douglass C., xii, 296
novelty, 218

occupations, 316
Oi, Walter Y., 308
opportunism, 292, 295, 325, 326
optimal utilization, *see* capital utilization
   and utilization, optimal
output: base rate, 107, 109; characteristics, 47–51; instantaneous, *see* output flow rates; maximum, 81, 150; off-peak, 123–4, 248, 263, 320; optimal duration of, 82, 103, *see also* utilization, optimal; optimal rate of, 240–8; peak rate, 105–13, 119, 121, 123; perishable 5, 100–27, 159, 227; rhythm, 115; speed of, 76–82, 84, 86, 103, 110, 308; storable, 67–99, 227; at *t*, 244; time-shaped, *see* time-shaped output; per unit time, *see* output flows, accumulated, output flow rates
output flow rates, 77–86, 103, 244–6, 308, 320 (*see also* output, speed of); amplitude of, 115, 118; duration-weighted, 110; strata, 105–10, 242–4
output flows, accumulated, 38–46, 67, 86, 101
output intensity, *see* output flow rates
output profile, equilibrium, 255
Over, Mead, xv
owner cost of capital, *see* capital stocks, owner cost of, *and* rental rate of capital
ownership, 47, 54, 131

Pack, Howard, 308
Pakistan, 153, 323, 324
Panzar, John C., 310
Pareto efficiency, 292
peaking capacity, 108–10
peaking technology, 107–10
perishability, 6, 47, 51–2, 100, 252, *see also* storability
Perlman, Mark, xv
Perry, George, 149, 152, 314
perspective time, *see* time, perspective
Phan-Thuy, N., 153
Phelps, E. S., 299
plant scale, optimal, 110, 117
pleasures: forgotten, 218; time-intensive, 201
Pollak, Robert A., 15, 158, 163, 164, 193, 196, 202, 217, 299
preference conflict, 196
preferences, 50, 159, 192, 206, 209, 231,

319, *see also* household preferences *and* utility; characteristics of, 194–7; nonrigid, 288; stable, 25; timing, 57
price: average, *see* prices, time-invariant; of capital, 54–6, 86, 135, 308; of capital service, 55, 60, 62, 64, 98, 113, 208, *see also* prices, duration-specific; constant, *see* prices, time-invariant; information, 137, 265, 273; of inputs, *see* input prices; rationing, 259, 262; stable disequilibrium, 259
price rhythms, amplitude of, 89
price schedule, time-conditional, 274
prices: duration-specific, 54–7, 58, 60, 62–6, 71–8, 90, 130, 133, 135, 208, 288, *see also* price of capital services; labor service, 57, 61, 64, 138, *see also* wage rate, time-specific prices; peak-load, 227, 231, 238–48, 261–2, 272, *see also* prices, time-specific; rhythmic, 57, 68–74, 89, 305, *see also* prices, time-specific; seasonal, 305, *see also* prices, time-specific, *and* prices, rhythmic; time-invariant, 54–63, 60, 71, 130, 133, 134, 136, 161, 206, 207, 228, 239, 240, 248, 259, 269, 288; time-specific, 54–60, 73, 78, 86, 90, 101, 108, 117, 119, 133, 207, 239, 258, 259, 261, 263, 267, 273–4, 288
pricing: average cost, 271; marginal cost, 119–25, 268–74; peak-load, *see* prices, time-specific; time-of-supply, 268–74, 289
process utility, *see* utility
product: perishable, 101, 107, 259, *see also* perishability; storable, 88, 233, 236
production: capital intensity of, 86; data, 312; duration of, 6, 7, 43, 60–4, 67–76, 78, 80–4, 88, 91, 103, 107, 121, 134, 149, 163, 230, 246, *see also* production schedule, utilization, *and* capital utilization; efficiency, 60, 69–89, 102–20, 244; environment, 160, 169, 176, 231; home, 202–7, 222, *see also* do-it-yourself; household, 157–80, 190; idleness of, *see* utilization, production schedule; intensity, *see* production speed; intermittent, 249; market, 202; office, 136, 138; schedule, 7, 44, 52, 60, 64, 67, 68, 71, 88, 90, 93, 96, 98, 101, 102, 134, 233, 252, 305, 311; seasonal, 145; speed, 43, 76–82, 84, 88, 149; storable, 67; technology, 26, 41–7, 64, 119, 133, 137, 206;

time-specific costs of, 242–4; timing, 6, 7, 82, 102, 134, 137, 140, see also production schedule
production costs, 58, 78, 93, 272; time-shape of, 59–66
production function, 42, 50, 96, 99–100, 112, 231, 302, 320; accumulated flow, 45, 130; Cobb-Douglas, 117; household, 159–62; instantaneous, 45, 55, 58, 64, 78, 90, 91, 100, 105, 111, 130, 160, 161, 218, 301, 303, 306; purely technological, 64, 129
productivity differentials, day-night, 274–9, 322
public goods, 123–6, 296, 325
purchasing office, 136, 138
putty clay, 308

quantity adjustments, time-specific, 259
quantity rationing, time-specific, 210, 259–69, 272, 320

rationality, 293; bounded, 26
Reder, M. W., xii, 296
relational exchange, 15, 22, 289–97
rental rate of capital, 55, 130, 305, see also capital stocks, owner cost of
rents, time-specific, 322
repetitive choice, 26, 293–5
repetitive events, xii, 24–6, 62, 159, 190, 227, 290, 293, 319; and neoclassical theory, 293–7
repetitive transactions, 293–5
repetitiveness, 57, 287, 292, 293–6
reputation, 295–6
resource owners, 52–4, 321, see also factor ownership
resources, 151, 314
rhythmic (see also time-specific): analysis, 26; environment, 159, 167, 210, 214, 215, 218, 220, 262; equilibrium, 90
rhythms, 50, 57, 58, 92, 306; geophysical, 31; multiple, 257, 289; tidal, 289
Ricardian rents, time-specific, 271
Riley, Terry, 26
Robbins, Lionel, 15, 165, 299
Robinson, Joan, 300
Rosen, Sherwin, 308
Rosenstein-Rodan, P. N., 4

Samuelson, Paul, 4, 26
satisfaction, see utility
scale, optimal, 111, 113, 115
schedule, optimal, 67–90, 218–21, see

also production schedule, household activity schedule
Schelling, Thomas C., 194, 196, 188, 191, 318
Scitovsky, Tibor, xi, 8, 202, 214, 217, 218, 300
seasons, 142, 306
self-control, 8, 193, 196, 214, 218–21, 288, 318
self-deception, 288, 325
self-interest, 290–6, 325, 326
self-selection, 266, 279
Sen, Amartya Kumar, xii, xv, 202, 324
sequence, 17, 18, 26, 290–3, see also temporal order
service flows, 47, 48, 206, see also labor services flows; source of, 47, 160, 207
Shackle, George L. S., xii, xiii, 7, 9, 15, 16, 17, 294, 299, 324
Shephard, Ronald W., 41, 42, 45, 129–39, 271, 307, 311, 312
shift working: multiple, 25, 44–5, 50, 88–9, 142–5, 280, 300; optimal, 89, see also utilization, optimal; physiological effects of, 278, 321, 322, see also welfare effects of shift working
short run, 14, 73, 76, 78, 304, 307
Simon, Herbert A., xi, xiii, 26, 294, 300
simultaneity, 48, 289–92
slavery, 56
sleep, 277–9, 323
Smith, Adam, 137, 300, 317
Söderström, Hans, xv
Solow, Robert M., 302
South Korea, 303
speed, see intensity and flow rates
speed tracking, see tracking and time-shaped output
Stafford, Frank P., 307
static analysis, 12, 13, 26
statistical mean, 18
Stigler, George J., 115, 221, 305, 317
stock-flow relationship, 13, 41, 47–51, see also capital utilization
stocks, 13, 41, 47–51
storability, 6, 50, 57, 67–90, 119, 167, 252, 257, see also perishability
storage costs, 51, 273–4
stratum-specific technology, see peaking technology
Strotz, R. H., 15, 214, 220, 299, 324
substitution, 72, 77, 78, 81, 86, 118, 123–5, 240, 243, 248, 307
substitution effect, 182–3, 315
substitution elasticity, 77, 81–3, 86, 89,

substitution elasticity (*cont.*)
93, 111, 118, 124, 236, 243, 262, 313;
ex ante, ex die, ex post, 77, 78, 86, 88,
108, 118–19, 120, 121, 124, 307
supply, instantaneous, 227, 228, 248,
249, 252
supply: perpetual excess, 272; time of,
272–4; time-shaped, time-specific, 11,
120, 227, 228, 240, 248–51, 268–77;
time-specific excess, 228, 237, 240,
246, 249, 259, 261, 320
supply elasticities, intertemporal, 248
supply profile, 229, 244–7, 249–57, *see
also* supply, time-specific
supply rhythm, *see* supply, time-specific
supply side policies, 313
supply variations, nonrhythmic, 274–7
Svensson, Lars E. O., 313
Sweden, 282, 308, 318, 322
switching, *see* activity, switching costs
switching time, optimal, 169–75

Taubman, Paul, 307, 308
taxes, income, *see* income taxes
technological flexibility, 108, 115, 121
technologies of output strata, 108, 109
technology, 42–6, 64, 68, 101, 115, 130,
131, 138, 142, 160, 242, 243, 272;
capital-intensive, 108, 121, 124
temporal: abstraction, 19, 27, 41, 58; aggregation, 21; hyperopia, 5, 303; information, 9, 17, 22; mobility, 6, 47,
51, 167; nihilism, 9; order, 17, 18, 26,
299; perspective, 12, 16, 26, 290, 299,
307; range, 13
Theil, H., 21
time: analytical, 13, 307; Becker's treatment of, 163; calendar, *see* calendar
time; characteristics of, 12–16, 299; as
context, 38–41; costs of adjustment,
17, 216; exogenous, 24–6, 67, 72, 76,
88, 158, 312; historical, 312; and household labor, 162–4; in economics, 7–10,
12, 16, 17; perspective, 12–16, 26,
290, 299, 307; preference, 17, 193,
299; reified, 162–4; relativity of, 298;
scarcity of, 299; unit, *see* unit time
time, value of, 157, 164, 171–80, 191,
193, 197, 210, 237, 319; in consumption and work, 171–4, 178, 192, 197–
202, 237, 264
time-allocation, 15, 157, 174, 184, 185,
299; analysis, 161–4, 168, 175, 178,
181, 190–1, 202, 212; lifetime, 315
time-intensive activities, 5, 185–7, 304

time-shaped output, 8, 100–26, 228;
least cost tracking of, 102–19
time-shaped processes, 38, 100, 101,
190, 291, *see also* time-specific
time-specific: environment, *see* environment; market distortions, 268; prices,
see prices, time-specific
time-specific models, neoclassical, 7–9,
38–64; structure of, 3–7, 9, 22–4;
time context of, 37–43
time units, analytical, 14, 19, 22, 23, 40,
163, 215–16, 222, 288–90; elementary analytical (ETU), 17, 22, 23, 24,
37–42, 89, 290, 301; endogenous,
22–4, 287–90; exogenous calendar,
16–22, 24–6, 193, 214; functional,
22, 23, 24, 287–90; nested, 24, 287
timing, 4, 23, 51, 76, 168, 177, 179, 206,
292 (*see also* time-specific *and* time-
shaped); and duality, 131–5
timing preferences, *see* household activity schedule *and* preferences
tracking: mixed, 118–19, 123; speed, 103,
104, 110–20, 122, 124; technology, 105,
108–9, 111, 115–19; time-shaped output of, 59, 103–20, 242: utilization, 103,
104, 105–10, 121–3, 240
trade, gains from, 164–7, 295–6
transactions, 290–5
transportation services, 119
trust, 292
turbines, gas-fired, 108
Tversky, Amos, xi

uncertainty, 9, 14, 26, 57
unemployment, 263
UNIDO, 141
unit time, 5, 13–21, 24, 37, 60, 130,
159, 249, 302 (*see also* time unit); and
information loss, 16–22, 26–33, 289–
92; length of, 19, 31, 32, 40, 299;
storability over, 50–2
U.S. Census Bureau, 143, 312, 313
utility: accumulated daily, 161, 173, 175,
182, 218, 219, 330, 222; diminishing
marginal, 178; goal, 193–7, 202–5,
221, 318; indirect, 173–4, 198, 206,
317; marginal, *see* marginal utility;
process, 193–7, 202–5, 221; sources
of, 192–7, 203, 221; time-shaped,
161; from work, 173–4, 175–80, 197–
202, 206, 237, *see also* job satisfaction
utility flow, net, 159, 170, 171, 172–4,
175, 176–9, 181, 194–7, 215, 219,
248, 263, 266, *see also* time, value of

utility flow profiles, 173, 175, 219, 228
utility function, instantaneous, 161, 217, 319, 320
utility maximization, dynamic, 214, 220, 299
utilization, 7, 25, 44, 49–55, 56, 59–64, 67–76, 130, 140–3, 192, 207, 213, 222, 236, 240–6, 262–3, 275, 283, 303, 304, 308, 309, 322; household capital, 206–13, 318; optimal, 7, 59–64, 68–76, 140–1, 145, 242, 262–3, 308, 309, 321
utilization effect on prices, 209, 213, 222, see also capital price effect
utilization of capacity, 53, 148–54, see also capacity
utilization rate, 46, 93, 106, 107, 138, 243, 248, 318
utilization tracking, see tracking, time-shaped output of

value of time, see time, value of
Varian, Hal R., 302, 311
Veblen, Thorstein, 193, 213
voluntary exchange, 291, 326
Vonnegut, Kurt, 299
Vroom, Victor H., 275

Wachter, Michael L., 158, 163, 164, 193, 196, 202, 326
wage payment, accumulated, 79
wage premium: night-time, 57, 227, 231, 252; overtime, 305, 307, 308
wage rate, 54, 55, 57, 93, 204, 305, 307; effective, 248; gross and net, 198; household response to time-specific, 181–90, 264; marginal utility of, 170; secularly rising, 187, 206; time-invariant, 233, 234; time-specific, 64, 72, 81, 137, 198, 234, 236, 237, 263, 315

wage rhythms, 93, 234, 248, 249, 310; amplitude of, 73, 84, 96, 98
Weitzman, Elliot D., 300
welfare, 123, 258–84; effects of shift working, 264–7, see also shift working, physiological effects of; effects of time-specific pricing, 238, 258–68
Wenders, John T., 310, 312
Whitrow, G. J., 298
Wilkinson, Maurice, 307, 308
Williamson, Jeffrey G., 54
Williamson, Oliver, xi, 15, 290, 292, 300, 326
Winston, Gene, xv
Winston, Gordon C., 7, 15, 25, 89, 141, 142, 196, 220, 265, 267, 275, 279, and *passim*
Winter, Sidney G., xii, 300
work: activities 157, 158, 173–4, 190, 192, 221; effort, 48; hours of, 175–8, 257, 278, 308, 316; household production of, 175; optimal duration of 174–9, 316; pain or pleasure of, 174–9, 192, 197–202, 221, 307, 317, see also job satisfaction, utility from work
work costs, time-specific, 279–82
work-leisure choice, 52–4, 141, 165, 177–81, 268, 307, see also labor, utilization of, time–allocation, and household activity choice
work satisfactions, direct, 174, 177, 197–202; indirect, 174–9, 197–202
work timing, 15, 57, 162, 178–81, 190, 249, 274, see also shift-working, labor supply, time-specific; altering, 238, 264–7, 274
work utility, process, 197–202
worker, average, 266, 321
World Bank, 141, 143, 144